# GRAMMAR FOR LANGUAGE LEARNING

# ELEMENTS of SUCCESS

**ANNE M. EDIGER**

**RANDEE FALK**

**MARI VARGO**

**JENNI CURRIE SANTAMARIA**

1

OXFORD

UNIVERSITY PRESS

# SHAPING *learning* TOGETHER

## We would like to thank the following classes for piloting *Elements of Success*:

**University of Delaware English Language Institute**
Teacher: Kathleen Vodvarka
Students: Ahmad Alenzi, Bandar Manei Algahmdi, Fadi Mohammed Alhazmi, Abdel Rahman Atallah, Anna Kuzmina, Muhanna Sayer Aljuaid, Coulibaly Sita

**ABC Adult School, Cerritos, CA**
Teacher: Jenni Santamaria
Students: Gabriela A. Marquez Aguilar, Yijung Chen, Laura Gomez, Terry Hahn, EunKyung Lee, Subin Lee, Sunmin Lee, Jane Leelachat, Lilia Nunezuribe, Gina Olivar, Young Park, Seol Hee Seok, Kwang Mi Song

During the development of *Elements of Success*, we spoke with teachers and professionals who are passionate about teaching grammar. Their feedback led us to create *Elements of Success: Grammar for Language Learning*, a course that solves teaching challenges by presenting grammar clearly, simply, and completely. We would like to acknowledge the advice of teachers from

**USA • BRAZIL • CANADA • COSTA RICA • GUATEMALA • IRAN • JAPAN • MEXICO • OMAN • RUSSIA**
**SAUDI ARABIA • SOUTH KOREA • TUNISIA • TURKEY • UKRAINE • THE UNITED ARAB EMIRATES**

**Mehmet Abi**, Mentese Anatolian High School, Turkey; **Anna-Marie Aldaz**, Doña Ana Community College, NM; **Diana Allen**, Oakton Community College, IL; **Marjorie Allen**, Harper College, IL; **Mark Alves**, Montgomery College, Rockville, MD; **Kelly Arce**, College of Lake County, IL; **Irma Arencibia**, Union City Adult Learning Center, NJ; **Arlys Arnold**, University of Minnesota, MN; **Marcia Arthur**, Renton Technical College, WA; **Alexander Astor**, Hostos Community College, NY; **Chris Atkins**, CHICLE Language Institute, NC; **Karin Avila-John**, University of Dayton, OH; **Ümmet Aydan**, Karabuk University, Iran; **Fabiana Azurmendi**; **John Baker**, Wayne State University, MI; **Sepehr Bamdadnia**; **Terry Barakat**, Missouri State University, MO; **Marie Bareille**, Borough of Manhattan Community College, NY; **Eileen Barlow**, SUNY Albany, NY; **Denise Barnes**, Madison English as a Second Language School, WI; **Kitty Barrera**, University of Houston, TX; **Denise Barsotti**, EID Training Solutions, FL; **Maria Bauer**, El Camino College; **Christine Bauer-Ramazani**, Saint Michael's College, VT; **Jamie Beaton**, Boston University, MA; **Gena Bennett**, Cornerstone University, NE; **Linda Berendsen**, Oakton Community College, IL; **Carol Berteotti**; **Grace Bishop**, Houston Community College, TX; **Perrin Blackman**, University of Kansas, KS; **Mara Blake-Ward**, Drexel University English Language Center, PA; **Melissa Bloom**, ELS; **Alexander Bochkov**, ELS, WA; **Marcel Bolintiam**, University of Colorado, CO; **Nancy Boyer**, Golden West College, CA; **T. Bredl**, The New School, NY; **Rosemarie Brefeld**, University of Missouri, MO; **Leticia Brereton**, Kingsborough Community College, NY; **Deborah Brooks**, Laney College, CA; **Kevin Brown**, Irvine Community College, CA; **Rachel Brown**, Center for Literacy, NY; **Tracey Brown**, Parkland College, IL; **Crystal Brunelli**, Tokyo Jogakkan Middle and High School, Japan; **Tom Burger**, Harris County Department of Education, TX; **Thom Burns**, Tokyo English Specialists College, Japan; **Caralyn Bushey**, Maryland English Institute, MD; **Gül Büyü**, Ankara University, Turkey; **Scott Callaway**, Community Family Centers, TX; **Adele Camus**, George Mason University, VA; **Nigel Caplan**, University of Delaware, DE; **Nathan Carr**, California State University, CA; **Christina Cavage**, Savannah College of Art and Design,

GA; **Neslihan Çelik**, Özdemir Sabancı Emirgan Anatolian High School, Turkey; **Shelley Cetin**, Kansas City Kansas Community College, KS; **Hoi Yuen Chan**, University of Wyoming, WY; **Esther Chase**, Berwyn Public Library, IL; **Suzidilara Çınar**, Yıldırım Beyazıt University, Turkey; **Diane Cirino**, SUNY Suffolk, NY; **Cara Codney**, Emporia State University, KS; **Catherine Coleman**, Irvine Valley College, CA; **Jenelle Collins**, Washington High School, AZ; **Greg Conner**, Orange Coast Community College, CA; **Ewelina Cope**, The Language Company, PA; **Jorge Cordon**, Colegio Montessori, Guatemala; **Kathy Cornman**, University of Michigan, MI; **Barry Costa**, Castro Valley Adult and Career Education, CA; **Cathy Costa**, Edmonds Community College, WA; **Julia Cote**, Houston Community College NE, TX; **Eileen Cotter**, Montgomery College, MD; **Winnie Cragg**, Mukogawa Fort Wright Institute, WA; **Douglas Craig**, Diplomatic Language Services, VA; **Elizabeth Craig**, Savannah College of Art and Design, GA; **Ann Telfair Cramer**, Florida State College at Jacksonville, FL; **R. M. Crocker**, Plano Independent School District, TX; **Virginia Cu**, Queens Adult Learning Center, CT; **Marc L. Cummings**, Jefferson Community and Technical College, KY; **Roberta Cummings**, Trinidad Correctional Facility, CO; **David Dahnke**, Lone Star College-North Harris, TX; **Debra Daise**, University of Denver, CO; **L. Dalgish**, Concordia College, NY; **Kristen Danek**, North Carolina State University, NC; **April Darnell**, University of Dayton, OH; **Heather Davis**, OISE Boston, MA; **Megan Davis**, Embassy English, NY; **Jeanne de Simon**, University of West Florida, FL; **Renee Delatizky**, Boston University, MA; **Sonia Delgadillo**, Sierra Community College, NY; **Gözde Burcu Demirkul**, Orkunoglu College, Turkey; **Stella L. Dennis**, Longfellow Middle School, NY; **Mary Diamond**, Auburn University, AL; **Emily Dibala**, Bucks County Community College, PA; **Cynthia Dieckmann**, West Chester East High School, PA; **Michelle DiGiorno**, Richland College, TX; **Luciana Diniz**, Portland Community College, OR; **Özgür Dirik**, Yıldız Technical University, Turkey; **Marta O. Dmytrenko-Arab**, Wayne State University, MI; **Margie Domingo**, Intergenerational Learning Community, CO; **Kellie Draheim**, Hongik University, South Korea; **Ilke Buyuk Duman**, Sehir University, Turkey; **Jennifer Eick-Magan**, Prairie State College, IL;

**Juliet Emanuel**, Borough of Manhattan Community College, NY; **David Emery**, Kaplan International Center, CA; **Patricia Emery**, Jefferson County Literacy Council, WI; **Eva Engelhard**, Kaplan International Center, WA; **Nancey Epperson**, Harry S. Truman College, IL; **Ken Estep**, Mentor Language Institute, CA; **Cindy Etter**, University of Washington, WA; **Rhoda Fagerland**, St. Cloud State University, MN; **Anrisa Fannin**, Diablo Valley College, CA; **Marie Farnsworth**, Union Public Schools, OK; **Jim Fenton**, Bluegrass Community Technical College, KY; **Lynn Filazzola**, Nassau BOCES Adult Learning Center, NY; **Christine Finck**, Stennis Language Lab; **Mary Fischer**, Texas Intensive English Program, TX; **Mark Fisher**, Lone Star College, TX; **Celeste Flowers**, University of Central Arkansas, AR; **Elizabeth Foss**, Washtenaw Community College, MI; **Jacqueline Fredericks**, West Contra Costa Adult Education, CA; **Patricia Gairaud**, San Jose City College, CA; **Patricia Gallo**, Delaware Technical Community College, DE; **Beverly Gandall**, Coastline Community College, CA; **Alberto Garrido**, The Community College of Baltimore County, MD; **Debbie Garza**, Park University, MO; **Karen Gelender**, Castro Valley Adult and Career Education, CA; **Ronald Gentry**, Suenos Compartidos, Mexico; **Kathie Madden Gerecke**, North Shore Community College, MA; **Jeanne Gibson**, Colorado State University, CO; **A. Elizabeth Gilfillan**, Houston Community College, TX; **Melanie Gobert**, The Higher Colleges of Technology, UAE; **Ellen Goldman**, West Valley College, CA; **Jo Golub**, Houston Community College, TX; **Maria Renata Gonzalez**, Colegio Montessori, Guatemala; **Elisabeth Goodwin**, Pima Community College, AZ; **John Graney**, Santa Fe College, FL; **Karina Greene**, CUNY in the Heights, NY; **Katherine Gregorio**, CASA de Maryland, MD; **Claudia Gronsbell**, La Escuelita, NY; **Yvonne Groseil**, Hunter College, NY; **Alejandra Gutierrez**, Hartnell College, CA; **Eugene Guza**, North Orange County Community College District, CA; **Mary Beth Haan**, El Paso Community College, TX; **Elizabeth Haga**, State College of Florida, FL; **Saeede Haghi**, Ozyegin University, Turkey; **Laura Halvorson**, Lorain County Community College, OH; **Nancy Hamadou**, Pima Community College, AZ; **Kerri Hamberg**, Brookline Community and Adult Education, MA;

ii

# Contents

# 4 | The Verb _Be_

# 5 | Nouns, Articles, and Quantifiers

# 9│Adjectives

# 10│Future Forms

# 11│Modals I

# 12 | Modals II

# 13 | Types of Verbs

# 14|Sentence Patterns

# 1

# Introduction to Parts of Speech

**IN THIS UNIT, WE STUDY** parts of speech.

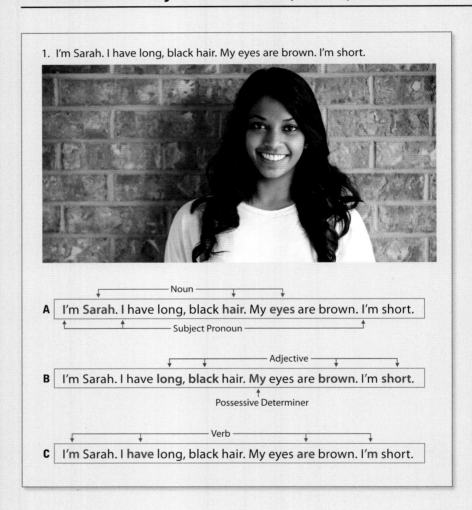

1. I'm Sarah. I have long, black hair. My eyes are brown. I'm short.

———— Noun ————

**A** I'm **Sarah**. I have long, black **hair**. My **eyes** are brown. I'm short.

———— Subject Pronoun ————

———— Adjective ————

**B** I'm Sarah. I have **long, black** hair. **My** eyes are **brown**. I'm **short**.

Possessive Determiner

———— Verb ————

**C** I'm Sarah. I **have** long, black hair. My eyes **are** brown. I'm short.

 **ONLINE**

For the Unit Vocabulary Check, go to the Online Practice.

2. These are my friends Joe and Paul. They're really tall. Joe's hair is black. Paul's hair is brown.

Noun

**A** | These are my **friends Joe** and **Paul**. **They**'re really tall. **Joe's hair** is black. **Paul's hair** is brown.

Subject Pronoun       Possessive Noun

Adjective

**B** | These are **my** friends Joe and Paul. They're really **tall**. Joe's hair is **black**. Paul's hair is **brown**.

Possessive Determiner

Verb

**C** | These **are** my friends Joe and Paul. They**'re** really tall. Joe's hair **is** black. Paul's hair **is** brown.

**Think about It** Check (✓) the words to complete the sentences about you. You may check more than one word.

1. I study ____.
   - ☐ English
   - ☐ science
   - ☐ Chinese
   - ☐ history
   - ☐ math
   - ☐ other: _____

2. My English class is ____.
   - ☐ big
   - ☐ difficult
   - ☐ small
   - ☐ fun
   - ☐ easy
   - ☐ other: _____

3. I have ____.
   - ☐ one brother
   - ☐ ____ brothers
   - ☐ one sister
   - ☐ ____ sisters
   - ☐ no (0) brothers or sisters

4. I have ____ hair.
   - ☐ brown
   - ☐ blond
   - ☐ black
   - ☐ red
   - ☐ other: _____

5. I have ____ hair.
   - ☐ short
   - ☐ curly
   - ☐ long
   - ☐ straight
   - ☐ other: _____

6. I have ____ eyes.
   - ☐ brown
   - ☐ green
   - ☐ blue
   - ☐ other: _____

## 1.1 Nouns

**A**

**Nouns** are words for:

| PEOPLE | PLACES | THINGS | | IDEAS |
|---|---|---|---|---|
| a **girl** | an **office** | an **apple** | an **orange** | biology |
| a **teacher** | a **school** | a **bicycle** | rice | an **example** |
| Mark | Paris | a **book** | a **street** | information |

**B**

SINGULAR NOUNS AND PLURAL NOUNS

| SINGULAR (= ONE) | PLURAL (= TWO OR MORE) | SINGULAR (= ONE) | PLURAL (= TWO OR MORE) |
|---|---|---|---|
| a book | book**s** | a woman | wom**e**n |
| a student | student**s** | a man | m**e**n |
| an orange | orange**s** | a person | p**eo**pl**e** |

For many nouns, we add **-s** or **-es** to form the plural.

Some nouns have **irregular** plural forms. For these nouns, we don't add **-s**. We change the word.

Notice: We can use *a* or *an* before many singular nouns.

For more information about nouns, see Unit 5.

## 1 | Noticing Groups of Nouns  Look at the groups of nouns. Add four nouns to each group.  `1.1 A`

| People | | Cities | | Foods | |
|---|---|---|---|---|---|
| mother | _teacher_ | London | _____ | pizza | _____ |
| father | _____ | Istanbul | _____ | chicken | _____ |
| sister | _____ | Hong Kong | _____ | salad | _____ |
| friend | _____ | San Francisco | _____ | fruit | _____ |

| School subjects | | Sports | | Days of the week | |
|---|---|---|---|---|---|
| science | _____ | soccer[1] | _____ | Sunday | _____ |
| math | _____ | basketball | _____ | Monday | _____ |
| history | _____ | tennis | _____ | Tuesday | _____ |
| literature | _____ | baseball | _____ | | _____ |

**Write about It** Complete each sentence with your favorite thing. Use a noun from the boxes above or a different noun. Compare your sentences with a partner.

MY FAVORITE THINGS[2]

1. My favorite city is _____.
2. My favorite food is _____.
3. My favorite subject is _____.

4. My favorite sport is _____.
5. My favorite day is _____.

## 2 | Writing Singular and Plural Nouns  Label the pictures with the words from the box.  `1.1 B`

THINGS AT SCHOOL

| a backpack | a computer | a desk | a notebook | a student | a teacher |
|---|---|---|---|---|---|
| a classroom | computers | desks | notebooks | students | a whiteboard |

1. _____ *a classroom* _____   2. _____   3. _____   4. _____

5. _____   6. _____   7. _____   8. _____

9. _____   10. _____   11. _____   12. _____

[1] **soccer:** the American English word for *football*        [2] **favorite thing:** a thing you like more than other things

**Think about It** Are the nouns in Activity 2 singular or plural? Write *S* above the singular nouns. Write *P* above the plural nouns.

*S*
*a classroom*

**Talk about It** Work with a partner. Look around your classroom. Circle the things you see. Then write four more things.

a desk / (desks)

a computer / computers

a notebook / notebooks

a whiteboard / whiteboards

a teacher / teachers

a backpack / backpacks

_____

_____

_____

_____

**3 | Spelling Note: *A* and *An*** Read the note. Then do Activity 4.

We can use *a* or *an* before many singular nouns.

| We usually use *a* when the next word starts with a **consonant sound**. | | We usually use *an* when the next word starts with a **vowel sound**. | |
|---|---|---|---|
| a banana | a letter | an apple | an object |
| a car | a nurse | an event | an umbrella |
| a jacket | a school | an idea | |

For more information on *a* and *an*, see Unit 5, page 115.

**4 | Using *A* or *An*** Look at the nouns in the box. Write the nouns under the correct group in the chart on page 7. Write *a* or *an* before each noun.

NOUNS

| answer | aunt | brother | exercise | office | school | table |
|---|---|---|---|---|---|---|
| apartment | banana | chair | friend | question | store | teacher |
| apple | bed | example | house | sandwich | street | uncle |

| Things in a grammar book | People | Food | Places | Things in a home |
|---|---|---|---|---|
| *an answer* | | | | |

**Write about It** Write two more nouns in each group above. Use *a* or *an* before each noun.

**5 | Forming Singular and Plural Nouns** Complete the sentences with the singular or plural form of the nouns in parentheses. Then listen and check your answers. **1.1 B**

**MY FAMILY AND FRIENDS**

1. I have a _____*mother*_____ , a _____ , three _____ , and a _____ .
   (mother)          (father)              (sister)              (brother)

2. My brother is a _____ .
   (teacher)

3. I have two _____ in London and a _____ in Paris.
   (friend)                      (friend)

**MY HOME**

4. My mother and father live in a _____ with three _____ .
   (house)                      (bedroom)

5. I live in an _____ .
   (apartment)

6. My apartment has one _____ .
   (bedroom)

**MY WORK**

7. I work in an _____ . I use a _____ .
   (office)              (computer)

8. We have eight _____ in my office.
   (person)

9. I bring my lunch to work. Today I have a _____ and an _____ for lunch.
   (sandwich)              (apple)

**MY SCHOOL**

10. I take two _____ at night: English and business.
    (course)

11. My school is ten _____ from my office.
    (minute)

12. My English class has 20 _____ : 12 _____ and 8 _____ .
    (student)              (woman)              (man)

**Think about It** Which nouns above have irregular plural forms?

**Write about It** Choose three sentences above. Make the sentences true for you. Use different nouns.

*I have a friend in Tokyo and two cousins in Seoul.*

## 1.2 Subject Pronouns and the Verb *Be*

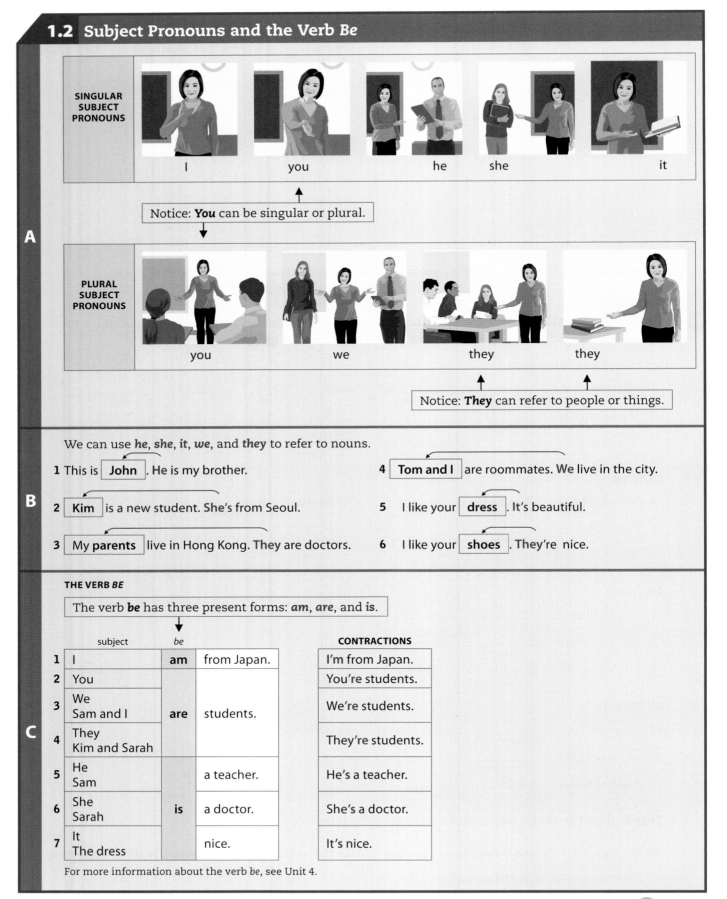

**A**

SINGULAR SUBJECT PRONOUNS

I    you    he   she    it

Notice: **You** can be singular or plural.

PLURAL SUBJECT PRONOUNS

you    we    they    they

Notice: **They** can refer to people or things.

**B**

We can use **he**, **she**, **it**, **we**, and **they** to refer to nouns.

1  This is | John | . **He** is my brother.

2  | Kim | is a new student. **She's** from Seoul.

3  My | **parents** | live in Hong Kong. **They** are doctors.

4  | Tom and I | are roommates. **We** live in the city.

5  I like your | dress | . **It's** beautiful.

6  I like your | shoes | . **They're** nice.

**C**

THE VERB *BE*

The verb **be** has three present forms: **am**, **are**, and **is**.

| | subject | be | | CONTRACTIONS |
|---|---|---|---|---|
| 1 | I | **am** | from Japan. | I'm from Japan. |
| 2 | You | | | You're students. |
| 3 | We / Sam and I | **are** | students. | We're students. |
| 4 | They / Kim and Sarah | | | They're students. |
| 5 | He / Sam | | a teacher. | He's a teacher. |
| 6 | She / Sarah | **is** | a doctor. | She's a doctor. |
| 7 | It / The dress | | nice. | It's nice. |

For more information about the verb *be*, see Unit 4.

**6 | Noticing Subject Pronouns** Circle the subject pronouns in these sentences. Is the pronoun singular or plural? Check (✓) the correct column. `1.2 A`

| STUDENTS AROUND THE WORLD | SINGULAR | PLURAL |
|---|:---:|:---:|
| 1. (I)'m Jorge. (I)'m a student in São Paolo. | ☐ | ☐ |
| 2. My classmates are from many different countries. They're very interesting. | ☐ | ☐ |
| 3. I'm Julia. I'm a high school student in Mexico. | ☐ | ☐ |
| 4. My brother Eduardo is a student, too. He's in college. | ☐ | ☐ |
| 5. I'm Yong Sook, and this is Hae Min. | ☐ | ☐ |
| 6. We're from Korea. We go to school in California. | ☐ | ☐ |
| 7. Our school is in San Diego. It's a big school! | ☐ | ☐ |
| 8. My sister is in Hong Kong. She's a student. | ☐ | ☐ |
| 9. Hong Kong is a great city. It's very crowded³. | ☐ | ☐ |
| 10. I'm Takuto. I'm a university student in Tokyo. | ☐ | ☐ |
| 11. My brother works at the university. He's a professor. | ☐ | ☐ |

**Think about It** Look at the sentences above with *he*, *she*, *it*, and *they*. Which nouns do these pronouns refer to? Underline the nouns.

> <u>My classmates</u> are from many different countries. (They)'re very interesting.

**7 | Using Subject Pronouns** Look at the **bold** words. Complete the sentences with the correct subject pronouns. `1.2 A–B`

A NEW SEMESTER

1. The **university** is great. _____*It*_____'s really big.
2. I like the **library**. _____'s really beautiful.
3. **Victoria and Karina** are from Russia. _____'re really good students.
4. I have a lot of **books** this semester. _____'re expensive!
5. I have **Mr. Cho** for English. _____'s a good teacher.
6. **Marcus and I** study a lot. _____'re biology students.
7. My friend **Jessica** is from Canada. _____'s in a lot of my classes.
8. **My parents** are here this weekend. _____'re from Haiti.
9. **Laura** is my new roommate. _____'s from Brazil.
10. **Laura and I** live on Downey Street. _____ have a small apartment.

**Write about It** Choose two of the items above. Write a new second sentence.

> The university is great. It's in a big city.

---

³ **crowded:** full of people

**8│Using the Verb *Be***  Complete each sentence with *am*, *is*, or *are*. Use contractions (*'m*, *'s*, or *'re*) with subject pronouns.  `1.2 C`

MAKING INTRODUCTIONS

1.  Susanna _____*is*_____ my sister. She___*'s*_____ a student at the high school.

2.  This is my cousin Beth. She lives in New York. She_____ a lawyer.

3.  My name _____ Tara. I _____ in college.

4.  Kayo and Feride _____ my friends. We _____ in the same classes.

5.  These are my new roommates. They_____ from China.

6.  Mr. Thompson _____ from Arizona. He _____ a teacher at my school.

7.  This is Luisa. She _____ from Peru. She _____ an amazing singer!

8.  Juan and Karina _____ in my English class. Juan _____ from Mexico, and Karina _____from Russia.

9.  Juan _____ a good cook. He makes delicious Mexican food!

10. Alex and Miguel _____ my neighbors. They live across the street.

a lawyer

**Talk about It**  Bring in a picture of someone (or some people) you know. Tell a partner about the people in the picture.

*"This is my roommate Binh. He's from Vietnam."*
*"These are my parents. They're in Poland."*

---

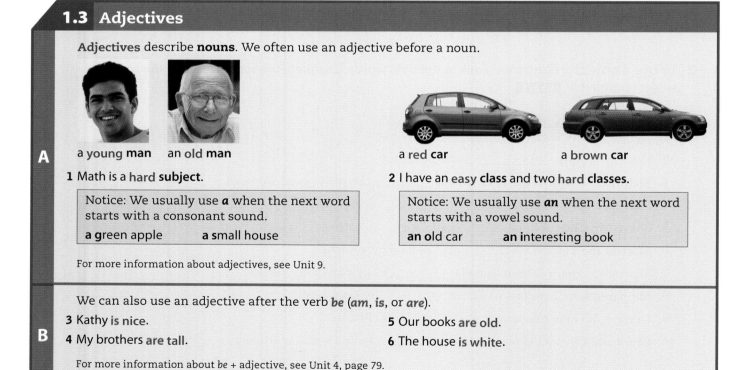

## 1.3  Adjectives

**Adjectives** describe **nouns**. We often use an adjective before a noun.

**A**

a young **man**    an old **man**

a red **car**    a brown **car**

1 Math is a **hard subject**.

Notice: We usually use **a** when the next word starts with a consonant sound.

**a g**reen apple    **a s**mall house

2 I have an **easy class** and two **hard classes**.

Notice: We usually use **an** when the next word starts with a vowel sound.

**an o**ld car    **an i**nteresting book

For more information about adjectives, see Unit 9.

**B**

We can also use an adjective after the verb **be** (*am*, *is*, or *are*).

3 Kathy **is nice**.

4 My brothers **are tall**.

5 Our books **are old**.

6 The house **is white**.

For more information about *be* + adjective, see Unit 4, page 79.

**9 | Understanding Adjectives** Look at these adjectives. Check (✓) the adjectives you know. Use a dictionary to look up the adjectives you don't know. `1.3 A`

☐ 1. angry
☐ 2. bad
☐ 3. beautiful
☐ 4. big
☐ 5. black
☐ 6. cold
☐ 7. early
☐ 8. easy

☐ 9. good
☐ 10. happy
☐ 11. hard
☐ 12. hot
☐ 13. interesting
☐ 14. late
☐ 15. new
☐ 16. nice

☐ 17. old
☐ 18. short
☐ 19. small
☐ 20. tall
☐ 21. white
☐ 22. young

Which adjectives above can you use to describe these things? Write the adjectives in the chart. Some adjectives may go in more than one column.

| a person | a class | an animal | a dinner | clothes (a shirt, jeans, etc.) | an apartment |
|---|---|---|---|---|---|
| *beautiful* | | *beautiful* | | *beautiful* | *beautiful* |

**Write about It** Write two more adjectives in each column in the chart above.

**10 | Using Adjective + Noun** Complete each sentence with a word from the box. Make the sentences true for you. Circle *a* or *an* where necessary. `1.3 A`

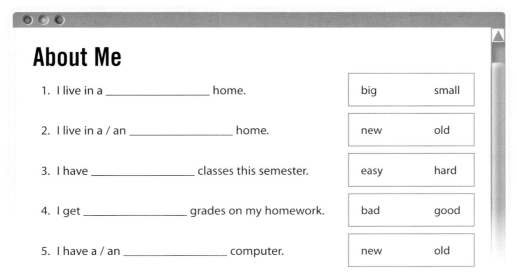

## About Me

1. I live in a _____ home.   | big | small |

2. I live in a / an _____ home.   | new | old |

3. I have _____ classes this semester.   | easy | hard |

4. I get _____ grades on my homework.   | bad | good |

5. I have a / an _____ computer.   | new | old |

6. I like a _____ breakfast.

7. I eat a / an _____ lunch.

8. I like _____ days.

9. I have _____ friends.

10. I like _____ shoes.

| big | small |
|---|---|
| early | late |
| cold | hot |
| interesting | nice |
| black | white |

**Think about It** Underline the noun that each adjective describes.

*I live in a big <u>home</u>.*

**Talk about It** Compare your answers with a partner. Are your answers similar or different?

**11 | Using *Be* + Adjective** Look at the photos. Complete the sentences with adjectives from the box. You will not use all of the adjectives. **1.3 B**

WHAT'S WRONG?

| angry | cold | easy | hot |
|---|---|---|---|
| broken | early | hard | late |

1. I'm _____*cold*_____!

2. The bus is _____!

3. I think Jim is _____.

4. My computer is _____.

5. It's _____ today!

6. This class is _____.

**Think about It** Underline the verb *be* in the sentences above.

12

**Write about It** Write three more sentences with the adjectives from the box in Activity 11 (page 12). Use *be* + adjective. Compare your sentences with a partner.

*My math class is easy.*

**Talk about It** How do you feel today? Tell a partner. Use the adjectives in this box or your own ideas.

| | | | | | | |
|---|---|---|---|---|---|---|
| cold | fine | great | happy | hot | sick | tired |

A: *I'm cold today.*
B: *Not me. I'm hot today.*

## 1.4 Possessives

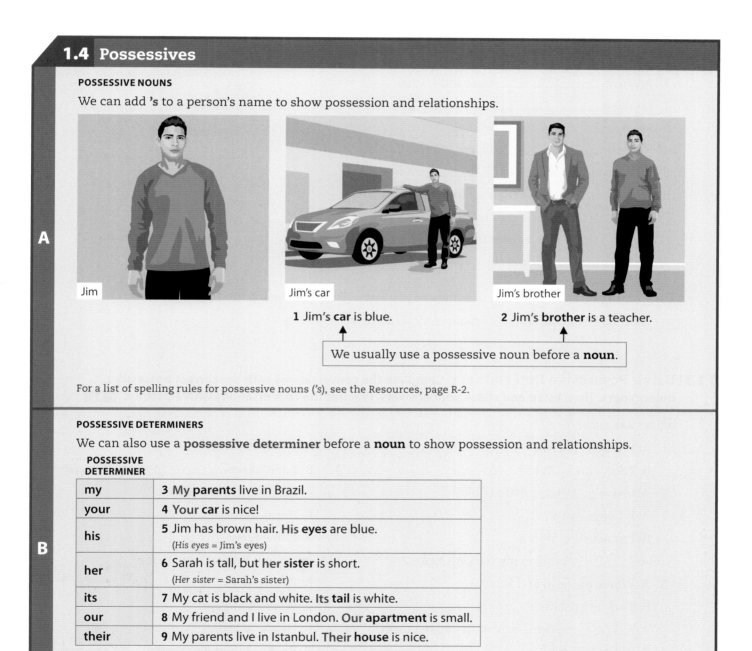

### POSSESSIVE NOUNS

We can add **'s** to a person's name to show possession and relationships.

Jim

Jim's car

Jim's brother

1 Jim's **car** is blue.

2 Jim's **brother** is a teacher.

We usually use a possessive noun before a **noun**.

For a list of spelling rules for possessive nouns ('s), see the Resources, page R-2.

### POSSESSIVE DETERMINERS

We can also use a **possessive determiner** before a **noun** to show possession and relationships.

| POSSESSIVE DETERMINER | |
|---|---|
| my | 3 **My parents** live in Brazil. |
| your | 4 **Your car** is nice! |
| his | 5 Jim has brown hair. **His eyes** are blue.<br>(*His eyes* = Jim's eyes) |
| her | 6 Sarah is tall, but **her sister** is short.<br>(*Her sister* = Sarah's sister) |
| its | 7 My cat is black and white. **Its tail** is white. |
| our | 8 My friend and I live in London. **Our apartment** is small. |
| their | 9 My parents live in Istanbul. **Their house** is nice. |

**GRAMMAR TERM: Possessive determiners** are also called **possessive adjectives**.

**12 | Using Possessive Nouns** Look at the family tree. Complete each sentence with a possessive noun. Then underline the noun after each possessive. **1.4 A**

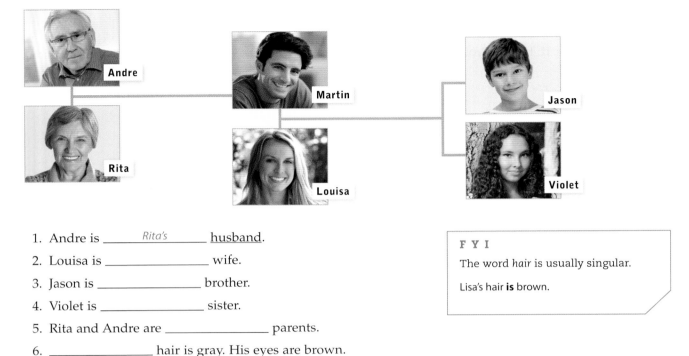

Andre | Martin | Jason | Rita | Louisa | Violet

1. Andre is _____*Rita's*_____ husband.
2. Louisa is _____ wife.
3. Jason is _____ brother.
4. Violet is _____ sister.
5. Rita and Andre are _____ parents.
6. _____ hair is gray. His eyes are brown.
7. _____ hair is gray. Her eyes are blue.
8. _____ eyes are blue. Her hair is blond.
9. _____ hair is curly and brown. Her eyes are brown.

> **F Y I**
> The word *hair* is usually singular.
> Lisa's hair **is** brown.

**Talk about It** Show a picture of someone you know. Describe the person to your partner.

*"This is my friend Dan. His hair is brown. His eyes are brown."*

**13 | Using Possessive Determiners** Complete the conversations with the correct possessive determiners. Then listen and check your answers. Practice the conversations with a partner. **1.4 B**

WHERE ARE THEY?

1. A: Where's Alberto?
   B: I don't know. Why?
   A: I have ____*his*____ math book.
2. A: Where's Amy?
   B: I'm not sure. Why?
   A: _____ car is in my parking space.
3. A: Where are Sean and Sam?
   B: They're upstairs.
   A: _____ sister is here. Can you tell them?
4. A: Where's Tina?
   B: She's in her room. Why?
   A: _____ mother is on the phone.
5. A: Where are we?
   B: I don't know. _____ phone is dead[4].
6. A: Kim? Where are you?
   B: I'm at the store.
   A: Come home. _____ pizza is here.
7. A: Oh, no! Where's my phone?
   B: I see it. It's in _____ pocket.
8. A: Where's Miguel?
   B: He's at school.
   A: Really? I think this is _____ backpack.

[4] **dead:** (electronics) not working because it doesn't have any power

## 1.5 Subjects, Verbs, and Sentences

**A**

Most **verbs** show an action.

1 I **eat** lunch at school.
2 We **drink** coffee with breakfast.
3 I **sleep** at my parents' house on weekends.
4 They **study** business.
5 I **walk** to my office.

Some verbs do not show an action. Here are some examples of **non-action verbs**:

| **be** | 6 I'm a new student. | **want** | 11 They want some water. |
| | 7 We're sisters. | | |
| | 8 She's Kim. | | |
| **have** | 9 I have three brothers. | **know** | 12 I know the answer. |
| **like** | 10 We like coffee. | | |

For more information about simple present verbs, see Units 2, 3, and 4.
For more information about action verbs and non-action verbs, see Unit 7, page 185.

**B**

Every sentence has a **subject** and a **verb**.

> The **subject** includes a **noun** or a **subject pronoun**.
> It can be one word or more than one word.

| | subject | verb | |
|---|---|---|---|
| 13 | My **friends** | drive | to school. |
| 14 | We | study | English. |
| 15 | Our **car** | is | old. |
| 16 | My **brother** and I | are | tall. |

GO ONLINE

**14 | Understanding Verbs** Look at the verbs in the box and at the phrases in the chart below. Which verbs can you use to complete the phrases? Write the verbs in the chart. Some verbs may go in more than one column. **1.5 A**

| buy | eat | make | speak |
| close | go | open | study |
| drive | learn | read | walk |

| ____ lunch | ____ English | ____ to school | ____ a book |
|---|---|---|---|
| *buy* | | | *buy* |

**Think about It** Write five more verbs you know. Share your verbs with your classmates.

**15 | Identifying Verbs in Sentences** Underline the verb in each sentence. Are the sentences true for you? Check (✓) *True* or *False*. **1.5 A**

## My Habits[5]

|   |   | TRUE | FALSE |
|---|---|------|-------|
| 1. | I <u>live</u> with my family. | ☐ | ☐ |
| 2. | I live with a roommate (or roommates). | ☐ | ☐ |
| 3. | I work in an office. | ☐ | ☐ |
| 4. | I drive a car to school. | ☐ | ☐ |
| 5. | I walk to school. | ☐ | ☐ |
| 6. | I use a backpack. | ☐ | ☐ |
| 7. | My teachers give a lot of homework. | ☐ | ☐ |
| 8. | I study with friends. | ☐ | ☐ |
| 9. | I drink coffee with breakfast. | ☐ | ☐ |
| 10. | I eat lunch at school. | ☐ | ☐ |
| 11. | I go to movies with friends. | ☐ | ☐ |
| 12. | I go on the Internet every day. | ☐ | ☐ |
| 13. | My friends come to my home. | ☐ | ☐ |
| 14. | I play video games. | ☐ | ☐ |
| 15. | I play tennis. | ☐ | ☐ |

**Talk about It** Compare your answers as a class. Which sentences are true for most students?

**Write about It** What other actions do you do? Write three sentences.

*I ride my bicycle.*     *I watch TV.*     *I exercise.*

**16 | Identifying Subjects and Verbs** Underline the verb in each sentence. Then circle the subject of the sentence. **1.5 B**

**AT HOME**

1. (My roommates) <u>are</u> from Venezuela and Algeria.

2. They make interesting food for dinner.

3. We talk about everything.

4. I have good roommates!

**AT SCHOOL**

5. Students study English at my school.

6. I learn many new words every week.

7. Our teachers help students after class.

8. My friends buy lunch in the cafeteria.

9. I bring my lunch to school.

---

[5] **habits:** things you do often

ON THE WEEKENDS

10. My friends and I play soccer in the park on Sundays.

11. Our team[6] is good!

12. We go to a restaurant after the game.

**Think about It** Look at the subjects in the sentences above. Which subjects include a subject pronoun (*I, you, . . .*)? Which subjects include a possessive determiner (*my, your, . . .*) + a noun?

**Think about It** Which verbs in Activity 16 are non-action verbs? Label these verbs *NA*.

**17 | Identifying Parts of Speech** Read the sentences. Put the **bold** words into the correct column in the chart below. (Review Charts 1.1–1.5 for help.)

HOW DO YOU PRACTICE ENGLISH?

1. I **have friends** in **Mexico. They speak** Spanish and English. **We talk** in English.
2. **I** travel a lot. I **meet people** from many **places.** Many people **speak** English.
3. **My favorite songs** are in English.
4. I **work** with **computers.** English **is important** for my job.
5. English is **easy.** I **learn new words** every day!
6. My **mother** is from the United States. English is **her** native language[7].
7. I **go** on the Internet a lot. I **read** websites in English.
8. **My friend** is an English **teacher. His class** is **interesting.**

| Nouns | Subject pronouns | Possessive determiners | Adjectives | Verbs |
|---|---|---|---|---|
| *friends* | | | | *have* |

**Talk about It** How do you practice English? Check (✓) the sentences above that are true for you.

**18 | Usage Note: Words That Are Nouns or Verbs** Read the note. Then do Activity 19.

Some words can be **nouns** or **verbs.**

**1a** Coffee is my favorite **drink.**    **1b** I **drink** coffee every morning.
**2a** Lisa is at **work.**    **2b** We **work** at the school.
**3a** This book has a lot of **exercises.**    **3b** I **exercise** after school.

---

[6] **team:** a group of people who play a sport against another group    [7] **native language:** your first language

INTRODUCTION TO PARTS OF SPEECH 17

**19 | Identifying Nouns and Verbs** Read the sentences. Is the **bold** word a noun or a verb? Check (✓) the correct column.

|  | NOUN | VERB |
|---|---|---|
| 1. I **drink** a lot of water. | ☐ | ☑ |
| 2. Lemonade is a delicious **drink** for summer. | ☐ | ☐ |
| 3. I **drink** coffee after dinner. | ☐ | ☐ |
| 4. I **work** on the weekends. | ☐ | ☐ |
| 5. My parents are at **work**. | ☐ | ☐ |
| 6. My friends **work** at a restaurant. | ☐ | ☐ |
| 7. I **exercise** every week. | ☐ | ☐ |
| 8. This **exercise** is hard for me. | ☐ | ☐ |

lemonade

**Talk about It** Check (✓) the statements above that are true for you. Compare your answers with a partner.

**20 | Using Nouns, Verbs, and Adjectives in Sentences** Complete the sentences with the words from the chart or your own ideas. Use the part of speech in parentheses. More than one answer is possible. (Review Charts 1.1–1.5)

| Nouns | | Verbs | | Adjectives | |
|---|---|---|---|---|---|
| bicycle/bicycles | parents | buy | talk | beautiful | good |
| book/books | pen/pens | drive | walk | big | hard |
| car/cars | person/people | eat | work | cold | interesting |
| cat/cats | question/questions | read | write | easy | small |
| computer/computers | student/students | study | | | |
| friend/friends | teacher/teachers | | | | |

1. _____Students_____ ask a lot of questions.
   (plural noun)
2. Paris is _____.
   (adjective)
3. I have a _____ in my backpack.
   (singular noun)
4. I have _____ _____.
   (number) (plural noun)
5. Students _____ books.
   (verb)
6. My classes are _____.
   (adjective)
7. Sports are _____.
   (adjective)
8. I like my _____.
   (singular noun)

9. _____ do a lot of work.
   (plural noun)
10. Students _____ in class.
    (verb)
11. Russia is a / an _____ country.
    (adjective)
12. I _____ to school.
    (verb)
13. _____ learn a lot of things.
    (plural noun)
14. A lot of people _____ with their friends.
    (verb)
15. My home is _____.
    (adjective)

**Talk about It** Compare your sentences as a class.

18

## 1.6 Imperatives

### A

**COMMANDS AND INSTRUCTIONS**

A command means "do this."

1 Call me tomorrow.
2 Go to the board.
3 Open the door.

4 Close the door.
5 Take out your books.
6 Put away your books.

7 **Start** your tests. (= You start your tests.)

Notice: With commands, the subject is *you*, but we don't say it.

### B

**NEGATIVE COMMANDS**

We use ***don't* + a verb** for negative commands.

8 **Don't use** the microwave. It's broken.
9 **Don't worry.** Everything is OK.

10 **Don't leave** without me. I want to go.
11 **Don't talk** to John. He's busy.

### C

***LET'S* FOR SUGGESTIONS AND INVITATIONS**

We can use ***Let's* + a verb** to make a suggestion or an invitation.

12 A: Are you hungry?
   B: Yes! **Let's have** lunch.

13 A: What do you want to do?
   B: **Let's go** to a movie.

14 A: I'm worried about the test.
   B: Me, too. **Let's study** together.

Notice: We don't use a subject with *let's*. (*Let's* = *let us*.)

## 21 | Using Commands  Match each picture with the instructions below.  `1.6 A`

**CLASSROOM INSTRUCTIONS**

a.

b.

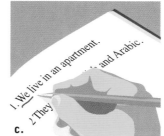
c.

d.

e.

f.

g.

h.

_b_ 1. Turn to page 24.
____ 2. Underline the subject pronoun.
____ 3. Circle the verb.
____ 4. Complete the sentence.

____ 5. Close the window.
____ 6. Put away your books.
____ 7. Close the door.
____ 8. Talk with a partner.

**Talk about It** Work in a group. Take turns giving commands to your classmates. Use commands 5–8 in Activity 21 or use your own ideas.

**22 | Giving Instructions** Complete the instructions with verbs from the box. `1.6 A`

| add | buy | cut | draw | erase | put | use | write |

**MAKE YOUR OWN CALENDAR**

1. _____Buy_____ a large picture frame.

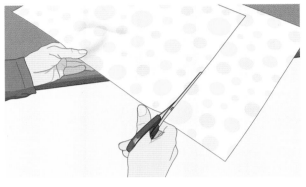

2. _____ a piece of paper to fit the frame.

3. _____ six rows and seven columns (42 boxes) on the paper. Use a ruler. Leave space at the top.

4. _____ the days of the week in the top row.

5. _____ the paper in the frame.

6. Write the month and the dates on the glass. _____ a whiteboard marker.

7. _____ activities to your calendar.

8. Next month, _____ your calendar and write new dates.

**23 | Using Positive and Negative Commands** Complete these tips for students. Use the verbs in parentheses to form positive or negative commands. `1.6 A–B`

TIPS[8] FOR STUDENTS

1. ___Don't do_____ your homework late at night.
   (do)
2. _____ new vocabulary in your notebook.
   (write)
3. _____ to your teacher in class.
   (listen)
4. _____ your cell phone in class.
   (use)
5. _____ a short break[9] every hour.
   (take)
6. _____ television when you study.
   (watch)
7. _____ notes in class.
   (take)
8. _____ for eight hours or more before a test.
   (sleep)
9. _____ awake all night before a test.
   (stay)
10. _____ in bed. You might fall asleep!
    (study)

**Think about It** Do you follow the tips above? Check (✓) the tips that you follow.

**Write about It** Write two more tips for students. Use commands.

**24 | Making Suggestions with *Let's*** Listen and write the missing words. Then practice the conversations with a partner. `1.6 C`

1. A: ___Let's go_____ . I'm tired.

   B: Really? I want to stay.

2. A: Dinner is ready. _____!

   B: Great! I'm hungry.

3. A: I don't want to cook dinner tonight.

   B: _____ a pizza.

---

[8] **tips:** pieces of advice

[9] **break:** a short time when you stop doing something

4. A: _____ a movie tonight.

   B: Sorry, I can't. I have to work.

5. A: I need new shoes.

   B: Me, too. _____ shopping.

6. A: I'm bored.

   B: Me, too. _____ a video game.

7. A: _____ a break.

   B: OK, good idea.

8. A: When is our test?

   B: I don't know. _____ the teacher.

**Talk about It**  Talk to a partner. Give three suggestions for this week. Use *Let's* + the verbs in this box or your own ideas.

| buy | eat | listen to | play | see | take |
|-----|-----|-----------|------|-----|------|
| cook | go | make | read | study | watch |

*A: Let's see a movie tonight.*
*B: OK!*

*A: Let's go to the mall tonight.*
*B: No, let's watch TV.*

## WRAP-UP

**A | GRAMMAR IN READING**  **Read the webpage. Then write the bold words in the chart below.**

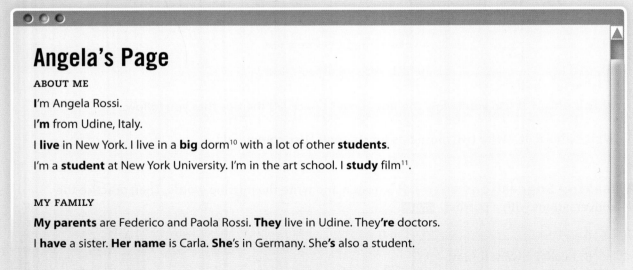

# Angela's Page

**ABOUT ME**

**I**'m Angela Rossi.

**I'm** from Udine, Italy.

I **live** in New York. I live in a **big** dorm[10] with a lot of other **students**.

I'm a **student** at New York University. I'm in the art school. I **study** film[11].

**MY FAMILY**

**My parents** are Federico and Paola Rossi. **They** live in Udine. They**'re** doctors.

I **have** a sister. **Her name** is Carla. **She**'s in Germany. She**'s** also a student.

[10] **dorm (or dormitory):**  a building at a university where students live

[11] **film:**  movies

**MY INTERESTS**

I **love** art! I **like old** art and **new** art. I go to museums a lot.

I like **beautiful** clothes. I have a lot of dresses!

I like **good** food. I **make** dinners for my friends on Sundays. They love Italian food.
**We** also **go** to restaurants. I love Indian, Chinese, Japanese, Turkish, and Mexican food!

I **run** in the park on the weekends. I also **ride** my **bicycle** in the park.

**MY FAVORITE THINGS**

Books: My **favorite** book is *The Filmmaker's Handbook*. It's a big **book**.

Movies: *Citizen Kane* (from 1941) is an **interesting movie** for film students.

**People:** Sarah Polley and Mia Hansen-Love are great directors[12]. They're interesting **women**.

Sports teams: Real Madrid is my favorite **team**. I also like Udinese. Udinese is the soccer team from my **city**.

| Subject pronouns | Possessive determiners | Adjectives | Nouns | | Verbs | |
|---|---|---|---|---|---|---|
| | | | Singular | Plural | *Be* | Other verbs |
| *I* | | | | | | |

**Think about It** Read the statements about Angela. Choose *True* or *False*. Then rewrite the false statements to make them true.

| | | TRUE | FALSE |
|---|---|---|---|
| 1. | Angela is from New York. | ☐ | ☑ |
| 2. | Angela lives in New York. | ☐ | ☐ |
| 3. | Angela's sister is a doctor. | ☐ | ☐ |
| 4. | Angela makes Italian food for her friends. | ☐ | ☐ |
| 5. | Angela runs in the park after class. | ☐ | ☐ |
| 6. | Angela studies biology. | ☐ | ☐ |

*Angela is from Udine, Italy.*

[12]**directors:** people in charge of movies who tell the actors what to do

**B | GRAMMAR IN SPEAKING** Complete the sentences with information about you. Then share your answers with the class.

**ABOUT ME**

I'm _____.

I'm from _____.

I study _____.

**MY FAMILY**

I have _____.

My _____ is / are

_____.

**MY INTERESTS**

I like _____.

I like _____.

I like _____.

**MY FAVORITE THINGS**

My favorite book is _____.

My favorite movie is _____.

My favorite people are _____

and _____.

My favorite team is _____.

**Talk about It** Compare your answers with a partner. Are your sentences similar or different?

# 1.7 Summary of Parts of Speech

## NOUNS

**Nouns** are words for people, places, things, and ideas.

| SINGULAR | PLURAL |
|---|---|
| a bicycle | bicycles |
| an example | examples |
| a girl | girls |
| an office | offices |
| a person | people |

## SUBJECT PRONOUNS

| SINGULAR | PLURAL |
|---|---|
| I | we |
| you | you |
| he | they |
| she | |
| it | |

## ADJECTIVES

**Adjectives** describe **nouns**.

They have a **big house**.     This **book** is **interesting**.

This is my **new car**.     My **classes** are **hard**.

**Possessive nouns and determiners** show possession and relationships.

### POSSESSIVE NOUNS

| NOUN | POSSESSIVE NOUN + NOUN |
|---|---|
| Jim | Jim's car |
| Sarah | Sarah's parents |

### POSSESSIVE DETERMINERS

| SUBJECT PRONOUN | POSSESSIVE DETERMINER |
|---|---|
| I | my |
| you | your |
| he | his |
| she | her |
| it | its |
| we | our |
| they | their |

## SUBJECTS AND VERBS

Every sentence has a **subject** and a **verb**. The subject includes a **noun** or a **subject pronoun**.

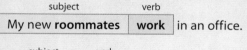

| subject | verb | |
|---|---|---|
| My new **roommates** | **work** | in an office. |

| subject | verb | |
|---|---|---|
| Your **parents** | **are** | here. |

| subject | verb | |
|---|---|---|
| **We** | **have** | a lot of homework. |

## IMPERATIVES

In commands and instructions, the subject is *you*, but we don't say it.

↓

### COMMANDS AND INSTRUCTIONS

**Open** your books.
**Don't start** your test.

### *LET'S* FOR SUGGESTIONS AND INVITATIONS

**Let's have** lunch.
**Let's go** to the game.

# 2

# The Verb *Have*

## **IN THIS UNIT, WE USE** the simple present of *have* to:

### Talk about food and drink

1. My family **has** coffee with every meal.

### Talk about family

2. I **have** a lot of cousins.

**GO ONLINE**

For the Unit Vocabulary Check, go to the Online Practice.

# Talk about activities and schedules

3. We **have** class at 11:00.

| 11 AM | |
| :-- | :-- |
| | **Class** |
| Noon | |
| 1 PM | |
| 2 PM | |

# Talk about possessions

4. Do you **have** a car?

5. Does your phone **have** a camera?

# Describe places

6. My apartment **has** lots of windows.

**Think about It**  Read these sentences. Check (✓) *Yes* or *No*.

|   | YES | NO |
| :-- | :--: | :--: |
| 1.  I have coffee with every meal. | ☐ | ☐ |
| 2.  I have two sisters. | ☐ | ☐ |
| 3.  I have class at 11:00. | ☐ | ☐ |
| 4.  I have a car. | ☐ | ☐ |
| 5.  My phone has a camera. | ☐ | ☐ |
| 6.  My apartment has lots of windows. | ☐ | ☐ |

## 2.1 Positive Statements with *Have* / *Has*

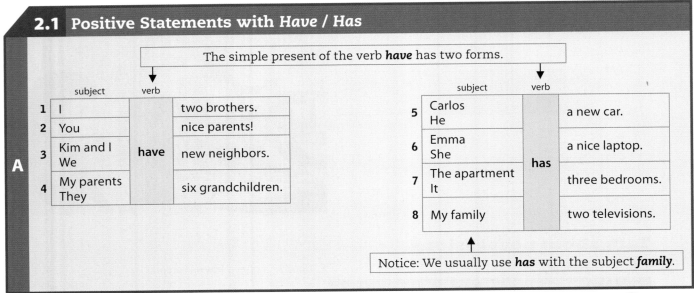

The simple present of the verb **have** has two forms.

**A**

| | subject | verb | |
|---|---|---|---|
| 1 | I | | two brothers. |
| 2 | You | | nice parents! |
| 3 | Kim and I / We | **have** | new neighbors. |
| 4 | My parents / They | | six grandchildren. |

| | subject | verb | |
|---|---|---|---|
| 5 | Carlos / He | | a new car. |
| 6 | Emma / She | | a nice laptop. |
| 7 | The apartment / It | **has** | three bedrooms. |
| 8 | My family | | two televisions. |

Notice: We usually use **has** with the subject *family*.

GO ONLINE

**1 | Noticing Forms of *Have*** Read the passages. Circle all forms of the verb *have*. Then underline the subject for each of these verbs. **2.1 A**

COFFEE OR TEA?

1. Turkey is famous for coffee! But at breakfast <u>we</u> (have) tea. The Turkish word for breakfast is *kahvalti*, or "before coffee." Turkish people have a lot of tea in the afternoon, too.

2. Norway has very good coffee. Norwegians love coffee! My sister and I have coffee with every meal. My little brother drinks milk.

3. British people drink a lot of tea. Many British people have six or seven cups of tea per day. We drink tea with milk. We also have a meal called "tea" between lunch and dinner.

4. In India, we have our coffee with a lot of milk and sugar. We drink coffee with very spicy food.

5. People in China drink tea every day. We have green tea and black tea. Tea is important for weddings and other events.

6. In Egypt, we have very sweet black tea. We put lots of sugar in our tea. My family has tea with breakfast and after lunch. We also make tea for visitors.

**Talk about It** Do you have coffee in the morning? Do you have tea? Talk to your classmates.

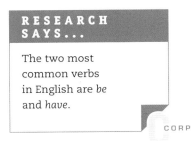

**RESEARCH SAYS...**

The two most common verbs in English are *be* and *have*.

CORPU

Chinese tea house

**2 | Choosing Forms of *Have*** Circle the correct form of *have* to complete each sentence. Then match each description with a picture below. **2.1 A**

**F Y I**

We often use the verb *have* to talk about food and drink.

Notice: We do NOT use the verb *take*.

✓ I **have** cereal in the morning.

✗ I **take** cereal in the morning.

WHAT'S FOR BREAKFAST?

1. In Germany, many people eat big breakfasts. My family (**have** / **has**) eggs, bread, cheese, cold meat, and cereal. We (**have** / **has**) coffee to drink.

2. In Spain, people (**have** / **has**) small breakfasts—maybe because we eat dinner very late. Most mornings I (**have** / **has**) bread and coffee. My roommate just (**have** / **has**) coffee.

3. For breakfast, many Vietnamese people (**have** / **has**) *pho*, a soup with noodles and meat. Sometimes we also (**have** / **has**) *pho* for lunch or dinner.

4. In the morning, I (**have** / **has**) a traditional Japanese breakfast: tea, rice, soup, and fish. My husband (**have** / **has**) the same thing. But my children (**have** / **has**) an American breakfast. They like cereal.

5. At college in the United States, my friends and I (**have** / **has**) eggs and toast. One roommate eats strange breakfasts. Sometimes he (**have** / **has**) cold pizza in the morning!

6. In Indonesia, I (**have** / **has**) chicken, eggs, and hot cereal for breakfast. Many people (**have** / **has**) chicken, tofu, and eggs with rice.

a. _____   b. _____   c. _____

d. _1_   e. _____   f. _____

**Talk about It** Which breakfast above looks good to you?

**Talk about It** What do you have for breakfast? Tell a partner.

*"I have tea and toast for breakfast."*

**3 | Using *Have* and *Has*** Look at this family tree. Complete the sentences below with *have* or *has*. `2.1 A`

FAMILY TREE

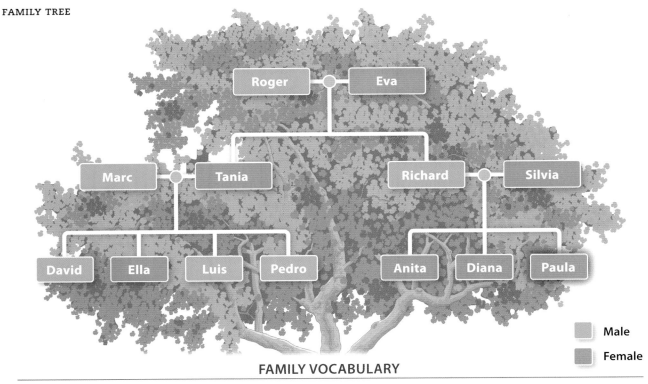

☐ Male
☐ Female

FAMILY VOCABULARY

**Your uncle** = your mother's or father's brother
**Your aunt** = your mother's or father's sister
**Your cousin** = your aunt's or uncle's son or daughter
**Your nephew** = your brother's or sister's son

**Your niece** = your brother's or sister's daughter
**Your grandparents** = your parents' parents
**Your grandchildren** = your children's children

1. Anita ____*has*____ two sisters.

2. She _____ four cousins.

3. Richard and Silvia _____ three daughters.

4. They _____ one niece and three nephews.

**Now complete these sentences with the people from the family tree and *have* or *has*. Then add two more sentences about the family.**

5. __*Tania*_____ ____*has*____ a husband, Marc.

6. _____ and _____ _____ seven grandchildren.

7. _____ _____ one brother.

8. _____ _____ three brothers.

9. Anita, Diana, and Paula _____ one _____, Tania.

10. Pedro _____ three _____: Anita, Diana, and Paula.

11. _____

12. _____

**Write about It** Draw a family tree for your family (or part of your family). Then write four sentences about your family. Use *have* or *has* in each sentence. Share your sentences with a partner.

*I have two brothers, Hassan and Khalid. My brother Khalid has a son, Nassir.*

## 2.2 Negative Statements with *Have*

**A**

We use **do / does** + **not** to form negative statements in the simple present.

| | subject | do / does + not | have | |
|---|---|---|---|---|
| 1 | I | do not<br>don't | have | friends here. |
| 2 | You | | | my phone number. |
| 3 | We<br>Sam and I | | | class tomorrow. |
| 4 | They<br>My friends | | | money. |
| 5 | He<br>Sam | does not<br>doesn't | | a laptop. |
| 6 | She<br>Maria | | | a car. |
| 7 | It<br>The apartment | | | a dining room. |

Notice: We do NOT use *has*.
✗ She doesn't has . . .

In speaking and informal writing, we often use contractions.

| | | contraction |
|---|---|---|
| do not | = | don't |
| does not | = | doesn't |

GO ONLINE

**4 | Using *Don't Have* and *Doesn't Have*** Read the riddles and look at the pictures below. Underline *don't/doesn't* + *have*. Circle *have/has* in positive statements. Then complete each riddle. **2.2 A**

RIDDLES

1. I (have) hands, but I <u>don't have</u> fingers. I have a face. But my face doesn't have eyes, a nose, or a mouth. It has numbers. I am a _____.

2. I have arms and legs. But I don't have a body or a head. I am a _____.

3. I have one foot. My foot doesn't have five toes. It has 12 inches (1 inch = 2.54 centimeters). I am a _____.

4. I have two legs. But my legs don't have feet. I am a _____.

chair                clock                pair of pants                ruler

**5 | Using *Don't Have* and *Doesn't Have*** Complete each sentence with *don't have* or *doesn't have*. Do you agree with the complaints? Check (✓) your complaints. **2.2 A**

COMMON COMPLAINTS FROM UNIVERSITY STUDENTS                                          MY COMPLAINTS

1. The cafeteria _____*doesn't have*_____ good food.                    ☐

2. And we only have the cafeteria. We _____ other choices here.    ☐

3. I _____ a lot of friends.                    ☐

4. My roommate and I _____ much in common.[1]    ☐

5. Our professors _____ time for us.    ☐

6. I _____ time for classes and my job!    ☐

7. I _____ a car, and the buses here _____ good schedules.    ☐

8. My school _____ activities for students.    ☐

9. I'm confused about my class. And my professor _____ advice for me.    ☐

## 6 | Error Correction  Find and correct the errors. (Some sentences may not have any errors.)  2.2 A

COMMON NEIGHBORHOOD[2] COMPLAINTS

1. The neighborhood *doesn't* ~~not~~ have many restaurants.

2. It don't have a park.

3. The children doesn't have a place to play.

4. Our streets no have parking places.

5. Many streets don't have trees.

6. My street don't have many streetlights.

7. The stores doesn't have good prices.

**Write about It**  Think of two other complaints about your neighborhood. Write two sentences with *don't have* or *doesn't have*.

*The neighborhood doesn't have sidewalks.*

## 7 | Writing Sentences with *Don't Have* and *Doesn't Have*  Look at Picture A carefully.  2.2 A

PICTURE A

[1] **have much in common:**  to be very similar    [2] **neighborhood:**  a part of a town or city

Now look at Picture B carefully.

PICTURE B

Write six sentences about how Picture B is different from Picture A. Use *don't have* or *doesn't have* in each sentence. You can use the words in this box.

| | | | | | | |
|---|---|---|---|---|---|---|
| apples | ball | boy | driver | houses | street | tree |
| baby | bicycle | cat | girl | leaves | street sign | truck |
| backpack | birds | children | helmet | nest | toy | windows |

*The street doesn't have a street sign.*

**8 | Using *Have/Has* and *Don't Have/Doesn't Have*** Look at these two apartments for rent. Complete the sentences below. Use *have, has, don't have,* or *doesn't have.* **2.2 A**

Two-Bedroom Apartment on Busy Main Street

closet
fireplace
bedrooms
living room

Other features:
Great city views!

**MAIN STREET APARTMENT**

1. The apartment _____*doesn't have*_____ a large kitchen.

2. The rooms _____ a lot of windows.

3. The bathroom _____ a bathtub.

4. The apartment _____ a fireplace.

5. The floors _____ carpets.

6. The bedrooms _____ closets.

7. The apartment _____ a garden.

### Two-Bedroom Apartment on Quiet Elm Street

garden
bathtub
dining room
kitchen
carpet

Other features:
A garage for your car!
A garden!

ELM STREET APARTMENT

8. The apartment _____ a large kitchen.

9. The rooms _____ lots of windows.

10. The bathrooms _____ bathtubs.

11. The apartment _____ a fireplace.

12. The bedroom floors _____ carpets.

13. The bedrooms _____ closets.

14. The apartment _____ a garden.

**Write about It** Write two sentences about your home. Then write two sentences about your dream home (the home you want). Use *have/has* and *don't have/doesn't have*.

*My home has two bathrooms. It doesn't have a garden.*
*My dream home has four bathrooms. It has a swimming pool.*

## 2.3 Yes/No Questions with *Have*

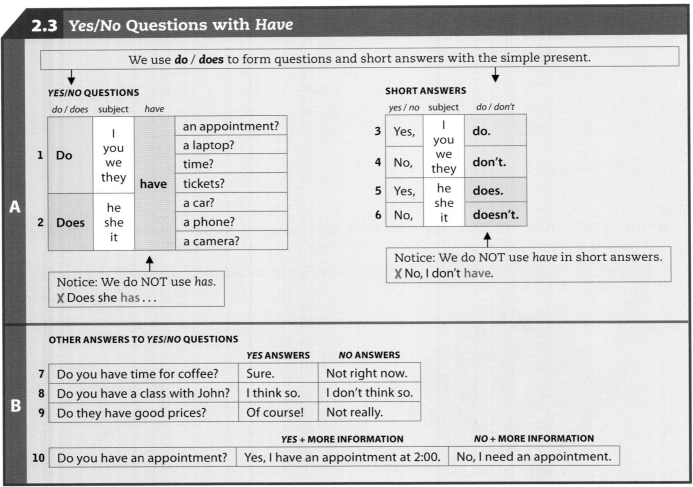

We use **do / does** to form questions and short answers with the simple present.

**YES/NO QUESTIONS**

| | do / does | subject | have | |
|---|---|---|---|---|
| 1 | **Do** | I you we they | **have** | an appointment? |
| | | | | a laptop? |
| | | | | time? |
| | | | | tickets? |
| 2 | **Does** | he she it | | a car? |
| | | | | a phone? |
| | | | | a camera? |

Notice: We do NOT use *has*.
✗ Does she has...

**SHORT ANSWERS**

| | yes / no | subject | do / don't |
|---|---|---|---|
| 3 | Yes, | I you we they | **do.** |
| 4 | No, | | **don't.** |
| 5 | Yes, | he she it | **does.** |
| 6 | No, | | **doesn't.** |

Notice: We do NOT use *have* in short answers.
✗ No, I don't have.

**A**

**B**

**OTHER ANSWERS TO *YES/NO* QUESTIONS**

| | | YES ANSWERS | NO ANSWERS |
|---|---|---|---|
| 7 | Do you have time for coffee? | Sure. | Not right now. |
| 8 | Do you have a class with John? | I think so. | I don't think so. |
| 9 | Do they have good prices? | Of course! | Not really. |

| | | YES + MORE INFORMATION | NO + MORE INFORMATION |
|---|---|---|---|
| 10 | Do you have an appointment? | Yes, I have an appointment at 2:00. | No, I need an appointment. |

GO ONLINE

**9 | Answering *Yes/No* Questions** Look at these ads for tablets. Answer the questions with the short answers in the box. Then practice the questions with a partner. `2.3 A`

QUESTIONS

1. Does the YouGo Tablet have a 7-inch screen?

   *No, it doesn't.*

2. Does the YouGo Tablet have a leather case?

3. Does the Star Tablet have a camera?

4. Does the Star Tablet have a leather case?

5. Do the tablets have keyboards?

6. Does Tech City have a discount for students?

7. Do the stores have sales on Monday?

| ANSWERS |
| --- |
| Yes, it does. |
| No, it doesn't. |
| Yes, they do. |
| No, they don't. |

**Talk about It** Talk about your cell phone, tablet, or other device. Ask and answer three questions with a partner. Use *does . . . have* in your questions. Answer with a short answer.

A: *Does your phone have a calendar?*
B: *Yes, it does.*

**10 | Asking Questions with *Have*** Complete these conversations with the words in parentheses. Then listen and check your answers. `2.3 A–B`

ASKING ABOUT PRODUCTS

1. A: ___*Does*___ this phone ___*have*___ a long battery life?
       (do / does)      (have / has)

   B: Yes, it _____ a ten-hour battery.
       (have / has)

2. A: _____ this television _____ a good sound system?
       (do / does)      (have / has)

   B: Not really. The other TV _____ a better sound system.
       (have / has)

battery life

3. A: _____ the laptops _____ webcams?
  (do / does)      (have / has)

  B: Yes, all of the laptops _____ webcams.
                            (have / has)

4. A: _____ this car _____ a stereo?
  (do / does)      (have / has)

  B: Of course! It _____ a stereo with a CD player and an MP3 player.
                   (have / has)

5. A: _____ these MP3 players _____ a lot of memory³?
  (do / does)               (have / has)

  B: Yes, they _____ 30 gigabytes⁴.
              (have / has)

6. A: These headphones are really small. _____ you _____ big headphones?
                                        (do / does)    (have / has)

  B: Sure, we _____ many kinds of headphones.
             (have / has)

**Talk about It** Practice the conversations above with a partner.

webcam

car stereo

---

**11 | Usage Note: Common Phrases with *Have*** Read the note. Then do Activities 12–13.

Notice these common phrases with **have**.

| | |
|---|---|
| have a (big / small) family | We **have a small family**. |
| have an appointment | Hello. I **have an appointment** with Dr. Chin. |
| have change | Do you **have change** for a dollar? |
| have children | We **have two children**. |
| have class / English / Math | I can't come. I **have class** today. |
| have (free) time | Do you **have free time** today? |
| have friends | I **have friends** all over the world. |
| have homework | Do we **have homework** today? |
| have trouble | I **have trouble** with languages. |

have an appointment

have change for a dollar

---

**12 | Using Common Phrases with *Have*** Complete these conversations with *do, does, have,* or *has.* Then listen and check your answers. Practice the conversations with a partner. **2.3 A–B**

1. A: Excuse me, ___*do*___ you ___*have*___ change for a dollar?

  B: Let me look. Yes, I _____ four quarters.

2. A: Hey, _____ we _____ a class together?

  B: I don't think so.

  A: I think we do. _____ you _____ chemistry class on
    Mondays and Wednesdays?

  B: Oh, yes, I do. Nice to meet you!

3. A: _____ Tomas _____ homework tonight?

  B: Yes, he _____ a lot of homework. He can't watch any TV.

4. A: _____ you _____ trouble with math?

  B: No, I like math.

  A: I _____ a lot of trouble. Can you help me with my homework?

5. A: _____ you _____ time for a cup of coffee?

  B: Not right now. I _____ class at 2:00. I'm free at 3:00.

  A: Great. Let's go at 3:00.

I have trouble with math.

³**memory (in electronics):** space for music, photos, and other information

⁴**gigabytes:** 1 gigabyte ("gig") = 1 billion bytes

## 13 | Asking Questions with *Have*  Ask and answer these questions with three classmates. Write their names in the chart. Answer the questions with short answers or with more information. Circle each classmate's answers. 2.3 A–B

TALKING TO FRIENDS

| | Name _____ | Name _____ | Name _____ |
|---|---|---|---|
| 1. Do you **have a big family**? | Yes / No | Yes / No | Yes / No |
| 2. Do you **have an appointment** today? | Yes / No | Yes / No | Yes / No |
| 3. Do you **have change** for a dollar? | Yes / No | Yes / No | Yes / No |
| 4. Do you **have children**? | Yes / No | Yes / No | Yes / No |
| 5. Do you **have class** tonight? | Yes / No | Yes / No | Yes / No |
| 6. Do you **have free time** today? | Yes / No | Yes / No | Yes / No |
| 7. Do you **have friends** in New York? | Yes / No | Yes / No | Yes / No |
| 8. Do you **have homework** tonight? | Yes / No | Yes / No | Yes / No |
| 9. Do you **have trouble** with math? | Yes / No | Yes / No | Yes / No |

A: *Do you have an appointment today?*
B: *No, I don't.*   OR   *Yes, I have a doctor's appointment.*

**Talk about It**  Work with a new partner. Trade books. What do you remember about your classmates? Quiz your partner. Use *does . . . have*.

A: *Does Ben have an appointment today?*
B: *No, he doesn't.*

## 14 | Pronunciation Note: Reduction of *Do You*  Listen to the note. Then do Activity 15.

Notice how we pronounce *Do you* in questions:

| **1 Do you** have friends in New York? | *sounds like* | "**D'you** have friends in New York?" |
| **2 Do you** have children? | *sounds like* | "**D'you** have children?" |
| **3 Do you** have a car? | *sounds like* | "**D'you** have a car?" |

## 15 | Reducing *Do You* in Questions  Listen and repeat these questions. 2.3 A–B

1. Do you have brothers or sisters?
2. Do you have a lot of cousins?
3. Do you have a pet?
4. Do you have a car?
5. Do you have a bike?

6. Do you have a TV at home?
7. Do you have an email address?
8. Do you have a laptop?
9. Do you have a smartphone?
10. Do you have a tablet?

**Talk about It**  Ask and answer the questions above with a partner. Pronounce *do you* like *d'you*. Answer the questions with short answers or with more information.

A: *Do you have brothers or sisters?*
B: *No, I don't.*   OR   *Yes, I have two brothers.*

🔊 **16｜Pronunciation Note: Intonation in *Yes/No* Questions**  Listen to the note. Then do Activity 17.

> Notice the rising intonation in these questions:
>
> **1** Do I have your phone number?
>
> **2** Does your brother have children?
>
> **3** Do we have time for lunch?

🔊 **17｜Using Intonation in *Yes/No* Questions**  Listen and repeat these questions.  `2.3 A–B`

1. Do you have friends at school?
2. Do you have friends at work?
3. Do you have family in Europe?
4. Does your best friend have a class with you?
5. Does your best friend have a car?
6. Do you have a lot of homework?
7. Does your school have a library?
8. Do you have free time today?
9. Does your school have a lot of students?
10. Do you have a TV?

**Talk about It**  Ask and answer the questions above with a partner. Use rising intonation. Answer the questions with short answers or with more information.

## 2.4  Questions with *When*, *What*, and *How Many*

*When*, *What*, and ***How many*** are **Wh- words.**

| | wh- word | (noun) | do | subject | have | |
|---|---|---|---|---|---|---|
| **1** | **When** | – | | I | **have** | class? |
| **2** | **What** | – | **do** | you | | for breakfast? |
| **3** | **What** | class | | we | **have?** | |
| **4** | **How many** | classes | | they | | |

| | wh- word | (noun) | does | subject | have | |
|---|---|---|---|---|---|---|
| **5** | **When** | – | | Marc | **have** | Math? |
| **6** | **What** | – | **does** | Kim | | in her bag? |
| **7** | **What** | classes | | she | **have?** | |
| **8** | **How many** | bedrooms | | it | | |

> Notice: We can use **What** + noun (singular or plural).
>
> We use **How many** + plural noun.

**A**

| TO ASK ABOUT: | USE *WH*- WORD: | | ANSWER WITH: |
|---|---|---|---|
| a time | **When** | **9** When **do** you **have** class?<br>**10** When **does** Marc **have** tennis? | **a day or time:**<br>On Monday.<br>At 10:00. |
| a thing | **What** | **11** What **do** you **have** for breakfast?<br>**12** What class **does** Sarah **have** now? | **a thing:**<br>Some coffee and toast.<br>She has English. |
| a number | **How many** | **13** How many classes **do** you **have?**<br>**14** How many bedrooms **does** the apartment **have?** | **a number:**<br>Three classes.<br>Two. |

Notice:

✓ How many bedrooms **does** the apartment have?    ✗ How many bedrooms do the apartment have?

**18 | Using Wh- Words** Complete these conversations with *When*, *What*, or *How many*. Then practice the conversations with a partner. ▨2.4A

1. A: _What_ do you have for dessert?

   B: We have apple pie, chocolate cake, and ice cream.

   A: Oh, I want the chocolate cake!

2. A: Does Karen have class today?

   B: I think so.

   A: _____ class does she have?

   B: I'm not sure.

3. A: _____ bathrooms does the apartment have?

   B: Just one.

   A: Oh, no, thank you. We need two bathrooms.

4. A: _____ do you have your doctor's appointment?

   B: At 9:30 in the morning.

5. A: _____ restaurants does this hotel have?

   B: Two—the Wellington and Joe's Grill. They're downstairs.

6. A: _____ do you have lunch?

   B: At 1:00.

   A: Me too! Let's eat together.

7. A: _____ do you have math?

   B: At 2:00.

   A: _____ class do you have after that?

   B: I have history at 3:30.

8. A: Do you have children?

   B: Yes, I do.

   A: _____ children do you have?

   B: I have two daughters.

**Think about It** There are two *yes/no* questions in the conversations above. Underline them.

**19 | Writing Wh- Questions** Put the words in the correct order to make *wh-* questions. ▨2.4A

**Fall Holidays**

1. Q: China/have/what/in the fall/big holiday/does/?

   _What big holiday does China have in the fall?_

   A: China has the Mid-Autumn Festival.

2. Q: foods/what/do/for the Mid-Autumn Festival/people/have/?

   _____

   A: They have mooncakes and taro.

Mooncakes for the Mid-Autumn Festival in China

3. Q: Americans/what/in the fall/have/holiday/do/?

   _____

   A: Americans have Thanksgiving in November.

4. Q: do/for dinner/people/on Thanksgiving/what/have/?

   _____

   A: They usually have turkey.

Thanksgiving in the U.S.

5. Q: does/what/Japan/in the fall/have/holiday/?

   _____

   A: Japan has Sports Day in the fall.

6. Q: national holidays/have/does/how many/Japan/?

   _____

   A: Japan has 15 national holidays.

Sports Day in Japan

7. Q: Mexico/holiday/does/in the fall/what/have/?

   _____

   A: Mexico has *Día de los Muertos*: "The Day of the Dead."

8. Q: days/does/how many/have/the holiday/?

   _____

   A: The holiday has two days of celebrations: November 1–2.

The Day of the Dead in Mexico

**Think about It** Which questions above use a *wh-* word + a noun? Circle them.

**20 | Usage Note: Time Expressions with *At*, *In*, and *On*** Read the note. Then do Activity 21.

Notice the words we use with different times.

| *at . . .* | *in . . .* | *on . . .* | |
|---|---|---|---|
| 8:00 | the morning | Monday | **1** We have English **at** 10:00 **in** the morning. |
| noon | the afternoon | Tuesday | **2** I have a meeting **at** 2:00 **on** Monday. |
| midnight | the evening | Monday morning | **3** He has tennis **on** Friday **in** the afternoon. |
| | | Tuesday evening | |

**GRAMMAR TERM:** *at*, *in*, and *on* are **prepositions**.

**21 | Talking about Schedules**  Look at these calendars. Complete the questions and answers below with the words in parentheses. Then draw lines to match the questions with the correct answers.  **2.4 A**

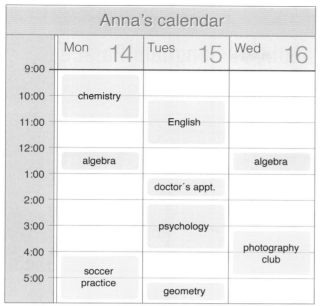

**QUESTIONS**

1. ___When___ does Anna ___have___ chemistry?
   (when / what)     (have / has)

2. _____ does Anna have _____
   (when / what)                    (on / in)
   Monday morning?

3. When _____ Sarah _____ guitar lessons?
        (do / does)        (have / has)

4. When _____ Anna and Sarah _____
         (do / does)                         (have / has)
   English?

5. _____ does Anna have _____ Monday
   (when / what)                 (on / in)
   afternoon?

6. What _____ Sarah have _____ Wednesday?
        (do / does)              (on / in)

7. _____ does Anna have _____ 1:00
   (when / what)                (on / at)
   _____ Tuesday?
   (on / in)

8. What _____ Anna and Sarah have _____
        (do / does)                              (on / at)
   12:00 _____ Wednesday?
         (on / at)

**ANSWERS**

a. She _____ them _____ Monday
       (have / has)         (on / at)
   _____ 1:00.
   (on / at)

b. They _____ it _____ Tuesday
        (have / has)     (on / at)
   _____ 10:00.
   (on / at)

c. She _____ soccer practice.
       (have / has)

d. She ___has___ it ___on___ Monday
       (have / has)   (on / in)
   ___at___ 9:00.
   (on / at)

e. They _____ algebra.
        (have / has)

f. She _____ chemistry.
       (have / has)

g. She _____ world history, algebra, and
       (have / has)
   tennis club.

h. She _____ a doctor's appointment.
       (have / has)

**Talk about It**  Anna and Sarah want to get together. When can they meet? Use *at* and *on* in your answer.

*"Anna and Sarah can meet ____."*

**Talk about It**  Write out your schedule for one week. (Use the schedules above for ideas.) Then work with a partner. Find a time to get together. Use these expressions or your own ideas.

*"What do you have on ____ at ____?"*
*"Do you have class on/at ____?"*
*"Do you have free time on/at ____?"*
*"Let's meet on ____ at ____."*

**22 | Writing Questions with *How Many*** Complete these questions. Use *how many* and the verb *have* in each question. **2.4 A**

# Frequently Asked Questions about Buckingham Palace and the British Royal Family

1. Q: _____ *How many rooms does* _____ Buckingham Palace ___*have*___?
   A: It has 775 rooms.

2. Q: _____ it _____?
   A: It has 240 bedrooms.

3. Q: _____ it _____?
   A: It has 78 bathrooms.

4. Q: _____ it _____?
   A: It has 1,514 doors.

5. Q: _____ it _____?
   A: It has 760 windows.

6. Q: _____ it _____?
   A: It has over 40,000 light bulbs.

7. Q: _____ the gardens _____?
   A: The gardens have over 350 kinds of flowers.

8. Q: _____
      Queen Elizabeth and Prince Philip _____?
   A: They have four children.

**Write about It** Choose a famous building from this box. Write four *How many* questions about the building. Then go online and find the answers. Share your answers with the class.

| Angkor Wat | Bangkok's Grand Palace | the Palace of Versailles | the White House |
| --- | --- | --- | --- |

*How many rooms does the Palace of Versailles have?*

**23 | Pronunciation Note: Intonation in *Wh-* Questions** Listen to the note. Then do Activity 24.

*Wh-* questions usually end with falling intonation. Notice the difference between *yes/no* questions and *wh-* questions.

| *YES/NO* QUESTIONS | *WH-* QUESTIONS |
|---|---|
| 1 Do you have class today? | 4 When do you have class? |
| 2 Does Carlos have sisters? | 5 How many sisters does he have? |
| 3 Do they have children? | 6 How many children do they have? |

**24 | Using Intonation in *Wh-* Questions and *Yes/No* Questions** Read these questions. Do you use rising intonation or falling intonation? Choose the correct intonation. Then listen and check your answers.

**2.4 A**

|  | (RISING INTONATION) | (FALLING INTONATION) |
|---|:---:|:---:|
| 1. Do you have a lot of classes? | ☑ | ☐ |
| 2. How many classes do you have? | ☐ | ☐ |
| 3. Do you have coffee every day? | ☐ | ☐ |
| 4. When do you have breakfast? | ☐ | ☐ |
| 5. How many bedrooms does your home have? | ☐ | ☐ |
| 6. Do you have a big house? | ☐ | ☐ |
| 7. Do you have nieces or nephews? | ☐ | ☐ |
| 8. How many brothers or sisters do you have? | ☐ | ☐ |
| 9. Does your classroom have computers? | ☐ | ☐ |
| 10. What kinds of computers does your school have? | ☐ | ☐ |
| 11. What do you have for lunch every day? | ☐ | ☐ |
| 12. Does your school have a cafeteria? | ☐ | ☐ |

**Talk about It** Complete these questions with your own ideas. Mark the questions ⤴ or ⤵ for the correct intonation. Then ask and answer your questions with a partner.

1. When do you have _____?

2. What _____ do you have?

3. How many _____ do you have?

4. How many _____ does your _____ have?

**Write about It** Write your partner's answers to the questions above. Use complete sentences.

*Sun-Hee has tennis lessons on Mondays at 2:00.*

**A | GRAMMAR IN READING** Read this discussion forum. Underline the forms of *have*. Then complete the sentences below with *have*, *has*, *don't have*, or *doesn't have*.

## What's In Your Bag?

| Joseph S. | 6/8/14   8:20 p.m. |
|---|---|
| | I start college in September, and I want to buy a backpack. Do I need a big backpack or a small one? What do college students <u>have</u> in their bags? Do they only have books and notebooks? Do they have computers? Are you a college student? What do you have in your bag? |
| Erin33 | 6/8/14   10:17 p.m. |
| | My sister is a college student. She has a lot of things in her backpack. She always has books, pens, and notebooks. She also has her wallet, her cell phone, and her tablet. |
| KenjiT92 | 6/9/14   7:22 a.m. |
| | I'm a freshman[5] in college. I usually have a laptop, books, notebooks, pens, my cell phone, my keys, and some money in my bag. Sometimes I have exercise clothes in my backpack because I play tennis. |
| Sonja445 | 6/9/14   9:18 a.m. |
| | I don't have a backpack. I have a big shoulder bag. At my school, a lot of students have shoulder bags. I usually have my tablet, notebooks, pencils, an eraser, and snacks in my bag. I don't usually have textbooks in my bag. They're really heavy, so I leave them at home. |

1. Erin33's sister and Sonja445 _____*have*_____ tablets in their bags.

2. Sonja445 _____ a backpack. She _____ a big shoulder bag.

3. KenjiT92 sometimes _____ clothes in his backpack.

4. A lot of Sonja445's classmates _____ shoulder bags.

5. Usually, Sonja445 _____ textbooks in her bag.

**B | GRAMMAR IN SPEAKING** Look at the survey on page 45. Follow these instructions.

1. Add two more items to the survey.

2. Interview your classmates. Ask questions with *have*.

   A: *Do you have a backpack?*
   B: *Yes, I do.*

3. Count your classmates' answers. Write sentences about the results.

   *14 students have backpacks.*

[5] **freshman:** a student in the first year of college

## A Student Backpack/Bag Survey

| | |
|---|---|
| 1. a backpack | 9. an eraser |
| 2. another kind of bag | 10. snacks |
| 3. textbooks | 11. water |
| 4. notebooks | 12. a cell phone |
| 5. a tablet | 13. keys |
| 6. a laptop | 14. some clothes |
| 7. pens | 15. _____ |
| 8. pencils | 16. _____ |

## 2.5 Summary of the Verb *Have*

### USES

We can use *have* when we:

- talk about food and drink
- talk about family
- talk about activities and schedules
- talk about possessions
- describe places

### STATEMENTS

| POSITIVE STATEMENTS | | | |
|---|---|---|---|
| | I You We They | have | a camera. |
| | He She It | has | |

| NEGATIVE STATEMENTS | | | | |
|---|---|---|---|---|
| | I You We They | do not don't | have | a camera. |
| | He She It | does not doesn't | | |

### QUESTIONS

| YES/NO QUESTIONS | | | | |
|---|---|---|---|---|
| | Do | I you we they | have | a camera? |
| | Does | he she it | | |

| SHORT ANSWERS | | | |
|---|---|---|---|
| | Yes, | you I | do. |
| | No, | we they | don't. |
| | Yes, | he she it | does. |
| | No, | | doesn't. |

| QUESTIONS WITH *WHEN* AND *WHAT* | When | do | I / you / we / they | have | class? |
|---|---|---|---|---|---|
| | What | does | he / she | | at 10:00? |

| QUESTIONS WITH *WHAT* AND *HOW MANY* + NOUN | What | classes | do | I / you / we / they | have? |
|---|---|---|---|---|---|
| | How many | children | does | he / she | |
| | | bedrooms | | it | |

# 3

# Simple Present

**For the Unit Vocabulary Check, go to the Online Practice.**

## IN THIS UNIT, WE USE the simple present to:

### Talk about facts

1. The equator **divides** the Earth around the center.

2. Baboons often **sleep** in trees.

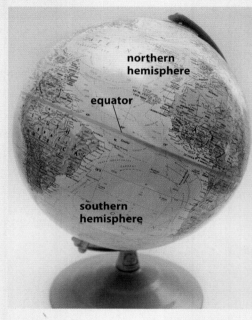

**Think about It** Complete these facts with the words from the box.

| Australia | Brazil | France | Russia |

1. _____ and _____ have summer in December.

| bats | bears | cows | owls |

2. _____ and _____ sleep during the day.

46

## Talk about habits and routines

3. I usually **ride** my bike to work.

4. My roommate often **cooks** dinner.

5. My brother **exercises** every morning.

6. I usually **study** on the weekends.

**Think about It**  Look at the photos above. What do you do? Check (✓) *True* or *False*.

|  | TRUE | FALSE |
|---|---|---|
| 1.  I ride a bike to school. | ☐ | ☐ |
| 2.  I cook dinner every night. | ☐ | ☐ |
| 3.  I often exercise in the morning. | ☐ | ☐ |
| 4.  I study on the weekends. | ☐ | ☐ |

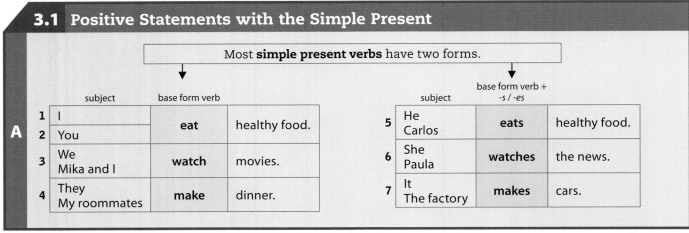

Most **simple present verbs** have two forms.

| A | | subject | base form verb | | | | subject | base form verb + -s / -es | |
|---|---|---|---|---|---|---|---|---|---|
| | 1 | I | **eat** | healthy food. | | 5 | He<br>Carlos | **eats** | healthy food. |
| | 2 | You | | | | | | | |
| | 3 | We<br>Mika and I | **watch** | movies. | | 6 | She<br>Paula | **watches** | the news. |
| | 4 | They<br>My roommates | **make** | dinner. | | 7 | It<br>The factory | **makes** | cars. |

**1 | Noticing the Simple Present** Circle all the simple present verbs in these sentences. Then underline the subject for each of these verbs.  3.1 A

INTERESTING FACTS ABOUT PLANTS

### Water Lilies

1. Water lilies (live) in water. They grow in the soil¹ under the water.

2. Frogs sit on water lily leaves.

3. Water lilies grow very quickly. Some water lilies grow in just 2–3 weeks.

4. Water lilies have big, colorful flowers. The flowers smell very nice.

5. The flowers bloom² for only 3–4 days.

water lilies

### Duckweed

6. Duckweed grows in water—not soil.

7. Frogs swim in duckweed. They hide from other animals.

8. Duckweed makes very small flowers.

9. Ducks eat duckweed. In Southeast Asia, some people eat duckweed, too.

10. Some people use duckweed for fuel³. They make electricity from dried duckweed.

**Talk about It** Which facts surprise you? Talk to a partner.

a frog in duckweed

¹**soil:** the dirt where plants and trees grow
²**bloom:** when a plant's flowers are open

³**fuel:** something that you burn to make heat or power

**2 | Choosing Simple Present Forms**  Read the passages. Circle the correct form of each verb.  `3.1 A`

FACTS ABOUT WEATHER

hurricane

blizzard

earthquake

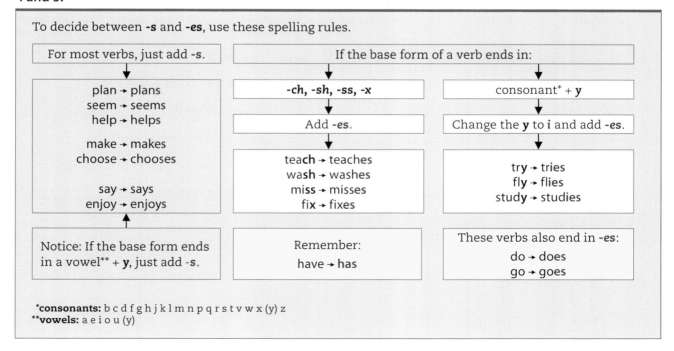
tornado

1. Hurricanes (**happen** / **happens**) in warm, wet places. The Atlantic Ocean (**produce** / **produces**) about 15 hurricanes each year. In Cuba, people (**see** / **sees**) a lot of hurricanes.

2. Blizzards (**happen** / **happens**) in cold places around the world. They're common in Russia and North America. A blizzard (**make** / **makes**) a lot of snow and wind.

3. Earthquakes (**happen** / **happens**) in many places all over the world. California (**has** / **have**) many small earthquakes every day. Japan also (**experience** / **experiences**) many earthquakes.

4. Tornadoes (**happen** / **happens**) in North America. They're common in the middle of the United States. Tornadoes (**has** / **have**) very strong winds. They (**destroy** / **destroys**) many homes and other buildings.

**Talk about It**  Do these weather events happen in your area? What other kinds of weather do you see?

**3 | Spelling Note: *-s* and *-es* Endings on Simple Present Verbs**  Read the note. Then do Activities 4 and 5.

To decide between **-s** and **-es**, use these spelling rules.

| For most verbs, just add **-s**. | If the base form of a verb ends in: | |
|---|---|---|
| plan → plans<br>seem → seems<br>help → helps<br><br>make → makes<br>choose → chooses<br><br>say → says<br>enjoy → enjoys | **-ch, -sh, -ss, -x**<br>↓<br>Add **-es**.<br>↓<br>tea**ch** → teaches<br>wa**sh** → washes<br>mi**ss** → misses<br>fi**x** → fixes | consonant* + **y**<br>↓<br>Change the **y** to **i** and add **-es**.<br>↓<br>tr**y** → tries<br>fl**y** → flies<br>stud**y** → studies |
| Notice: If the base form ends in a vowel** + **y**, just add **-s**. | Remember:<br>have → **has** | These verbs also end in **-es**:<br>do → does<br>go → goes |

*consonants: b c d f g h j k l m n p q r s t v w x (y) z
**vowels: a e i o u (y)

**4 | Spelling Simple Present Verbs** Add -s or -es to each verb in the box. Write the verb in the correct part of the chart. `3.1 A`

| bring | finish | rush |
|---|---|---|
| brush | fix | say |
| care | fly | seem |
| carry | help | stay |
| catch | hold | study |
| change | kiss | sweep |
| come | make | take |
| cost | miss | talk |
| cross | mix | teach |
| cry | pay | throw |
| discuss | plan | touch |
| draw | press | try |
| drink | pull | want |
| dry | push | wash |
| enjoy | reply | watch |
| find | review | |

| Verbs ending in -ch, -sh, -ss, -x | Verbs ending in consonant + y | Other verbs |
|---|---|---|
| | | *brings* |

**Think about It** Do you know the words above? Use a dictionary to look up the words you don't know.

**5 | Choosing -s or -es for Simple Present Verbs** Look at the jobs. Complete the sentences below with a job and the verb in parentheses. Use the correct spelling of the verb. `3.1 A`

DESCRIBING JOBS

a cashier        a nurse        an IT person        a waiter (or waitress)        a salesperson        an elementary school teacher

1. _A nurse_ _____ _helps_ sick people.
   (help)
2. _____ _____ things for you in a store.
   (find)
3. _____ _____ young children.
   (teach)
4. _____ _____ your food in a restaurant.
   (bring)
5. _____ _____ your money and gives you change.
   (take)
6. _____ _____ computer systems.
   (fix)

| an engineer | a manager | a professor | a journalist | an astronomer | a counselor |

7. _____ _____ at a university.
(teach)

8. _____ _____ to people and writes about events.
(talk)

9. _____ _____ buildings and roads.
(plan)

10. _____ _____ the stars and planets.
(watch)

11. _____ _____ people's plans and problems.
(discuss)

12. _____ _____ decisions about the work in an office.
(make)

**Talk about It** Look at the jobs above and on page 50. What are the three best jobs? Compare your ideas with a partner.

*"The best jobs are an engineer, a nurse, and an astronomer."*

🔊 **6 | Pronunciation Note: -s and -es Endings on Simple Present Verbs** Listen to the note. Then do Activities 7 and 8.

Notice how we pronounce the **-s** and **-es** endings on simple present verbs.

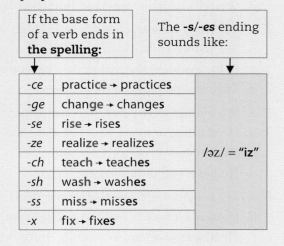

| If the base form of a verb ends in **the sound:** | | The **-s/-es** ending sounds like: |
|---|---|---|
| /f/ | laugh → laughs | |
| /k/ | make → makes | /s/ = "ss" |
| /p/ | stop → stops | |
| /t/ | put → puts | |

| /b/ | grab → grabs | |
|---|---|---|
| /d/ | decide → decides | |
| /g/ | drag → drags | |
| /l/ | smile → smiles | |
| /m/ | swim → swims | |
| /n/ | turn → turns | /z/ = "zz" |
| /r/ | care → cares | |
| /v/ | save → saves | |
| /w/ | show → shows | |
| a vowel sound | fly → flies | |
| | go → goes | |
| | do → does* | |

| If the base form of a verb ends in **the spelling:** | | The **-s/-es** ending sounds like: |
|---|---|---|
| -ce | practice → practices | |
| -ge | change → changes | |
| -se | rise → rises | |
| -ze | realize → realizes | /əz/ = "iz" |
| -ch | teach → teaches | |
| -sh | wash → washes | |
| -ss | miss → misses | |
| -x | fix → fixes | |

The /s/ and /z/ endings sound very similar. It's often difficult to hear the difference.

*We pronounce *does* "duz."

**◀)) 7 | Listening for -s Endings** Listen to the sentences. Do the verbs have an -s ending? Circle the form you hear. `3.1 A`

| | | | | |
|---|---|---|---|---|
| 1. stop | (stops) | 11. help | helps | |
| 2. sleep | sleeps | 12. clean | cleans | |
| 3. need | needs | 13. cost | costs | |
| 4. come | comes | 14. drink | drinks | |
| 5. get | gets | 15. swim | swims | |
| 6. laugh | laughs | 16. design | designs | |
| 7. work | works | 17. play | plays | |
| 8. want | wants | 18. make | makes | |
| 9. open | opens | 19. put | puts | |
| 10. seem | seems | 20. live | lives | |

> **F Y I**
>
> Make sure you pronounce the -**s** ending. The -**s** ending shows that you are using the correct form of the verb.

**Talk about It** Check your answers above with a partner. Then say each verb both ways. Try to pronounce the -s ending as /s/ or /z/.

**◀)) 8 | Pronouncing -s and -es Endings on Simple Present Verbs** Read these sentences. Choose the correct pronunciation for the -s/-es ending of the **bold** verb. Then listen and check your answers. `3.1 A`

| DESCRIBING A SPECIAL PERSON | /s/ | /z/ | /əz/ |
|---|---|---|---|
| 1. a. My Grandma Rosa **lives** with us. | ☐ | ☑ | ☐ |
| b. She **pronounces** English words with a Spanish accent. | ☐ | ☐ | ☐ |
| c. She **kisses** people on both cheeks. | ☐ | ☐ | ☐ |
| d. She **tells** us interesting and funny stories. | ☐ | ☐ | ☐ |
| 2. a. My wife Maria **teaches** science to high school students. | ☐ | ☐ | ☐ |
| b. She **works** a lot. | ☐ | ☐ | ☐ |
| c. In the evening, she **makes** delicious dinners. | ☐ | ☐ | ☐ |
| d. Then she **prepares** for her classes. | ☐ | ☐ | ☐ |
| 3. a. My brother Henry **has** problems with schoolwork. | ☐ | ☐ | ☐ |
| b. He **studies** for many hours at night and on the weekend. | ☐ | ☐ | ☐ |
| c. He **finishes** all of his homework. | ☐ | ☐ | ☐ |
| d. He **passes** all of his classes. | ☐ | ☐ | ☐ |
| 4. a. My neighbor Mr. Lee **fixes** computers. | ☐ | ☐ | ☐ |
| b. He **reads** lots of books and newspapers. | ☐ | ☐ | ☐ |
| c. He **discusses** many interesting things with me. | ☐ | ☐ | ☐ |
| d. He also **gives** me good advice. | ☐ | ☐ | ☐ |

**Talk about It** With a partner, take turns reading the sentences above. Use correct pronunciation.

We use **adverbs of frequency** to say how often something happens.

| never | hardly ever | | sometimes | | often | usually | always |
|---|---|---|---|---|---|---|---|
| 0% | 1–10% | | 50% | | 75–90% | 90–99% | 100% |

**A**

| | subject | adverb of frequency | verb | |
|---|---|---|---|---|
| 1 | I | always<br>usually<br>often | eat | healthy food. |
| 2 | He | sometimes<br>hardly ever<br>never | eats | |

We can use the adverb *sometimes* in different places in a sentence.

**3** We **sometimes** take the bus.

**4** **Sometimes** we take the bus.

**5** We take the bus **sometimes**.

GO ONLINE

**9 | Choosing Adverbs of Frequency** Read Isabel's food diary. Then complete each sentence below and on page 54 with an adverb of frequency. (More than one answer may be possible.) **3.2 A**

## LIFESTYLE FITNESS PLANNER

_____Isabel_____'S FOOD DIARY — week of _March 10-16_

Remember: Write down **all** food.

| | MONDAY | TUESDAY | WEDNESDAY | THURSDAY | FRIDAY | SATURDAY | SUNDAY |
|---|---|---|---|---|---|---|---|
| BREAKFAST | coffee<br>cereal | coffee<br>cereal | coffee<br>cereal | coffee<br>cereal | coffee<br>cereal | coffee<br>eggs | coffee<br>eggs |
| MORNING SNACK | fruit | | fruit | | fruit | | |
| LUNCH | salad | salad | salad | salad | pizza | salad | fruit and cheese |
| AFTERNOON SNACK | tea | tea<br>cookies | tea | tea<br>cookies | tea | tea<br>cookies | |
| DINNER | chicken<br>rice | fish | pasta | soup<br>salad | fish<br>vegetables | pasta | chicken<br>cake<br>ice cream |

Visit our website for diet and exercise tips.

1. Isabel _____*often*_____ has cereal for breakfast.

2. Isabel _____ drinks coffee at breakfast.

3. Isabel _____ has fruit as a snack.

4. Isabel _____ drinks tea in the morning.

5. Isabel _____ has pizza for lunch.

6. Isabel _____ eats a salad for lunch.

7. Isabel _____ has a cup of tea in the afternoon.

8. Isabel _____ has cookies with her tea.

9. Isabel _____ has cake and ice cream at dinner.

10. Isabel _____ has a hamburger for dinner.

**Write about It** Write three sentences about your food habits. Use an adverb of frequency in each sentence. Compare your sentences with a partner. How are your habits similar or different?

*I usually have cereal for breakfast.*

**10 | Placing Adverbs of Frequency** Read these statements about study habits. Insert adverbs of frequency. Make the sentences true for you. `3.2 A`

MY STUDY HABITS
   *always*
1. I go to class.

2. I ask questions in class.

3. I take notes in class.

4. I review my notes after class.

5. I compare my notes with a classmate.

6. I schedule⁴ time for homework and studying.

7. I study in a quiet place.

8. I study for tests.

9. I do my homework on time.

10. I study with a group.

**Talk about It** Compare your answers above with a partner. Do you have good study habits?

**11 | Using Adverbs of Frequency** Take the survey. Choose an adverb of frequency for each statement below. Then tell a partner your answers. `3.2 A`

*"I hardly ever wake up before 7:00 a.m."*

## Are You a "Morning Lark" or a "Night Owl"?

"Morning Larks" love the morning.

"Night Owls" have more energy at night.

| | ALWAYS | OFTEN | SOMETIMES | HARDLY EVER | NEVER |
|---|---|---|---|---|---|
| 1. I wake up before 7:00 a.m. | ☐ | ☐ | ☐ | ☐ | ☐ |
| 2. I hear the alarm clock and get up right away. | ☐ | ☐ | ☐ | ☐ | ☐ |

⁴ **schedule:** (verb) to plan to do something at a specific time

| | ALWAYS | OFTEN | SOMETIMES | HARDLY EVER | NEVER |
|---|---|---|---|---|---|
| 3. I hear the alarm clock and stay in bed. | ☐ | ☐ | ☐ | ☐ | ☐ |
| 4. I do many things before breakfast. | ☐ | ☐ | ☐ | ☐ | ☐ |
| 5. I have a lot of energy in the morning. | ☐ | ☐ | ☐ | ☐ | ☐ |
| 6. I feel tired in the morning. | ☐ | ☐ | ☐ | ☐ | ☐ |
| 7. I like morning classes. | ☐ | ☐ | ☐ | ☐ | ☐ |
| 8. I study in the daytime. | ☐ | ☐ | ☐ | ☐ | ☐ |
| 9. I have a lot of energy at night. | ☐ | ☐ | ☐ | ☐ | ☐ |
| 10. I get tired at night. | ☐ | ☐ | ☐ | ☐ | ☐ |
| 11. I go to bed before 11:00. | ☐ | ☐ | ☐ | ☐ | ☐ |
| 12. I go to bed after midnight. | ☐ | ☐ | ☐ | ☐ | ☐ |

**Talk about It** Is your partner a morning lark or a night owl? Why? Tell the class three things about your partner.

*"Lena is a morning lark. She likes morning classes."*

## 12 | Forming Simple Present Sentences with Adverbs of Frequency Put the words in order to form simple present sentences. Use the correct form of the **bold** verb. `3.2 A`

TRANSPORTATION HABITS

1. **drive**/my brother/always/to class

   _My brother always drives to class._

2. he/**have** trouble/with parking/often

   _____

3. I/the bus/**take**/usually

   _____

4. **come** late/sometimes/the bus

   _____

5. I/**walk**/hardly ever/home

   _____

6. my friend Jamal/a ride/**give** me/sometimes/home

   _____

7. to the city/often/the train/**take**/my friends and I

   _____

8. never/**drive**/I/to the city

   _____

9. her bike/to work/my sister/**ride**/always

   _____

10. she/**take**/the bus/never

   _____

> **FYI**
>
> We often use the verb **take** to talk about public transportation.
>
> take ⎡ the train
> ⎢ the bus
> ⎢ the subway
> ⎣ a taxi

**Write about It** Write four sentences about transportation habits. Use the words and phrases from this chart or your own ideas. Then compare your sentences with a partner.

| I<br>My friends and I<br>My family<br><br>_____<br>(classmate's name) | always<br>usually<br>sometimes<br>hardly ever<br>never | walk<br>drive<br>take the bus<br>take the train<br>ride a bike / ride bikes<br>take a taxi | to school<br>to work<br>to the supermarket<br>to the mall<br>to my friend's place<br>downtown / to the city |
| --- | --- | --- | --- |

**13 | Usage Note: Time Expressions with the Simple Present** Read the note. Then do Activities 14 and 15.

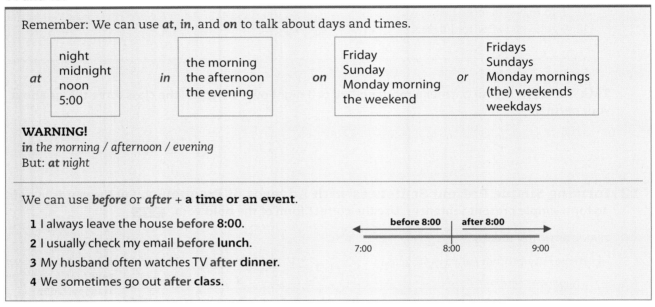

Remember: We can use **at**, **in**, and **on** to talk about days and times.

| **at** | night<br>midnight<br>noon<br>5:00 | **in** | the morning<br>the afternoon<br>the evening | **on** | Friday<br>Sunday<br>Monday morning<br>the weekend | **or** | Fridays<br>Sundays<br>Monday mornings<br>(the) weekends<br>weekdays |

**WARNING!**
*in* the morning / afternoon / evening
But: *at* night

We can use *before* or *after* + **a time or an event**.

**1** I always leave the house **before 8:00**.

**2** I usually check my email **before** lunch.

**3** My husband often watches TV **after** dinner.

**4** We sometimes go out **after** class.

before 8:00 | after 8:00
7:00          8:00          9:00

**14 | Using Time Expressions with the Simple Present** Complete the sentences below with the words from the box. You will use some words more than once.

| after | at | before | in | on |
| --- | --- | --- | --- | --- |

## A Counselor's Busy Routine

I usually see my first patient ____at____ 7:30. I see about 10 patients
(1)

_____ the morning _____ lunch. I see 10 more patients
(2)                                    (3)

_____ lunch. _____ Wednesdays, we're closed _____
(4)                      (5)                                              (6)

the morning and we open _____ noon. I have phone calls with
(7)

patients and doctors _____ the evening and sometimes _____
(8)                                                              (9)

night. _____ the weekends, I get some sleep!
(10)

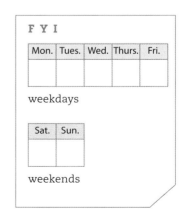

F Y I

| Mon. | Tues. | Wed. | Thurs. | Fri. |
| --- | --- | --- | --- | --- |
|  |  |  |  |  |

weekdays

| Sat. | Sun. |
| --- | --- |
|  |  |

weekends

## 15 | Using Time Expressions with the Simple Present One phrase in each sentence is incorrect. Cross it out.

### DAILY ROUTINES

1. I get up (a) before 6:00; (b) at 6:00; ~~(c) in 7:00;~~ (d) after 8:00.
2. I go to school (a) on weekdays; (b) in the evenings; (c) on Mondays; (d) at the afternoon.
3. I have classes (a) on Monday and Wednesday; (b) on Tuesday and Thursday; (c) in weekends; (d) at night.
4. I often study and do homework (a) at evening; (b) in the morning; (c) in the afternoon; (d) at night.
5. I usually check email (a) in the morning; (b) before class; (c) after dinner; (d) in night.
6. I usually eat lunch (a) before noon; (b) at noon; (c) in 1:00; (d) after 1:00.
7. I drink coffee or tea (a) at the morning; (b) in the afternoon; (c) after dinner; (d) at night.
8. I usually watch TV (a) in the morning; (b) at the afternoon; (c) in the evening; (d) at night.
9. I often go to sleep (a) before 10:00; (b) at 11:00; (c) in midnight; (d) after midnight.
10. I get together with friends (a) before class; (b) after class; (c) in the evenings; (d) in the weekends.
11. I shop for clothes and other things (a) at weekdays; (b) on the weekend; (c) on Saturdays; (d) in the morning.
12. I exercise or play a sport (a) in the morning; (b) on weekdays; (c) on weekends; (d) in the night.

**Write about It** Choose six of the sentences above. Write sentences about your routines. Compare your routines with a partner.

*I usually get up at 7:30.*

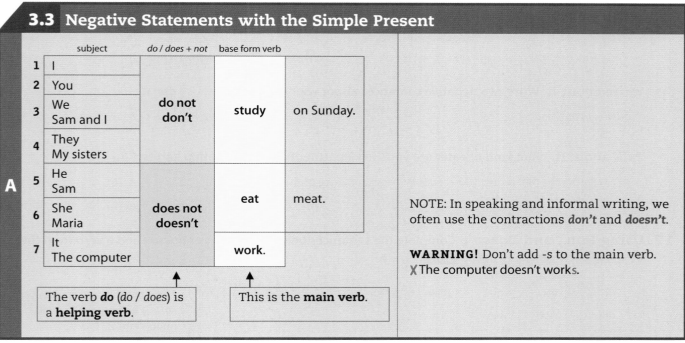

### 3.3 Negative Statements with the Simple Present

| | subject | do / does + not | base form verb | |
|---|---|---|---|---|
| 1 | I | | | |
| 2 | You | **do not** **don't** | study | on Sunday. |
| 3 | We Sam and I | | | |
| 4 | They My sisters | | | |
| 5 | He Sam | **does not** **doesn't** | eat | meat. |
| 6 | She Maria | | | |
| 7 | It The computer | | work. | |

The verb **do** (*do / does*) is a **helping verb**.

This is the **main verb**.

NOTE: In speaking and informal writing, we often use the contractions *don't* and *doesn't*.

**WARNING!** Don't add *-s* to the main verb.
✗ The computer doesn't works.

**16 | Forming Negative Statements** Complete these sentences with *doesn't* and the verb in parentheses. `3.3 A`

## Different Kinds of Eaters

1. **The snacker:** Adam _____doesn't like_____ meals—breakfast, lunch, or dinner. He likes snacks.
   (like)
   Cookies, nuts, and potato chips are his favorite kinds of food.

2. **The "all-the-time" eater:** Kimberley _____ big meals. But she eats food all day—
   (eat)
   an apple, some cheese, some bread, a cookie, some yogurt . . .

3. **The big eater:** At meals, Fernando eats, and he _____. He finishes everything on
   (stop)
   his plate. Then he usually has more food.

4. **The healthy eater:** Riko eats fruits and vegetables every day. She _____ unhealthy
   (eat)
   food. She hardly ever has cookies or potato chips.

5. **The adventurous⁵ eater:** Food is exciting for Amir. He looks for new kinds of food.
   He _____ unusual food.
   (avoid⁶)

6. **The timid⁷ eater:** Mina _____ new kinds of food. She usually eats the same things
   (try)
   every day.

7. **The regular eater:** Megan _____ a meal. She has breakfast, lunch, and dinner
   (miss)
   every day. She usually eats her meals at the same time every day.

8. **The "it-doesn't-matter"⁸ eater:** Jared _____, and food _____
   (cook)                                    (matter)
   to him. He _____ good food, and he _____ about bad food.
   (enjoy)                            (complain)

---

**Write about It** Write two negative sentences about your eating habits. Use *don't*.

   *I don't eat sweets.*

---

**Talk about It** What kind of eater are you? Tell a partner two of your eating habits.

   *"I'm an 'all-the-time' eater. I don't eat big meals. I eat a lot of small snacks."*

---

**17 | Using *Don't* and *Doesn't*** Complete the sentences below with *don't* or *doesn't* and a verb from the box. Use each verb only once. `3.3 A`

| do | eat | go | help |
|------|------|------|------|
| drive | give | have | live |

**FYI**
Some negative statements use **do** as a **helping verb** and as a **main verb**.

He **doesn't do** his homework every evening.

**MY ROUTINES**

1. I just have juice in the morning. I _____don't eat_____ breakfast.

2. I walk to school. I _____.

3. My English class is easy and fun. My teacher _____ a lot of homework.

---

⁵ **adventurous:** liking to do exciting things
⁶ **avoid:** to stay away from someone or something

⁷ **timid:** easily afraid; not wanting to do exciting things
⁸ **matter:** to be important

4. After school I _____ home right away. I usually spend time with my friends.

5. My friend Nick takes classes and works in a store. He _____ a lot of free time!

6. I do all of the cleaning. My roommate _____ me.

7. On weekends I _____ homework or chores. I enjoy my free time!

8. My parents _____ near me. We stay in touch⁹ through Skype and emails.

**Write about It** Write positive and negative statements with the verbs in Activity 17. Write three true statements and one false statement. Work with a partner. Your partner guesses the false statement.

*I drive a truck.*    *I don't have a brother.*    *I live with my parents.*    *I have class on Tuesdays.*

**18 | Writing Positive and Negative Statements about Habits** Read these roommate questionnaires. Then complete the chart below. Write positive and negative statements. **3.3 A**

| Roommate Questionnaire | Yes | No |
|---|---|---|
| Student's name: _Mia_ | | |
| I wake up early. | X | ☐ |
| I go to bed early. | X | ☐ |
| I keep my room neat. | X | ☐ |
| I study in a quiet room. | X | ☐ |
| I play my music loud. | X | ☐ |
| I like a lot of friends in my room. | ☐ | X |

| Roommate Questionnaire | Yes | No |
|---|---|---|
| Student's name: _Destiny_ | | |
| I wake up early. | X | ☐ |
| I go to bed early. | ☐ | X |
| I keep my room neat. | ☐ | X |
| I study in a quiet room. | X | ☐ |
| I play my music loud. | X | ☐ |
| I like a lot of friends in my room. | X | ☐ |

| Roommate Questionnaire | Yes | No |
|---|---|---|
| Student's name: _Kayla_ | | |
| I wake up early. | ☐ | X |
| I go to bed early. | ☐ | X |
| I keep my room neat. | ☐ | X |
| I study in a quiet room. | ☐ | X |
| I play my music loud. | ☐ | X |
| I like a lot of friends in my room. | X | ☐ |

| | Positive statement | Negative statement |
|---|---|---|
| 1. wake up early | *Mia and Destiny wake up early.* | *Kayla doesn't wake up early.* |
| 2. go to bed early | | |
| 3. keep the room neat | | |
| 4. study in a quiet room | | |
| 5. play loud music | | |
| 6. like a lot of visitors | | |

⁹**stay in touch:** to meet, call, or write to someone often

**Talk about It** Work with a partner. Look at the questionnaires from Mia, Destiny, and Kayla on page 59. Which people seem like good roommates? Why? Choose two roommates.

**Write about It** Take the roommate questionnaire. Then write six sentences about yourself. Compare your answers with a partner.

| Roommate Questionnaire | | |
|---|---|---|
| | Yes | No |
| I wake up early. | ☐ | ☐ |
| I go to bed early. | ☐ | ☐ |
| I keep my room neat. | ☐ | ☐ |
| I study in a quiet room. | ☐ | ☐ |
| I play my music loud. | ☐ | ☐ |
| I like a lot of friends in my room. | ☐ | ☐ |

*I don't wake up early.*

**19 | Error Correction** Find and correct the errors. (Some sentences may not have any errors.)

1. The children ~~no~~ *don't* visit their grandparents.

2. I wake up early always in the morning.

3. Most people doesn't exercise enough.

4. That plant need water.

5. My brother don't have a car.

6. She never complain.

7. He doesn't do his homework.

8. We often go grocery shopping at the evening.

9. That store hardly never stays open late.

10. The class usually meets on Monday evenings.

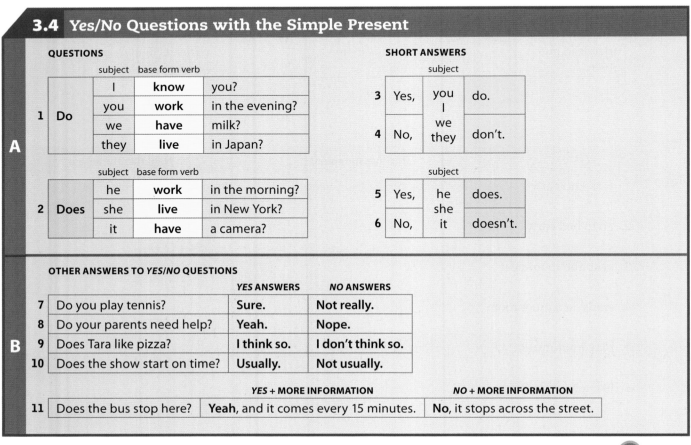

**3.4  Yes/No Questions with the Simple Present**

**A**

**QUESTIONS**

| | | subject | base form verb | |
|---|---|---|---|---|
| **1** | **Do** | I | **know** | you? |
| | | you | **work** | in the evening? |
| | | we | **have** | milk? |
| | | they | **live** | in Japan? |

| | | subject | base form verb | |
|---|---|---|---|---|
| **2** | **Does** | he | **work** | in the morning? |
| | | she | **live** | in New York? |
| | | it | **have** | a camera? |

**SHORT ANSWERS**

| | | subject | |
|---|---|---|---|
| **3** | Yes, | you / I | do. |
| **4** | No, | we / they | don't. |

| | | subject | |
|---|---|---|---|
| **5** | Yes, | he / she | does. |
| **6** | No, | it | doesn't. |

**B**

**OTHER ANSWERS TO *YES/NO* QUESTIONS**

| | | *YES* ANSWERS | *NO* ANSWERS |
|---|---|---|---|
| **7** | Do you play tennis? | Sure. | Not really. |
| **8** | Do your parents need help? | Yeah. | Nope. |
| **9** | Does Tara like pizza? | I think so. | I don't think so. |
| **10** | Does the show start on time? | Usually. | Not usually. |

| | | *YES* + MORE INFORMATION | *NO* + MORE INFORMATION |
|---|---|---|---|
| **11** | Does the bus stop here? | **Yeah**, and it comes every 15 minutes. | **No**, it stops across the street. |

GO ONLINE

**20 | Forming *Yes/No* Questions and Short Answers** Complete each question and short answer with *do* or *does*. Then practice the conversations with a partner. **3.4 A**

DO YOU HAVE A SCARY HOUSE?

1. A: ___Does___ the house feel cold?

   B: No, it ___doesn't___ .

2. A: _____ the house make loud noises?

   B: Yes, it _____ .

3. A: _____ you sometimes hear strange sounds?

   B: Yes, I _____ .

4. A: _____ things often break?

   B: Yes, they _____ .

5. A: _____ animals like your house?

   B: No, they _____ .

6. A: _____ your friends see strange things?

   B: Yes, they _____ .

7. A: _____ the roof leak[10]?

   B: Yes, it _____ .

8. A: _____ your friends believe you?

   B: No, they _____ .

> **PRONUNCIATION**
>
> Remember: *Yes/No* questions usually end with rising intonation.
>
> Do you want milk?
>
> Does she have a car?

a scary house

**Think about It** Which two questions have an adverb of frequency? Does the adverb of frequency come before or after the main verb?

**21 | Using *Yes/No* Questions and Short Answers** Ask and answer these questions with a partner. Use short answers. Check (✓) your partner's answers. **3.4 A**

*A: Do you watch TV?*
*B: Yes, I do.*

---

## Leisure Time[11] Activities Survey

Partner's name: _____

| WHEN YOU HAVE FREE TIME... | YES | NO |
|---|:---:|:---:|
| 1. Do you watch TV? | ✓ | ☐ |
| 2. Do you listen to music? | ☐ | ☐ |
| 3. Do you play a sport? (basketball, football, other?) | ☐ | ☐ |
| 4. Do you exercise? | ☐ | ☐ |
| 5. Do you play chess? | ☐ | ☐ |
| 6. Do you play video games? | ☐ | ☐ |
| 7. Do you go to movies? | ☐ | ☐ |

---

[10] **leak:** to have a hole that water goes through          [11] **leisure time:** free time; time for fun activities

|  | YES | NO |
|---|---|---|
| 8. Do you play a musical instrument? (piano, guitar, other?) | ☐ | ☐ |
| 9. Do you read books? | ☐ | ☐ |
| 10. Do you go on social networking sites? | ☐ | ☐ |
| 11. Do you get together with friends? | ☐ | ☐ |
| 12. Do you go out to dinner? | ☐ | ☐ |
| 13. Do you go to museums and art galleries? | ☐ | ☐ |
| 14. Do you go to the shopping mall with friends? | ☐ | ☐ |

**Talk about It** Work with a new partner. Trade books. What do you remember about your first partner? Quiz each other.

A: *Does Marsha watch TV?*
B: *Yes, she does.*

## 22 | Asking and Answering *Yes/No* Questions Complete each conversation with the verbs from the box. Add *do* or *does* for questions. Then practice the conversations with a partner. 3.4 A–B

TALKING TO AN ACQUAINTANCE[12]

1. A: ___Do___ you ___exercise___ at night?

    B: Not usually. At night I'm tired. I usually _____ TV

    or _____ to music.

| exercise | watch |
|---|---|
| listen | |

2. A: _____ you _____ here often?

    B: Not really. It's a beautiful park. But I _____ far away.

    A: My office is nearby. In the summer I often _____ on a bench

    and _____ my lunch.

| come | live |
|---|---|
| have | sit |

3. A: _____ your son _____ any sports?

    B: Nope. He _____ video games. But sometimes he

    _____ to the gym with me.

| go | prefer |
|---|---|
| play | |

4. A: _____ you and your roommate _____

    dinner together?

    B: Yeah. He and I _____ the same schedule. And we

    _____ the same kinds of food.

| eat | like |
|---|---|
| have | |

5. A: _____ your cats _____ outside?

    B: Sure. I sometimes _____ them for days!

    A: My cat is an apartment cat. She always _____ inside.

| go | stay |
|---|---|
| not see | |

6. A: _____ that store _____ good prices?

    B: I _____. I never _____ there.

| go | not know |
|---|---|
| have | |

[12] **acquaintance:** someone you know a little (not a close friend)

**Think about It** Look at how B says *yes* and *no* in the conversations in Activity 22 (page 62). Write the phrases in this chart.

| *Yes* answers | *No* answers | Not *yes* or *no* |
|---|---|---|
|  | *Not usually.* |  |
|  |  |  |
|  |  |  |

## 23 | Forming *Yes/No* Questions and Long Answers
Write *yes/no* questions with *do* or *does* and the words in parentheses. Then complete the answers with the extra information in the box. **3.4 A–B**

ANSWERS FOR B

| | |
|---|---|
| every day | thank you |
| it fits you really well | we also have it in blue, black, and brown |
| it's only one size | we close at 6:00 |
| it's on the second floor | we have some beautiful belts |

DEPARTMENT STORE CONVERSATIONS

1. A: _Do you stay open late today?_ (you/stay open/late today/?)

   B: No, _we close at 6:00_.

2. A: _____ (this dress/look/good on me/?)

   B: Yes, _____!

3. A: _____ (you/need/help/?)

   B: No, _____.

4. A: _____ (this jacket/come/in a large size/?)

   B: No, _____.

5. A: _____ (you/always/open at 10:00/?)

   B: Yes, _____.

6. A: _____ (the hat/come/in other colors/?)

   B: Yes, _____.

7. A: _____ (you/have/a restroom/?)

   B: Yes, _____.

8. A: _____ (you/have/more accessories[13]/?)

   B: Yes, _____.

**Talk about It** Listen and check your answers. Then practice the conversations with a partner.

**Write about It** Write a different response for each question in Activity 23. Add new information.

A: *Do you stay open late today?*
B: *Yes, we stay open until 9:00.*

---

[13] **accessories:** items such as jewelry, belts, purses, etc.

## 24 | Usage Note: Frequency Expressions with the Simple Present  Read the note. Then do Activities 25 and 26.

We can use **frequency expressions** to say how often something happens.

We usually put the frequency expression at the end of the sentence.

↓

**1** I eat breakfast **every day.**

**2** My wife runs **every morning.**

**3** We have class **every Monday and Wednesday.**

**4** My family goes to Mexico **every summer.**

| every | day, week, month, year<br>weekend, weekday<br>Sunday, Monday…<br>January, February…<br>morning, afternoon, evening, night<br>summer, fall, winter, spring<br>semester |
|---|---|

**5** I brush my teeth **twice a day.**

**6** Our class meets **three times a week.**

**7** We have a test **once a month.**

**8** I see my cousins **three or four times a year.**

| once a<br>twice a*<br>two times a<br>three times a<br>four times a | day, week, month, year |
|---|---|

*twice = two times

| Mon. | Tues. | Wed. | Thurs. | Fri. |
|---|---|---|---|---|
| ✓ | ✓ | ✓ | ✓ | ✓ |

every day

| Mon. | Tues. | Wed. | Thurs. | Fri. |
|---|---|---|---|---|
|  |  | ✓ |  |  |

once a week

| Mon. | Tues. | Wed. | Thurs. | Fri. |
|---|---|---|---|---|
| ✓ |  | ✓ |  |  |

twice a week / two times a week

| Mon. | Tues. | Wed. | Thurs. | Fri. |
|---|---|---|---|---|
| ✓ |  | ✓ |  | ✓ |

three times a week

## 25 | Using Frequency Expressions  Rewrite each sentence below. Replace the **bold** words with a frequency expression from the box.

| | | |
|---|---|---|
| about five times a week | every Saturday | twice a day |
| about three times a week | every spring | twice a month |
| every night | once a week | two times a week |

**F Y I**

*About* means "a little more or less than."

I exercise about three times a week.
(= I usually exercise three times a week. Sometimes I exercise two or four times a week.)

THE OWENS FAMILY'S SCHEDULE OF CHORES[14]

1. Nina **sometimes** makes breakfast.

   *Nina makes breakfast about three times a week.*

2. Yolanda washes the dishes **after breakfast and after dinner**.

   _____

3. Nina **always** does laundry **on Monday**.

   _____

---

[14] **chores:** small jobs you do around the house

4. Theo **always** takes out the garbage **on Tuesday and Friday**.

_____

5. Gary and Nina **usually** cook dinner.

_____

6. Gary **always** locks the house **at night**.

_____

7. The family **always** cleans the house **on Saturday**.

_____

8. Gary and Nina pay bills¹⁵ **at the beginning and the middle of the month**.

_____

9. The family **always** cleans the garage **in the spring**.

_____

**Write about It**  Write three sentences about chores that you do. Explain how often you do them.

_I take out the garbage twice a week._

## 26 | Asking and Answering Questions about Frequency  Ask and answer these questions with a partner. For *no* answers, give the correct information. Use frequency expressions.  `3.4 A–B`

1. Do you make breakfast every morning?

   _Yes, I do._  **OR**  _No, I don't. I make breakfast about three or four times a week._

2. Do you shop for food every day?
3. Do you cook dinner every night?
4. Do you do laundry every day?
5. Do you clean your house every week?
6. Do you have homework every day?
7. Do you have class every day?
8. Do you see your parents every day?
9. Do you see your best friend every day?
10. Do you talk to your best friend every day?
11. Do you spend time with friends every weekend?
12. Do you exercise every week?

**Write about It**  Write four sentences about your routines. Use phrases from the box.

| | |
|---|---|
| every January | once a month |
| every semester | once a week |
| every summer | twice a year |

_I call my grandparents once a week._

---

¹⁵ **bills:** money you must pay (for example: electricity bill, phone bill, Internet bill)

## 3.5 *Wh-* Questions with the Simple Present

*Wh-* questions begin with a **wh- word**.

**A**

| TO ASK ABOUT: | USE *WH-* WORD: | | ANSWER WITH: |
|---|---|---|---|
| a time | *When* | 1 When do you have English? | **A day or time:** On Monday and Wednesday. At 10:00. |
| | *What time* | 2 What time do you have English? | **A time:** At 10:00. |
| a thing | *What* (+ noun) | 3 What do you study? <br> 4 What **food** do you have? | **A thing:** Algebra. Some fruit. |
| | *What kind of* + noun | 5 What kind of **car** do you drive? | **A kind of thing:** A Ford. |
| a place | *Where* | 6 Where do you study English? | **A place:** In Room 203. At the Academy School. |
| a number | *How many* + plural noun | 7 How many **sports** do you play? | **A number:** Three. |
| frequency | *How often* | 8 How often do you exercise? | **A frequency expression:** Twice a week. Every day. |

**GRAMMAR TERM:** "*Wh-* words" include *how*.

**B**

**WH- QUESTIONS WITH *DO* / *DOES***

| | wh- word | do | subject | base form verb |
|---|---|---|---|---|
| 9 | Where | | you | exercise? |
| 10 | When | do | I | start? |
| 11 | What time | | we | meet? |
| 12 | How often | | they | play? |

| | wh- word | does | subject | base form verb |
|---|---|---|---|---|
| 13 | When | | he | work? |
| 14 | Where | does | she | study? |
| 15 | What | | it | mean? |
| 16 | What time | | the bus | leave? |

In conversation, we usually answer **wh-** questions with short answers. Sometimes we use full sentences.

| | QUESTIONS | ANSWERS | |
|---|---|---|---|
| | ***Wh-* Question** | **Short Answer** | **Full Sentence** |
| 17 | **What** do we need? | Bread and milk. | We need bread and milk. |
| 18 | **Where** does the class meet? | In the lecture hall. | It meets in the lecture hall. |
| 19 | **How many** tickets do you want? | Two, please. | I want two tickets, please. |

**27 | Using *Wh-* Words** Complete these conversations with the words from the box. (You will use some words more than once.) Then practice the conversations with a partner. `3.5 A`

1. A: _When_____ do you have your exams?

   B: Next week, on Tuesday and Wednesday.

2. A: _____ do you fly to Bangkok?

   B: About once a month.

   A: _____ do you stay in Bangkok?

   B: At my friend's house. I have lots of friends there.

| |
|---|
| how many |
| how often |
| what |
| when |
| where |

3. A: _____ do your children study Spanish?

   B: At their school. They're in a bilingual school.

   A: _____ do they have Spanish class?

   B: Every day.

4. A: _____ subway do you take to work?

   B: I usually take the red line.

   A: _____ does it go?

   B: To Fifth Avenue.

5. A: I'm always tired.

   B: _____ hours do you usually sleep?

   A: Just five or six hours.

   B: _____ do you go to sleep?

   A: About 1:00 or 2:00.

6. A: _____ do you go to the gym?

   B: Three or four times a week.

   A: That's great! _____ do you do there?

   B: I usually swim.

**Think about It** Look at the questions above with *when*. In which question can you also say *what time*?

**28 | Matching *Wh-* Questions and Answers** Read the answers on the left. Match each answer with a question on the right to complete the conversations. `3.5 A`

**Interview with a Musician**

1. Q: _____*g*_____

   A: We play jazz.

2. Q: _____

   A: I play the drums.

3. Q: _____

   A: Every day.

4. Q: _____

   A: Six right now.

5. Q: _____

   A: About twice a year.

6. Q: _____

   A: A lot of places: West Africa, Asia, South America, Europe, and the United States.

7. Q: _____

   A: The musicians from other countries—and the audiences!

a. How often do you practice?

b. How many musicians does your band have?

c. How often do you go on tour[16]?

d. What instrument do you play?

e. What do you like about your travels?

f. Where do you travel?

g. What kind of music do you play?

[16] **go on tour:** (for musicians) to travel and give concerts in different places

**Think about It** Which answers in Activity 28 are full sentences?

**Talk about It** Interview a partner about his or her schoolwork. Ask the questions below. Answer with short answers or with full sentences.

A: *What classes do you like a lot?*
B: *I like English and Psychology.*

INTERVIEW A STUDENT

1. What classes do you like a lot?
2. What do you like about school?
3. Where do you do your homework?
4. How often do you study?
5. When do you study?

**Write about It** Look at the jobs in Activity 5 (pages 50–51). What job do you want to know more about? Write three questions for an interview with someone in that job.

**29 | Asking and Answering Questions with *How Often*** Go back to the survey in Activity 21 (pages 61–62). Work with a new partner. Take the survey again. For each *yes* answer, ask your partner *how often*. Answer with a frequency expression. **3.5 A**

A: *Do you watch TV?*
B: *Yes, I do.*
A: *How often do you watch TV?*
B: *About four times a week.*

**Talk about It** Tell the class one interesting thing you learned about your new partner.

**30 | Forming *Wh-* Questions** Complete the *wh-* questions. Use *do* or *does* and the words in parentheses. Then practice the conversations with a partner. **3.5 B**

CONVERSATIONS IN A UNIVERSITY CAFETERIA

1. A: How often _____ *do you eat* _____ (you/eat) in the cafeteria?
   B: Hardly ever. We usually go off-campus[17] for lunch.
   A: Where _____ (you/go)?
   B: Different places. We often go to Café Milano.

2. A: What time _____ (the meeting/start)?
   B: I don't know. Ask Roberta.
   A: Hey, Roberta. When _____ (we/have) our meeting?
   C: In 15 minutes—at 3:00.

3. A: What _____ (your sister/study)?
   B: She studies medicine.
   A: How many classes _____ (she/have)?
   B: Five. They're all science classes.

[17] **off-campus:** not at the university

4. A: Where _____ (Yusuf/live)?

   B: He lives off-campus. He has an apartment with his brothers.

   A: Oh. How many brothers _____ (he/have)?

   B: He has two brothers.

5. A: What _____ (you/do) in the evening?

   B: I often study. And I work in a restaurant.

   A: How often _____ (you/work)?

   B: I usually work two nights a week.

6. A: What time _____ (Lana and Rika/have) tennis?

   B: Around 4:00.

   A: How often _____ (they/play) tennis?

   B: Three days a week.

7. A: What bus _____ (you/take) to school?

   B: The M15 bus.

   A: Where _____ (the bus/stop)?

   B: On Second Avenue, right by my apartment.

8. A: Let's have dinner later. When _____ (your classes/end)?

   B: At 6:00.

   A: What _____ (you/want) for dinner?

   B: Hmm. Maybe some pizza.

**Think about It** Which question above uses *do* twice—as a helping verb and a main verb?

## 31 | Asking and Answering *Wh-* Questions Match the questions with the answers. `3.5 A–B`

### World Facts Quiz

___c___ 1. When does summer start in Argentina?          a. About 1.3 billion.

_____ 2. When does the "midnight sun" start in Iceland?    b. In the Mediterranean Sea.

_____ 3. Where does the Nile River end?                c. In December.

_____ 4. How many people does the world have?          d. In the Arctic Circle.

_____ 5. How many people does China have?              e. Six.

_____ 6. Where do polar bears live?                    f. Ecuador.

_____ 7. What country does the equator divide?         g. About 7 billion.

_____ 8. How many states does Australia have?          h. In May.

1.c, 2.h, 3.b, 4.g, 5.a, 6.d, 7.f, 8.e

**Write about It** Write complete sentences for the answers above.

*Summer starts in December in Argentina.*

**32 | Forming *Wh-* Questions** Put the words in the correct order to create *wh-* questions about animals. Then match the questions with the answers. `3.5 B`

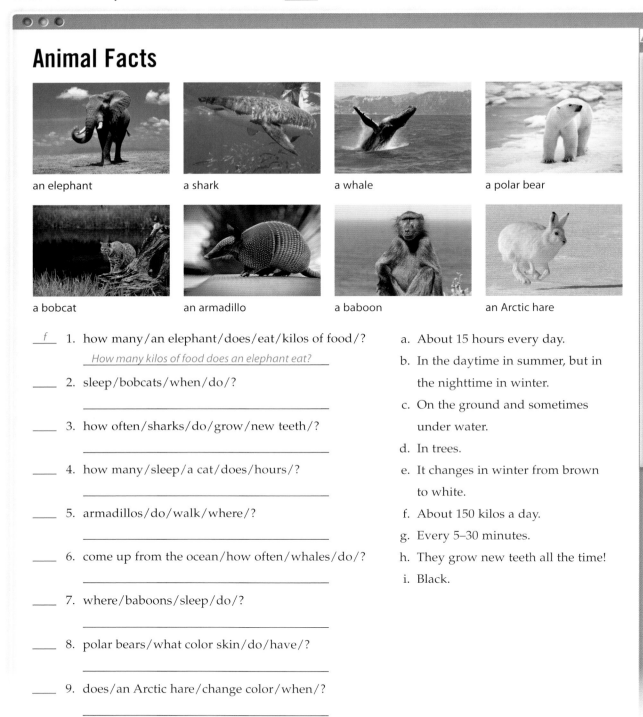

# Animal Facts

an elephant          a shark          a whale          a polar bear

a bobcat          an armadillo          a baboon          an Arctic hare

___f___ 1. how many/an elephant/does/eat/kilos of food/?

*How many kilos of food does an elephant eat?*

_____ 2. sleep/bobcats/when/do/?

_____

_____ 3. how often/sharks/do/grow/new teeth/?

_____

_____ 4. how many/sleep/a cat/does/hours/?

_____

_____ 5. armadillos/do/walk/where/?

_____

_____ 6. come up from the ocean/how often/whales/do/?

_____

_____ 7. where/baboons/sleep/do/?

_____

_____ 8. polar bears/what color skin/do/have/?

_____

_____ 9. does/an Arctic hare/change color/when/?

_____

a. About 15 hours every day.

b. In the daytime in summer, but in the nighttime in winter.

c. On the ground and sometimes under water.

d. In trees.

e. It changes in winter from brown to white.

f. About 150 kilos a day.

g. Every 5–30 minutes.

h. They grow new teeth all the time!

i. Black.

**Talk about It** Choose an animal from this box. Write four *wh-* questions about the animal. Go online to find the answers. Present the information to the class.

| a bald eagle | a giant squid | a lynx | a Komodo dragon | a river dolphin |

*What does a lynx eat?*

## 33 | Writing *Wh-* Questions  Look at the **bold** words in the answers. Write a *wh-* question for each answer. `3.5 B`

### Trips to Antarctica

1. Q: *Where do the ships go?*

   A: The ships go **to Antarctica**.

2. Q: _____

   A: They go to Antarctica **from December through February**.

3. Q: _____

   A: They leave **twice a month**.

4. Q: _____

   A: The ships carry **100 people**.

5. Q: _____

   A: The trips begin **in Ushuaia, Argentina**.

6. Q: _____

   A: The ships stop **once or twice a day**.

7. Q: _____

   A: People see **beautiful land and interesting animals**.

## 34 | Error Correction  Find and correct the errors. (Some conversations may not have any errors.)

1. A: Does Yuki leaves work early?
   B: Not really. She usually works late.

2. A: Do it rain a lot in Miami?
   B: Yes, all the time!

3. A: Does Carla know your friends?
   B: Yes, she knows.

4. A: When you usually have lunch?
   B: Around noon.

5. A: What do your children do after school?
   B: They usually play with their friends.

6. A: How many stamps do Ali need?
   B: He needs two.

7. A: Where does Jim usually parks the car?
   B: In a garage.

8. A: How often you do drive to work?
   B: About once a week.

## WRAP-UP

### A | GRAMMAR IN READING  Read about two job routines. Underline the simple present verbs.

#### Jobs in the Arts

**Interior Designer:** Interior designers <u>plan</u> the inside of many kinds of places: homes, offices, and other buildings. A space[18] with a good design looks good and fits people's needs. Lisa Garcia is an interior designer. First, she talks to the client[19]. What does the client want? What budget[20] does the client have? Lisa looks at the space. Then she makes plans and drawings. She thinks about floors, windows, lights, colors, furniture, art, and

[18] **space:** an area
[19] **client:** the person or group that pays for the designer's work
[20] **budget:** the money available for a project

plants. She usually works with painters, furniture makers, and other people. The project stays on schedule and in the budget. Sometimes the design changes a lot. In the end, the client usually feels happy about the space.

**Television Producer:** Television producers plan TV shows. They usually work on a project (a possible TV show) from beginning to end. Sam Wu is a producer. He reads ideas for shows and chooses a project. He makes the budget and finds money for the project. Then he finds actors and camera people. He makes the schedule. The camera people shoot[21] the video for the show. The project stays on schedule and in the budget. Sam checks the final video. Then the show goes on TV.

**Read the phrases about the two job routines. Write sentences for each job routine in the correct order. Use the correct form of the bold verbs.**

| **make** a schedule | **finish** the design | **make** plans and drawings | **read** ideas for shows |
|---|---|---|---|
| **find** actors and camera people | **look** at the space | **find** money for the project | **check** the final video |
| **work** with painters and furniture makers | **talk** to the client | | |

INTERIOR DESIGNER (LISA)

1. _Lisa talks to the client._
2. _____
3. _____
4. _____
5. _____

TV PRODUCER (SAM)

1. _____
2. _____
3. _____
4. _____
5. _____

**B | GRAMMAR IN SPEAKING** Work with a partner. Ask your partner *yes/no* questions about his or her interests and skills. Check (✓) your partner's *yes* answers.

A: *Do you like math?*     B: *No, I don't.*

INTERESTS AND SKILLS SURVEY

| Partner's name: _____ | *Yes* answers | | *Yes* answers |
|---|---|---|---|
| 1. likes math | ☐ | 10. works well with children | ☐ |
| 2. likes languages | ☐ | 11. builds things | ☐ |
| 3. understands computers | ☐ | 12. thinks of good solutions[22] to problems | ☐ |
| 4. loves nature and the outdoors | ☐ | 13. tells good stories | ☐ |
| 5. loves to travel | ☐ | 14. explains things clearly | ☐ |
| 6. loves adventure | ☐ | 15. plans everything carefully | ☐ |
| 7. likes video games | ☐ | 16. likes to be a leader or manager | ☐ |
| 8. follows directions well | ☐ | 17. communicates[23] well with people | ☐ |
| 9. likes to read | ☐ | 18. sings or plays a musical instrument | ☐ |

[21] **shoot:** to make a video with a camera
[22] **solutions:** answers to a question or problem

[23] **communicate:** to write, speak, or share information with other people

**Look at the jobs below. Add four more jobs.**

JOBS

| | | | |
|---|---|---|---|
| actor | doctor | filmmaker | journalist |
| astronomer | elementary school teacher | graphic designer | musician |
| counselor | engineer | interior designer | television producer |
| _____ | _____ | _____ | _____ |

**Think about your partner's answers to the Interests and Skills Survey in Activity B (page 72). What are some good jobs for your partner? Write three possible jobs.**

_____  _____  _____

## 3.6 Summary of the Simple Present

**USES**

We use the simple present to:
- talk about facts (**1**)
- talk about habits and routines (**2**)

**1** The apartment **has** four rooms.
**2** I usually **wake up** at 6:00.

**STATEMENTS**

| POSITIVE STATEMENTS | I You We They | leave | early. |
|---|---|---|---|
| | He She It | leaves | early. |

| NEGATIVE STATEMENTS | I You We They | do not don't | leave | early. |
|---|---|---|---|---|
| | He She It | does not doesn't | | early. |

**QUESTIONS**

| YES/NO QUESTIONS | Do | I you we they | leave | early? |
|---|---|---|---|---|
| | Does | he she it | | |

| SHORT ANSWERS | Yes, | you I we they | do. |
|---|---|---|---|
| | No, | | don't. |
| | Yes, | he she it | does. |
| | No, | | doesn't. |

| WH-QUESTIONS | When | | I | start? |
|---|---|---|---|---|
| | What | do | you | do? |
| | How often | | we | meet? |
| | How many classes | | they | teach? |
| | What time | | it | start? |
| | Where | does | she | live? |
| | | | he | |

# 4

# The Verb *Be*

## IN THIS UNIT, WE USE the verb *be* to:

### Introduce and identify people and things

1. I**'m** Tina.

2. This **is** my house.

### Describe people and things

3. Lisa **is** 22. She**'s** a good runner.

4. My cousin **is** from Brazil. He**'s** very tall.

**GO ONLINE**

For the Unit Vocabulary Check, go to the Online Practice.

## Talk about locations

5. A: Where's John?
   B: He's at work.

6. A: Where are my keys?
   B: They're on the counter.

## Talk about the weather

7. A: **Is** it hot out?

B: Yes, it **is**!

**Think about It**   Read these sentences. What is true about you? Check (✓) *True* or *False*.

|  | TRUE | FALSE |
|---|---|---|
| 1. I'm a student. | ☐ | ☐ |
| 2. I'm tall. | ☐ | ☐ |
| 3. I'm a good student. | ☐ | ☐ |
| 4. I'm at work now. | ☐ | ☐ |
| 5. It's hot today. | ☐ | ☐ |

## 4.1 Positive Statements with *Be* + Noun Phrase

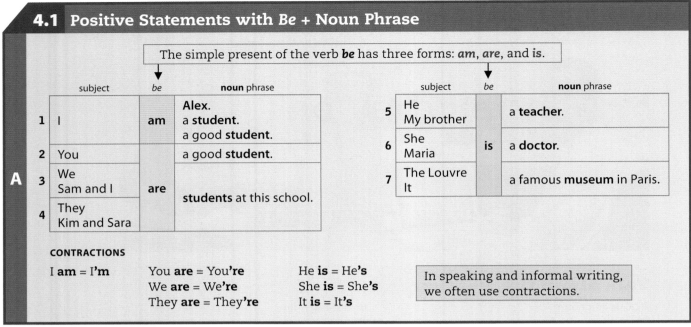

The simple present of the verb *be* has three forms: *am*, *are*, and *is*.

| | subject | be | noun phrase |
|---|---|---|---|
| 1 | I | am | Alex.<br>a **student**.<br>a good **student**. |
| 2 | You | | a good **student**. |
| 3 | We<br>Sam and I | are | students at this school. |
| 4 | They<br>Kim and Sara | | |

| | subject | be | noun phrase |
|---|---|---|---|
| 5 | He<br>My brother | | a **teacher**. |
| 6 | She<br>Maria | is | a **doctor**. |
| 7 | The Louvre<br>It | | a famous **museum** in Paris. |

**A**

**CONTRACTIONS**

I **am** = I'm

You **are** = You're
We **are** = We're
They **are** = They're

He **is** = He's
She **is** = She's
It **is** = It's

In speaking and informal writing, we often use contractions.

 GO ONLINE

**1 | Noticing Forms of *Be*** Read these sentences. Circle all the forms of *be*. Then underline the subjects.

4.1 A

INTERESTING SIBLINGS[1]

1. Ethan and Joel Coen are famous filmmakers. They're brothers. People often call them "the Coen brothers."

2. Jessica Jung is a singer. She's a member of the band Girls' Generation. Her sister Krystal is a singer, too. She's a member of the band f(x).

3. Christophe and Olivier Rochus are brothers. They are both tennis players.

4. Brothers Emilio and Javier Sánchez are tennis players. Their sister Arantxa is a tennis player, too.

5. Jake and Maggie Gyllenhaal are siblings. They are both famous actors. They're in a lot of movies.

6. Jim and John Harbaugh are brothers. They're both American football coaches[2]. Jim Harbaugh is the coach for the San Francisco 49ers. John is the coach for the Baltimore Ravens.

7. Masao and Naoto Suenaga are race car drivers. They're also brothers.

8. Ann and Nancy Wilson are famous sisters. They are musicians in the band Heart.

9. Daniel and Henrik Sedin are hockey players. They're twins. They play with the Vancouver Canucks.

**Talk about It** Do you know about the people above? Put a check (✓) next to the people you know about. Which siblings are the most interesting?

[1] **siblings:** brothers or sisters

[2] **coach (*pl.* coaches):** someone who leads a sports team

## 2 | Usage Note: Making Introductions  Read the note. Then do Activity 3.

We can use **This is** + a **name** to introduce someone.

> **1** Ling: **This is Anna.** Anna, this is my friend **Jen.**
> Jen: It's nice to meet you, Anna.
> Anna: Nice to meet you, too.

> Notice: Sometimes we leave out the subject + *be* in the response.
> *Nice to meet you.* = **It's** *nice to meet you.*

We can use **am** / **is** / **are** + **from** + a **place** to talk about a person's hometown or country.

> **2** Anna **is from Mexico.**
> **3** My parents **are from Tokyo.**

## 3 | Using Forms of *Be*  Complete each conversation with the correct form of *be*. Use contractions when possible.  `4.1 A`

INTRODUCING PEOPLE

1. Erin: Kay, this _____*is*_____ Linda. She __*'s*_____ an artist. She makes beautiful paintings.

   Kay: Hi, Linda. I _____ Erin's sister. Nice to meet you. What do you paint?

2. Linda: Kay, come meet my new neighbors. Sam _____ an engineer and Wes _____ a

   construction worker. They _____ from Chicago.

   Kay: Oh, my parents _____ from Chicago. It _____ a great city.

3. Wes: Kay, meet my parents. This _____ my mother Sue, and this _____ my father Bob.

   Mom, Dad, this_____ Kay. She _____ a gardener.

   Sue: Oh, hi Kay! We _____ so happy to meet you. We need a gardener.

4. Sue: Erin, this _____ my son Wes.

   Erin: Oh, hi Wes. You _____ Linda's neighbor, right?

   Wes: Yeah. You know Linda?

   Erin: Yes. Linda _____ my good friend.

**Now label the pictures with the people from the conversations above. Use the names in the box.**

| Kay | Linda | Sam | Sue and Bob | Wes |

a.

b.

c.

d.

e.

_____  _____  _____  _____  _____

**Talk about It** Work in a group of six. Take turns: introduce two people to each other.

A: *Sam, this is Mark.*
B: *Hi Mark. Nice to meet you.*
C: *Nice to meet you, too.*

**Write about It** Look at the "Interesting Siblings" in Activity 1. Where are the people from? Work with a partner. Do an online search. Write sentences about the people. Then share your sentences with the class.

*Joel and Ethan Coen are from the United States.*

**4 | Using *Be* + Noun Phrase** What do you know about famous places around the world? Complete each sentence below with a place from this box and the correct form of *be*. `4.1 A`

| | | |
|---|---|---|
| the Guggenheim Museum Bilbao | Luxembourg | Pompeii |
| Ipanema Beach | the Nile River | Table Mountain |
| Loch Ness | the Petronas Twin Towers | the White House and Capitol |

1.  ___The Nile River is___
    a long river in Africa.

2.  _____
    an ancient[3] city in Italy.

3.  _____
    a small country in Europe.

4.  _____
    two tall buildings in Malaysia.

5.  _____
    a lake in Scotland.

6.  _____
    two buildings in the U.S.

7.  _____
    a beach in Brazil.

8.  _____
    a mountain in South Africa.

9.  _____
    a museum in Spain.

[3]**ancient:** very old

**Write about It**  Work with a partner. Complete these statements with facts about places you know. Share your sentences with a partner.

1. _____ is an ancient city in _____.
2. _____ and _____ are museums in _____.
3. _____ is a _____ in _____.

*Rome is an ancient city in Italy.*

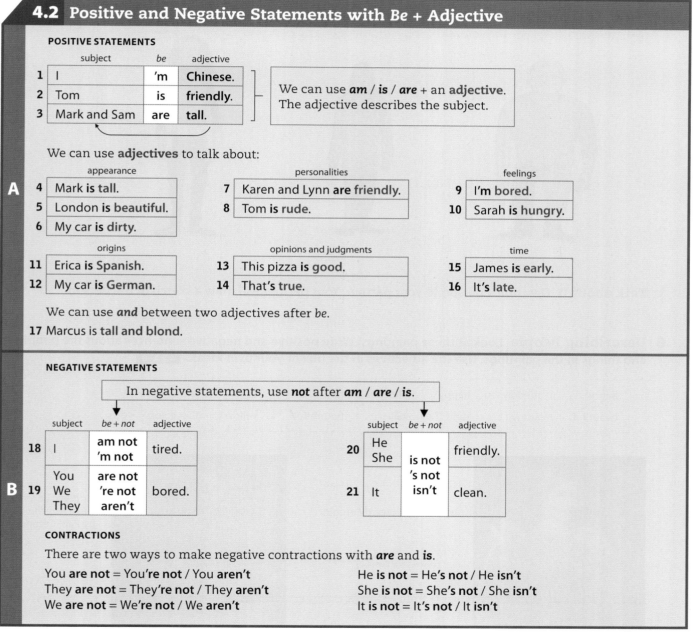

### 4.2 Positive and Negative Statements with *Be* + Adjective

**POSITIVE STATEMENTS**

| | subject | *be* | adjective |
|---|---|---|---|
| 1 | I | 'm | Chinese. |
| 2 | Tom | is | friendly. |
| 3 | Mark and Sam | are | tall. |

We can use **am** / **is** / **are** + an **adjective**. The adjective describes the subject.

We can use **adjectives** to talk about:

**A**

appearance
| | |
|---|---|
| 4 | Mark **is tall.** |
| 5 | London **is beautiful.** |
| 6 | My car **is dirty.** |

personalities
| | |
|---|---|
| 7 | Karen and Lynn **are friendly.** |
| 8 | Tom **is rude.** |

feelings
| | |
|---|---|
| 9 | I'm **bored.** |
| 10 | Sarah **is hungry.** |

origins
| | |
|---|---|
| 11 | Erica **is Spanish.** |
| 12 | My car **is German.** |

opinions and judgments
| | |
|---|---|
| 13 | This pizza **is good.** |
| 14 | That's **true.** |

time
| | |
|---|---|
| 15 | James **is early.** |
| 16 | It's **late.** |

We can use **and** between two adjectives after *be*.

17  Marcus is **tall and blond.**

**NEGATIVE STATEMENTS**

In negative statements, use **not** after **am** / **are** / **is**.

**B**

| | subject | be + not | adjective |
|---|---|---|---|
| 18 | I | am not / 'm not | tired. |
| 19 | You We They | are not / 're not / aren't | bored. |

| | subject | be + not | adjective |
|---|---|---|---|
| 20 | He She | is not / 's not / isn't | friendly. |
| 21 | It | | clean. |

**CONTRACTIONS**

There are two ways to make negative contractions with **are** and **is**.

You **are not** = You're **not** / You **aren't**
They **are not** = They're **not** / They **aren't**
We **are not** = We're **not** / We **aren't**

He **is not** = He's **not** / He **isn't**
She **is not** = She's **not** / She **isn't**
It **is not** = It's **not** / It **isn't**

**5 | Noticing *Be* + Adjective** Read this article. Underline each use of *be*. Circle the adjectives after *be*. Then number the police sketches *1*, *2*, or *3*. 4.2 A

## Late-Night Robbery⁴ on Monroe Street

The police have three sketches⁵ of the robbers from a robbery last night. (1) The leader of the group is tall and thin. His hair is long and wavy. (2) The second man is short. His hair is short and blond, and his face is round. (3) The third man is short and thin. His face is thin, and he has long, straight, black hair. All three men are in their 20s.

a. _____          b. _____          c. _____

**Talk about It** Describe a person to your partner. Your partner will draw a sketch of the person.

**6 | Describing People** Look at these paintings. Write positive and negative sentences about the people and things in the paintings. Use the adjectives in the box or your own ideas. 4.2 A–B

| angry | friendly | happy | short | thin | tired |
| beautiful | funny | sad | tall | thoughtful⁶ | yellow (or other colors) |

*Dressing Up*
by Charles Edward Perugini

*Madame Cézanne in
a Red Armchair*
by Paul Cézanne

*She's happy. Her dress is red. She's not angry.*

⁴**robbery:** when someone steals (takes things or money) from a place.
⁵**sketches:** pictures that you draw quickly

⁶**thoughtful:** thinking about something or someone

*American Gothic*
by Grant Wood

*Dr. Paul Gachet*
by Vincent Van Gogh

**Talk about It** Share your sentences with a partner. Do you agree with your partner's descriptions?

**7 | Using Positive and Negative Statements with *Be*** Complete these conversations with the correct form of *be* or *be* + *not*. Use contractions when possible. Then practice the conversations with a partner. `4.2 A–B`

GOING OUT WITH FRIENDS

1. A: Can we go inside?

   B: I __*'m not*__ sure. The theater looks closed.

   A: You __*'re*__ right. It opens at 5:00.

2. A: This movie _____ really funny!

   B: I know. Vince Vaughan and Owen Wilson _____ great!

3. A: I _____ hungry. Let's go out for pizza.

   B: I _____ hungry right now. Let's go later.

4. A: I like this restaurant. The food _____ good and the servers[7] _____ friendly.

   B: Yeah, the food _____ bad. I like their sandwiches.

5. A: Do you like this place?

   B: Not really.

   A: Why not?

   B: Well, I like the food. The pizza and burgers _____ good. But I don't like the servers.

   They _____ rude[8].

   A: That's true. The servers _____ friendly.

6. A: My brother loves this restaurant. He thinks it _____ the best pizza place in the city.

   B: He _____ right. The pizza is amazing. But it _____ cheap.

   A: I'll pay. I _____ really hungry and I want to try it.

> **RESEARCH SAYS...**
>
> The four most common adjectives after the verb *be* are *right*, *good*, *sure*, and *true*. Other common adjectives are *nice*, *funny*, *useful*, *necessary*, and *available*.
>
> CORPUS

**Write about It** Write three sentences about your favorite restaurant for an online review site. Describe the food, the servers, and the prices.

*The Tomato Garden is my favorite restaurant. The food is delicious, and the waiters are fast. The prices are cheap.*

---

[7] **servers:** waiters and waitresses          [8] **rude:** not polite

THE VERB BE   81

**8 | Usage Note: *Very* and *Really*** Read the note. Then do Activity 9.

We can put the words **very** and **really** before certain adjectives.

In positive statements, we can use **very** and **really** to make a statement stronger.

regular meaning

| 1 | Maria is **friendly**. |
| 2 | I'm **tired** today. |

stronger meaning

| 3 | Maria is **very friendly**. |
| 4 | I'm **really tired** today. |

In negative statements, we can use **very** and **really** to make a statement softer. This can sound more polite.

stronger meaning

| 5 | I'm **not hungry**. |
| 6 | The book **isn't interesting**. |

softer meaning (more polite)

| 7 | I'm **not really hungry**. |
| 8 | The book **isn't very interesting**. |

**GRAMMAR TERM:** *Very* and *really* are called **adverbs of degree**. For more information on adverbs of degree, see Unit 9, page 000.

**9 | Using *Very* and *Really*** Put the words in order to make sentences. Circle *very* and *really* in each sentence. Then check (✓) if the adverb makes the meaning stronger or softer. `4.2 A–B`

|  | | STRONGER MEANING | SOFTER MEANING |
|---|---|---|---|
| **PLANNING A BEACH VACATION** | | | |
| 1. really/are/the beaches in Cozumel/beautiful | | ☐ | ☐ |
| *The beaches in Cozumel are (really) beautiful.* | | | |
| 2. flight/is/the/expensive/very/not | | ☐ | ☐ |
| 3. are/cheap/not/the/very/hotels | | ☐ | ☐ |
| 4. very/nice/is/the Blue Sea Hotel | | ☐ | ☐ |
| 5. it/really/is/close to the beach/not | | ☐ | ☐ |
| 6. is/far from the beach/it/really | | ☐ | ☐ |
| 7. really/beautiful, too/the beaches in Hawaii/are | | ☐ | ☐ |
| 8. really/the/flights/are/expensive/to Hawaii | | ☐ | ☐ |
| 9. the K Hotel/is/not/nice/very | | ☐ | ☐ |

**Write about It** Describe a city you know. Write two positive statements and two negative statements. Use *very* and *really*.

*The art museum is really nice.*
*The parks aren't very big.*

## 10 | Writing Sentences with Adjectives
Look at the pictures below. Write three statements with *be* (positive and negative) about each photo. Use the adjectives from this box or your own ideas. Use *very* and *really* to make your statements stronger or softer. `4.2 A–B`

| | | | | |
|---|---|---|---|---|
| angry | bored | excited | hungry | quiet |
| annoyed | confused | happy | impatient | tired |

DESCRIBING FEELINGS

1. *They're really happy.*
2. _____
3. _____

4. _____
5. _____
6. _____

7. _____
8. _____
9. _____

10. _____
11. _____
12. _____

**Talk about It** How do you feel right now? Tell a partner. Describe three or more feelings.

*"I'm hungry."*

## 11 | Pronunciation Note: *He's* vs. *His*
Listen to the note. Then do Activity 12.

Notice the difference in sound between **he's** and **his**.

*He's*: "ee" /i/ like "tree"
1 He's really nice.
2 He's funny.
3 He's a good student.

*His*: "i" /ɪ/ like "big"
4 His brother is nice.
5 His teacher is good.
6 His parents are professors.

**12 | Listening for *He's* and *His*** Listen to the sentences. Circle the word you hear. `4.2 A–B`

1. (he's)   his
2. he's   his
3. he's   his
4. he's   his
5. he's   his
6. he's   his

7. he's   his
8. he's   his
9. he's   his
10. he's   his
11. he's   his
12. he's   his

**Talk about It** Think about a man or boy you know. Write three sentences about him with *he's* and three sentences with *his*. Look at Pronunciation Note 11 for ideas. Then give your sentences to a partner. Practice reading your partner's sentences.

Person: _____My friend Kenji_____

*He's from Tokyo. His wife is from Osaka.*

**13 | Usage Note: Adverbs of Frequency with *Be*** Read the note. Then do Activity 14.

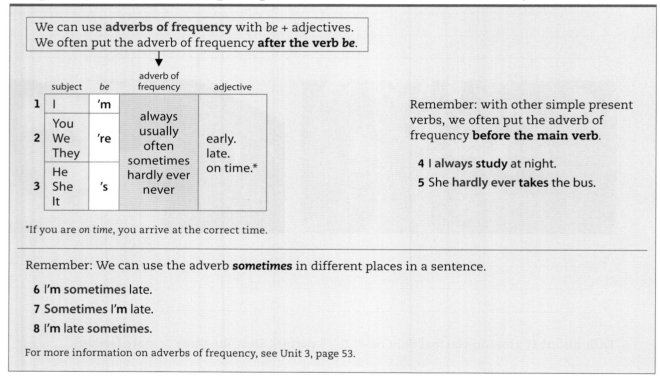

We can use **adverbs of frequency** with *be* + adjectives.
We often put the adverb of frequency **after the verb *be***.

| subject | be | adverb of frequency | adjective |
|---|---|---|---|
| 1 I | 'm | | |
| 2 You We They | 're | always usually often sometimes hardly ever never | early. late. on time.* |
| 3 He She It | 's | | |

*If you are *on time*, you arrive at the correct time.

Remember: with other simple present verbs, we often put the adverb of frequency **before the main verb**.

4 I **always study** at night.
5 She **hardly ever takes** the bus.

Remember: We can use the adverb ***sometimes*** in different places in a sentence.

6 I'm sometimes late.
7 Sometimes I'm late.
8 I'm late sometimes.

For more information on adverbs of frequency, see Unit 3, page 53.

**14 | Using Adverbs of Frequency with *Be*** Complete these sentences with *be* + an adverb of frequency and *early*, *late*, or *on time*. Make the sentences true for you. `4.2 A`

EARLY OR LATE?

1. I ___'m usually on time___ for class.
2. I _____ for a doctor's appointment.
3. I _____ for a job interview.
4. I _____ for a test.
5. I _____ for a movie.

6. I _____ for dinner with my friends.

7. I _____ for plans with my family.

8. I _____ for a wedding.

9. I _____ for a train.

10. I _____ for a flight.

11. I _____ for a game (for example: basketball, soccer, or tennis).

12. I _____ for a concert.

**Talk about It** Compare your answers above with a partner. How are your habits similar? How are they different?

**Write about It** Write four sentences about your partner. Then write the sentences in a different way.

*Kim is always early for a job interview. = Kim is never late for a job interview.*

## 15 | Using *Be* in Sentences with Adjectives  Add the correct form of *be* to each sentence.  `4.2 A–B`

1. I <u>am</u> very excited about my vacation.
   ∧

2. My friends always late!

3. Jack never on time for movies.

4. My parents always polite to my friends.

5. My neighbor hardly ever friendly to me.

6. The kids very hungry.

7. Justin not usually late for work.

8. Alex really tall.

9. My town not very big.

10. My neighborhood usually quiet.

11. The downtown area not very safe.

12. The stores downtown really expensive.

**Write about It** Write three true positive statements and three true negative statements about yourself, your town, and people you know. Use the verb *be*, *very*, *really*, adverbs of frequency, and your own adjectives. Then share your sentences with a partner.

## A

A **prepositional phrase** starts with a **preposition** and includes a **noun**.
It can answer the question *where*.

| | subject | *be* | prepositional phrase |
|---|---|---|---|
| **1** | The paintings | are | above the **desk**. |
| **2** | The black chair | is | behind the **desk**. |
| **3** | The computer | is | on the **desk**. |
| **4** | The phone | is | next to the **computer**. |
| **5** | The pens | are | in the **cup**. |
| **6** | The blue chair | is | in front of the **desk**. |
| **7** | The cat | is | under the **desk**. |

## B

We use the prepositions *at*, *in*, and *on* with certain places.

| **8** | *at* + | a street address | Her office is **at 42 Main Street**. |
|---|---|---|---|
| | | home / school / work / the office | We're **at school**. |
| | | the hospital* | Lynn is **at the hospital**. |

| **9** | *in* + | a city | He's **in London**. |
|---|---|---|---|
| | | a country | My mother is **in Thailand**. |
| | | class | Marta is **in class**. |
| | | the hospital ** | Kim is **in the hospital**. |

| **10** | *on* + | a street name | The bookstore is **on First Street**. |
|---|---|---|---|
| | | a floor in a building | It's **on the third floor**. |

*Lynn is **at** the hospital. = Lynn is not sick. She works there or she is visiting someone.
**Kim is **in** the hospital. = Kim is sick.

## C

**OTHER COMMONPLACE WORDS**

Mark

here

Jim

(over) there

inside

outside

**11** Mark **is here** today.

**12** Jim **is over there**.

**13** Kim **is inside** the house.

**14** Jenny **is outside**.

## 16 | Using Prepositions
Match the conversations below with these pictures. Then complete the conversations with the correct prepositions. Practice the conversations with a partner. `4.3 A`

WHERE'S MY STUFF?

1. A: Where are my keys?

   B: I think they're _____*on*_____ the counter.

2. A: Where are my sunglasses?

   B: I think they're _____ the dresser.

3. A: Oh, no! Where's my phone?

   B: Maybe it's _____ your pocket.

4. A: Where are my shoes?

   B: They're _____ the door.

5. A: Where's the cat?

   B: He's _____ the refrigerator!

6. A: Where's your book?

   B: It's _____ my backpack.

7. A: Where's your backpack?

   B: I think it's _____ the table.

8. A: Where is the coffee pot?

   B: It's _____ the stove.

9. A: Where's my hat?

   B: It's _____ your jacket.

## 17 | Using *At*, *In*, and *On* with Places
Complete these sentences with *at*, *in*, or *on*. `4.3 B`

AMAZING HOMES

1. The Nautilus House is ___*in*___ Mexico City, Mexico. It's a beautiful home. It looks like a seashell!

2. The Slide[9] House is _____ Tokyo, Japan. It has stairs, but it also has a slide. The top of the slide is _____ the third floor, and the bottom is _____ the first floor. The living room is _____ the first floor, and the bedrooms are _____ the third floor.

The Nautilus House

---

[9] **slide:** a long, smooth thing that children play on: they climb up steps, sit down, and then *slide* down.

3. The Keret House is a very strange building. It's _____ Warsaw, Poland, _____ Żelazna Street. It's less than five feet (1.5 meters) wide! The kitchen and bathroom are _____ the first floor. The bedroom is _____ the second floor.

4. The Transparent House is _____ a small street _____ Tokyo, Japan. People outside can see everything inside. The kitchen is _____ the second floor. The living room is _____ the top floor.

5. The Spaceship[10] House is _____ Chattanooga, Tennessee. It looks like a spaceship. Do you want to visit the Spaceship House? It's _____ 1408 Palisades Road.

The Transparent House

**Talk about It** Talk with a partner. Do you want to live in the houses above? Why or why not?

**Write about It** Write sentences about places in your area. Give the location. Use the places in this box or your own ideas.

| hospital | library | museum | school |
|---|---|---|---|

*The museum is on Main Street. The modern paintings are on the top floor. . . .*

**18 | Talking about Locations** Complete these conversations with the correct words in parentheses. Then practice the conversations with a partner. `4.3 B–C`

WHERE IS EVERYBODY?

1. A: Where is Emma today? I need to talk to her.

   B: She's ___*in*___ class.
   (in / at / on)

2. A: Where's Tom? He's late for work.

   B: He's _____ the hospital. He's very sick.
   (in / at / on)

3. A: Where are Jack and Ana? Their car isn't in the driveway.

   B: They're on vacation. I think they're _____ Hong Kong.
   (in / at / on)

4. A: Excuse me. Where's Dr. Jung's office?

   B: Her office is _____ the tenth floor. The elevator is just around the corner.
   (in / at / on)

5. A: Come in! I'm so happy you're _____. Where's Mike?
   (there / on / here)

   B: Oh, he's _____ home. He doesn't feel well tonight.
   (in / at / on)

6. A: I can pick you and Sonja up tonight. Where are you?

   B: We're _____ 5232 Lark Street. Our house is blue.
   (in / at / on)

[10] **spaceship:** a ship that travels in space

7. A: Where's Mark? I need to talk to him.

   B: He's _____. I think he's in the garden.
   (at / inside / outside)

8. A: Where's Tammy?

   B: She's in her office.

   A: No, she's not _____.
   (on / outside / there)

   B: Maybe she's in a meeting.

9. A: Where's Terri? We have plans for lunch.

   B: She isn't _____ today. She's _____ the hospital. Her daughter is sick.
   (here / there / inside)                (in / at / on)

10. A: Where is everybody? No one is _____ today.
    (here / there / outside)

    B: Edgar is _____ work and Janice is _____ school.
    (in / at / on)                    (in / at / on)

**Talk about It** Where are you during the week? Complete these sentences. Then share your schedule with a partner.

1. On Mondays at 2:00, I'm _____.

2. On Tuesdays at noon, I'm _____.

3. On Saturday mornings, I'm _____.

## 4.4 Yes/No Questions and Short Answers with *Be*

**A**

**YES/NO QUESTIONS**

| | *be* | subject | noun phrase / place / adjective |
|---|---|---|---|
| 1 | Are | you | a good cook? |
| 2 | Are | we they | in class? |
| 3 | Am | I | late? |
| 4 | Is | he she | a student? |
| | | it | on Market Street? |

**SHORT ANSWERS**

| | *yes / no* | subject | *be* (+ *not*) |
|---|---|---|---|
| 5 | Yes, | I | am. |
| 6 | No, | | am not. 'm not. |
| 7 | Yes, | we they you | are. |
| 8 | No, | | are not. aren't. 're not. |
| 9 | Yes, | he she it | is. |
| 10 | No, | | is not. isn't. 's not. |

Notice: We do NOT use contractions for short *yes* answers.
X Yes, I'm.

**B**

**OTHER ANSWERS TO *YES/NO* QUESTIONS**

| | | *YES* + MORE INFORMATION | *NO* + MORE INFORMATION |
|---|---|---|---|
| 11 | Am I late? | Yes, but it's OK. | No, you're right on time. |
| 12 | Are you a cook? | Yes, I work at Mick's Cafe. | No, I'm a server. |
| 13 | Is it fun? | Yes, it is. I really like it. | No, not really. It's kind of boring. |

**19 | Asking *Yes/No* Questions** Complete these quiz questions with the correct form of *be*. Then take the quiz. Add up your points and read your results below.  `4.4 A`

## Personality Quiz

1. _____ you talkative in a group of people?
   a. Yes, always.
   b. Yes, sometimes.
   c. No, never.

2. Someone looks you in the eye[11] during a conversation. _____ you comfortable?
   a. Yes, always.
   b. Yes, sometimes.
   c. No, not really.

3. You're busy and someone calls or texts you. _____ you happy?
   a. Yes, always.
   b. Yes, sometimes.
   c. No, hardly ever.

4. _____ your voice loud?
   a. Yes, always.
   b. Yes, sometimes.
   c. No, hardly ever.

5. _____ you a fast talker?
   a. Yes, always.
   b. Yes, sometimes.
   c. No, hardly ever.

6. You're asleep in bed. _____ you on your stomach?
   a. No, hardly ever.
   b. Yes, sometimes.
   c. Yes, usually.

7. You're watching TV. _____ your legs crossed[12]?
   a. No, hardly ever.
   b. Yes, sometimes.
   c. Yes, usually.

8. In the morning, _____ you very awake?
   a. No, never.
   b. Yes, sometimes.
   c. Yes, always.

9. You're talking to someone. _____ your arms crossed?
   a. No, never.
   b. Yes, sometimes.
   c. Yes, always.

10. _____ your friends very quiet?
    a. No, hardly ever.
    b. Yes, sometimes.
    c. Yes, always.

CHECK YOUR SCORE:

a = 1 point      b = 2 points      c = 3 points

My Score: _____

21–30 points: You are careful and you like to plan things. You make decisions slowly. You're very kind to your friends. You are a little shy with new people.

11–20 points: You are a good listener and a good friend. But sometimes you don't trust[13] people. You don't usually like to talk to new people.

1–10 points: You are popular and people like you. You are a good leader and you make decisions quickly. But sometimes you are a little bossy[14]. Sometimes people don't trust you.

**Think about It** Do you think your quiz results above are correct? In your opinion, which set of results describes you best?

---

[11] **look you in the eye:** to look at your eyes
[12] **legs crossed:** one leg on top of the other leg

[13] **trust:** to believe that someone is good and honest
[14] **bossy:** often telling other people what to do

**20 | Usage Note: *It* for Weather**  Read the note. Then do Activity 21.

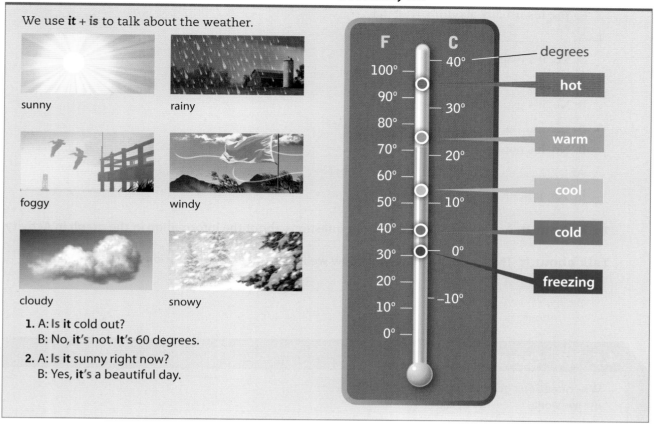

We use **it** + **is** to talk about the weather.

sunny

rainy

foggy

windy

cloudy

snowy

F    C

degrees

hot

warm

cool

cold

freezing

1. A: **Is it** cold out?
   B: No, **it's** not. **It's** 60 degrees.

2. A: **Is it** sunny right now?
   B: Yes, **it's** a beautiful day.

**21 | Asking about the Weather**  Look at this graph about the weather in Seoul, South Korea. Complete the questions below with *is it* and an adjective from the box. More than one question might be possible.  `4.4 A–B`

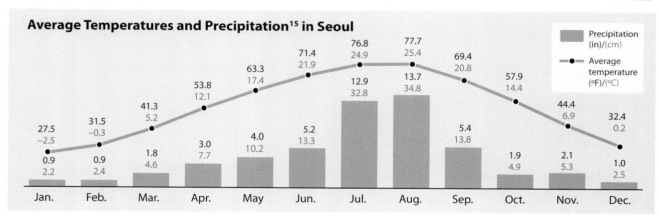

**Average Temperatures and Precipitation¹⁵ in Seoul**

Precipitation (in)/(cm)

Average temperature (°F)/(°C)

| | Jan. | Feb. | Mar. | Apr. | May | Jun. | Jul. | Aug. | Sep. | Oct. | Nov. | Dec. |
|---|---|---|---|---|---|---|---|---|---|---|---|---|
| Temp (°F) | 27.5 | 31.5 | 41.3 | 53.8 | 63.3 | 71.4 | 76.8 | 77.7 | 69.4 | 57.9 | 44.4 | 32.4 |
| Temp (°C) | −2.5 | −0.3 | 5.2 | 12.1 | 17.4 | 21.9 | 24.9 | 25.4 | 20.8 | 14.4 | 6.9 | 0.2 |
| Precip (in) | 0.9 | 0.9 | 1.8 | 3.0 | 4.0 | 5.2 | 12.9 | 13.7 | 5.4 | 1.9 | 2.1 | 1.0 |
| Precip (cm) | 2.2 | 2.4 | 4.6 | 7.7 | 10.2 | 13.3 | 32.8 | 34.8 | 13.8 | 4.9 | 5.3 | 2.5 |

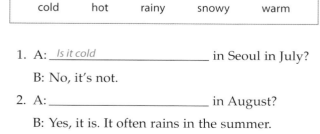

| cold | hot | rainy | snowy | warm |
|---|---|---|---|---|

1. A: _Is it cold_____ in Seoul in July?

   B: No, it's not.

2. A: _____ in August?

   B: Yes, it is. It often rains in the summer.

**PRONUNCIATION**

Remember: *Yes/No* questions usually end with rising intonation.

Are you a student?

Is it rainy?

Is Ben your brother?

¹⁵**precipitation:** rain or snow that falls to the ground

3. A: _____ in Seoul in August?

   B: Yes, it's usually about 78°F (25°C).

4. A: _____ in February?

   B: No, it's really cold.

5. A: _____ in June?

   B: No, it's usually warm.

6. A: _____ in December?

   B: No, it's not very rainy.

7. A: _____ in September?

   B: Yes, it is.

**Talk about It** Ask and answer three more questions about the information in the graph in Activity 21.

**Talk about It** Think about a place you know well. Ask and answer questions about the weather.

*A: Is it humid in Thailand in April?*
*B: Yes, it is. It's very hot and humid.*

---

## 4.5 Wh- Questions with Be

**Wh- questions** begin with a **wh- word**.

| | USE *WH-* WORD: | TO ASK ABOUT: | |
|---|---|---|---|
| 1 | **Where** | a place | A: **Where is** the restaurant?<br>B: It's on Main Street. |
| 2 | **Where ... from** | where someone is from | A: **Where are** John and Kim **from**?<br>B: They're from Texas. |
| 3 | **Who** | a person | A: **Who is** your teacher?<br>B: Mark Silver. |
| 4 | **What** | a thing | A: **What are** your favorite kinds of food?<br>B: I like Italian and Chinese food. |
| 5 | **What time** | a time | A: **What time is** the show?<br>B: It's at 5:30. |
| 6 | **What ... like** | a description | A: **What is** John **like**?<br>B: He's nice and friendly. |
| 7 | **How** | a person's health or well-being | A: **How are** you?<br>B: I'm fine, thanks. And you? |
| 8 | **How old** | age | A: **How old are** your brothers?<br>B: Ten and fourteen. |
| 9 | **How much** | prices | A: **How much is** the shirt?<br>B: It's $35. |

In conversation and informal writing, we often use contractions for **wh- words** + **is**.

10 **Where's** the restaurant?     12 **What's** John like?

11 **Who's** your teacher?          13 **How's** your brother?

Remember: We use *do* in questions with other verbs. We DON'T use *do* when the main verb is *be*.

| BE | OTHER VERBS |
|---|---|
| ✓Where **is** the restaurant? | ✓Where **do** you **work**? |
| ✗Where **do** the restaurant? | |

**22 | Answering Wh- Questions** Match each question with the correct answer. Then listen and check your answers. `4.5 A`

CLASSROOM CONVERSATIONS

1. How are you? _c_              a. It's next to the library.
2. Who is your English teacher this semester? ____    b. She's from London.
3. What time is your English class? ____    c. I'm fine, thanks.
4. Where is your English class? ____    d. He's 22.
5. What is your teacher like? ____    e. Professor Miller.
6. Where is your teacher from? ____    f. It's at 2:30.
7. What is your brother's name? ____    g. It's really small.
8. How old is your brother? ____    h. It's $15.
9. Where are your parents? ____    i. In Japan.
10. How big is your family? ____    j. She's really nice and patient.
11. How much is your English book? ____    k. Tom.

**Talk about It** Choose six of the questions above. Ask and answer the questions with a partner. Answer with your own information.

A: *What time is your class?*
B: *It's at 10:00.*

**23 | Understanding Wh- Questions** Listen to the questions and check (✓) the best answers. `4.5 A`

1. ☐ a. It's 8:30.
   ☑ b. Laura.
2. ☐ a. I'm fine, thanks.
   ☐ b. I'm Laura.
3. ☐ a. It's on Eighth Street.
   ☐ b. It's really nice.
4. ☐ a. I'm fine, thanks.
   ☐ b. I'm 22.
5. ☐ a. At 1552 First Street.
   ☐ b. Lima, Peru.
6. ☐ a. He's at work.
   ☐ b. His name is Miguel.

7. ☐ a. It's a comedy.
   ☐ b. It's at 7:15.
8. ☐ a. She's great.
   ☐ b. Professor Wong.
9. ☐ a. They're $45.
   ☐ b. We have three.
10. ☐ a. He's outside.
    ☐ b. He's my brother.
11. ☐ a. He's fine.
    ☐ b. He's 18.
12. ☐ a. Joseph.
    ☐ b. He's a teacher.

**24 | Asking about Events** Read about the events at the Sydney Opera House. Complete the questions below with a *wh-* word and a form of *be*. Then check (✓) the correct answers. `4.5 A`

### The Australian World Orchestra (AWO)

See world-famous Zubin Mehta conduct[16] the Australian World Orchestra (AWO). The AWO includes over 110 musicians from over 47 orchestras around the world.

| Shows: | Prices: |
|---|---|
| Fri. 6:00 p.m. | Regular: $125 |
| Sat. 7:00 p.m. | Students: $89 |

### Henry IV

Experience this exciting new production of the classic Shakespeare play.

| Shows: | Prices: |
|---|---|
| Fri. 8:00 p.m. | Regular: $89 |
| Sat. 8:00 p.m. | Students: $79 |
| Sun. 2:00 p.m. | |

The Opera House is located at Bennelong Point in Sydney, Australia.

**CUSTOMER QUESTIONS**

1. _Where is_ _____ the opera house?

   ☑ a. It's at Bennelong Point.

   ☐ b. It's in Sydney, Canada.

2. _____ the Australian World Orchestra show on Friday?

   ☐ a. It's at 6:00 p.m.

   ☐ b. It's at 8:00 p.m.

3. _____ student tickets for the Orchestra?

   ☐ a. They're $79.

   ☐ b. They're $89.

4. _____ one regular ticket for the Orchestra?

   ☐ a. It's $89.

   ☐ b. It's $125.

5. _____ show _____ on Sunday?

   ☐ a. The Australian World Orchestra.

   ☐ b. Henry IV.

6. _____ one regular ticket for Henry IV?

   ☐ a. It's $89.

   ☐ b. It's $125.

7. _____ Henry IV on Friday?

   ☐ a. It's at 8:00 p.m.

   ☐ b. It's at 2:00 p.m.

8. _____ two student tickets for Henry IV?

   ☐ a. They're $158.

   ☐ b. They're $178.

9. _____ the conductor of the AWO?

   ☐ a. Zubin Mehta.

   ☐ b. Shakespeare

[16] **conduct:** to stand in front of a group of musicians and control what they do (the person who does this is the **conductor**)

**Talk about It** Go online and look up information about a show in your area. Complete this chart with information about the show. Then ask and answer questions about the show with a partner.

| Name of the show | |
|---|---|
| Performers in the show | |
| Name of the place | |
| Address | |
| Times | |
| Ticket prices | |

A: *Where is the show?*
B: *It's at the Jackson Theater.*
A: *How much are the tickets?*
B: *They're $30.*

**25 | Error Correction** Find and correct the errors in the questions. (Some questions may not have any errors.)

1. Q: What time *is* the movie?

   A: It's at 9:00.

2. Q: Who do the stars of the movie?

   A: Joan Chen and Lucy Liu.

3. Q: Where's the theater?

   A: It's on Market Street.

4. Q: How much do the tickets?

   A: They're $10 each.

5. Q: Who are those girls?

   A: They're my friends from class.

6. Q: What is their names?

   A: Sue and Ling.

7. Q: Where they are from?

   A: They're from China.

8. Q: Where are the restaurant?

   A: It's on Second Avenue.

9. Q: How much is the book?

   A: It's $30.

10. Q: Where your car?

    A: It's in the parking garage.

> **PRONUNCIATION**
> Remember: *Wh-* questions usually end with falling intonation.
>
> **Yes/No Question**
> Is he 21?
>
> ***Wh-* Question**
> How old is he?

## 4.6 The Simple Present of *Be* vs. Other Verbs

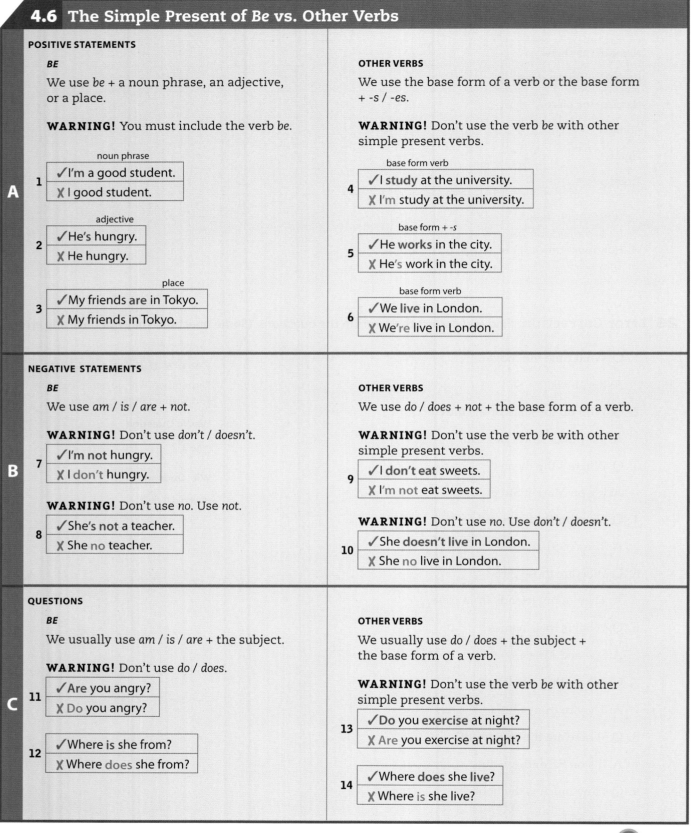

**A**

**POSITIVE STATEMENTS**

*BE*

We use *be* + a noun phrase, an adjective, or a place.

**WARNING!** You must include the verb *be*.

noun phrase
1 ✓ I'm a good student.
✗ I good student.

adjective
2 ✓ He's hungry.
✗ He hungry.

place
3 ✓ My friends are in Tokyo.
✗ My friends in Tokyo.

**OTHER VERBS**

We use the base form of a verb or the base form + -s / -es.

**WARNING!** Don't use the verb *be* with other simple present verbs.

base form verb
4 ✓ I **study** at the university.
✗ I'm study at the university.

base form + -s
5 ✓ He **works** in the city.
✗ He's work in the city.

base form verb
6 ✓ We **live** in London.
✗ We're live in London.

**B**

**NEGATIVE STATEMENTS**

*BE*

We use *am / is / are + not*.

**WARNING!** Don't use *don't / doesn't*.

7 ✓ I'm **not** hungry.
✗ I **don't** hungry.

**WARNING!** Don't use *no*. Use *not*.

8 ✓ She's **not** a teacher.
✗ She **no** teacher.

**OTHER VERBS**

We use *do / does + not +* the base form of a verb.

**WARNING!** Don't use the verb *be* with other simple present verbs.

9 ✓ I **don't eat** sweets.
✗ I'm **not** eat sweets.

**WARNING!** Don't use *no*. Use *don't / doesn't*.

10 ✓ She **doesn't live** in London.
✗ She **no** live in London.

**C**

**QUESTIONS**

*BE*

We usually use *am / is / are +* the subject.

**WARNING!** Don't use *do / does*.

11 ✓ **Are** you angry?
✗ **Do** you angry?

12 ✓ Where **is** she from?
✗ Where **does** she from?

**OTHER VERBS**

We usually use *do / does +* the subject + the base form of a verb.

**WARNING!** Don't use the verb *be* with other simple present verbs.

13 ✓ **Do** you **exercise** at night?
✗ **Are** you exercise at night?

14 ✓ Where **does** she **live**?
✗ Where **is** she live?

**GO ONLINE**

**26 | Noticing Errors with *Be*** Find and correct the errors in this job description. Add or remove forms of the verb *be*. 4.6 A

# Wanted: Office Manager for Law Office

           *is*

Our office⌃downtown. We ~~are~~ need a new office manager five days a week,

eight hours a day.

### What does the office manager do?

The manager is makes schedules and answers emails from clients[17]. He/she also

is buys equipment, works with new employees, and pays bills.

### Are you the right person for this job?

The right person reliable[18] and comes to work on time every day. He/she friendly

and hard-working. The right person is works well on a team.

Are you interested? Please email your resume.

**Talk about It** Are you the right person for this job? Why or why not? Discuss your answers with a partner.

**27 | Using *Be* and *Do* in Negative Statements** Complete each negative statement with the correct form of *be + not* or *do + not*. 4.6 B

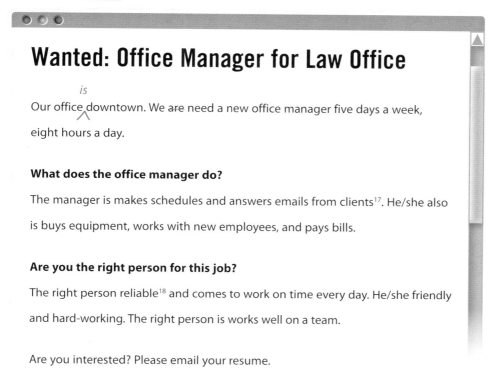

# The Ocean's Amazing Creatures[19]

The **leafy sea dragon** is an interesting creature. It looks like seaweed[20],

but it \_\_\_\_\_*isn't*\_\_\_\_\_ a plant. It's an animal. It _____ look
           1                      2

like a fish, so other animals _____ eat it. The leafy sea dragon
                               3

only lives in southern Australia. It _____ live in other parts of
                                    4

the world.

    The **viperfish** _____ a beautiful fish, and it _____ very
                    5                          6

friendly! It has very long teeth. It has a light above its head. Other fish swim toward the

light, and the viperfish eats them. The viperfish _____ live in cold water.
                                            7

It only lives in warm oceans.

a leafy sea dragon

a viperfish

---

[17] **clients:** people who pay a professional or a business for help or advice
[18] **reliable:** someone that you can trust

[19] **creatures:** living things that are not plants
[20] **seaweed:** a plant that grows in the ocean

**Write about It** Go online and learn about an interesting animal. Write three sentences about it. Use the simple present of *be* and other verbs. Choose an animal from this box or use your own idea.

| blobfish | glass frog | narwhal | peacock spider | tarsier |

## 28 | Using *Be* and *Do* in Questions and Answers Complete these conversations with the correct form of *be* or *do*. Then circle the correct answer for each question. 4.6 C

WHAT'S FOR LUNCH?

1. A: _Are_ you hungry?

   B: (Yes, I'm very hungry.) / Yes, I do.

2. A: _____ you want to go to Mia's Bistro?

   B: Yes, let's go. / Yes, I am.

3. A: What _____ your favorite dish there?

   B: Yes, it's my favorite. / I like the chicken salad.

4. A: _____ they have good soup?

   B: Yes, they do. / Yes, they are.

5. A: _____ you ready to go now?

   B: No, I don't right now. / No, I need ten minutes.

6. A: _____ you want to walk there?

   B: No, it's far. Let's drive. / Yes, I am. Let's walk.

LET'S DO SOMETHING

7. A: _____ you busy right now?

   B: No, I'm not. / No, I don't.

8. A: _____ you want to do something with me?

   B: Sure. / Yes, I am.

9. A: _____ you want to play basketball in the park?

   B: No, let's do something else. / No, I'm not.

10. A: _____ it nice out?

    B: No, it doesn't. / No, it's a little cloudy.

11. A: _____ you like video games?

    B: Yes, I do. / Yes, I am.

12. A: _____ you want to come over to my place?

    B: Yes, I am. / Sure.

**Talk about It** Listen and check your answers. Then practice the conversations with a partner.

## 29 | Usage Note: Answering *Be* Questions with Other Verbs Read the note. Then do Activity 30.

We sometimes answer **be** questions with **other verbs** to give more information.

**1** A: **Is** your daughter a student?

B: No, she **doesn't go** to school.

**2** A: **Are** you a server?

B: Yes, I **work** at Dino's Diner.

**3** A: What's your favorite food?

B: I **love** sushi.

**30 | Answering *Be* Questions with Other Verbs** Match the questions with the answers. `4.6 C`

1. Are you a student? _g_
2. Is your brother here? ____
3. Are we late? ____
4. Is Anna at work? ____
5. Where are my shoes? ____
6. What are your favorite colors? ____
7. Who is your math teacher? ____
8. How much is a bus ticket? ____
9. When is the movie? ____
10. What's your address? ____

a. It starts at 7:00.
b. No, the meeting starts at 10:30.
c. Yes, she works from noon to 5:00.
d. No, he works in the evenings.
e. It costs $1.00.
f. I live at 1818 Oak Street.
g. Yes, I go to City College.
h. I like purple and blue.
i. You usually put them in your closet.
j. I have Professor Kwok.

**Write about It** Write answers with *be* for the questions above.

*1. Yes, I am.*     *2. No, he's in class.*

**31 | Error Correction** Find and correct the errors. (Some sentences may not have any errors.)

1. I don't tired right now.   [*am not*]
2. Are your teachers give you a lot of homework?   [*Do*]
3. It isn't very sunny today.
4. I no have my umbrella.   [*don't*]
5. We are live in Santiago.
6. Do you tired?   [*Are*]
7. He's not feel good today.   [*ing*]
8. We don't work on Sundays.
9. The restaurant don't be open on Mondays.   [*isn't*]
10. What class are you have right now?   [*do*]

**32 | Writing a Paragraph** Write a short paragraph (5–8 sentences) about yourself. Use words from this chart or your own ideas. Use the verb *be* and other simple present verbs. `4.6 A–C`

| VERBS | | | ADJECTIVES | | | ADVERBS | | |
|---|---|---|---|---|---|---|---|---|
| be | like | study | friendly | outgoing | reliable | never | really | usually |
| have | live | want | happy | quiet | talkative | often | sometimes | very |

*I'm Sun-Hee. I'm from Korea. Now I live in Los Angeles. I'm very talkative. I like to meet new people.*

## WRAP-UP

**A | GRAMMAR IN READING** Read the article about personality types. Then complete the sentences on page 100 with the positive or negative form of the verbs in parentheses.

## Introverts and Extroverts

Psychologists sometimes use the words *extrovert* and *introvert* to describe personalities. People are usually either extroverts or introverts, but sometimes they act both ways.

Extroverts are outgoing. They're happy in social situations[21]. They like to be with a lot of people, and they have large groups of friends. They like to be the center of attention[22]. They often do a lot of different activities at one time. Extroverts are not very good planners[23].

Introverts are not very outgoing. They enjoy some social situations, but they are very happy to be alone. They often feel tired after social activities. Introverts are *not* always shy. Shy people are often afraid in social situations. Introverts are not afraid, but they have more energy when they're alone.

1. Sarah is an extrovert. She is home alone on a Friday night, and she ___*is*___ bored. She ___*isn't*___
   (be)                                        (be)
   happy to be alone. She _____ to go out with her friends.
                            (want)

2. Roommates Mike and Luis are introverts. They are at a social event. They don't know the other people

   in the room. They _____ to meet the other people. They _____ very happy. The event
                       (want)                                     (be)
   _____ fun for them.
    (be)

3. Ken is an extrovert. He's at a restaurant with a large group of friends. At dinner, Ken _____ really
                                                                                            (be)
   talkative. He _____ the dinner.
                  (enjoy)

4. Alison is an introvert. Tonight, she's at home reading a book. Her roommates are out for the evening.

   She _____ lonely. She _____ happy to be home alone.
        (be)                    (be)

**B | GRAMMAR IN SPEAKING** Ask and answer these survey questions with a partner. Count your partner's *yes* and *no* answers. Then look at the results on page 101. Is your partner an introvert or an extrovert?

A: *Do you like to talk to new people?*
B: *Yes, I do.*

## WHAT'S YOUR PERSONALITY TYPE?

My partner: _____

|  | Yes | No |
|---|---|---|
| 1. Do you like to talk to new people? | | |
| 2. Do you like large groups of people? | | |
| 3. Do you talk on the phone a lot? | | |
| 4. Are you often the center of attention? | | |
| 5. Do you have a lot of energy? | | |
| 6. On weekends, do you usually go out with friends? | | |
| 7. In classes, is your desk usually in the center of the room? | | |
| 8. Are you in a lot of social groups and clubs? | | |
| 9. You're home alone. Are you bored? | | |
| 10. Do you often talk to people about your problems? | | |
| 11. Are you often excited? | | |
| Total: | | |

[21] **social situations:** things and events with other people
[22] **center of attention:** someone who everyone in a group watches and listens to
[23] **planners:** people who plan things

**Talk about It**  Do you agree with your results? Why or why not?

**Write about It**  Write six statements about your partner. Use your partner's answers to the survey.

*Valentin doesn't like to talk to new people.*

## 4.7 Summary of the Verb *Be*

**USES**

We can use *be* to:
- introduce people
- identify people and things
- describe people and things
- talk about locations
- talk about the weather

**POSITIVE STATEMENTS**

| | | |
|---|---|---|
| I | am<br>'m | Alex.<br>tired.<br>at work. |
| You<br>We<br>They | are<br>'re | my classmate(s).<br>friendly.<br>outside. |
| He<br>She | is<br>'s | a good doctor.<br>late.<br>at home. |
| It | | my bag.<br>beautiful.<br>on the table. |

**NEGATIVE STATEMENTS**

| | | |
|---|---|---|
| I | am not<br>'m not | a teacher.<br>bored.<br>in New York. |
| You<br>We<br>They | are not<br>'re not / aren't | my classmate(s).<br>confused.<br>in class. |
| He<br>She | is not<br>'s not / isn't | a good doctor.<br>late.<br>at home. |
| It | | my phone.<br>new.<br>here. |

**YES/NO QUESTIONS**

| | | |
|---|---|---|
| Are | you | a teacher? |
| | we | early? |
| | they | from Brazil? |
| Am | I | late? |
| Is | he | a student? |
| | she | a painter? |
| | it | a good book? |

**SHORT ANSWERS**

| | | |
|---|---|---|
| Yes,<br>No, | I | am.<br>am not / 'm not. |
| | you<br>we<br>they | are.<br>are not / 're not / aren't. |
| | he<br>she<br>it | is.<br>is not / 's not / isn't. |

**WH- QUESTIONS**

| | | |
|---|---|---|
| **What** | are | their names? |
| **Who** | is | your doctor? |

| | | |
|---|---|---|
| **Where** | am | I? |
| **How much** | is | it? |

| | | |
|---|---|---|
| **How** | are | you? |
| **What time** | is | the show? |

# 5

# Nouns, Articles, and Quantifiers

**GO ONLINE**

For the Unit Vocabulary Check, go to the Online Practice.

## IN THIS UNIT, WE STUDY nouns. Nouns are names for:

### People

1. **Emiko** is my good **friend**.

2. I have two **brothers** and a **sister**.

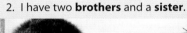

### Places

3. I study at a **university** and work in an **office**.

### Things

4. My **closets** and **drawers** are very full.

5. My **bicycle** is my favorite **thing**.

# Ideas

6. Sometimes I have **problems**.

7. My friends help me. They give good **advice**.

**Think about It** What people, places, things, and ideas are part of your life? In each row, cross out nouns that are **not** in your life.

1. **People:** neighbor, boss, brother, sister, friend
2. **Places:** store, park, movie theater, office, library
3. **Things:** bicycle, car, computer, smartphone, apartment
4. **Ideas:** problems, fun, education, work, health

## WE USE articles and quantifiers to:

## Give more information about nouns

A SHORT PICNIC

**a** picnic

12:00

**the** sun

12:15

**a** cloud

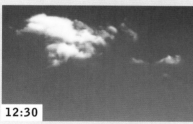

12:30

**many** clouds

12:45

**some** rain

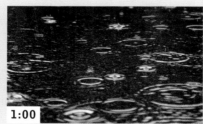

1:00

**a lot of** rain

1:15

**Think about It** Look out the window. Circle the things you see. Write two more things.

| | | | |
|---|---|---|---|
| a bicycle | some clouds | some students | the sun |
| many bicycles | some grass | some trees | a _____ |
| many cars | some stars | the moon | some _____ |

## 5.1 Introduction to Nouns

**Nouns** are words for people, places, things, and ideas.

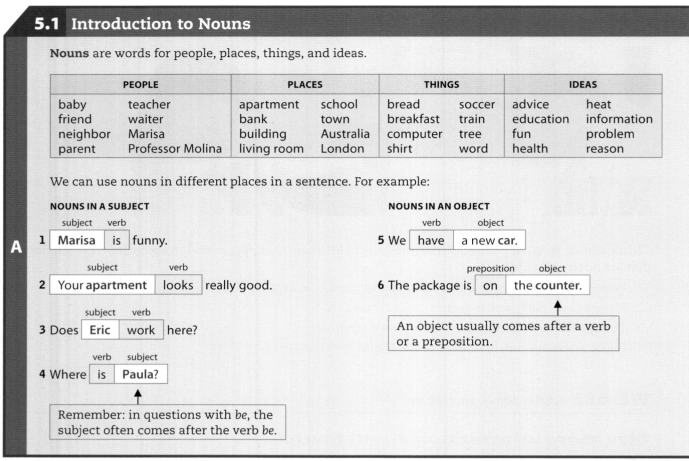

| PEOPLE | | PLACES | | THINGS | | IDEAS | |
|---|---|---|---|---|---|---|---|
| baby | teacher | apartment | school | bread | soccer | advice | heat |
| friend | waiter | bank | town | breakfast | train | education | information |
| neighbor | Marisa | building | Australia | computer | tree | fun | problem |
| parent | Professor Molina | living room | London | shirt | word | health | reason |

We can use nouns in different places in a sentence. For example:

**NOUNS IN A SUBJECT**

**A**

1 | subject | verb | 
  Marisa | is | funny.

2 | subject | verb |
  Your **apartment** | looks | really good.

3 Does | subject | verb | here?
  Eric | work |

4 Where | verb | subject |
  is | Paula?

Remember: in questions with *be*, the subject often comes after the verb *be*.

**NOUNS IN AN OBJECT**

5 We | verb | object |
  have | a new **car**.

6 The package is | preposition | object |
  on | the **counter**.

An object usually comes after a verb or a preposition.

 **GO ONLINE**

---

## 1 | Identifying Nouns  In each group of words, cross out the one word that is not a noun. `5.1 A`

| | | | |
|---|---|---|---|
| 1. classroom | hat | ~~write~~ | laptop |
| 2. after | brother | grass | soccer |
| 3. at | child | kitchen | doctor |
| 4. aunt | eat | restaurant | waiter |
| 5. before | education | professor | son |
| 6. advice | beach | problem | enter |
| 7. pasta | dining room | on | dinner |
| 8. describe | hospital | town | vegetable |
| 9. reason | science | partner | live |
| 10. and | office | shirt | health |

**Think about It**  Work with a partner. Are the nouns above people, places, things, or ideas? Write the nouns in the correct group in the chart.

| People | Places | Things | Ideas |
|---|---|---|---|
| | *classroom* | | |
| | | | |
| | | | |
| | | | |

## 2 | Identifying Nouns in Subjects

Underline the nouns in the subject in each question and answer. (One sentence has two subject nouns.) **5.1 A**

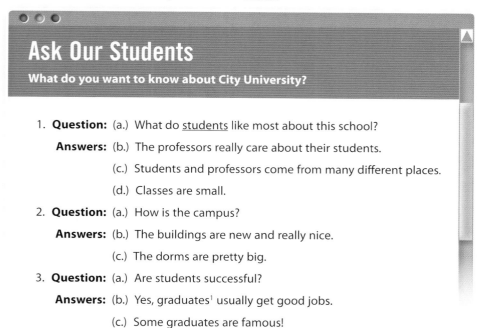

**Ask Our Students**

**What do you want to know about City University?**

1. **Question:** (a.) What do <u>students</u> like most about this school?

   **Answers:** (b.) The professors really care about their students.

   (c.) Students and professors come from many different places.

   (d.) Classes are small.

2. **Question:** (a.) How is the campus?

   **Answers:** (b.) The buildings are new and really nice.

   (c.) The dorms are pretty big.

3. **Question:** (a.) Are students successful?

   **Answers:** (b.) Yes, graduates[1] usually get good jobs.

   (c.) Some graduates are famous!

**Think about It** Four sentences above have nouns in the object (after a preposition or verb other than *be*). Circle these nouns.

## 3 | Identifying Nouns in Objects

Look at the **bold** nouns. Does the noun come after a verb or a preposition? Underline the verbs. Circle the prepositions. **5.1 A**

1. A: Where's Ryan?

   B: He's ⓐt **practice**. He <u>plays</u> **soccer** after work.

   His team has a **game** tomorrow.

2. A: Does the P3 bus stop in front of the **supermarket**?

   B: No, that bus stops across from the **bank**.

3. A: What does your new apartment look like?

   B: Well, the kitchen is really big. The living room

   is behind the **kitchen**.

4. A: You always order **steak** in restaurants.

   B: Yeah, I like **meat**.

5. A: Wow! You have a **balcony**[2]!

   B: Yeah. And I often eat my **breakfast** here.

6. A: Where are the lemons? They're not in the **refrigerator**.

   B: Look again. They're on that **shelf**, behind the **oranges**.

> **F Y I**
> Some prepositions have more than one word.
>
> across from
> in front of
> next to

---

[1] **graduates (noun):** people who finish school or university

[2] **balcony:** a small area outside, above ground, attached to an apartment

## 5.2 Singular Nouns and Plural Nouns

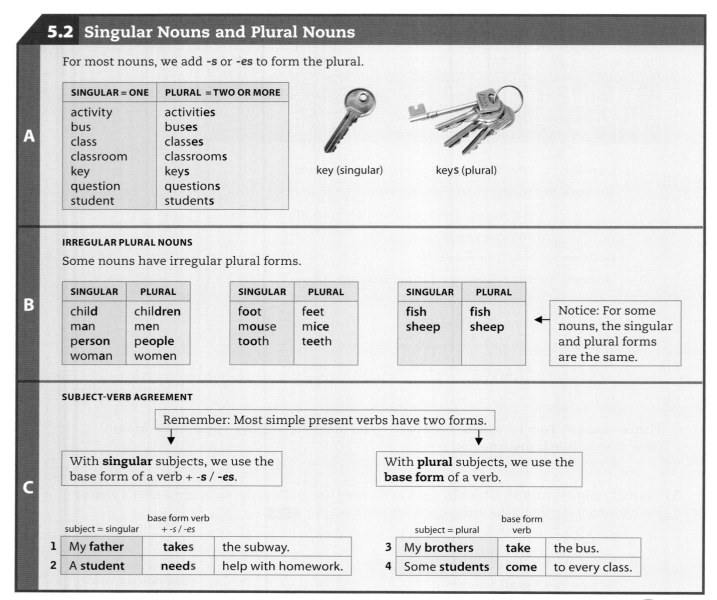

**A**

For most nouns, we add **-s** or **-es** to form the plural.

| SINGULAR = ONE | PLURAL = TWO OR MORE |
|---|---|
| activity | activities |
| bus | buses |
| class | classes |
| classroom | classrooms |
| key | keys |
| question | questions |
| student | students |

key (singular)     keys (plural)

**B**

**IRREGULAR PLURAL NOUNS**

Some nouns have irregular plural forms.

| SINGULAR | PLURAL |
|---|---|
| child | children |
| man | men |
| person | people |
| woman | women |

| SINGULAR | PLURAL |
|---|---|
| foot | feet |
| mouse | mice |
| tooth | teeth |

| SINGULAR | PLURAL |
|---|---|
| fish | fish |
| sheep | sheep |

Notice: For some nouns, the singular and plural forms are the same.

**C**

**SUBJECT-VERB AGREEMENT**

Remember: Most simple present verbs have two forms.

With **singular** subjects, we use the base form of a verb + **-s / -es**.

With **plural** subjects, we use the **base form** of a verb.

| | subject = singular | base form verb + -s / -es | |
|---|---|---|---|
| 1 | My **father** | **takes** | the subway. |
| 2 | A **student** | **needs** | help with homework. |

| | subject = plural | base form verb | |
|---|---|---|---|
| 3 | My **brothers** | take | the bus. |
| 4 | Some **students** | come | to every class. |

**4 | Identifying Singular Nouns and Plural Nouns** Write *sg* over each **bold** noun that is singular and write *pl* over each **bold** noun that is plural. Then practice the conversations with a partner. **5.2 A**

AT A FAST-FOOD RESTAURANT

1. A: I'd like a *sg* **hamburger** and some **fries**, please.

   B: And to drink?

   A: Umm . . . a **soda**.

   B: And for you, sir?

   C: I'll have an Italian **sandwich** with **onions** and **peppers**.

   And a small **salad**. Nothing to drink. Thanks.

2. A: I'll take a **peach**, please. No, wait . . . they look so good! Make that

   four **peaches**.

   B: OK. Anything else? How about some **blueberries**? Today's **special**³ is

   two **boxes** of **blueberries** for the **price** of one.

   A: No, thanks. But maybe a **box** of **strawberries**.

3. A: Attention, **shoppers**! Don't miss our great **specials** on **fruits** and

   **vegetables**! . . .

   . . . Try our delicious **salads** and **sandwiches** . . .

   . . . And now, you can shop from your **computer**. Go to our **website**

   and order your groceries⁴ online.

   B: Those loud **announcements** make me crazy!

**Talk about It** Imagine that you and your partner are at each of the places above—a fast-food restaurant, a market, and a supermarket. What food do you get?

🔊 **5 | Listening for Singular Nouns and Plural Nouns** Listen to the sentences. Are the nouns singular or plural? Circle the noun you hear. **5.2 A**

1. Larisa sees her **brother** / (**brothers**) almost every weekend.
2. Rashid works two **job** / **jobs** and takes classes.
3. We don't have the **book** / **books** for class.
4. I usually drink seven or eight **glass** / **glasses** of water a day.
5. The lemons are from the **tree** / **trees** in my yard.
6. Turn in your **assignment** / **assignments** on Monday.
7. I live next to the tall **building** / **buildings** on Elm Street.
8. I really like the **rug** / **rugs** in your office.
9. Fatima likes her new **roommate** / **roommates**.
10. Leave your **bicycle** / **bicycles** outside.
11. Don't park your **car** / **cars** on the street at night.
12. Lina loves **video game** / **video games**.

🔊 **Talk about It** Listen again and repeat the sentences.

---

³ **special (noun):** a price or sale that is offered for a short time          ⁴ **groceries:** food and other things for the home that you buy regularly

**6 | Spelling Note: -s and -es Endings on Plural Nouns** Read the note. Then do Activity 7.

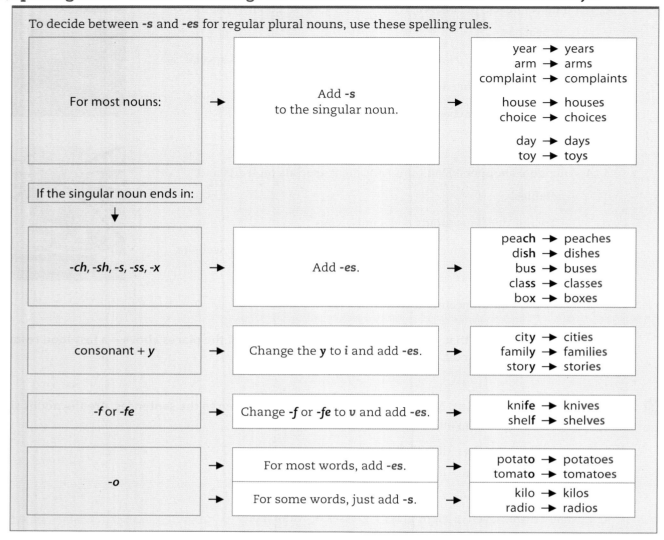

To decide between **-s** and **-es** for regular plural nouns, use these spelling rules.

| For most nouns: | → | Add **-s** to the singular noun. | → | year → years<br>arm → arms<br>complaint → complaints<br>house → houses<br>choice → choices<br>day → days<br>toy → toys |

If the singular noun ends in:

| -ch, -sh, -s, -ss, -x | → | Add -es. | → | peach → peaches<br>dish → dishes<br>bus → buses<br>class → classes<br>box → boxes |
| consonant + y | → | Change the **y** to **i** and add **-es**. | → | city → cities<br>family → families<br>story → stories |
| -f or -fe | → | Change **-f** or **-fe** to **v** and add **-es**. | → | knife → knives<br>shelf → shelves |
| -o | → | For most words, add **-es**.<br>For some words, just add **-s**. | → | potato → potatoes<br>tomato → tomatoes<br>kilo → kilos<br>radio → radios |

**7 | Spelling Plural Nouns** For each singular noun in the box, write the plural form in the correct part of the chart on page 109. **5.2 A–B**

| | | | | |
|---|---|---|---|---|
| address | class | guest | neighbor | story |
| baby | cookie | holiday | path | tax |
| backpack | dish | knife | peach | tomato |
| beach | dress | leaf | person | tooth |
| berry | family | library | project | toy |
| box | fly | man | reason | university |
| bus | foot | monkey | sandwich | way |
| child | glass | month | shelf | woman |

| Nouns ending in -ch, -sh, -x, -s, -ss | Nouns ending in consonant + y | Nouns ending in -f or -fe | Irregular plural nouns | Other nouns |
|---|---|---|---|---|
| *addresses* | | | | |

**Write about It** Use plural nouns from the chart on page 108 to complete these sentences. Share your sentences with a partner.

*I like tomatoes.*

1. I like _____.

2. Many _____ like _____.

3. _____ are interesting.

4. _____ are annoying.

**8 | Spelling Plural Nouns** Complete the passage with the plural form of each noun in parentheses.

5.2 A–B

## Wedding Gifts in Countries around the World

Around the world, _____brides_____ and _____ get _____
(1. bride)                        (2. groom)              (3. gift)
from their _____ and _____. Different _____
(4. friend)                  (5. family)                 (6. country)
have different _____, but money is a common gift. _____
(7. tradition)                                              (8. thing)
for the home are also common. In many countries, the bride and groom often

post[5] a list of _____ for _____. After the wedding, the
(9. suggestion)              (10. gift)
bride and groom open many _____. They often get _____,
(11. box)                                    (12. pot)
_____, and _____ for their new home.
(13. dish)           (14. glass)
   Today some _____ and _____ marry at a later age.
(15. man)              (16. woman)
Sometimes they ask for unusual _____. For example, some
(17. thing)
couples ask for language _____, and some couples ask for money
(18. class)
for _____.
(19. charity[6])

A bride and groom in South Korea

A bride and groom in Egypt

**Talk about It** Imagine it's your wedding. What gifts do you want? Compare your ideas with the class.

[5] **post:** put on the Internet

[6] **charity:** a group that collects money to help people

## 9 | Pronunciation Note: -s and -es Endings on Plural Nouns Listen to the note. Then do Activity 10.

Notice how we pronounce the **-s** and **-es** endings on plural nouns.

| If the word ends in the **sound**: | | The **-s/-es** ending sounds like: |
|---|---|---|
| /f/ | coughs, laughs | |
| /k/ | clocks, ducks | /s/ = "ss" |
| /p/ | ships, tips | |
| /t/ | adults, pots | |

| | | |
|---|---|---|
| /b/ | clubs, jobs | |
| /d/ | bands, heads | |
| /g/ | bags, mugs | |
| /l/ | examples, pencils | |
| /m/ | exams, arms | |
| /n/ | lessons, pens | |
| /r/ | neighbors, summers | /z/ = "zz" |
| /v/ | sleeves, knives | |
| /w/ | windows, cows | |
| a vowel sound | boys, toys | |
| | umbrellas, bananas | |
| | tomatoes, radios | |
| | activities, cities | |

| If the word ends in the **letter(s)**: | | The **-s/-es** ending sounds like: |
|---|---|---|
| -ce | prices, races | |
| -ge | pages, bridges | |
| -se | houses, horses | |
| -ze | prizes, sizes | |
| -ch | beaches, benches | /əz/ = "iz" |
| -sh | dishes, wishes | |
| -s | buses, gases | |
| -ss | glasses, classes | |
| -x | boxes, taxes | |

The /s/ and /z/ endings sound very similar. It's often difficult to hear the difference.

## 10 | Pronouncing -s and -es Endings On Plural Nouns Read these sentences. Choose the correct pronunciation for the -s/-es ending of the **bold** noun. Then listen and check your answers. `5.2 A–B`

LEARNING LANGUAGES

| | /s/ | /z/ | /əz/ |
|---|---|---|---|
| 1. **Babies** and young children learn their language easily. | ☐ | ☑ | ☐ |
| 2. They're like **sponges**[7]—they soak up[8] language. | ☐ | ☐ | ☐ |
| 3. By age two they can make simple **sentences**. | ☐ | ☐ | ☐ |
| 4. By age six they are fluent[9] **speakers** of their language. | ☐ | ☐ | ☐ |
| 5. For an adult, new **languages** aren't so easy! | ☐ | ☐ | ☐ |
| 6. But adults have some **advantages**[10]. | ☐ | ☐ | ☐ |
| 7. Adults already know many **things** about language. | ☐ | ☐ | ☐ |
| 8. They can take **classes**. | ☐ | ☐ | ☐ |
| 9. They can read **books** in the language. | ☐ | ☐ | ☐ |
| 10. Many **adults** ask a friend for help. | ☐ | ☐ | ☐ |
| 11. They have **difficulties**, but they learn a new language with lots of practice. | ☐ | ☐ | ☐ |

Babies are like sponges.

[7] **sponge (pl. sponges):** a soft thing with holes in it that you use to wash things
[8] **soak up:** to take in easily (such as a liquid)
[9] **fluent:** able to speak easily and correctly
[10] **advantages:** things that help you or are useful

**Talk about It** Work with a partner. Take turns reading the sentences in Activity 10 (page 110). Use correct pronunciation.

**Talk about It** Is a new language difficult? Why or why not? What is difficult for you—the words, the grammar, or the pronunciation? What is easy for you?

**11 | Using Subject-Verb Agreement** Complete the conversations with the singular or plural form of the noun in parentheses. (Look at the verbs in the sentences to help you.) Then match each conversation with the correct situation. **5.2 C**

  a. two friends in a store
  b. a worker and customer at the dry cleaners[11]
  c. a waiter and customer in a restaurant
  d. two friends at home
  e. a parent and son at home
  f. a parent and a babysitter[12] on the phone
  g. two coworkers at an office

__e__ 1. A: Your _____notebooks_____ are under the table.
        (notebook)

  B: Thanks, Dad! Now where's my _____book_____?
                                    (book)

____ 2. A: The _____ look perfect on you!
               (shoe)

  B: I agree. But my _____ are too big! Ouch!
                        (foot)

____ 3. A: I'm sorry. Your _____ isn't ready yet.
                    (dress)

  B: It's OK. I have something for you . . . two _____.
                                                    (shirt)

____ 4. A: How is everything?

  B: The _____ is perfect! And the _____ are great!
           (steak)                              (vegetable)

____ 5. A: Where is everyone? Our _____ starts at 9:00.
                                        (meeting)

  B: Two _____ are sick—Alex and Jenna. I don't know about the others.
           (person)

____ 6. A: Do you like my new things?

  B: They're great! The _____ looks great there. And the _____ really
                            (chair)                                    (rug)
  goes with your furniture.

____ 7. A: Hi, Ms. Smith, it's Lisa. . . . The _____ are fine. But they don't want dinner—
                                                  (child)
  just cookies.

  B: _____ come after dinner. That's the rule!
        (cookie)

**Talk about It** Listen and check your answers. Then practice the conversations with a partner.

---

[11] **dry cleaners:** a place where people clean your clothes with chemicals, not water

[12] **babysitter:** a person who takes care of another person's children

**A**

| COUNT NOUNS | |
|---|---|
| singular | plural |
| one friend | two friends |
| one olive | three olives |
| one year | five years |

three olives

| NONCOUNT NOUNS |
|---|
| bread |
| money |
| rain |

rain

Notice:

• **Count nouns** have singular and plural forms.

• We can use numbers (*two*, *three*) with count nouns.

Notice:

• **Noncount nouns** usually do not have plural forms.

• We do not use numbers with noncount nouns.
  ✗ moneys      ✗ two money

**EXAMPLES OF NONCOUNT NOUNS**

| LIQUIDS | | FOODS | | ABSTRACT THINGS | | NATURAL THINGS | |
|---|---|---|---|---|---|---|---|
| coffee | soup | bread | rice | advice | information | air | heat |
| milk | tea | cheese | salt | fun | time | cold | rain |
| oil | water | flour | sugar | health | work | electricity | weather |

For a list of common noncount nouns, see the Resources, page R-2.

Some **noncount nouns** describe groups of things. The things in the group are often **count nouns**.

| GROUP (NONCOUNT NOUNS) | THINGS IN THE GROUP (COUNT NOUNS) |
|---|---|
| furniture | chairs, tables |
| jewelry | necklaces, rings |
| luggage | bags, suitcases |
| mail | letters, packages |
| money | dollars, coins |
| traffic | cars |

Furniture

 chair

 table

 desk

**B**

**SUBJECT-VERB AGREEMENT WITH COUNT AND NONCOUNT NOUNS**

We use a **singular verb form** with **singular count nouns** and **noncount nouns**.

We use a **plural verb form** with **plural count nouns**.

1 The **computer works**.

2 The **ring is** nice.

3 The **coffee smells** good.

4 The **jewelry is** nice.

5 My **friends work** here.

6 The **rings are** nice.

 **GO ONLINE**

**12 | Identifying Plural Count Nouns and Noncount Nouns** Read the passage. Label each **bold** noun: write *pl* if it is a plural count noun and *nc* if it is a noncount noun. **5.3 A**

Oymyakon

## Extreme[13] Weather

*pl* *nc*

Some **places** often have extreme **weather**. Here are some **examples**:

The **towns** of Oymyakon (pronounced *oy-mia-KONE*) and Verkhoyansk (pronounced *verka-YANsk*) are in the far north of Russia. In the winter,

[13] **extreme:** very great or strong

Death Valley

The Atacama Desert

Lloró

**temperatures** there are often below −58°F (−50°C)! The **cold** makes life very difficult for the **people** of Oymyakon and Verkhoyansk. **Snow** and **ice** cover the **roads** and the **buildings**.

Daliol, Ethiopia, and Death Valley, California, are both **deserts**[14]. They have very dry **air**. In the summer, the **heat** is extreme. In Death Valley, summer **temperatures** sometimes reach about 122°F (50°C)!

The Atacama Desert in South America is extremely dry. It gets almost no **rain**. Some **parts** of this desert get only .01 cm of rain in a year! The high Andes **mountains** keep **clouds** away.

Lloró (pronounced *yo-RO*) is a town in Colombia. It rains almost every day in Lloró. Most years the town gets over 40 **feet** (1,200 cm) of **rain**!

**Think about It**  We often use *the* with nouns. Underline *the* in the sentences in Activity 12. What nouns come after *the*? Write the nouns in the chart below.

| Count nouns after *the* | Noncount nouns after *the* |
|---|---|
| *towns* | |

**Talk about It**  What weather do you like? Do you want to go to any of the places above?

**13 | Identifying Singular, Plural, and Noncount Nouns**  Read these conversations. Then write each **bold** noun in the correct group in the chart on the right.  `5.3 A`

PREPARING DINNER

1. A: Do you need some **help**?
   B: I'm OK for now. . . . Are you hungry? Have some **cheese** and **crackers**.

2. A: What's next?
   B: Get an **onion** and chop it up. Then put the onion in a **pan** with some **oil**.

3. B: Add the **water** and the **rice**.
   A: Do we put **butter** in the rice?

4. B: What do we have for **salad**?
   A: I see some **tomatoes**, some **carrots**, a **pepper**, and a **cucumber**.
   B: Let's use the tomatoes and the cucumber.

5. B: Put the **bowls** on the **table**. Put the **bread** and the **soup** on the table, too. OK?
   A: OK. It looks great, and I'm hungry. Let's eat!

| Singular count nouns |
|---|
| |

| Plural count nouns |
|---|
| |

| Noncount nouns |
|---|
| *help* |

[14] **deserts:** large dry areas with few plants

**Think about It** Circle *a*, *an*, *some*, and *the* in Activity 13 (page 113). Then read these statements. Check (✓) *True* or *False*.

| IN ACTIVITY 13, WE USE . . . | TRUE | FALSE |
|---|:---:|:---:|
| 1. *a/an* before plural count nouns. | ☐ | ☐ |
| 2. *a/an* before singular count nouns. | ☐ | ☐ |
| 3. *some* before plural count nouns and noncount nouns. | ☐ | ☐ |
| 4. *some* before singular count nouns. | ☐ | ☐ |
| 5. *the* before singular count nouns, plural count nouns, and noncount nouns. | ☐ | ☐ |

**14 | Using Count and Noncount Nouns with Similar Meanings** Complete these conversations with words from the boxes. Use each word only once. Then practice the conversations with a partner.

`5.3 A–B`

1. A: My students are always late to class. You're an experienced teacher. Do you
   have some _____*advice*_____ for me?

   B: I have one _____: Don't let late students come to class.

| advice |
|---|
| suggestion |

2. A: These jeans cost a hundred _____.

   B: The _____ isn't the problem. It's the style. The jeans look terrible!

| dollars |
|---|
| money |

3. A: Do you need some _____ for your trip?

   B: I don't think so. I just have one _____, but it's big.

| luggage |
|---|
| suitcase |

4. A: Does my new _____ look OK?

   B: Sure! It's great! Your new _____ are very comfortable.

| chairs |
|---|
| furniture |

5. A: The _____ are beautiful. Let's get them for Mom.

   B: I like them too, but _____ isn't Mom's favorite thing.
   Let's look at scarves.

| necklaces |
|---|
| jewelry |

6. A: Are my _____ here?

   B: Not yet. The _____ doesn't come on Sundays.

| mail |
|---|
| packages |

**Write about It** These sentences have noncount nouns. Rewrite the sentences with the plural count nouns in parentheses.

1. I have some money. (dollars)
2. The mail is here. (bills)
3. Your new furniture is beautiful. (chairs)

**15 | Using Subject-Verb Agreement** Read the email. Complete the sentences with the correct form of the verb in parentheses. `5.3 B`

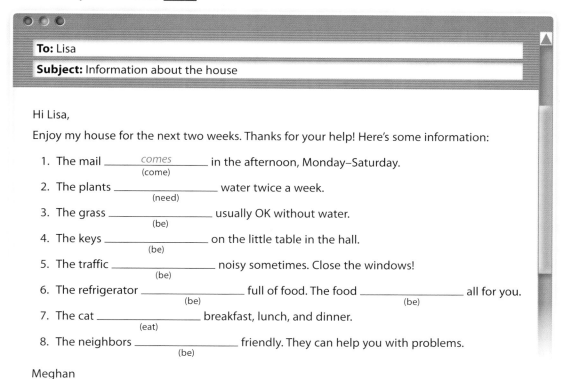

To: Lisa

Subject: Information about the house

Hi Lisa,

Enjoy my house for the next two weeks. Thanks for your help! Here's some information:

1. The mail _____*comes*_____ in the afternoon, Monday–Saturday.
   (come)

2. The plants _____ water twice a week.
   (need)

3. The grass _____ usually OK without water.
   (be)

4. The keys _____ on the little table in the hall.
   (be)

5. The traffic _____ noisy sometimes. Close the windows!
   (be)

6. The refrigerator _____ full of food. The food _____ all for you.
   (be)                                                       (be)

7. The cat _____ breakfast, lunch, and dinner.
   (eat)

8. The neighbors _____ friendly. They can help you with problems.
   (be)

Meghan

---

## 5.4 A and *An* with Singular Count Nouns

**A AND *AN* + NOUN**

We use *a* and *an* with **singular count nouns**.

| If a noun begins with a **consonant** sound, use *a*. | | |
|---|---|---|
| a bicycle | a job | a vacation |
| a day | a shirt | a year |

| If a noun begins with a **vowel** sound, use *an*. | | |
|---|---|---|
| an apartment | an insect | an orange |
| an email | an ocean | an uncle |

**WARNING!** The letters *u* and *h* can sound like a consonant or a vowel.

**A**

| *u* = a **consonant** sound (sounds like /y/) | *u* = a **vowel** sound |
|---|---|
| a university | an umbrella |

| *h* = a **consonant** sound | *h* is silent, and a **vowel** sound follows |
|---|---|
| a house | an hour |

**WARNING!** Don't use *a* / *an* with plural nouns or noncount nouns.

✗ We don't have **a** keys.          ✗ I need **a** money.

**GRAMMAR TERM:** *a* and *an* are **indefinite articles**.

**A AND *AN* + ADJECTIVE + NOUN**

Sometimes we use an **adjective** before a singular count noun.

**B**

| If the adjective begins with a **consonant** sound, use *a*. | If the adjective begins with a **vowel** sound, use *an*. |
|---|---|
| a big umbrella | an interesting job |

GO ONLINE

**16 | Choosing _A_ or _An_ with Singular Count Nouns** Write _a_ or _an_ in front of each singular count noun. Do not write anything in front of a plural count noun or a noncount noun. `5.4 A`

SOME COMMON ENGLISH NOUNS

1. _a_ man
2. ____ woman
3. ____ child
4. ____ people
5. ____ thing
6. ____ hand
7. ____ arm
8. ____ eyes
9. ____ student
10. ____ information

11. ____ hour
12. ____ day
13. ____ numbers
14. ____ house
15. ____ activity
16. ____ fact
17. ____ area
18. ____ water
19. ____ idea
20. ____ program

> **RESEARCH SAYS...**
>
> The nouns in Activity 16 are some of the most common nouns in English. All of the words are part of the Oxford 3000™.

CORPUS

**Think about It** Which noun above is a plural count noun? Which nouns are noncount nouns?

**17 | Using _A_ and _An_ with Singular Count Nouns** Complete these conversations with _a_ and _an_. Then listen and check your answers. Practice the conversations with a partner. `5.4 A`

GOING PLACES

1. A: Sam, you live pretty close to your office. Do you take _a_ bus to work?

   B: Yeah, but it makes so many stops. The trip takes ____ hour. Sometimes I'm in ____ hurry, and I just call ____ taxi.

2. A: It's very cloudy. Take ____ umbrella.

   B: I don't need one. I have ____ hat.

3. A: Let's visit Mom and Dad today.

   B: How about Friday? Today I have ____ appointment and ____ interview for ____ job. And tomorrow I have ____ exam and ____ assignment for English class.

TALKING ABOUT PEOPLE

4. A: How is your friend Lara?

   B: She's fine. She's at ____ university in England . . . in London, I think.

   A: Oh, really?

   B: Yeah. She has ____ aunt and ____ uncle there.

5. A: Guess what—I have ____ roommate now. And he seems really interesting.

   B: What does he do?

   A: He's ____ actor. He's in ____ play and some TV commercials. And he works at ____ restaurant.

6. A: Where does your friend Lina live?

   B: She lives in ____ apartment on Spring Street.

**Talk about It** Work with a partner. Practice conversation 6 again. Talk about your own friend.

_A: Where does your friend Josh live?_
_B: He lives in a house on Second Avenue._

**18 | Using _A/An_ + Adjective + Noun** Complete each description below with _a_ or _an_ and an adjective from the box. Use each adjective one time. Use a dictionary to help you. **5.4 B**

| | | | |
|---|---|---|---|
| female | male | ~~small~~ | yellow |
| large | orange | sweet-smelling | young |

1. An ant is _____ _a small_ _____ insect.
2. An elephant is _____ animal.
3. A banana is _____ fruit.
4. A carrot is _____ vegetable.
5. A rose is _____ flower.
6. A kitten is _____ cat.
7. A hen is _____ chicken.
8. A rooster is _____ chicken.

a hen

**19 | Using _A_ and _An_** Read the two choices in each situation below. Write _a_ or _an_ before each choice. Then circle your choice. **5.4 A–B**

**It's Your Choice**

**Example:** You want to buy new electronics. You buy _a_ laptop / _a_ tablet.

1. You want to eat dinner in a restaurant. You choose ____ Chinese restaurant / ____ Italian restaurant.
2. You want to move. You prefer ____ apartment / ____ house.
3. You need furniture for your living room. You choose ____ expensive couch / ____ cheap couch and some chairs.
4. After a very busy week, it's the weekend. You prefer ____ quiet evening at home / ____ evening with friends.
5. You need to choose a school. You prefer ____ small college / ____ big university.
6. You need to choose your classes. You choose ____ interesting class / ____ easy class.
7. You want to take a summer course. You register for ____ online course / ____ face-to-face[15] course.
8. A course is available at different times. You register for ____ early-morning class / ____ night class.
9. You want to take a short vacation. You prefer ____ exciting vacation / ____ relaxing vacation.
10. You need to take a trip across the Atlantic Ocean. You take ____ airplane / ____ ship.

**Talk about It** Compare your choices above with a partner. Are most of your choices the same or different?

[15] **face-to-face:** in a classroom with other students and a teacher

## 5.5 Some and Any

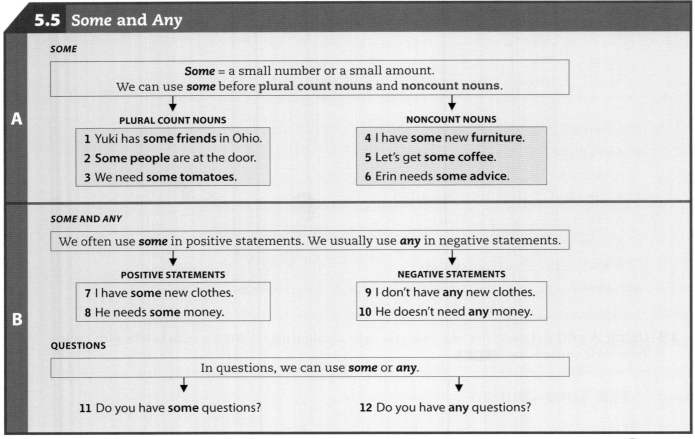

**SOME**

> **Some** = a small number or a small amount.
> We can use **some** before **plural count nouns** and **noncount nouns**.

**A**

| PLURAL COUNT NOUNS | NONCOUNT NOUNS |
|---|---|
| **1** Yuki has **some friends** in Ohio. | **4** I have **some** new **furniture**. |
| **2 Some people** are at the door. | **5** Let's get **some coffee**. |
| **3** We need **some tomatoes**. | **6** Erin needs **some advice**. |

**SOME AND ANY**

> We often use **some** in positive statements. We usually use **any** in negative statements.

**B**

| POSITIVE STATEMENTS | NEGATIVE STATEMENTS |
|---|---|
| **7** I have **some** new clothes. | **9** I don't have **any** new clothes. |
| **8** He needs **some** money. | **10** He doesn't need **any** money. |

**QUESTIONS**

> In questions, we can use **some** or **any**.

| **11** Do you have **some** questions? | **12** Do you have **any** questions? |
|---|---|

**20 | Noticing *Some* + Noun** Underline each *some* + noun combination. Then label the noun *pl* for plural count noun or *nc* for noncount noun. Then practice the conversations with a partner. **5.5 A**

TALKING ABOUT FOOD

1. A: What do you want on your pizzas?
   B: <u>Some olives</u> and some mushrooms for me, please.
   *pl*
   C: Just some cheese. Thanks.

2. A: We need some groceries.
   B: What do we need?
   A: Milk, eggs, and some rice. Oh, and some coffee for tomorrow.

3. A: What's for lunch?
   B: Just some pasta and bread. Is that OK?
   A: It's perfect. Pasta is my favorite food.

4. A: What do you want in your smoothies[16]?
   B: Some blueberries and a banana for me. And some milk, please.
   C: I want strawberries and some yogurt in my smoothie.

---

[16] **smoothie (*pl.* smoothies):** a thick drink made of fruit or fruit juice with milk, ice cream, or yogurt

**Talk about It** Ask and answer these questions with a partner. Use *some* in your answers.

1. What groceries do you need now?
2. What do you usually eat for lunch?


**21 | Using *A, An*, and *Some*** What do you pack for different situations? Fill in the chart below with the nouns from the box or your own ideas. If necessary, make the nouns plural. Use *a/an* with singular count nouns. Use *some* with plural count nouns and noncount nouns. **5.5 A**

| | | | | |
|---|---|---|---|---|
| bandage | coffee | jeans | music | tablet |
| book | dictionary | jewelry | pen | toothbrush |
| camera | flashlight | laptop | pencil | toothpaste |
| cell phone | food | medicine | shirt | umbrella |
| charger | jacket | money | sweater | water |

| For... | You pack... |
|---|---|
| 1. your school backpack | *a pen, some pencils, some water, a snack* |
| 2. a camping trip | |
| 3. an overnight¹⁷ trip | |
| 4. a trip to a far-away place | |

**Talk about It** Compare your answers with a partner. Are your answers similar or different?


**22 | Using *Some* and *Any* in Statements** Complete these statements with *some* or *any*. **5.5 B**

STATEMENTS FROM THE MIDDLE OF CONVERSATIONS

1. We have _____*some*_____ problems. We don't have _____ easy solutions.
2. Sorry—I don't have _____ tickets for that night. But I have _____ tickets for next Monday and Tuesday.
3. OK, now you have _____ homework. It's due on Monday. This time I don't want _____ excuses.
4. No, I don't have _____ plans for the weekend. I'm really busy. I don't have _____ free time.
5. I don't have _____ money. I really need a job! But most places don't have _____ jobs. Maybe the career counselor¹⁸ has _____ advice for me.
6. It's cold out! I have _____ nice shirts, but I need _____ sweaters for this cold weather!

**Talk about It** What is the topic of each conversation above? Who is the speaker and who is the listener? Discuss your ideas with a partner.

*"In 1, maybe the speaker is a boss in an office and the listeners are some workers. Maybe the topic is a problem at work."*


¹⁷**overnight:** including one night            ¹⁸**career counselor:** a person who helps people find good jobs

## 23 | Using *Some* and *Any* in Statements and Questions  Complete these conversations with *some* or *any*.  **5.5 B**

**A HEALTHY PICNIC**

1.  A: Mom, I'm thirsty. Do we have _____*any*_____ soda?

    B: I'm sorry, we don't have _____ soda. Have _____ water instead[19].

2.  B: Do you want a cheese sandwich?

    A: OK. I like potato chips. Do we have _____ potato chips?

    B: Nope! We don't have _____ potato chips. We have _____ nuts

    and _____ raisins.

    A: OK, I guess I'll have raisins.

3.  A: It's time for dessert! I want _____ cookies, please!

    B: We don't have _____ cookies. But you like fruit, and we have _____ delicious apples.

    A: Oh, OK.

**Think about It**  In which places above are both *some* and *any* possible? Why?

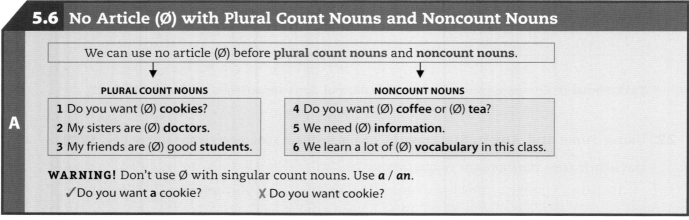

### 5.6 No Article (Ø) with Plural Count Nouns and Noncount Nouns

We can use no article (Ø) before **plural count nouns** and **noncount nouns**.

**A**

| PLURAL COUNT NOUNS | NONCOUNT NOUNS |
|---|---|
| **1** Do you want (Ø) **cookies**? | **4** Do you want (Ø) **coffee** or (Ø) **tea**? |
| **2** My sisters are (Ø) **doctors**. | **5** We need (Ø) **information**. |
| **3** My friends are (Ø) good **students**. | **6** We learn a lot of (Ø) **vocabulary** in this class. |

**WARNING!** Don't use Ø with singular count nouns. Use *a / an*.

✓ Do you want **a** cookie?          ✗ Do you want cookie?

## 24 | Choosing *A*, *An*, or No Article  Label each **bold** noun *sg* for singular count noun, *pl* for plural count noun, or *nc* for noncount noun. Then add *a* or *an* before each singular count noun.  **5.6 A**

# Tips for Learning a Foreign Language

For adult learners, ____ *pl* **languages** aren't easy. But here are some tips:

1.  Buy __*a*__ *sg* good **book** about grammar.

2.  Take ____ **class**.

3.  Use ____ good **dictionary**.

---

[19] **instead:** in place of

120

4. Make ____ **time** every day for studying.

5. Work on ____ **vocabulary**. To figure out the meaning of ____ difficult **word**, use other words in the sentence. Write down and review ____ new **words**.

6. Work on ____ **pronunciation**.

7. Listen to the language. Watch ____ **movies**. Listen to ____ **music**.

8. Talk to ____ **people** in the language. Don't worry about ____ **mistakes**.

9. Look online for ____ good **materials**. Read ____ **websites** and ____ **blogs**.

**Talk about It** Read the tips again. Check (✓) all the tips you use. Compare your answers with a partner. Which tips are the most useful?

**Write about It** Work with a partner. Write three more tips for learning English. Share your sentences with your classmates.

**25 | Error Correction** Find and correct the errors. (Some sentences may not have any errors.)

1. We need ~~an~~ *some* advice about a problem.

2. She has new computer.

3. Do you want any coffee?

4. We have a hour before class.

5. My uncle is dentist.

6. Good furniture are often expensive.

7. My favorite snack are potato chips.

8. He studies at an university in France.

9. Let's get some informations about classes for next semester.

10. We don't have some homework for the weekend.

## 5.7 The

**A**

We use the article **the** with all three types of nouns.

| SINGULAR COUNT NOUN | PLURAL COUNT NOUN | NONCOUNT NOUN |
|---|---|---|
| **1** Our friends are at **the restaurant**. | **2 The children** are at a friend's house. | **3 The water** is cold. |

**GRAMMAR TERM:** *The* is called the **definite article**.

**B**

**USES OF *THE* AND OTHER ARTICLES**

> Does the listener know which noun you mean?
> Listener doesn't know ➔ Use **a / an** or **some**.
> Listener knows ➔ Use **the**.

- We often use **a / an** or **some** the **first time** we mention something. We use **the** when we mention the same thing again.

**4** Ken has | a new **car** | . | **The car** | is really expensive.

first mention: The listener doesn't know about the car.

second mention: The listener knows about the car.

second mention

**5** I have | **some news** | . | **The news** | isn't good.

first mention

- We often use **the** when there is **only one** of something. (The listener knows.)

**6 The Earth** moves around **the Sun**.

There is only one Earth.

There is only one Sun.

**7** A: Where's Amy?
B: She's in **the kitchen**.

In this house, there is only one kitchen.

- If the noun is **not specific**, use **a / an** or **some**.

**8** I need a big **closet**.

*Closet* is not specific. The speaker means "any big closet."

**C**

***THE* VS. NO ARTICLE**

Notice: We don't usually use **the** to talk about things in general. We use no article (Ø).

| GENERAL | NOT GENERAL |
|---|---|
| **9a** Water is a liquid. | **9b The** water isn't cold. I don't want it. |
| **10a** Bananas are my favorite fruit. | **10b The** bananas are old. Don't eat them. |

122

**26 | Identifying _The_ + Noun** Underline each _the_ + noun combination. Then write each phrase in the correct column in the chart below. **5.7 A**

## Don't Rent From These Guys!

<u>The advertisement</u> is a lie. This house is terrible! The roof leaks[20], so the rain comes in! The water is always cold. We have NO HOT WATER. Sometimes the electricity doesn't work, and the lights go out. The house has three bedrooms. But the bedrooms are tiny! The furniture is really old. The chairs and the beds are uncomfortable. Outside, the grass comes up to our shoulders. Also, the stairs are really dangerous, especially at night.

| _the_ + singular count noun | _the_ + plural count noun | _the_ + noncount noun |
|---|---|---|
| _the advertisement_ | | |

**Write about It** Complete these sentences about your home. You can write about bad things (complaints) or good things. Use _the_ in each sentence. Share your sentences with a partner.

1. My house/apartment _____.
2. The rooms _____.
3. The _____.

**27 | Pronunciation Note: Pronouncing _A_, _An_, and _The_** Listen to the note. Then do Activity 28.

Notice how we often pronounce **a**, **an**, and **the**:

**1** I have a stomachache.     **a** sounds like "uh"
**2** I have an earache.     **an** sounds like "uhn"
**3** I have the flu.     **the** sounds like "thuh"

Sometimes **the** and **a** sound similar.

---

[20] **leak:** to have a hole that liquid can go through

**28│Listening for *A*, *An*, and *The*** Listen and write the missing words in these conversations. Then practice the conversations with a partner. **5.7 B**

EVERYDAY CONVERSATIONS

1. A: Pass _____*the*_____ bread.

   B: OK. Do you need _____ knife?

2. A: What's _____ problem?

   B: I just have _____ headache.

3. A: Let me take _____ trash out. Where does it go?

   B: Outside, behind _____ house. We have _____ garbage can

   next to _____ back door.

4. A: Do you have _____ needle and some thread?

   B: Sure. What for?

   A: _____ button on my sweater is loose.

5. A: Finally! I don't need _____ umbrella today!

   B: Right! _____ weather's perfect . . . not _____ cloud in

   _____ sky.

   A: Yeah. And _____ temperature is perfect!

6. A: _____ bus isn't here yet.

   B: I have _____ idea. Let's take _____ cab.

7. A: Do you have _____ minute?

   B: Sure. Come in and close _____ door.

8. A: I have _____ note from _____ neighbors.

   B: What does _____ note say?

a headache

a button

**29│Using *A*, *An*, and *The*** Each group of sentences is the beginning of a paragraph. Complete the sentences with *a*, *an*, or *the*. Remember to use *a/an* for the first mention of a noun and *the* to mention the noun again. **5.7 B**

### A Special Person, Place, or Thing

1. My brother Paul is a "stay-at-home dad." He and his wife have two children: _____*a*_____ daughter and _____ son. _____ daughter is five years old, and _____ son is two. . . .

2. My parents have _____ car, and they let me use it. _____ car is just an old Chrysler, but it gives me my freedom. . . .

3. Most summers I spend a month at _____ farmhouse in the country. _____ farmhouse is near _____ pond. I often swim in _____ pond. . . .

4. I have _____ great new video game. _____ video game is actually from my dad. He loves video games. . . .

124

5. My brothers aren't at school with me. They live in _____ small town. _____ town is called Orlek. My brothers own _____ store with fresh fruits and vegetables. _____ store gets a lot of customers. . . .

6. I spend many hours at _____ table in _____ café. _____ table is in the back of _____ café. _____ café is noisy, but I do my work there and drink some great coffee. . . .

**Write about It** Write a short paragraph (3–4 sentences) about a special thing or place in your life. Use *a/an* + noun to introduce the thing or place, and use *the* + noun for the next mention. Read your paragraph to a partner.

> Possible paragraph beginnings:
> I have a/an . . .
> I often go to a/an . . .

*I have a very old photo. The photo shows a boy and a girl. The boy and the girl are my parents. But in the photo they're children.*

## 30 | Usage Note: Common Phrases with *The* Read the note. Then do Activity 31.

We often use **the** with certain nouns:

| | | | | |
|---|---|---|---|---|
| **the** bank | **the** (shopping) mall | **the** mail | **the** newspaper | **the** bus |
| **the** beach | **the** park | **the** movies | **the** phone/**the** telephone | **the** train |
| **the** hospital | **the** store | **the** news | **the** radio | |

**1** A: Where is Koji?
B: He's at **the doctor.** (the doctor = Koji's doctor)

## 31 | Using Common Phrases with *The* Complete the blog entry with phrases from Usage Note 30. More than one phrase may be possible. 5.7 A–B

School is over! It's June, and I'm relaxing. Here's my routine: I sleep late and wake up around 10 a.m.

First I read ___the newspaper___ or listen to _____. Then I go to _____ for
             1                        2                        3

food, and I have a late breakfast. Around this time, _____ usually rings. It's a friend, and
                4

we make some plans. Some days we go to _____ and play soccer. Other days we take
                        5

_____ and go to _____. I love to swim in the ocean! Sometimes we go
   6                      7

shopping for clothes and other things at _____ near my house. It has lots of stores and
                8

restaurants. At night we often go to _____. I like action movies the best! Next month I
                9

start work—but that seems very far away!

**Write about It** Write five sentences about your routines. Use the phrases in Usage Note 30.

*I don't read the newspaper. I often listen to music on the radio. Every summer I go to the beach.*

**32 | Using *The* or No Article (Ø)** Complete each sentence with the correct word or words from the box. Remember to use no article for general statements and *the* for specific statements. `5.7 C`

1. a. _Pizza_____ is my favorite food.

   b. _____ is from Antonio's Pizzeria.

2. a. _____ is not so important in life.

   b. _____ is on the dresser. Give it to the babysitter.

3. a. _____ isn't hot. Can you heat it up?

   b. _____ is the world's most popular drink.

4. a. _____ in my kitchen are old.

   b. _____ are good for you.

5. a. People need _____ to live.

   b. Today _____ feels really nice.

6. a. _____ freezes at 32°F (0°C).

   b. _____ in the sink is dirty.

| |
|---|
| 1. Pizza/The pizza |
| 2. Money/The money |
| 3. Coffee/The coffee |
| 4. Bananas/The bananas |
| 5. air/the air |
| 6. Water/The water |

**33 | Using *A/An*, *Some*, *Any*, and *The*** Some words are missing from these conversations. Listen and add *a*, *an*, *some*, *any*, or *the*. Then practice the conversations with a partner. `5.7 A–C`

ROOMMATES—SOME DIFFICULT MOMENTS

1. A: We each have shelf, and my shelf is bottom shelf, right?
   
   *a* ^    *the* ^

   B: Yeah. Why?

   A: I see stuff on my shelf, and it's not my stuff.

2. A: kitchen is really messy. Why are all these dirty dishes

   in sink?

   B: I don't know. They're not my dishes.

3. A: people are at front door. Do you know them?

   B: They're deliverymen from store. They have our groceries.

4. A: I have test tomorrow. I need to study. Turn down radio please!

   B: radio isn't loud. Just shut your door.

5. A: My printer's out of paper. Do you have paper?

   B: Sorry! I don't have paper.

6. A: Guess what? I have new bike!

   B: That's great, but where do we put bike? We have so many things here!

7. A: Do you see book around here? I need my book for class.

   B: What does book look like?

8. A: We have big apartment. But sometimes apartment feels small.

   B: With four roommates, any apartment feels small!

> **F Y I**
>
> In speech we sometimes use the count noun **thing/things** or the noncount noun **stuff** instead of other words. For example:
>
> Put your **things** down.
> OR = Put your **books and bags** down.
> Put your **stuff** down.

We use **quantifiers** with nouns to describe the quantity (amount) of something. We use different quantifiers with **plural count nouns** and **noncount nouns**.

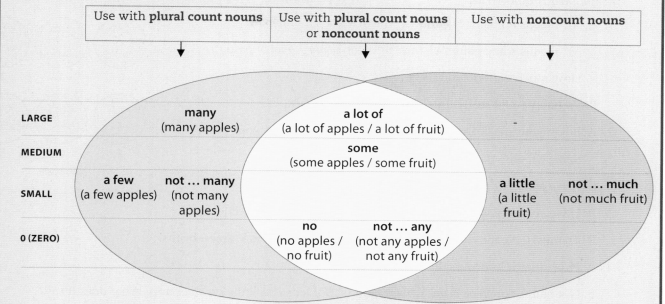

| Use with **plural count nouns** | Use with **plural count nouns** or **noncount nouns** | Use with **noncount nouns** |

| | | |
|---|---|---|
| LARGE | **many**<br>(many apples) | **a lot of**<br>(a lot of apples / a lot of fruit) | |
| MEDIUM | | **some**<br>(some apples / some fruit) | |
| SMALL | **a few**<br>(a few apples)   **not … many**<br>(not many apples) | | **a little**<br>(a little fruit)   **not … much**<br>(not much fruit) |
| 0 (ZERO) | | **no**<br>(no apples / no fruit)   **not … any**<br>(not any apples / not any fruit) | |

Notice: We don't usually use **much** in positive statements. We use **a lot of** instead.

1 We have **many / a lot of** forks and knives.
2 We have **a lot of** water.

3 We have **some** eggs.
4 We have **some** cereal.

5a We have **a few** apples.
5b We **don't** have **many** apples.

6a We have **a little** oil.
6b We **don't** have **much** oil.

7a We have **no** milk.
7b We **don't** have **any** milk.

### QUESTIONS WITH *HOW MANY* AND *HOW MUCH*

|   |  | plural count noun |  |  |
|---|---|---|---|---|
| 8 | How many | people | does he know there? | A lot. / Not many. |
| 9 | How many | eggs | do we need for the cake? | Three. |

|   |  | noncount noun |  |  |
|---|---|---|---|---|
| 10 | How much | homework | does he get? | A lot. / Not much. |
| 11 | How much | milk | do we need for the cake? | One cup. |

**34 | Using Quantifiers with Plural Count and Noncount Nouns** Label each **bold** noun: write *pl* if it is a plural count noun and *nc* if it is a noncount noun. Then circle the correct word to complete the sentence. `5.8 A`

1. A: "0" means no pain. "1" and "2" mean *a few* / (*a little*) **pain**.    *nc*

   "3" means some pain. "4" and "5" mean *many* / *a lot of* **pain**.

   How much pain do you feel?

   B: Probably "1." I really don't feel *many* / *much* **pain**.

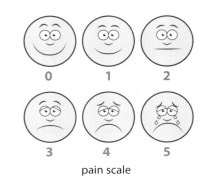

0   1   2

3   4   5

pain scale

2. A: Enjoy your meal! Do you want some black pepper for your pasta?

   Some cheese?

   B: Just *a few* / *a little* **pepper**, please.

3. A: Have some chicken. And can I give you some rice and green beans?

   B: Thanks! Give me *many* / *a lot of* **rice** but just *a few* / *a little* **green beans**.

4. A: How does it look outside?

   B: Not bad. I don't see *many* / *much* **clouds**. But let's check the weather app. What does it say?

   A: *A few* / *A little* **rain** throughout the day. Let's take some umbrellas.

5. A: Let's go to a restaurant.

   B: I don't know. I don't have *many* / *much* **money**.

   A: How much money do you have?

   B: I just have *a few* / *a little* **dollars**. Let's find a bank first.

6. A: Does Sapna know a lot of people at her school in England?

   B: Yes, she knows a lot of people there. But she doesn't have *many* / *much* close **friends**.

7. A: How often do you go to the gym?

   B: I usually go *a few* / *a little* **times** a week. And you?

   A: Don't ask! I just don't have *many* / *much* **time** these days.

8. A: How are you?

   B: Really busy! I have *a lot of* / *many* **work**! I stay late at the office *a few* / *a little* **days** each week.

9. A: Mom, I need some clothes for summer—*a few* / *a little* **pairs** of pants and maybe a dress.

   B: OK. Let's get *a few* / *a little* **things** this weekend.

10. A: Another win! Congratulations! How do you do it?

    B: *Many* / *A lot of* hard **work**!

## 35 | Using Quantifiers Look at the Mediterranean Diet pyramid below. Complete the sentences with a quantifier from this box. Use *much* only in negative sentences. More than one answer may be possible. 5.8 A

| a few | a little | a lot of | many | much | no | some |
|-------|----------|----------|------|------|-----|------|

### A MEDITERRANEAN DIET

1. _Many / A lot of_ doctors recommend a Mediterranean diet.

2. In a Mediterranean diet, people don't eat _____ meat.

3. They also don't eat _____ sweets.

4. They eat only _____ cheese and _____ yogurt.

5. Mediterranean yogurt often has _____ fat (0% fat).

6. Eggs are OK—but only _____ eggs a week.

7. In a Mediterranean diet, people eat _____ fish.

8. They eat _____ vegetables and beans.

9. They also eat _____ rice.

10. In a Mediterranean diet, people use _____ olive oil.

Meats
Sweets

Chicken
Eggs
Cheese
Yogurt

Fish
Seafood

Fruit
Vegetables
Rice
Pasta
Olive Oil
Beans
Nuts
Spices

**Talk about It** Talk about your eating habits. Complete these sentences with different foods. Compare your answers with a partner.

*I eat a lot of . . .*      *I don't eat a lot of . . .*      *I don't eat any . . .*

## 36 | Using *No* and *Not Any* Complete each sentence below with *no* + a word from the box. Then rewrite the sentence with *not . . . any*. More than one answer may be possible. 5.8 A

| food | friends | fun | help | information | money | sleep | time |
|------|---------|-----|------|-------------|-------|-------|------|

### WHAT'S THE PROBLEM?

1. This computer is really old. I need a new computer. But I have _____ _no money_ _____.
   _But I don't have any money._

2. I like my classes. But I feel a little lonely. I have _____ here.
   _____

3. I clean the house, and my kids just play video games. I get _____ from them.
   _____

4. My brother's plane is really late. I don't know the reason. The airline has _____.
   _____

5. I usually work at my parents' restaurant, but this semester I have six classes. I have _____.

_____

6. What can we eat? The refrigerator is empty. We have _____.

_____

7. My friends often go to the beach. But I don't swim, so I have _____ at the beach.

_____

8. On the weekends my neighbors make a lot of noise at night. So I get _____.

_____

**Talk about It** Do you have any problems like the ones in Activity 36? Tell a partner. Use *no* or *not . . . any*.

*"My roommates are really loud at night. I don't get any sleep."*

**37 | Asking and Answering Questions with *How Many* and *How Much*** Complete these survey questions with *How many* or *How much*. Then circle your answer. ▮5.8 A–B▮

---

## A University Food Survey

In a typical week . . .

| | | |
|---|---|---|
| 1. _How much_____ water do you drink? | 1. (a lot of / some / a little / no) water |
| 2. _____ coffee do you drink? | 2. (a lot of / some / a little / no) coffee |
| 3. _____ juice do you drink? | 3. (a lot of / some / a little / no) juice |
| 4. _____ meat do you eat? | 4. (a lot of / some / a little / no) meat |
| 5. _____ fish do you eat? | 5. (a lot of / some / a little / no) fish |
| 6. _____ vegetables do you eat? | 6. (a lot of / some / a few / no) vegetables |
| 7. _____ pasta do you eat? | 7. (a lot of / some / a little / no) pasta |
| 8. _____ rice do you eat? | 8. (a lot of / some / a little / no) rice |
| 9. _____ bread do you eat? | 9. (a lot of / some / a little / no) bread |
| 10. _____ eggs do you eat? | 10. (a lot of / some / a few / no) eggs |
| 11. _____ cheese do you eat? | 11. (a lot of / some / a little / no) cheese |
| 12. _____ fruit do you eat? | 12. (a lot of / some / a little / no) fruit |
| 13. _____ sweets do you eat? | 13. (a lot of / some / a few / no) sweets |
| 14. _____ salty snacks (like potato chips) do you eat? | 14. (a lot of / some / a few / no) salty snacks |

---

**Talk about It** Ask and answer the questions above with a partner. Then discuss your answers as a class. Do the students in the class have a healthy diet?

## 38 | Usage Note: Measure Words Read the note. Then do Activity 39.

We often use a **measure word** + ***of*** before plural nouns and noncount nouns.

**1** Let's get **a bunch of** bananas.

**2** Most days I drink **eight glasses of** water.

> Notice: Measure words can be singular (*a glass*) or plural (*eight glasses*).
> We use measure words to change noncount nouns to count nouns.

Common measure words include:

**bag**

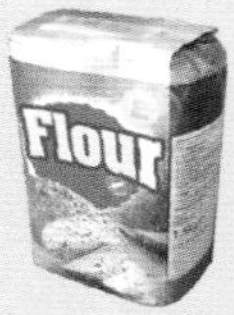

*a bag of flour*

**can**

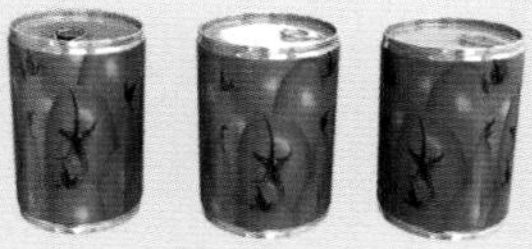

*three cans of tomatoes*

**loaf**

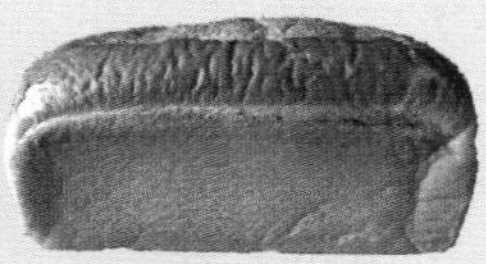

*a loaf of bread*

**bottle**

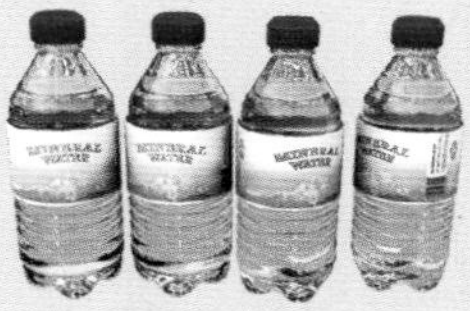

*four bottles of water*

**glass**

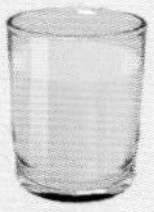

*a glass of juice*

**jar**

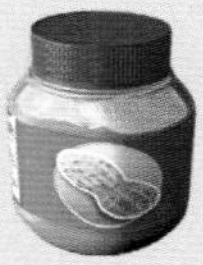

*a jar of peanut butter*

**bowl**

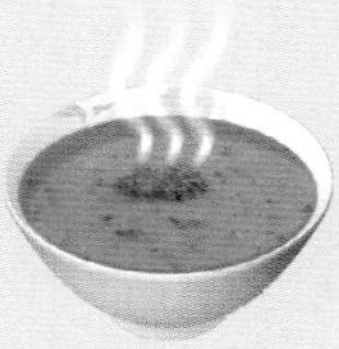

*a bowl of soup*

**cup**

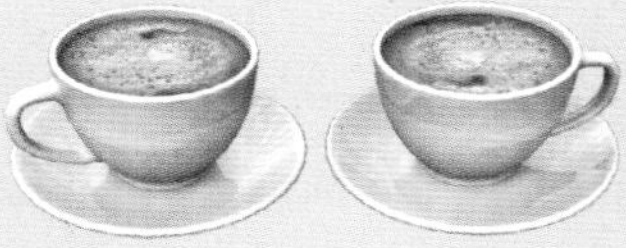

*two cups of coffee*

**slice**

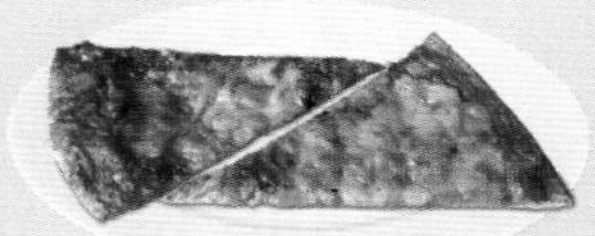

*two slices of pizza*

**box**

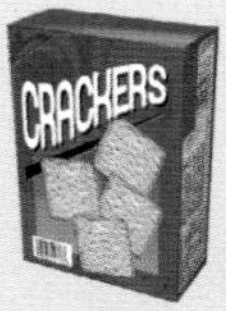

*a box of crackers*

**carton**

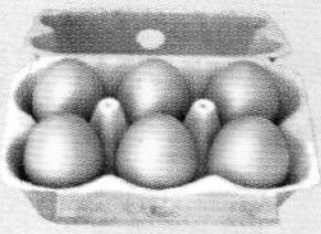

*a carton of eggs*

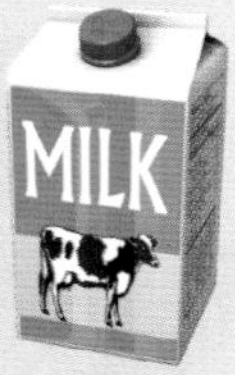

*a carton of milk*

**bunch**

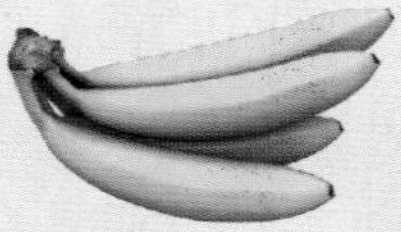

*a bunch of bananas*

**piece**

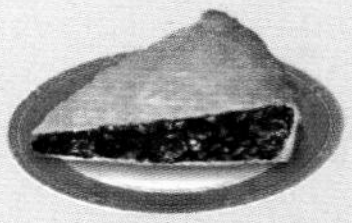

*a piece of pie*

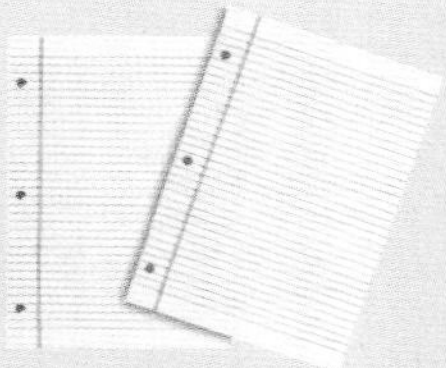

*two pieces of paper*

**39 | Using Measure Words** Complete these conversations with a measure word + *of*. Then listen and check your answers. Practice the conversations with a partner.

1. A: Are you ready to order?

   B: Yes, thanks. I'd like three _____*pieces of*_____ chocolate cake, two _____

   coffee, and one _____ tea.

2. A: Spaghetti and tomato sauce sounds great. And let's have brownies for dessert. Do we need any

   ingredients?

   B: Yes, we need a _____ spaghetti and a _____ eggs.

   A: OK. I can go to the store. Do we need anything else?

   B: Yeah. A _____ milk, two _____ tuna fish, a

   _____ cereal, and a _____ bananas.

   A: That's a lot of stuff! I need a shopping list.

3. A: I'm hungry. Do you have anything?

   B: Yes, I have some snacks. I have a _____ crackers, a big

   _____ potato chips, and two _____ water.

4. A: Please set the table for breakfast. Put out a _____ jam, a

   _____ bread, and some butter.

   B: OK. And we need four _____ juice.

**Write about It** Your refrigerator and kitchen cabinets are almost empty. What food do you need for breakfast, lunch, and dinner tomorrow? Write a shopping list. Use measure words from Usage Note 38.

## WRAP-UP

**A | GRAMMAR IN READING** Read the comic. Then complete the activities on page 134.

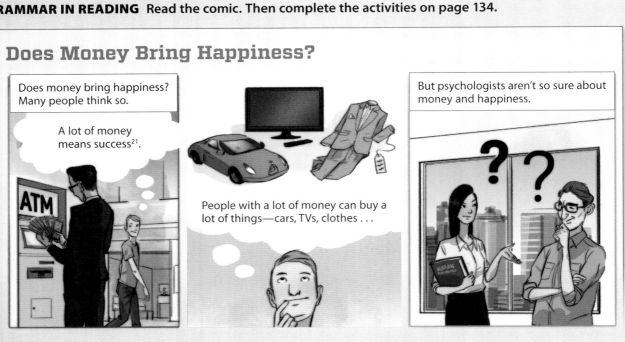

**Does Money Bring Happiness?**

Does money bring happiness? Many people think so.

A lot of money means success[21].

People with a lot of money can buy a lot of things—cars, TVs, clothes . . .

But psychologists aren't so sure about money and happiness.

[21] **success:** doing well

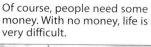

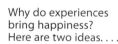

[22] **possessions:** things you have or own

**What are the psychologist's ideas about happiness? Circle the correct choices.**

1. People **need** / **don't need** a lot of money.

2. **Things** / **Experiences** are very important.

**Read two responses to the psychologist's ideas. Circle the correct words to complete the passages.**

**Evan:** I agree: experiences (**is** / **are**) important. (**Thing** / **Things**) don't interest me. I have just (**a little** / **a few**) things. I have (**a** / **an**) small apartment. I use my money for (**a** / **Ø**) trips to new places. I go on (**a** / **some**) trip, and then I remember (**a** / **the**) trip for many years!

**Jared:** I don't agree with (**the** / **Ø**) psychologist. My (**possession** / **possessions**) are important in my life. I have (**a** / **the**) nice house. I buy (**a lot of** / **much**) things for (**a** / **the**) house. I look at my things, and I feel happy.

**Talk about It** Who do you agree with—Evan or Jared? Discuss your ideas as a class.

**B | GRAMMAR IN SPEAKING** Read some people's answers to the question "What makes you happy?" Put a check (✓) next to the answers you agree with.

# WHAT MAKES YOU HAPPY?

| Yes, I agree! | | Yes, I agree! | |
|---|---|---|---|
| ☐ | good weather | ☐ | good art |
| ☐ | my family | ☐ | a good book |
| ☐ | a good friend | ☐ | a good grade on a test |
| ☐ | the moon and stars at night | ☐ | a wedding |
| ☐ | nice clothes | ☐ | a clean house |
| ☐ | a glass of water on a hot day | ☐ | a trip to new a place |
| ☐ | a funny joke | ☐ | ice cream |
| ☐ | a good dinner | ☐ | a day at the beach |
| ☐ | the sound of rain | ☐ | new shoes |
| ☐ | the smell of bread | ☐ | a new smartphone |
| ☐ | a happy memory | ☐ | help from a stranger[24] |
| ☐ | a beautiful sunset[23] | ☐ | a lot of snow |
| ☐ | my cat | ☐ | a big TV |
| ☐ | chocolate | ☐ | comfortable jeans |
| ☐ | a sports game | ☐ | my car |

**Talk about It** Discuss your answers as a class. Which answers are the most popular?

[23] **sunset:** the time in the evening when the sun goes down       [24] **stranger:** a person you do not know

## 5.9 Summary of Nouns, Articles, and Quantifiers

NOUNS CAN BE:

**COUNT NOUNS**

singular
**chair**

plural
**chairs**

**NONCOUNT NOUNS**
**furniture**

**ARTICLES**

|  | SINGULAR COUNT NOUNS | PLURAL COUNT NOUNS | NONCOUNT NOUNS |
|---|---|---|---|
| *a / an* | a car<br>an automobile | - | - |
| *some* | - | some cars | some traffic |
| *Ø* | - | cars | traffic |
| *the* | the car | the cars | the traffic |

**QUANTIFIERS FOR PLURAL COUNT NOUNS AND NONCOUNT NOUNS**

|  | USE WITH PLURAL COUNT NOUNS | USE WITH PLURAL COUNT NOUNS AND NONCOUNT NOUNS | USE WITH NONCOUNT NOUNS |
|---|---|---|---|
| | **many** bananas | **a lot of** bananas<br>**a lot of** fruit | - |
| | - | **some** bananas<br>**some** fruit | - |
| | **a few** bananas | - | **a little** fruit<br>**not much** fruit |
| | - | **no** bananas<br>**no** fruit | - |

# 6

# There Is/There Are and Pronouns

**ONLINE**

For the Unit Vocabulary Check, go to the Online Practice.

## IN THIS UNIT, WE USE *there is* and *there are* to:

### Introduce new information

1. **There's** an interesting movie on TV.

2. **There are** a lot of new restaurants on Miller Street.

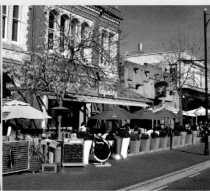

3. **There aren't** any parking spots.

4. A: **Is there** class today?
   B: No, it's a holiday.

**Think about It** Read the statements. Check (✓) *True* or *False*.

|  | TRUE | FALSE |
|---|---|---|
| 1. There's a good restaurant nearby. | ☐ | ☐ |
| 2. There are a lot of computers in our classroom. | ☐ | ☐ |
| 3. There's a museum in our town. | ☐ | ☐ |
| 4. There are a few hotels in the area. | ☐ | ☐ |

## WE USE *this*, *that*, *these*, and *those* to:

## Point out things and people nearby

5. A: Is **this** your phone?
   B: Yes, thank you!

6. **These** are my daughters.

## Point out things and people far away

7. A: Who is **that**?
   B: **That**'s our new manager.

8. A: What are **those**?
   B: **Those** are seals.

## WE USE object pronouns to:

## Refer to people and things

9. This is **Maria's book**. Please give **it** to **her**.

10. These **shoes** are nice. I really like **them**.

**Think about It** Circle the nouns in sentences 5–10 above. Which nouns are singular? Which nouns are plural?

## 6.1 Positive Statements with *There Is* and *There Are*

**A**

| We use *there is* to introduce a **singular** noun. | We use *there are* to introduce a **plural** noun. |

**1** A: **There's** a new restaurant across the street.
B: Is it nice?

**2** A: **There are** a lot of nice stores.
B: Are they expensive?

Notice: In speaking, we usually use the contraction *there's*. (*There's* = *There is*.)

**B**

We often use **there is** and **there are** with **prepositional phrases**. They describe where something is.

**PREPOSITIONS OF LOCATION**

**3** **There's** a mall **on** 2ⁿᵈ Street.

**4** **There's** a museum **across from** the park.

**5** **There's** a parking lot **behind** the Good Earth Market.

**6** **There's** an ATM **in front of** the bank.

**7** **There's** a cafe **between** Lion Street and King Street.

**8** **There's** a library **on the corner of** Lion Street and Main Street.

**9** **There are** two markets **in** this neighborhood.

**GO ONLINE**

---

**1 | Describing Locations with *There Is* and *There Are*** Complete each sentence with *is* or *are*. Then look at the map on page 139. Check (✓) *True* or *False* for each statement. **6.1 A**

| | TRUE | FALSE |
|---|---|---|
| 1. There _____*is*_____ a hospital on E 53ʳᵈ St. | ☐ | ✓ |
| 2. There _____ a pharmacy on the corner of S Kimbark Ave. and E 53ʳᵈ St. | ☐ | ☐ |
| 3. There _____ two ATMs between S Kimbark Ave. and S Blackstone Ave. | ☐ | ☐ |
| 4. There _____ four hotels in this area. | ☐ | ☐ |
| 5. There _____ a park across from the Walgreens pharmacy. | ☐ | ☐ |
| 6. There _____ a parking lot behind the CVS pharmacy. | ☐ | ☐ |
| 7. There _____ a few parks in this neighborhood. | ☐ | ☐ |

**FYI**

We often write abbreviations for the words in street names.

**E** 51ˢᵗ **St.** = East 51ˢᵗ Street

Summit **Ave.** = Summit Avenue

Grand **Dr.** = Grand Drive

Sunset **Blvd.** = Sunset Boulevard

|  | TRUE | FALSE |
|---|---|---|
| 8. There _____ a bookstore in front of Bixler Park. | ☐ | ☐ |
| 9. There _____ a park across from the Provident Hospital of Cook County. | ☐ | ☐ |
| 10. There _____ a hotel between E 52ⁿᵈ St. and E Hyde Park Boulevard. | ☐ | ☐ |
| 11. There _____ two hospitals in this area. | ☐ | ☐ |
| 12. There _____ two pharmacies on E 53ʳᵈ St. | ☐ | ☐ |

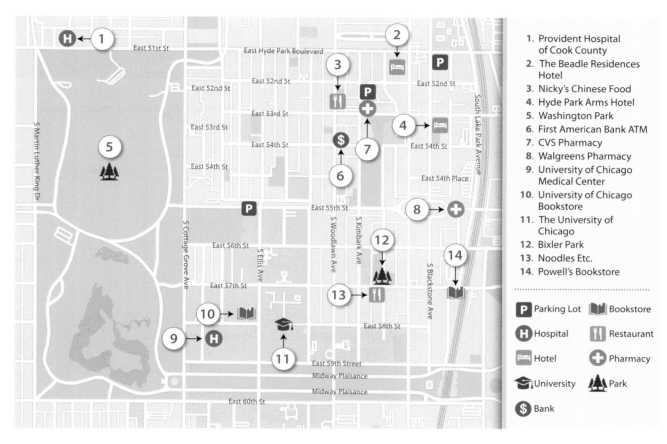

1. Provident Hospital of Cook County
2. The Beadle Residences Hotel
3. Nicky's Chinese Food
4. Hyde Park Arms Hotel
5. Washington Park
6. First American Bank ATM
7. CVS Pharmacy
8. Walgreens Pharmacy
9. University of Chicago Medical Center
10. University of Chicago Bookstore
11. The University of Chicago
12. Bixler Park
13. Noodles Etc.
14. Powell's Bookstore

P Parking Lot  📖 Bookstore
H Hospital  🍴 Restaurant
🛏 Hotel  ➕ Pharmacy
🎓 University  🌲 Park
$ Bank

## 2 | Using Preposition  Look at the map above again. Complete the tips below with the correct prepositions.  6.1 B

TIPS FOR NEW STUDENTS

1. Don't forget to buy your books! There's a bookstore _____on_____
   E 57ᵗʰ St. There's also one _____on_____ the corner of S Ellis Ave.
   and E 58ᵗʰ St.

2. Coffee shops are great places to study and meet new people. There are
   a lot of cafes _____ the neighborhood. There are also some
   cafes on campus.

3. There are a few hotels _____ the area. They're great for visitors. The Hyde Park Arms Hotel is
   _____ E 53ʳᵈ St. and E 54ᵗʰ St.

4. There are a lot of great restaurants in the neighborhood. There's a noodle restaurant _____
   E 57ᵗʰ St. _____ Bixler Park. There's a good restaurant _____
   S Woodlawn Ave. and E 53ʳᵈ St.—Nicky's Chinese Food. There are a lot of places all along E 53ʳᵈ St.

> **FYI**
>
> We can use the pronoun *one* in place of a noun.
>
> There's also **a bookstore** on S Ellis Ave. = There's also **one** on S Ellis Ave.

**Talk about It** Work with a partner. Take turns describing the locations of places in your city or town. Make some descriptions true and some false. Your partner says *That's true* or *That's false*.

A: *There's a bank on First St.*
B: *That's false.*

**Write about It** Imagine a friend is in town for a visit. Write some tips for your friend about places in your neighborhood or town.

*There's a good Chinese restaurant across from Myer Park.*

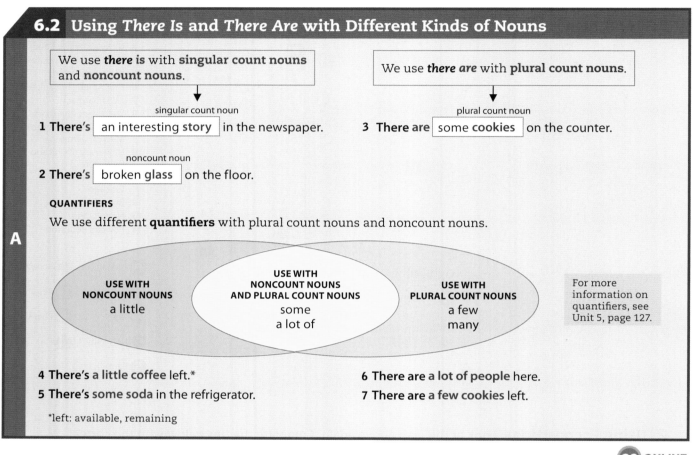

**6.2** Using *There Is* and *There Are* with Different Kinds of Nouns

We use *there is* with **singular count nouns** and **noncount nouns**.

We use *there are* with **plural count nouns**.

singular count noun
**1 There's** | an interesting **story** | in the newspaper.

plural count noun
**3 There are** | some **cookies** | on the counter.

noncount noun
**2 There's** | broken **glass** | on the floor.

**QUANTIFIERS**

We use different **quantifiers** with plural count nouns and noncount nouns.

**USE WITH NONCOUNT NOUNS**
a little

**USE WITH NONCOUNT NOUNS AND PLURAL COUNT NOUNS**
some
a lot of

**USE WITH PLURAL COUNT NOUNS**
a few
many

For more information on quantifiers, see Unit 5, page 127.

**4 There's a little coffee** left.*
**5 There's some soda** in the refrigerator.

**6 There are a lot of people** here.
**7 There are a few cookies** left.

*left: available, remaining

**A**

GO ONLINE

**3 | Using *There's* and *There Are* in Conversation** Write *sg* (singular), *pl* (plural), or *nc* (noncount) above each **bold** noun. Then complete the conversations with *there's* or *there are*. Do the speakers know each other? Check (✓) the correct column. **6.2 A**

| | KNOW EACH OTHER | DON'T KNOW EACH OTHER |
|---|---|---|
| 1. A: _There's_ ^sg^ a **man** at the door. | ✓ | ☐ |
| B: Really? Who is he? | | |
| 2. A: _____ some **glass** on the floor. Be careful! | ☐ | ☐ |
| B: OK, thanks, Mom. | | |
| 3. A: Please wait for the doctor. _____ some **magazines** on the table by the door. | ☐ | ☐ |
| B: All right. Thank you. | | |

4.  A: Do you have any **cereal**?

    B: _____ a lot of cereal in the kitchen. It's in the cabinet

       above the stove.

5.  A: Are you hungry? _____ some **pizza** in the kitchen.

    B: Yes, I am. It looks delicious!

6.  A: I need paper for my printer. Do you have any?

    B: _____ a little **paper** on my desk. You can have it.

7.  A: _____ some **keys** on the table. Are they your car keys?

    B: No, my car keys are in my pocket.

8.  A: Excuse me. Where's the restroom?

    B: _____ two **restrooms**. They're both upstairs.

9.  A: Excuse me. Does this hotel have a restaurant?

    B: _____ a few **restaurants** on the fourth floor.

       They're all great.

10. A: Do we have any milk?

    B: Yes, _____ a little **milk** in the refrigerator.

**Talk about It** Listen and check your answers. Then practice the conversations with a partner.

**Think about It** There are eight quantifiers in the conversations above. Write each quantifier + noun in the correct part of the chart below.

| quantifier + plural count noun | quantifier + noncount noun |
| --- | --- |
| | *some glass* |
| | |
| | |
| | |
| | |

**4 | Pronunciation Note: *There Are* vs. *They're*** Listen to the note. Then do Activity 5.

> ***There are*** and ***they're*** (they are) sound similar. Pay attention to the words around them.
>
> **1** There are two **packages** on your desk.     **3** They're on your desk.
> **2** There are a lot of **stores** on 8ᵗʰ Street.     **4** They're open from 10 a.m. to 8 p.m.

**5 | Listening for *There Are* vs. *They're*** Listen to the conversations. Does the second speaker say *there are* or *they're*? Check (✓) the words you hear.

| | | | | | |
|---|---|---|---|---|---|
| 1. ☐ there are | ☑ they're | | 8. ☐ there are | ☐ they're |
| 2. ☐ there are | ☐ they're | | 9. ☐ there are | ☐ they're |
| 3. ☐ there are | ☐ they're | | 10. ☐ there are | ☐ they're |
| 4. ☐ there are | ☐ they're | | 11. ☐ there are | ☐ they're |
| 5. ☐ there are | ☐ they're | | 12. ☐ there are | ☐ they're |
| 6. ☐ there are | ☐ they're | | 13. ☐ there are | ☐ they're |
| 7. ☐ there are | ☐ they're | | 14. ☐ there are | ☐ they're |

**Talk about It** Write two sentences with *there are* and two sentences with *they're*. Then read your sentences to a partner. Your partner listens for *there are* or *they're*.

**6 | Usage Note: Using Subject Pronouns** Read the note. Then do Activity 7.

Notice the **subject pronoun** in the second sentence in each of these examples.

subject pronoun
**1** There's | a spider | on the wall. | **It** | 's really big!

subject pronoun
**2** There's | a man | in your office. | **He** | 's a new employee.

subject pronoun
**3** There's | a woman | on the phone. | **She** | wants to talk to Joan.

subject pronoun
**4** There are | some people | at the door. | **They** | have some questions for you.

subject pronoun
**5** There are | two restaurants | on 14th Street. | **They** | 're across from the park.

**7 | Using Subject Pronouns** Read the sentences below. Use the words in each box to write a second sentence. More than one answer may be possible.

| SUBJECT PRONOUN | VERB + INFORMATION | | |
|---|---|---|---|
| It | is/are a blue Ford | is/are hot | is/are turkey and cheese |
| He | is/are chocolate | is/are my roommate's friends | speak/speaks three languages |
| She | is/are diet cola | is/are on the counter | want/wants to talk to Jack |
| They | have/has a letter for you | | |

1. There's a car in the driveway. *It's a blue Ford.* _____.

2. There are some sandwiches in the refrigerator. _____.

3. There's a man on the phone. _____.

4. There are a few cupcakes left. _____.

5. There's a man outside. _____.

6. There's some soda in the kitchen. _____.

7. There's a new woman in my class. _____.

8. There's ice cream in the freezer. _____.

9. There are some people downstairs. I think _____.

10. There's coffee in the break room. _____.

**Write about It** Complete these sentences with your own information. Then write another sentence with more information. Use subject pronouns.

1. There's a ____coffee shop____ near the park. _It has really good coffee!_ _____

2. There are two _____ downtown. _____

3. There are two _____ in my neighborhood. _____

4. There's a _____ restaurant on _____ Street. _____

---

## 6.3 Negative Statements with *There Is* and *There Are*

| We can use *there isn't* with noncount nouns. | We can use *there aren't* with plural count nouns. |

**1** There isn't | any fruit | in the refrigerator.    **3** There aren't | any seats | left.

**2** There isn't | much food | in the kitchen.    **4** There aren't | many people | here.

Notice: It's more common to use a **plural form** (not a **singular count noun**) to make a general negative statement.

More common: There aren't any **seats** left.    Less common: There isn't **a seat** left.

**QUANTIFIERS IN NEGATIVE STATEMENTS**

A

|  | USE WITH NONCOUNT NOUNS | USE WITH PLURAL COUNT NOUNS OR NONCOUNT NOUNS | USE WITH PLURAL COUNT NOUNS |
|---|---|---|---|
| **SMALL AMOUNT** | not much | not a lot of | not many |
| **0 (ZERO)** |  | not any / no |  |

**5a** There aren't a lot of chairs in the kitchen.    **7a** There isn't a lot of furniture in the apartment.

**5b** There aren't many chairs in the kitchen.    **7b** There isn't much furniture in the apartment.

**6a** There aren't any chairs in the kitchen.    **8a** There isn't any furniture in the apartment.

**6b** There are no chairs in the kitchen.    **8b** There is no furniture in the apartment.

Notice: We use a positive verb (**is** / **are**) with **no**.

**WARNING!** Don't use *isn't* / *aren't* + *no*.

✓There aren**'t any** cars in the parking lot.    ✗ There aren't no cars in the parking lot.

✓There **are no** cars in the parking lot.

**8 | Using *There Isn't* and *There Aren't* with Count and Noncount Nouns** Complete these conversations with the correct words in parentheses. `6.3 A`

**A HOME KITCHEN**

1. A: There _____*isn't any*_____ coffee left.
      (isn't any / aren't any)
   Can you get some?

   B: Sure.

2. A: There _____ tea, either.
      (isn't much / aren't many)
   B: OK. I'll get coffee and tea. Anything else?

3. A: Where's the sugar?

   B: There _____ sugar. We need to
      (isn't any / aren't any)
   buy some.

4. A: There _____ flour left.
      (isn't any / aren't any)
   B: Yes, there is. It's on the top shelf.

   A: Oh, you're right.

**A RESTAURANT KITCHEN**

5. A: There _____ cartons of milk left.
      (isn't much / aren't many)
   We need 50 cartons for the week.

   B: OK, I'll order more milk.

6. A: There _____ cheddar cheese.
      (isn't much / aren't many)
   B: How much do we have?

   A: Only half a pound.

7. A: There _____ beef in the
      (isn't any / aren't any)
   refrigerator.

   B: I think it's in the freezer.

8. A: There _____ vegetables left.
      (isn't much / aren't many)
   B: What vegetables do we have?

   A: Just peppers and onions.

**Write about It** Four of the sentences above use *isn't/aren't* + *any*. Rewrite these sentences with *no*.

*There is no coffee left.*

**9 | Describing Quantities with *There Is* and *There Are*** Look at the picture. Write positive and negative sentences about the things in each box on page 145. Use *there is/there are* and quantifiers. `6.3 A`

PLANNING A PICNIC

| QUANTIFIERS | | | |
|---|---|---|---|
| a lot of | a few | not many | not any |
| some | two, three ... | not much | no |

1. *There are a lot of forks.*
2. _____.
3. _____.
4. _____.
5. _____.

| forks |
|---|
| knives |
| spoons |
| plates |
| cups |

6. _____.
7. _____.
8. _____.

| water |
|---|
| soda |
| lemonade |

9. _____.
10. _____.
11. _____.
12. _____.
13. _____.
14. _____.
15. _____.
16. _____.

| hot dogs |
|---|
| hamburgers |
| hamburger buns |
| hot dog buns |
| cake |
| pie |
| chicken |
| strawberries |

**Write about It**  Look at the picture on page 144 and at your sentences above. What do we need to buy for the picnic? Write a shopping list. Use quantifiers in your list.

SHOPPING LIST

| | |
|---|---|
| | *a lot of knives* |
| | |
| | |
| | |
| | |
| | |

**Write about It**  Think about things in your kitchen at home. Write four sentences with *there is/there are* or *there isn't/there aren't*.

*There's a lot of pasta.*
*There aren't any snacks.*

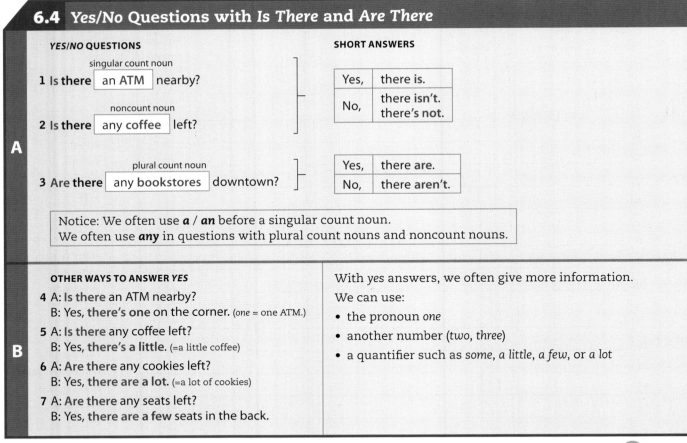

## 6.4 Yes/No Questions with *Is There* and *Are There*

**A**

**YES/NO QUESTIONS**

singular count noun

**1** Is there | an ATM | nearby?

noncount noun

**2** Is there | any coffee | left?

plural count noun

**3** Are there | any bookstores | downtown?

**SHORT ANSWERS**

| Yes, | there is. |
| No, | there isn't. there's not. |

| Yes, | there are. |
| No, | there aren't. |

Notice: We often use **a / an** before a singular count noun.
We often use **any** in questions with plural count nouns and noncount nouns.

**B**

**OTHER WAYS TO ANSWER *YES***

**4** A: Is there an ATM nearby?
B: Yes, **there's one** on the corner. (one = one ATM.)

**5** A: Is there any coffee left?
B: Yes, **there's a little**. (=a little coffee)

**6** A: Are there any cookies left?
B: Yes, **there are a lot**. (=a lot of cookies)

**7** A: Are there any seats left?
B: Yes, **there are a few** seats in the back.

With *yes* answers, we often give more information.
We can use:

• the pronoun *one*
• another number (*two, three*)
• a quantifier such as *some, a little, a few,* or *a lot*

 **GO ONLINE**

---

**10 | Asking Questions with *Is There* and *Are There*** Complete the questions with *is there* or *are there*. 6.4 A

ASKING ABOUT THE NEIGHBORHOOD

1. _Is there_____ a bank around here?

2. _____ any coffee shops around here?

3. _____ a post office in this neighborhood?

4. _____ a movie theater nearby?

5. _____ any good Chinese food around here?

6. _____ a gas station nearby?

7. _____ any grocery stores in the area?

8. _____ a bus stop near here?

9. _____ any drugstores in this neighborhood?

10. _____ any good Italian food in this area?

**Talk about It** Ask and answer the questions above with a partner. Use short answers.

A: *Is there a bank around here?*
B: *Yes, there is. / No, there isn't.*

**Think about It** Underline *a* + singular noun in the questions in Activity 10. Then rewrite the questions with *any* + plural noun.

*Is there <u>a bank</u> around here?* ➔ *Are there any banks around here?*

146

**11 | Asking and Answering Questions with *Is There* and *Are There*** Complete these questions and answers with *there + is/isn't/are/aren't*. Then check (✓) where each conversation takes place. **6.4 A**

1. A: _Are there_ any seats left in the front row?

   B: No, _there aren't_ .

   ☑ at a theater
   ☐ at home

2. A: _____ any money in the cash register?

   B: Yes, _____.

   ☐ at a store
   ☐ at home

3. A: _____ any cookies left?

   B: No, _____. The cookies sell out fast.

   ☐ at a bakery
   ☐ at home

4. A: _____ any coffee?

   B: Yes, _____ a lot. It's in the kitchen.

   ☐ at a store
   ☐ at home

5. A: _____ any tables available?

   B: No, _____. I'm sorry.

   ☐ at a restaurant
   ☐ at home

6. A: _____ any mail today?

   B: Yes, _____. It's in your office.

   ☐ at work
   ☐ at home

7. A: _____ any homework tonight?

   B: Yes, _____. Please read pages 30–45.

   ☐ at school
   ☐ at home

8. A: _____ any students in the classroom?

   B: Yes, _____ a few.

   ☐ at school
   ☐ at home

🔊 **Talk about It** Listen and check your answers. Then practice the conversations with a partner.

**12 | Answering Questions with Pronouns** Complete these conversations with the correct words in parentheses. **6.4 B**

QUESTIONS FOR A HOTEL

1. A: Is there a hair dryer in the room?

   B: Yes, there's ____*one*____ in the bathroom.
   (one / some)

2. A: Is there a coffee machine?

   B: Yes, there's _____ in every room.
   (one / a few)

3. A: Is there any shampoo in the room?

   B: Yes, there's _____ in the bathroom.
   (many / some)

4. A: Is there an ice machine on my floor?

   B: Yes, there's _____ on every floor.
   (one / a little)

5. A: Is there a coffee shop in the hotel?

   B: Yes, there's _____ in the lobby.
   (one / a few)

6. A: Is there an elevator near my room?

   B: Yes, there's _____ next to your room.
   (one / a little)

7.  A: Are there any good restaurants in the area?

    B: Yes, there are _____ on Main Street.
    (one / a lot)

8.  A: Are there any buses to the airport in the morning?

    B: Yes, there are _____ between
    (one / a few)
    6 a.m. and 10 a.m.

**Write about It** Write two more questions for a hotel. Use *is there* or *are there*.

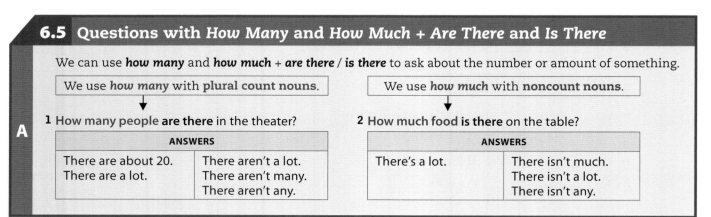

**6.5 Questions with *How Many* and *How Much* + *Are There* and *Is There***

We can use **how many** and **how much** + **are there** / **is there** to ask about the number or amount of something.

| We use *how many* with **plural count nouns**. | We use *how much* with **noncount nouns**. |

**A**

**1 How many people are there in the theater?**

| ANSWERS | |
|---|---|
| There are about 20.<br>There are a lot. | There aren't a lot.<br>There aren't many.<br>There aren't any. |

**2 How much food is there on the table?**

| ANSWERS | |
|---|---|
| There's a lot. | There isn't much.<br>There isn't a lot.<br>There isn't any. |

**13 | Asking *How Much/How Many*** Complete these questions with *how much* or *how many*. Then match the questions with the answers. **6.5 A**

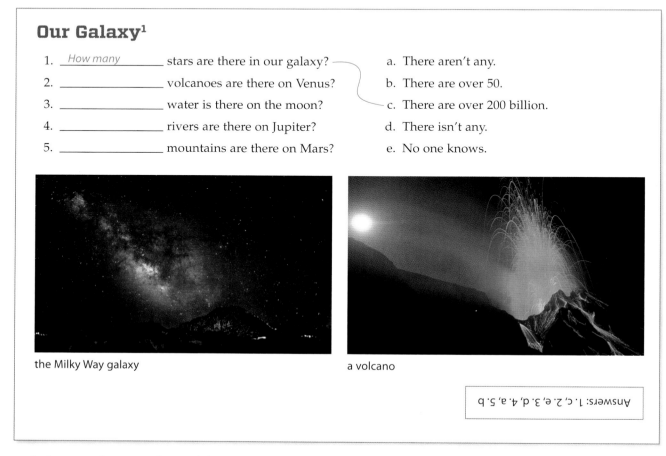

**Our Galaxy¹**

1.  _How many_____ stars are there in our galaxy? ⎤      a.  There aren't any.
2.  _____ volcanoes are there on Venus?  ⎟      b.  There are over 50.
3.  _____ water is there on the moon?    ⎦      c.  There are over 200 billion.
4.  _____ rivers are there on Jupiter?          d.  There isn't any.
5.  _____ mountains are there on Mars?          e.  No one knows.

the Milky Way galaxy

a volcano

Answers: 1. c, 2. e, 3. d, 4. a, 5. b

¹ **galaxy:** a very large group of stars and planets

148

**Complete these questions with *how much* or *how many* and *is* or *are*. Then match the questions with the answers.**

## Our Earth

6. _____ lakes _____ there in the world?

7. _____ water _____ there in the oceans?

8. _____ garbage _____ there in the oceans?

9. _____ large rivers _____ there on Earth?

10. _____ water _____ there in the rivers?

f. There are about 165.

g. 509 cubic miles.

h. More than 320 million cubic miles.

i. There are 307 million.

j. No one knows.

Answers: 6. i, 7. h, 8. j, 9. f, 10. g

1 mile

1 mile

a cubic mile

**Talk about It** Write six questions with *how much/how many* and *is there/are there*. Use the ideas in the box or your own ideas. Then ask and answer your questions with a partner.

| houses on your street | restaurants in your neighborhood | parks in your neighborhood |
| people in your family | bedrooms in your home | food in your home |

A: *How many houses are there on your street?*
B: *There are a few.*

**14 | Pronunciation Note: Stress in Questions with *How Much* and *How Many*** Listen to the note. Then do Activity 15.

In questions with *how much* and *how many*, we usually put the stress on the **noun**.

**1** A: How many **PEOPLE** are there in the room?
B: There are 30.

**2** A: How much **WATER** is there?
B: There are 10 bottles.

**15 | Using Stress in Questions with *How Much* and *How Many*** Listen and repeat these questions. Underline the stressed noun in each question.

1. How many <u>cars</u> are there in the driveway?
2. How many people are there in the house?
3. How much time is there?
4. How much homework is there?
5. How much coffee is there?
6. How many cups are there?
7. How many students are there in the class?
8. How much money is there in our checking account?
9. How many tables are there in the restaurant?
10. How many customers are there in the store?

11. How many books are there in your backpack?
12. How many pens are there in your backpack?
13. How much money is there in your pocket?
14. How much change² is there in your wallet?
15. How much food is there in your refrigerator?
16. How many shopping malls are there in your town?

17. How many supermarkets are there in your neighborhood?
18. How many movie theaters are there in your town?
19. How many museums are there in your town?
20. How many parks are there in your neighborhood?

**Talk about It** Ask and answer questions 11–20 with a partner.

## 6.6 This, That, These, and Those

We can use the pronouns **this**, **that**, **these**, and **those** to point out people or things.

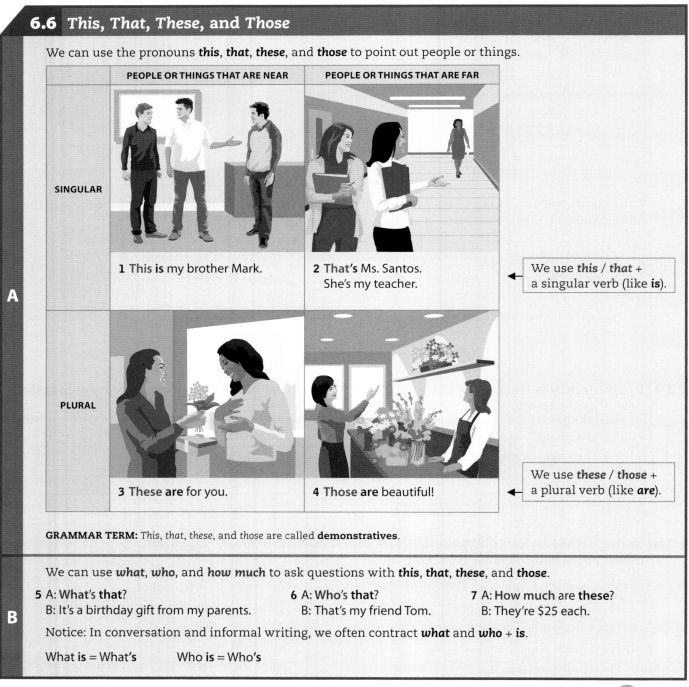

| | PEOPLE OR THINGS THAT ARE NEAR | PEOPLE OR THINGS THAT ARE FAR | |
|---|---|---|---|
| **SINGULAR** | **1** This **is** my brother Mark. | **2** That**'s** Ms. Santos. She's my teacher. | We use **this** / **that** + a singular verb (like **is**). |
| **PLURAL** | **3** These **are** for you. | **4** Those **are** beautiful! | We use **these** / **those** + a plural verb (like **are**). |

**A**

**GRAMMAR TERM:** *This, that, these,* and *those* are called **demonstratives**.

**B**

We can use **what**, **who**, and **how much** to ask questions with **this**, **that**, **these**, and **those**.

**5** A: What's **that**?
B: It's a birthday gift from my parents.

**6** A: Who's **that**?
B: That's my friend Tom.

**7** A: How much are **these**?
B: They're $25 each.

Notice: In conversation and informal writing, we often contract **what** and **who** + **is**.

What **is** = What**'s**       Who **is** = Who**'s**

² **change:** small pieces of money; coins

**16 | Using *This*, *That*, *These*, and *Those*** Look at the pictures. Circle the correct words to complete the conversations. `6.6 A`

GOING ON A TRIP

1. A: Do you want to pack ((these) / those)?
   B: No, I don't want to take (these / those).

2. A: Is (this / that) a good shirt?
   B: Yes, it's perfect.

3. A: Is (this / that) your bag?
   B: Yes, it is.

4. A: Excuse me. (Those / That) are our seats.
   B: Oh, you're right.

5. A: (This / These) aren't our bags.
   B: They aren't?

6. A: (Those / These) are our bags.
   B: Oh, no!

**Talk about It** Bring some photos to class. Describe your photos to a partner. Use *this*, *that*, *these*, and *those*.

*"This is my sister Lisa. These are my friends."*

**17 | Asking Questions with *What*, *Who*, and *How Much*** Complete the questions with *what*, *who*, or *how much* and *is* or *are*. Then practice the conversations with a partner. **6.6 B**

SHOPPING CONVERSATIONS

1.  A: _What's_____ this?

    B: It's a seashell.

2.  A: _____ those?

    B: They're $14 each.

    A: Wow, that's cheap.

3.  A: _____ this?

    B: It's $55.

    A: Oh, that's expensive!

4.  A: _____ that?

    B: That's my friend Alex. He's here on vacation, too.

    A: That's funny!

5.  A: _____ these?

    B: They're scarves.

6.  A: _____ those?

    B: They're $40 each.

7.  A: _____ this?

    B: This is our son, Peter.

8.  A: _____ these?

    B: They're tickets for the show.

9.  A: _____ these?

    B: They're $3.

10. A: _____ that?

    B: That's Sandy. She works at the hotel.

11. A: _____ this?

    B: It's a jewelry box.

    A: Oh, I see now. Cool!

12. A: _____ those?

    B: They're $100 each.

    A: Oh, no thanks. That's too much.

a seashell

> **FYI**
>
> In conversation, we can use *that* to refer to something that someone just said.
>
> A: I love my new job!
>
> B: **That's** great!

**Think about It** Look at the conversations above. Which subject pronoun does speaker B use? Why? (For more information about subject pronouns, see Unit 1, page 8.)

**Talk about It** Have a garage sale³. Put some items on your desk. Ask and answer questions about the items. Use *this*, *that*, *these*, or *those* in your questions.

A: What's this?        A: How much is this?
B: It's a smartphone.  B: It's $20.
                       A: That's cheap.

³ **garage sale:** a sale in someone's yard or garage of used things that people do not want anymore

## 6.7 Object Pronouns

We can use **object pronouns** to refer to people and things.

**A**

1 A: **Sandra** is here.
  B: Oh, good. I want to talk to **her**.
  (*her* = Sandra)

2 A: Do you like **John and Eddie**?
  B: Yes, I like **them** a lot.
  (*them* = John and Eddie)

3 A: Where's **my book**?
  B: I have **it**.
  (*it* = the book)

| SUBJECT PRONOUN | OBJECT PRONOUN | USE FOR PEOPLE | USE FOR THINGS |
|---|---|---|---|
| I | me | ♂ or ♀ | X |
| you | you | ♂ or ♀ or ♂♂♀♀ | X |
| he | him | ♂ | X |
| she | her | ♀ | X |
| it | it | X | ✏ |
| we | us | ♂♂♂♀ | X |
| they | them | ♂♂♂♀ | ✏✏✏ |

**B**

An **object pronoun** usually comes after a **verb** or a **preposition**.

verb
4 **Call** me tomorrow.

verb
5 Do you **know** them?

preposition
6 I have a message **for** you.

**C**

Notice how we use the pronouns *me*, *you*, and *us* in conversations.

7 Lisa: Call **me** tomorrow. (*me* = Lisa)
  Hannah: I can't call **you** tomorrow. (*you* = Lisa)

me ➜ you

8 Bill: Is Sam your roommate?
  Shaun: No, Paul is my roommate. But Sam lives near **us**. (*us* = Shaun and Paul)
  Bill: Does he visit **you** often? (*you* = Shaun and Paul)

us ➜ you

18 | **Noticing Object Pronouns** These conversations tell a story. Read the conversations. Underline the object pronouns that refer to the **bold** nouns. 6.7 A–B

A FRIEND'S BIRTHDAY

9:00 A.M.    1. Lisa: Where's my new **sweater**?
             I want to wear <u>it</u> tonight.
             Petra: Hmm, I'm not sure.

10:00 A.M.   2. Petra: Where's **Ann**?
             Lisa: She's not in the living room?
             Petra: No, I can't find her.

> **RESEARCH SAYS...**
>
> Object pronouns are more common in conversation than in academic writing.
>
> CORPUS

| 11:00 A.M. | 3. Lisa: Do you want to go to the mall? I want to buy a gift for **Katie**. |
| | Petra: Sure, I want to get something for her, too. Let's go. |

| 11:30 A.M. | 4. Petra: Where are my **sunglasses**? |
| | Lisa: I don't know. I don't have them. |

| 7:00 P.M. | 5. Lisa: Do you have Katie's **address**? |
| | Petra: Yes, I have it in my phone. |
| | Lisa: Great. Let's go. |

| 7:30 P.M. | 6. Lisa: Oh, Ann is here too. |
| | Ann: Happy birthday, **Katie**! I have a gift for you. |
| | Katie: Thanks, Ann. What is it? |
| | Ann: Open it. |

| 7:35 P.M. | 7. Katie: This is a beautiful **sweater**, Ann. I love it! |
| | Lisa: Hey! That's my sweater! |
| | Petra: And look! Those are my sunglasses! |

**Talk about It** Read the statements about the story above. Check (✓) *True* or *False*. Discuss your answers with a partner.

| | TRUE | FALSE |
|---|---|---|
| 1. Lisa, Petra, and Ann are roommates. | ☑ | ☐ |
| 2. Lisa, Katie, and Petra are roommates. | ☐ | ☐ |
| 3. It's Ann's birthday. | ☐ | ☐ |
| 4. Ann is a good roommate. | ☐ | ☐ |

**19 | Pronunciation Note: Reducing *Him*, *Her*, and *Them***  Listen to the note. Then do Activity 20.

Notice how we often pronounce **him**, **her**, and **them** in conversation. *Him* and *them* often sound similar.

**1** A: Do you know Ken?   **2** A: Do you know Sheila?   **3** A: Do you know Ken and Sheila?
  B: Yes, I know **him** (*'im*).   B: Yeah, I know **her** (*'er*).   B: Yeah, I know **them** (*'em*).

**20 | Pronouncing *Him*, *Her*, and *Them***  Listen to the sentences. Circle the word you hear.

1. him / her / (them)
2. him / her / them
3. him / her / them
4. him / her / them
5. him / her / them
6. him / her / them
7. him / her / them
8. him / her / them
9. him / her / them
10. him / her / them

**Talk about It** Talk to a partner. Ask about people you know. Use *him*, *her*, and *them* in your answers.

*A: Do you know Jorge Gonzales?*   *A: Do you know Kate and Sarah?*
*B: Yes, I know him. I have a class with him.*   *B: No, I don't know them.*

**21 | Using Object Pronouns** Complete the conversations with the correct pronouns. Underline the noun that the pronoun refers to. Then choose where each conversation takes place. **6.7 A–B**

1. A: Is there a textbook for this class?

   B: Yes, there are two <u>textbooks</u>. You can buy ___*them*___ at the campus bookstore.

   > a. in class ⬭
   > b. at a store
   > c. with a friend

2. A: I need to send this package.

   B: OK. Do you want to send _____ express[4] or regular mail?

   > a. in class
   > b. at the post office
   > c. at a store

3. A: There's a new cafe on Franklin Street. Do you want to go?

   B: Yeah, let's try _____ today.

   > a. at a restaurant
   > b. at a store
   > c. with a friend

4. A: Tran and Joe want to go out for pizza tonight. Let's go with _____.

   B: I can't. I have work tonight.

   > a. at a restaurant
   > b. with a friend
   > c. at a store

5. A: Those two men want to buy some running shoes. Can you help _____?

   B: Of course.

   > a. at the post office
   > b. at a store
   > c. with a friend

6. A: Excuse me. Do you have these shoes in a different color?

   B: Yes, we have _____ in blue and red.

   > a. in class
   > b. with a friend
   > c. at a store

7. A: I get headaches a lot.

   B: Do you get _____ every day?

   > a. at a store
   > b. at a restaurant
   > c. at a doctor's office

8. A: Oh, no. I have John's phone.

   B: He's in my class. I can give it to _____.

   > a. at a restaurant
   > b. in class
   > c. at a store

🔊 **Talk about It** Listen and check your answers. Then practice the conversations with a partner.

**Think about It** Look at the word before each pronoun in the sentences above. Is it a verb or a preposition? Write *V* above the verb or *P* above the preposition.

         *V*
*You can buy <u>them</u> at the campus bookstore.*

**Think about It** The pronoun *them* can refer to people or things. Look at the conversations in Activity 21. Where does *them* refer to people? Where does *them* refer to things?

---

[4]**express:** very quick

**22 | Using *Me*, *You*, and *Us*** Complete the conversations with the correct pronouns. Then listen and check your answers. Practice the conversations with a partner. `6.7 C`

1. Alison: This is for you.

   Margie: For ____*me*____? Thank you!

2. Jim: Hi, guys.

   Lucas: Hi, Jim.

   Marco: Hi, Jim. There's an extra chair here. Sit with _____.

3. Lisa: Something smells good!

   Soon Jin: Marta and I are making chicken. Are you hungry?

   Lisa: Yeah, I am.

   Marta: Great! Have dinner with _____.

4. Michael: Excuse me. Can you help _____?

   Tony: Sure. What do you need?

   Michael: I need a new printer.

5. Anna: Lunch is here! I have a salad and a soda for _____.

   George: Thank you.

6. Carol: Kim, there's a lot of mail for _____ today.

   Kim: Thanks, Mom.

7. Sam: Do you want to watch this movie with _____?

   Luis: What kind of movie is it?

   Sam: It's an action movie.

8. Ming: Is Dr. West in the office today?

   Brian: No, he isn't here today.

   Ming: OK. Can he call _____ back tomorrow, please?

9. Cara: Oh, no! I don't have my notes. The test is today!

   Emily: Don't worry. I have my notes here. You can study with _____.

10. Jessica: I need to talk to _____. Can you call _____ tomorrow?

    Sarah: OK. I'll call _____ in the morning.

**Think about It** Look at the conversations again. Which person or people does each object pronoun refer to?

*1. me = Margie*

**Think about It** Circle the subject pronouns in the conversations above. Which subject pronouns refer to people? Which refer to things?

## 6.8 Possessive Pronouns and Questions with *Whose*

A **possessive pronoun** refers to a **possessive determiner*** + a **noun**.

| POSSESSIVE DETERMINER | + | NOUN | = | POSSESSIVE PRONOUN |
|---|---|---|---|---|
| my | | car | | mine |
| your | | phone | | yours |
| his | | jacket | | his |
| her | | book | | hers |
| our | | food | | ours |
| their | | food | | theirs |

**A**

**1** A: Is this your car?
B: Yes, it's **mine.** (=It's my car.)

**2** That's **his.**
(= That's **his** jacket.
= That's **Paul's** jacket.)

**3** That's not mine. It's **hers.**
(= It's **her** book.
= It's **Kim's** book.)

**4** Is this **yours?**
(= Is this **your** phone?)

**5** That's not **ours.**
(=That's not **our** food.)

**6** It's **theirs.** (= It's their food.)

*For more information on possessive determiners, see Unit 1, page 13.

**B**

### QUESTIONS WITH *WHOSE*

We can use **whose** to ask about possession.

Whose bag is this?

We can use **whose** + noun + **verb** OR **whose** + **verb**.

**7a** Whose bag **is** this?
**7b** Whose car **is** this? } = **7c** Whose **is** this?

**8a** Whose books **are** these?
**8b** Whose flowers **are** these? } = **8c** Whose **are** these?

### ANSWERING *WHOSE* QUESTIONS

We often answer *whose* questions with a **possessive pronoun** or a **possessive noun**.

**9** A: **Whose** bag is this?
B: It's **mine**.

**10** A: **Whose** phone is this?
B: It's **Jim's**.

A name + **'s** is a possessive noun.*

*For more information on possessive nouns, see Unit 1, page 13 and the Resources, page R-2.

**23 | Using Possessive Pronouns** Complete each conversation with the correct possessive pronouns.
6.8 A

1. Jack:    Excuse me. Are these your sunglasses?

   Luna:    No, they're not ___mine___. Do you see
            the girl in the red coat? I think they're
            _____.

2. Jack:    Excuse me. I think these are your
            daughter's sunglasses.

   Alan:    No, they're not _____. See the
            boy on the bench? Maybe they're
            _____.

3. Jack:    Hi. Are these your son's sunglasses?

   Pedro:   No, they're not _____. Sorry.

4. Ken:    Hey, Jack! Those are _____.

   Jack:   Really? They're yours?

   Ken:    Don't laugh. They're a gift for my niece.

**24 | Using Possessive Pronouns** Complete each conversation with the correct possessive pronoun.
Do the speakers know each other? Check (✓) the correct column. Then listen and check your answers. 6.8 A

|  | KNOW EACH OTHER | DON'T KNOW EACH OTHER |
|---|---|---|
| 1. A: Is this your suitcase, sir?<br>B: Yes. That's ___mine___. | ☐ | ☑ |
| 2. A: Are these Mom's sunglasses?<br>B: No, I don't think they're _____. | ☐ | ☐ |
| 3. A: Are these our tickets, ma'am?<br>B: Yes, those are _____. Your movie is in theater 3. | ☐ | ☐ |
| 4. A: Oh no! The door is locked, and my keys are in the house.<br>B: That's OK. I have _____. | ☐ | ☐ |
| 5. A: How old are your children?<br>B: They're twelve and fourteen. How old are _____?<br>A: They're six and eight. | ☐ | ☐ |

| | KNOW EACH OTHER | DON'T KNOW EACH OTHER |
|---|---|---|

6. A: Lisa, your dress is beautiful!

   B: Oh, thank you. I like _____, too.

☐ ☐

7. A: Hi, Ann. Hi, Trina. Our hotel rooms are on the 10ᵗʰ floor. Where are _____?

   B: _____ are on the 11ᵗʰ floor. We're right above you!

☐ ☐

8. A: Excuse me. We need the 5:00 train to Bakersfield. Is this our train?

   B: No, this is the 4:50 train. _____ is the next train.

☐ ☐

9. A: Are these your glasses, sir?

   B: No, they're not _____.

☐ ☐

10. A: How much is your apartment?

    B: It's $1,200 a month.

    A: Wow, that's expensive.

    B: Well, Peter's apartment is really expensive. _____ is $2,000 a month.

☐ ☐

**25 | Asking and Answering Questions with _Whose_** Look at the picture. Then look at the objects below. Complete each question with an object from the box + _is/are_ + _this/these_. Then complete the answers with a possessive noun. `6.8 A–B`

CAMPUS LOST AND FOUND

| backpack | books | skateboard | shopping bags |
|---|---|---|---|

1. A: Whose _____*backpack is this*_____?

   B: It's _____*Ji-young's*_____.

2. A: Whose _____?

   B: They're _____.

3. A: Whose _____?

   B: It's _____.

4. A: Whose _____?

   B: They're _____.

THERE IS/THERE ARE AND PRONOUNS  159

| book | flowers | jacket | sweater |

5. A: Whose _____?
   B: It's _____.

6. A: Whose _____?
   B: It's _____.

7. A: Whose _____?
   B: They're _____.

8. A: Whose _____?
   B: It's _____.

**Talk about It** Practice the conversations in Activity 25 with a partner.

**Talk about It** Work in a group of five. Follow these instructions.

WHOSE IS IT?

1. Everyone puts five things on the table (for example: a book, a notebook, a pen, an eraser, a phone).
2. Mix the things around.
3. Take turns. Choose a thing. Ask and answer questions about the thing. Use *whose*.
4. If you're correct, you get a point. Take the thing off the table.
5. If you're wrong, you don't get a point. The thing stays on the table.
6. Write down the number of points for each person. Who is the winner?

A: Whose is this?
B: It's yours!
A: That's right.

A: Whose is this?
B: It's his. / It's Jamal's.
C: No, it's not mine.

**26 | Error Correction** Find and correct the errors in these conversations. (Some conversations may not have any errors.) `6.8 A–B`

1. Gina: Is this your phone, Ben?
   Ben: Yes, it's ~~me~~. *mine*

2. Erin: Does Sarah have your jacket?
   Kay: No, that's not mine. It's she's.

3. Lin: That's Felipe's house, right?
   Mara: No, that's not him. He lives in
   the blue house.

4. James: Is this Mike's phone?
   Ann: No, it's not his.

5. Ken: Here are your keys.
   Wei-chi: These aren't mine. I think
   they're Amy.

6. Kay: Is this your laptop?
   James: No, my is at home. I think it's Ken's.

7. Lin: Whose water are this?
   Erin: It's Ben's water.

8. Lin: Whose shoes is these?
   James: They're mine.

9. Felipe: Whose coffee is this?
   Mara: It's your.

10. Lin: Whose books is these, Kay?
    Kay: They're mine.

# WRAP-UP

**A | GRAMMAR IN READING** Read these riddles. Underline the uses of *there is/there are* (statements and questions). Circle the subject of each of these sentences. Then talk to a partner. Guess the answers to the riddles.

## Riddles

1. <u>There is</u> (a house) with four walls. There is a window in each wall. Through each window, you can look south. Where is the house?

2. There are six men carrying a box. In the box, there are six cats. Each cat has six kittens. How many legs are there?

3. There are two girls in front of one girl. There are two girls behind one girl. There is one girl in the middle. How many girls are there?

4. There are two people in a house. No one comes in and no one goes out. Five minutes later, there are three people in the house. Why?

5. You need a haircut. There are two hair stylists[5] in town: Anna and Belinda. Anna has beautiful hair. Belinda's hair is terrible. Which hair stylist do you choose?

6. There is a man alone on an island[6] in the middle of a lake. He cannot swim. There are no bridges. One day, he leaves the island. No one helps him. How does he do it?

7. There is a green house on Green Street. It has one floor[7]. The walls are green. The furniture is green. The floors are green. The doors are green. What color are the stairs?

8. There are two mothers and two daughters. They go out to eat. Everyone eats a hamburger. They eat three hamburgers. Why?

Look on page 162 for the answers.

**B | GRAMMAR IN SPEAKING** Take this survey. Underline the object pronouns in the questions and answers.

WHAT WOULD YOU DO?

1. An old man on the street asks <u>you</u> for money. You ____.
   a. give <u>him</u> money
   b. say, "Sorry," and don't give <u>him</u> money
   c. ignore[8] <u>him</u>
   d. do something else

2. You see a five-year-old girl on the sidewalk. She is alone and crying. You ____.
   a. call the police
   b. look for her parents
   c. stay with her until her parents come
   d. do something else

---

[5] **stylists:** people who cut and shape other people's hair
[6] **island:** a piece of land with water all around it
[7] **floor:** all the rooms at the same height in a building (for example, *first floor, second floor*, etc.)

[8] **ignore:** to know about someone or something, but to not do anything about it

3. You find $20 on the street in front of your house. There is no one around[9]. You ____.
   a. keep it and spend it
   b. look for the owner of the money
   c. give it to the police
   d. do something else

4. You find $1,000 on the street in front of your house. There is no one around. You ____.
   a. keep it and spend it
   b. look for the owner of the money
   c. give it to the police
   d. do something else

5. You see a woman in front of your neighbor's house. She has your neighbor's bicycle. You ____.
   a. call the police
   b. tell your neighbor
   c. take the bicycle from her
   d. do nothing

6. You see a man in front of your neighbor's house. The living room window is broken. The man has two laptop computers in his hands. You ____.
   a. call the police
   b. tell your neighbor
   c. take the laptops from him
   d. do nothing

**Think about It** The object pronouns *him*, *her*, *it*, and *them* refer to nouns. In the questions and answers in the survey, which nouns do these pronouns refer to?

   *1. him = an old man*

**Talk about It** Ask three classmates the questions above. Record their answers and your answers in the chart below.

| My Answer | _____'s Answer | _____'s Answer | _____'s Answer |
|---|---|---|---|
| 1. | | | |
| 2. | | | |
| 3. | | | |
| 4. | | | |
| 5. | | | |
| 6. | | | |

**Talk about It** Share your survey results with the class. Which answers do most people agree with?

**Answers to Riddles on page 161:**
1. The North Pole.
2. 180.
3. Three (The girls are in a line).
4. They're married. Their baby is born.
5. Belinda. She cuts Anna's hair, and Anna's haircut is beautiful.
6. He leaves in the winter. The lake is frozen.
7. There are no stairs. The house has one floor.
8. There are three women: a grandmother, a mother, and a daughter.

[9]**no one around:** no people nearby

*THERE IS* AND *THERE ARE*

We can use **there is** (**there's**) and **there are** to introduce new information.

| | POSITIVE STATEMENTS | NEGATIVE STATEMENTS |
|---|---|---|
| **SINGULAR COUNT NOUNS** | There's an interesting **movie** on TV. | There **isn't** a **movie** on.<br>(not very common) |
| **NONCOUNT NOUNS** | There's some **coffee** in the kitchen. | There **isn't** much **coffee** in the kitchen. |
| **PLURAL COUNT NOUNS** | There are many good **restaurants** on Bleecker Street. | There **aren't** any good **restaurants** around here. |

| | YES/NO QUESTIONS | SHORT ANSWERS |
|---|---|---|
| **SINGULAR COUNT NOUNS** | Is **there** a **bookstore** nearby? | Yes, **there is.** |
| **NONCOUNT NOUNS** | Is **there** any tea left? | No, **there isn't.** / No, **there's not.** |
| **PLURAL COUNT NOUNS** | Are **there** any **parking spaces**? | Yes, **there are.**<br>No, **there aren't.** |

| | HOW MUCH/HOW MANY QUESTIONS | ANSWERS |
|---|---|---|
| **NONCOUNT NOUNS** | How much **food is there**? | **There's** a lot. |
| **PLURAL COUNT NOUNS** | How many **chairs are there**? | **There aren't** many. |

*THIS, THAT, THESE,* AND *THOSE*

We can use **this**, **that**, **these**, and **those** to point out people or things.

| | PEOPLE OR THINGS THAT ARE NEAR | PEOPLE OR THINGS THAT ARE FAR |
|---|---|---|
| **SINGULAR** | **This is** my sister Marla. | **That's** Richard. He's my assistant. |
| **PLURAL** | **These are** delicious. | **Those are** beautiful! |

OBJECT PRONOUNS AND POSSESSIVE PRONOUNS

| | singular | | | | | plural | |
|---|---|---|---|---|---|---|---|
| **SUBJECT PRONOUN** | I | he | she | it | you | we | they |
| **OBJECT PRONOUN** | me | him | her | it | you | us | them |
| **POSSESSIVE DETERMINER** | my | his | her | its | your | our | their |
| **POSSESSIVE PRONOUN** | mine | his | hers | — | yours | ours | theirs |

QUESTIONS WITH *WHOSE*

A: **Whose car** is that? / **Whose** is that?
B: It's Lisa's.

A: **Whose keys** are these? / **Whose** are these?
B: They're mine.

# Present Progressive

**IN THIS UNIT, WE USE** the present progressive to talk about

## Things in progress now—at this moment

1. I**'m sitting** outside with some friends.
2. We**'re talking** about sports.

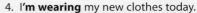

3. We**'re eating** dinner at the moment.
4. I**'m wearing** my new clothes today.

**GO ONLINE**

For the Unit Vocabulary Check, go to the Online Practice.

## Things in progress now—over a longer time

5. I'm **exercising** a lot these days.

6. My sister **is taking** college classes this semester.

7. I'm **living** in Paris this year.

8. My friends **are traveling** this month.

**Think about It** What are you doing now? Check (✓) *True* or *False*.

| | TRUE | FALSE |
|---|:---:|:---:|
| 1. I'm eating some food at the moment. | ☐ | ☐ |
| 2. I'm talking to friends at the moment. | ☐ | ☐ |
| 3. I'm wearing some new clothes today. | ☐ | ☐ |
| 4. I'm exercising a lot these days. | ☐ | ☐ |
| 5. I'm taking good classes this semester. | ☐ | ☐ |
| 6. I'm living with roommates this year. | ☐ | ☐ |

## 7.1 Positive Statements with the Present Progressive

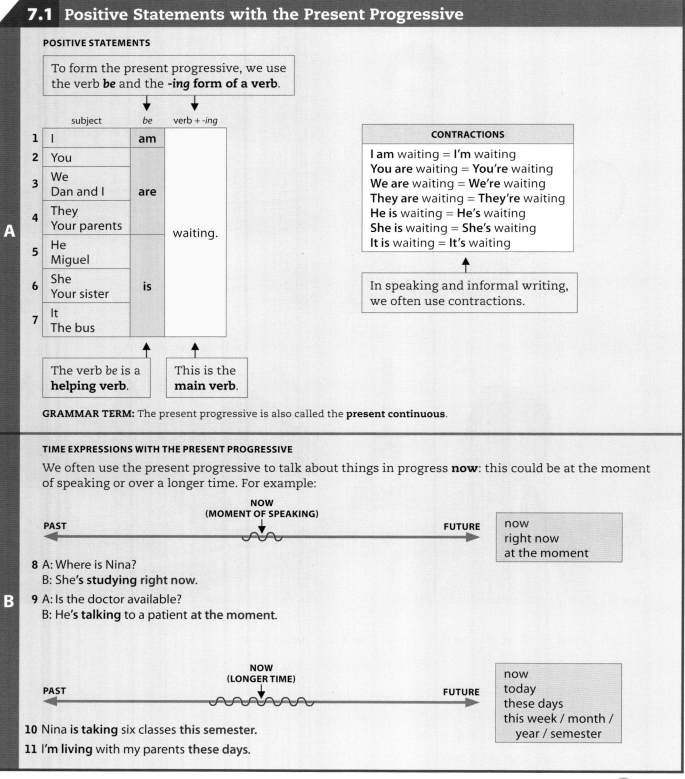

**POSITIVE STATEMENTS**

To form the present progressive, we use the verb **be** and the **-ing form of a verb**.

| | subject | be | verb + -ing |
|---|---|---|---|
| 1 | I | am | |
| 2 | You | are | |
| 3 | We / Dan and I | are | |
| 4 | They / Your parents | are | waiting. |
| 5 | He / Miguel | is | |
| 6 | She / Your sister | is | |
| 7 | It / The bus | is | |

The verb *be* is a **helping verb**.

This is the **main verb**.

**CONTRACTIONS**

**I am** waiting = **I'm** waiting
**You are** waiting = **You're** waiting
**We are** waiting = **We're** waiting
**They are** waiting = **They're** waiting
**He is** waiting = **He's** waiting
**She is** waiting = **She's** waiting
**It is** waiting = **It's** waiting

In speaking and informal writing, we often use contractions.

**GRAMMAR TERM:** The present progressive is also called the **present continuous**.

**TIME EXPRESSIONS WITH THE PRESENT PROGRESSIVE**

We often use the present progressive to talk about things in progress **now**: this could be at the moment of speaking or over a longer time. For example:

PAST ← NOW (MOMENT OF SPEAKING) → FUTURE

now
right now
at the moment

**8** A: Where is Nina?
B: She**'s studying right now.**

**9** A: Is the doctor available?
B: He**'s talking** to a patient **at the moment.**

PAST ← NOW (LONGER TIME) → FUTURE

now
today
these days
this week / month / year / semester

**10** Nina **is taking** six classes **this semester.**

**11** I**'m living** with my parents **these days.**

**1 | Noticing Present Progressive Verbs** Read one student's updates. Underline the present progressive verbs (*be* + *-ing* verb). Then circle the subject for each of these verbs. `7.1 A`

## Lisa's Status Updates

ON VACATION

1. We're at the airport in New York. (I)'m feeling excited! *#paris*
2. We're drinking coffee at a street café. I look Parisian. ☺
3. This line is moving so slowly! *#thelouvre*
4. I'm eating French cheese now. I love all the food here! *#yum*
5. We're climbing the Eiffel Tower. The sun is setting.
6. My feet are killing¹ me!
7. We're flying home already. *#sad*

BACK AT SCHOOL

8. I'm putting up my posters from Paris. *#dormroom*
9. I'm looking for the psychology section of the bookstore. This bookstore is too big!
10. My study group is reviewing for the French test.
11. Yuck! A huge spider is hanging from the ceiling!

the Eiffel Tower
at sunset

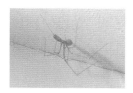

a spider

**Think about It** Which verbs above are *not* present progressive verbs?

**Write about It** What is happening in class right now? Complete these status updates with your own information.

1. We're learning about _____.
2. I'm sitting next to _____.
3. _____ is wearing _____.

**2 | Forming the Present Progressive** Complete the present progressive verbs with the correct form of *be*. Use contractions with pronouns. Underline the *-ing* verb that follows *be*. `7.1 A`

## What Are You Doing These Days?

INTERNATIONAL CLUB ALUMNI², CLASS OF 2013

1. **Elsa:** My program at school ____is____ giving me some more time for my studies. So I __'m__
   living in Brazil this year. I _____ studying Portuguese.

---

¹ **are killing me:** (informal) hurt a lot

² **alumni:** (plural) people who graduated from a particular school or university

2. **Abdul:** I _____ working at a bank. I often see other people from our class! For example, these days Carla Morel and Miguel Sanchez _____ working for a lawyer in my building.

3. **Shanna:** I _____ dieting and I _____ losing a lot of weight. My big news is about my brother Alex. He and Anna Ivanova are married, and they _____ traveling in Russia now. Alex _____ learning a lot about Russia. He and Anna _____ having a great time!

4. **Marisha:** These days I _____ looking for a new job. I _____ living with my parents now.

5. **Matt:** This summer I _____ exercising a lot. I go to the gym six days a week. My brother and I _____ playing basketball on a team from the neighborhood.

6. **Daniel:** My wife and I _____ cooking lots of Ethiopian food. We have our own restaurant in Cleveland, Ohio! We _____ working hard, but we love it.

**Think about It** There are six time expressions in the sentences in Activity 2. Circle them.

**Talk about It** Tell a partner three things that you are doing these days. Use the the present progressive form of the verbs in this box or other verbs.

| do | exercise | go | listen | make | study | travel |
|----|----------|-----|--------|------|-------|--------|

*"These days I'm spending lots of time with my nephews, Jordy and Martin."*

**3 | Spelling Note: Adding –ing to Verbs** Read the note. Then do Activities 4 and 5.

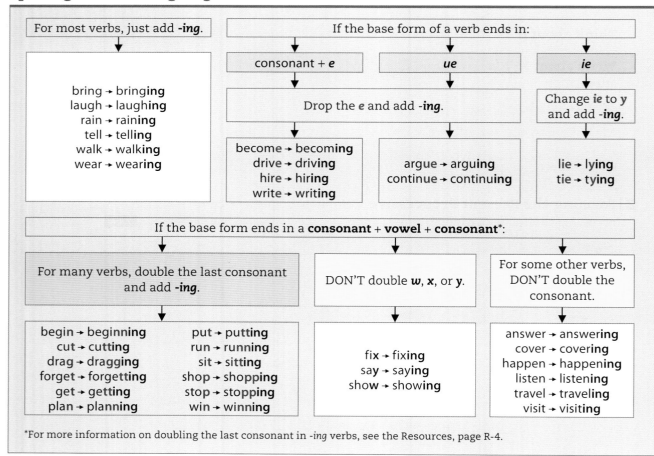

*For more information on doubling the last consonant in -ing verbs, see the Resources, page R-4.

## 4 | Spelling -ing Verbs
Write the -ing form of these verbs. Write the verbs in the correct part of the chart below. `7.1 A`

| agree | burn | cut | fit | help | lie | put | say | take |
| ask | buy | die | fix | hit | lose | relax | show | tell |
| become | change | drop | get | keep | make | rise | shut | tie |
| begin | complain | eat | go | laugh | plan | run | sleep | use |
| break | continue | feel | grow | let | play | save | stop | write |

| Add -ing | Drop the e and add -ing | Change the ie to y and add -ing | Double the consonant and add -ing |
|---|---|---|---|
| *agreeing* | | | |

**Think about It** Do you know the verbs above? Use a dictionary to look up the words you don't know.

## 5 | Forming Present Progressive Verbs
Read the diagrams about climate change. Then complete the sentences on page 170 with the present progressive form of the verbs in parentheses. `7.1 A`

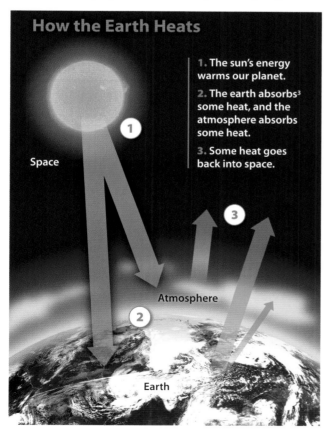

**How the Earth Heats**

1. The sun's energy warms our planet.

2. The earth absorbs[3] some heat, and the atmosphere absorbs some heat.

3. Some heat goes back into space.

Space

Atmosphere

Earth

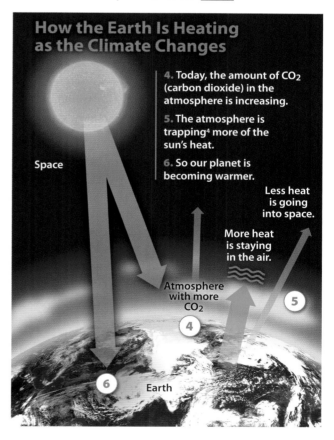

**How the Earth Is Heating as the Climate Changes**

4. Today, the amount of $CO_2$ (carbon dioxide) in the atmosphere is increasing.

5. The atmosphere is trapping[4] more of the sun's heat.

6. So our planet is becoming warmer.

Less heat is going into space.

More heat is staying in the air.

Space

Atmosphere with more $CO_2$

Earth

[3] **absorb (absorbs):** to take something in and hold it

[4] **trap (trapping):** to hold something so it can't get away

STATEMENTS FROM A SPEECH ABOUT CLIMATE CHANGE

1. Climate change is real: our planet _____*is getting*_____ warmer.
   (get)

2. We _____ too much oil and gas—at home, at work,
   (use)
   and on the road.

3. Our air _____ more polluted[5]. For example, there is
   (become)
   more carbon dioxide ($CO_2$) in the air.

4. In many parts of the world, summers _____ hotter.
   (get)
   Very hot summers _____ more common.
   (become)

5. In the Arctic and the Antarctic, more ice _____ each summer.
   (melt)

6. The oceans _____.
   (rise)

7. Storms _____ stronger.
   (get)

8. Many types of plants and animals _____ out[6].
   (die)

9. We _____ our planet in danger.
   (put)

10. Many scientists _____ to slow climate change.
    (plan)

11. We _____ for your help.
    (ask)

**Think about It** Check your spelling. Look at the Spelling Note on page 168.

**Think about It** Look at the two diagrams in Activity 5. Which diagram uses the simple present? Which diagram uses the present progressive? Why?

**6 | Usage Note: Using Two -*ing* Verbs with One Subject** Read the note. Then do Activity 7.

> We can use **and** to connect two **-ing** verbs with the same subject.
> **1** I'm **eating** dinner **and watching** TV.
> **2** Yasuko **is taking** pictures **and posting** them on the Web.
>
> Notice: We don't repeat **am / is / are** before the second verb.
> X I'm eating dinner and am watching TV.

**7 | Writing Sentences with Present Progressive Verbs** Look at the pictures on page 171. Use the phrases in the box to write sentences with present progressive verbs. **7.1 A**

MULTITASKING[7]

| | | | |
|---|---|---|---|
| drink coffee | make dinner | put on makeup[8] | read a magazine |
| drive | play a videogame | read a book | ride the subway |

---

[5] **polluted:** dirty with dangerous gases and chemicals
[6] **die out:** disappear

[7] **multitasking:** doing two or more things at the same time
[8] **makeup:** things you put on your face to look beautiful

FYI

We often use the present progressive to talk about things that are changing. We often use the verbs *get* and *become* in these sentences.

He **is becoming** annoyed.
My English **is getting** better.
Prices **are getting** really high.

1. _____She's riding the subway_____ and

_____ .

2. _____ and
_____ .

3. _____ and

_____ .

4. _____ and
_____ .

**8 | Using Time Expressions with the Present Progressive** Circle the words to make the statements true for you. Then underline the time expression in each sentence. `7.1 B`

WHAT ARE YOU DOING RIGHT NOW?

1. I'm sitting (**in class** / **in the library** / **at home**) <u>right now</u>.

2. I'm thinking about (**the present progressive** / **other things**) at the moment.

3. I'm feeling (**hungry** / **tired** / **fine**) right now.

4. I'm feeling (**excited** / **interested** / **bored**) at the moment.

WHAT ARE YOU DOING THESE DAYS?

5. I'm spending (**a lot of time** / **a little time**) on homework this week.

6. I'm doing my homework (**in the library** / **at home** / **at cafes**) these days.

7. I'm taking (**easy classes** / **difficult classes**) this semester.

8. I'm getting (**OK grades** / **good grades**) this semester.

9. I'm learning (**a little English** / **a lot of English**) this year.

**Write about It** Write two more sentences about yourself with the present progressive. Use one time expression from Box A and one time expression from Box B. Then share your sentences with the class.

| A | | | B | | |
|---|---|---|---|---|---|
| now | right now | at the moment | these days | this semester | this week/month/year |

*I'm studying at the library these days.*

## 7.2 Negative Statements with the Present Progressive

### A

**NEGATIVE STATEMENTS**

| | subject | be + not | verb + -ing |
|---|---|---|---|
| **1** | I | am not<br>'m not | |
| **2** | You<br>We<br>They | are not<br>'re not<br>aren't | waiting. |
| **3** | He<br>She<br>It | is not<br>'s not<br>isn't | |

Remember: There are two ways to make negative contractions with **are** and **is**.

They**'re not** **waiting.** = They **aren't** **waiting.**

She**'s not** **reading.** = She **isn't** **reading.**

**9 | Writing Present Progressive Negative Statements** Listen and complete the sentences with the words you hear. Use contractions. Then practice the conversations with a partner. `7.2 A`

**TALKING ABOUT PROBLEMS**

1. A: _You're not eating_ your food. What's wrong?

   B: I'm not hungry.

2. A: Where's Anne? She usually gets here on time.

   B: _____ well today. She's at home.

3. A: The buses _____ a normal schedule today.
   Let's take a taxi.

   B: There's a taxi! But _____ for us.

4. A: _____ much this semester.

   B: Yeah. Maybe this class is too easy.

5. A: The new computer system _____.

   B: Tell the manager about it.

6. A: Those kids are fighting!

   B: _____. They're just playing.

7. A: _____ those shirts in the right place.

   B: I'm sorry! Where do they go?

8. A: I don't believe you.

   B: _____ to you.

   A: Maybe not. But _____ me everything!

9. A: _____ much money.

   B: We spend a lot of money in restaurants. Let's cook more meals at home.

10. A: It's cold. Can you close the window?

    B: I'm trying. But _____.

11. A: This knife isn't good. _____ the bread.

    B: Sorry! I'll give you a different knife.

**RESEARCH SAYS...**

We use the present progressive more often in speaking than in writing.

CORPUS

**Think about It** Check your answers with a partner. Use the chart on page 168 to check your spelling.

**Write about It** What are two problems in your life? Write two negative statements with the present progressive. Then share your sentences with a partner.

*My car isn't working.*
*My son isn't studying.*

**🔊 10 | Understanding Positive and Negative Verbs** Choose the positive or negative verb to complete each conversation. Then listen and check your answers. **7.2 A**

CONVERSATIONS ABOUT SCHOOL

1. A: How's your schedule this semester?

   B: It's hard. (**I'm taking**) / **I'm not taking** a lot of classes.

2. A: Do students like the new English language program?

   B: Yes, I think so! **They're complaining** / **They aren't complaining**.

3. A: How does your son feel about his new school?

   B: **He's having** / **He's not having** an easy year.

   A: What's wrong?

   B: I'm not sure. But **we're getting** / **we aren't getting** worried.

4. A: Is your science class hard?

   B: Yeah, **I'm having** / **I'm not having** some problems. But I'm working with a tutor.

      **He's helping** / **He's not helping** me.

5. A: Your sister is studying here too now! How does she like it?

   B: I don't know. **She's meeting** / **She isn't meeting** a lot of people. She feels a little lonely.

6. A: What is the science program like this year?

   B: The program **is changing** / **isn't changing** a lot. There are a lot of new classes and professors now.

**11 | Forming Negative Statements with the Present Progressive** Complete the statements with the negative present progressive form of the verbs in parentheses. Then practice the conversations with a partner. **7.2 A**

SOME SMALL PROBLEMS

1. A: I'm looking around Grand Central Station, but I don't see Tim anywhere!

   B: Grand Central? He _____*isn't waiting*_____ for you there! He's at Penn Station!
                                    (wait)

2. A: You _____ to me.
              (listen)

   B: Sorry! You're right! I'm thinking about my interview tomorrow.

3. A: We're all waiting for you. Where are you?

   B: I'm on the road. But the cars _____.
                                          (move)

4. A: It _____ much this summer.
            (rain)

   B: That's for sure! My grass is turning brown. And the plants don't look great.

5. A: How's Teena?

   B: I don't know. She's angry at me, and she _____ to me.
                                                     (talk)

6. A: How are the apartments near school?

   B: They're expensive! I _____ anything for under $800 a month!
   (find)

7. A: Ji-hoon really likes his new school. He talks about it a lot.

   B: He _____ the truth. He's not happy there!
   (tell)

8. A: Let's get some dinner.

   B: I _____ hungry right now. Let's wait an hour or two.
   (feel)

9. A: Turn off the TV, and do your homework!

   B: Don't worry, Mom! The TV is on, but we _____ it.
   (watch)

**Think about It** In the conversations above, there are five negative statements with the **simple present—** one with the verb *be* and four with other verbs. Underline the verbs in these statements.


**12 | Using Present Progressive Verbs to Talk about Change** Complete the statements with the present progressive form of the verbs in parentheses. Use contractions where possible. `7.2 A`

## How Are Our Lives Changing?

1. People _____*are working*_____ too many hours. They _____*'re not enjoying*_____ life!
   (work)                                          (not / enjoy)

2. Children _____ inside with their smartphones and tablets. They
   (sit)
   _____ outdoors with their friends.
   (not / play)

3. The Internet _____ the way we communicate. Young people
   (change)
   _____ a lot of time with their online "friends." They _____
   (spend)                                                      (not / get)
   together with their real friends.

4. These days we _____ our friends a lot, but we _____ them
   (text)                                        (not / call)
   very often.

5. Some fathers _____ very long hours. They _____ more
   (not / work)                                  (spend)
   time with their children.

6. Many mothers _____ at jobs and _____ time with
   (work)                              (spend)
   their children.

7. People _____ at home every night. They _____ in
   (not / cook)                                  (eat)
   restaurants more.

8. People _____ more. These days I _____ a bike to school.
   (exercise)                              (ride)
   I _____ so much.
   (not / drive)

9. People _____ online more. They _____ so much TV.
   (go)                                  (not / watch)

10. People _____ in one place. More people _____ to other
    (not / stay)                                  (move)
    cities or countries for school and work.

**Talk about It**  Do you agree with the statements in Activity 12? Discuss your ideas with a partner.

**Write about It**  What are you doing these days? Write two positive sentences and two negative sentences with the present progressive. Use the verbs in this box or other verbs.

| buy | eat | learn | meet | play | read | sleep | watch | work |
|-----|-----|-------|------|------|------|-------|-------|------|

*I'm buying lots of things online. I'm not eating a lot of sweets.*

**13 | Error Correction**  Find and correct the errors. (Some sentences might not have any errors.)

      *is*
1. He ⌃staying with us for a few days.
2. The baby no is eating his food.
3. They not doing that the right way.
4. Nora is living with her parents now.
5. The children are sleep now.

6. Shuji and I waiting for some answers.
7. We are use a new computer now.
8. Tanya isn't taking any classes this semester.
9. They be having a good time.
10. She's makeing dinner at the moment.

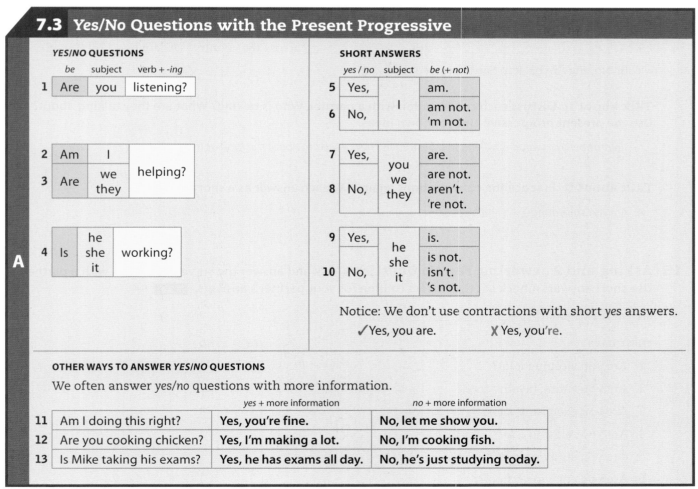

**A**

**7.3  Yes/No Questions with the Present Progressive**

**YES/NO QUESTIONS**

| | be | subject | verb + -ing |
|---|-----|---------|-------------|
| 1 | Are | you | listening? |
| 2 | Am | I | helping? |
| 3 | Are | we / they | |
| 4 | Is | he / she / it | working? |

**SHORT ANSWERS**

| | yes / no | subject | be (+ not) |
|---|----------|---------|------------|
| 5 | Yes, | I | am. |
| 6 | No, | | am not. / 'm not. |
| 7 | Yes, | you / we / they | are. |
| 8 | No, | | are not. / aren't. / 're not. |
| 9 | Yes, | he / she / it | is. |
| 10 | No, | | is not. / isn't. / 's not. |

Notice: We don't use contractions with short *yes* answers.
✓Yes, you are.     ✗ Yes, you're.

**OTHER WAYS TO ANSWER *YES/NO* QUESTIONS**

We often answer *yes/no* questions with more information.

| | | *yes* + more information | *no* + more information |
|---|---|---|---|
| 11 | Am I doing this right? | Yes, you're fine. | No, let me show you. |
| 12 | Are you cooking chicken? | Yes, I'm making a lot. | No, I'm cooking fish. |
| 13 | Is Mike taking his exams? | Yes, he has exams all day. | No, he's just studying today. |

## 14 | Forming *Yes/No* Questions with the Present Progressive

Complete the conversations with the words in parentheses. Make present progressive *yes/no* questions. Then practice the conversations with a partner. **7.3 A**

1. A: _____*Are you*_____ still _____*eating*_____? (you/eat)

   B: Yes—this food is delicious!

2. A: _____ these days? (Carla/work)

   B: No, she's just taking classes.

3. A: _____ you at a bad time? (I/call)

   B: No, it's a good time. We're not doing anything.

4. A: _____ to me? (you/listen)

   B: Of course!

5. A: _____ their summer vacation? (your friends/enjoy)

   B: Yes, they're having a great time!

6. A: _____ too much noise? (we/make)

   B: No, it's fine. I'm just writing an email.

7. A: _____ a lot of English this year? (you/learn)

   B: Sure! I understand all my favorite songs now!

8. A: _____ you? (Sam/help)

   B: Not really. I'm doing most of the work.

9. A: _____ still _____ across the country? (Adam and Phil/travel)

   B: No, they're back in San Francisco now.

> **FYI**
>
> We often use **still** with the present progressive to show that an action is continuing longer. We put it between **be** and the **main verb**.
>
> He**'s still studying** in England.

**Talk about It** Discuss each conversation with a partner. Who is talking? What are they talking about? Use the present progressive and your own ideas.

*"In number 1, a waiter is talking to a customer. They're talking about the food at the restaurant."*

**Talk about It** Practice the conversations again. Say each answer as a short answer.

*A: Are you still eating?     B: Yes, I am.*

## 15 | Asking and Answering *Yes/No* Questions

Ask and answer the survey questions with a partner. Use short answers. Check (✓) the correct column for your partner's answers. **7.3 A**

MY PARTNER'S NAME: _____

| THESE DAYS . . . | YES | NO |
|---|---|---|
| 1. Are you sleeping a lot? | ☐ | ☐ |
| 2. Are you eating healthy food? | ☐ | ☐ |
| 3. Are you exercising a lot? | ☐ | ☐ |
| 4. Are you relaxing a lot? | ☐ | ☐ |
| 5. Are you studying a lot? | ☐ | ☐ |
| 6. Are you enjoying school? | ☐ | ☐ |

|  |  | YES | NO |
|---|---|---|---|
| 7. | Is your English teacher giving you a lot of homework? | ☐ | ☐ |
| 8. | Are your teachers helping you? | ☐ | ☐ |
| 9. | Is your schoolwork taking a lot of time? | ☐ | ☐ |
| 10. | Are you and your friends getting together often? | ☐ | ☐ |
| 11. | Are you spending time with your family? | ☐ | ☐ |
| 12. | Are you meeting interesting people at school? | ☐ | ☐ |
| 13. | Are you playing any sports? | ☐ | ☐ |
| 14. | Are you saving money? | ☐ | ☐ |
| 15. | Are you working outside of school? | ☐ | ☐ |

*A: Are you sleeping a lot these days?*     *B: Yes, I am. / No, I'm not.*

**Talk about It** **Discuss your answers with your partner. Add some information to the short answer.**

*"No, I'm not. I'm only sleeping about 5 or 6 hours most nights."*

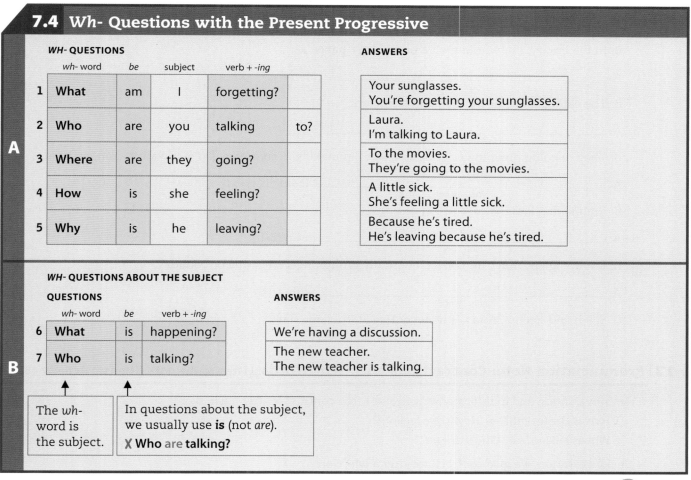

### 7.4 *Wh-* Questions with the Present Progressive

**WH- QUESTIONS**

**A**

| | *wh-* word | *be* | subject | verb + *-ing* | |
|---|---|---|---|---|---|
| 1 | What | am | I | forgetting? | |
| 2 | Who | are | you | talking | to? |
| 3 | Where | are | they | going? | |
| 4 | How | is | she | feeling? | |
| 5 | Why | is | he | leaving? | |

**ANSWERS**

| |
|---|
| Your sunglasses.<br>You're forgetting your sunglasses. |
| Laura.<br>I'm talking to Laura. |
| To the movies.<br>They're going to the movies. |
| A little sick.<br>She's feeling a little sick. |
| Because he's tired.<br>He's leaving because he's tired. |

**WH- QUESTIONS ABOUT THE SUBJECT**

**QUESTIONS**

**B**

| | *wh-* word | *be* | verb + *-ing* |
|---|---|---|---|
| 6 | What | is | happening? |
| 7 | Who | is | talking? |

**ANSWERS**

| |
|---|
| We're having a discussion. |
| The new teacher.<br>The new teacher is talking. |

The *wh-* word is the subject.

In questions about the subject, we usually use **is** (not *are*).
✗ Who **are** talking?

**16 | Forming *Wh-* Questions with the Present Progressive** Write present progressive questions with a *wh-* word from the box and the words in parentheses. Then listen and check your answers.  `7.4 A`

| what | who | where | how | why |

**ROOMMATE CONVERSATIONS**

1.  A: _What are you doing?_____?
        (you / do)

    B: Just playing a video game. _____?
                                          (you / ask)

    A: Because we're going to the gym now. Come with us!

2.  A: _____ to?
           (Brianna / talk)

    B: The neighbor from downstairs. He's complaining about us.

    A: _____?
           (he / complain)

    B: Because he thinks our TV is too loud.

3.  A: _____ today?
           (you / feel)

    B: I'm still feeling sick. Stay away from me. You don't want this cold!

4.  A: _____ these days? We never see you.
           (you / study)

    B: In the library. I'm working on a psychology paper.

    A: _____ about?
           (you / write)

    B: The eating habits of children and teenagers.

5.  A: _____?
           (Elise and Perri / go)

    B: They're going downtown for dinner. But I'm making dinner here. Do you want to join me?

    A: _____? It smells good!
           (you / make)

    B: I'm making lasagna.

6.  A: _____ in English?
           (you / do)

    B: I'm doing OK. But I'm worried about my group project. It's due on Monday.

    A: _____ with?
           (you / work)

    B: Seiko and Reema. And we're never free at the same time.

**17 | Pronunciation Note: Contractions with *Wh-* Words** Listen to the note. Then do Activity 18.

In conversation and in informal writing, we often contract **is** after a ***wh-*** word:

**1 How is** she feeling? ➜ "**How's** she feeling?"

**2 Who is** talking? ➜ "**Who's** talking?"

In conversation, we also contract ***are*** after a ***wh-*** word.

**3 Who are** you talking to? ➜ "**Who're** you talking to?"

**4 Where are** they going? ➜ "**Where're** they going?"

It's often difficult to hear the **'s** or **'re**.

**18 | Understanding Contractions with *Wh-* Words** Listen and complete the questions. Write the full form of the words you hear. Then choose the correct answer for each question. `7.4 A`

1. <u>*Where is*</u> he going?
   - (a.) To school.
   - b. Right now.
   - c. Because he's tired.

2. _____ you going?
   - a. Because it's late.
   - b. To school.
   - c. On the bus.

3. _____ you eating?
   - a. In the kitchen.
   - b. Soup and salad.
   - c. We're hungry!

4. _____ they traveling?
   - a. They're traveling for 2 months.
   - b. They're taking the train.
   - c. They have vacation now.

5. _____ they playing?
   - a. At a football stadium.
   - b. Soccer.
   - c. Manchester United.

6. _____ you standing?
   - a. For almost an hour.
   - b. There aren't any seats.
   - c. At the corner of Main Street.

7. _____ happening?
   - a. It's in a few minutes.
   - b. It's at the student center.
   - c. Jason and Matt are arguing.

8. _____ buying it?
   - a. Only when it's on sale.
   - b. At the store near us.
   - c. Because it tastes really good on bread.

9. _____ we forgetting?
   - a. The bread—we need some bread.
   - b. Aunt Martha— send her an invitation.
   - c. Because we're so tired!

10. _____ you painting the room?
    - a. Because the walls are so dirty!
    - b. Blue—it's my favorite color.
    - c. Today and tomorrow.

11. _____ talking on the phone?
    - a. Liam.
    - b. About Liam.
    - c. To Liam.

**Talk about It** Practice the conversations above with a partner. Contract the *wh-* word and *is* or *are*.

**19 | Forming *Wh-* Questions about the Subject** Complete each question with *who* or *what* and a verb from the box. Use the present progressive with contractions. Then listen and check your answers. `7.4 B`

1. Sandra: _____<u>*What's cooking*</u>_____ in that big pot?
   Lisa: It's a Spanish fish soup.

2. Sandra: _____ at the movie theater?
   Lisa: Some really old horror movies⁹—*Godzilla* and *King Kong*.

3. Lisa: _____ in the movie?
   Sandra: He's still climbing the mountain. It's snowing a lot now.

| cook |
| happen |
| play |

⁹**horror movies:** scary movies

PRESENT PROGRESSIVE   179

4. Sandra: _____?

   Lisa: My neighbor. She's a singer, and she practices a lot.

5. Sandra: _____ that noise?

   Lisa: The refrigerator. It's old and really noisy.

6. Lisa: Do you know of any apartments for rent?

   Sandra: There's one in this building. _____ for an apartment?

   Lisa: My friend Joelle.

7. Sandra: _____? I smell smoke.

   Lisa: Oh, no! The chocolate cake! It's still in the oven!

8. Lisa: _____ the game?

   Sandra: Real Madrid. The score is 1–0.

9. Sandra: Your phone is ringing. _____ so late?

   Lisa: It's probably a wrong number.

## 20 | Using Present Progressive Questions in Conversation  Complete the questions in the chart. Use the words to write *wh-* questions with the present progressive. Use contractions with *is*.  7.4 A–B

CONVERSATIONAL QUESTIONS

| Question | Meaning | Possible Answers |
|---|---|---|
| 1. how / everything / go<br>*How's everything going*  ? | "How are you?" | Great!<br>Pretty well.<br>Not bad.<br>OK.<br>Not great. |
| 2. how / it / go<br>_____ ? | | |
| 3. how / you / do<br>_____ ? | | |
| 4. what / you / do / these days<br>_____ ? | "Tell me about your life." | Not much.<br>I'm taking classes and … |
| 5. what / happen / with you<br>_____ ? | | |
| 6. what / go on<br>_____ ? | | |

**Think about It**  Which two questions above are *wh-* questions about the subject?

**Talk about It**  Ask and answer the questions above with a partner.

*A: How's everything going?*
*B: Pretty well.*

## 21 | Asking and Answering Questions with the Present Progressive  Look at the pictures. What are the people saying? Write questions and answers with the present progressive. Use the verbs in the box.  `7.4 A–B`

| argue about | eat | go | happen | look for | talk to |
|---|---|---|---|---|---|

1.  A: _What are you looking for?_

    B: _I'm looking for my wedding ring._

2.  A: _____

    B: _____

3.  A: _____

    B: _____

4.  A: _____

    B: _____

5.  A: _____

    B: _____

6.  A: _____

    B: _____

## 22 | Error Correction  Find and correct the errors. (Some sentences might not have any errors.)

1.  A: Joaquin and Rafael eating lunch now?
    B: No, they always eat lunch late.

2.  A: Who are they talking to?
    B: Their boss.

3.  A: Am I getting the answer right?
    B: Yes, you're.

4.  A: What we are forgetting now?
    B: Nothing!

5.  A: Who are taking the class with you?
    B: My friends Matt and Henry.

6.  A: Why Abel leaving early today?
    B: Because he's sick.

7.  A: What is it happening?
    B: I don't know.

8.  A: Where they going?
    B: To the mall.

## 7.5 Simple Present vs. Present Progressive

**A**

### SIMPLE PRESENT

For **simple present** positive statements, we use the **base form of a verb** or the base form + **-s** / **-es**.

We use **do** / **does** in negative statements and questions.

#### POSITIVE STATEMENTS

1 I **work** at a school.
2 Sam **works** five days a week.

#### NEGATIVE STATEMENTS

5 We **don't work** here.
6 The computer **doesn't work**.

#### YES/NO QUESTIONS AND SHORT ANSWERS

9 A: **Do** you **work** here?
   B: Yes, I **do**.
10 A: **Does** Paul **work** at a restaurant?
   B: No, he **doesn't**.

#### WH- QUESTIONS

13 A: Where **do** you **work**?
   B: At the bank.
14 A: Who **works** here?
   B: Jim works here.

### PRESENT PROGRESSIVE

For the **present progressive**, we always use a form of **be** (**am** / **is** / **are**) and the **-ing** form of a verb.

3 I'm **working**. Please be quiet.
4 Sam **is working** right now.

7 Carla **isn't working**.
8 My parents **aren't working** these days.

11 A: **Is** Sam **working**?
   B: Yes, he **is**.
12 A: **Are** your roommates **working**?
   B: No, they **aren't**.

15 A: Where **is** Jim **working** these days?
   B: At an office downtown.
16 A: Who **is working** now?
   B: The manager is working.

> Questions about the subject

For more information about the simple present, see Unit 3.

**B**

### COMMON USES OF THE SIMPLE PRESENT

Facts (things that are generally true):
17 Water **freezes** at 32° F (0° C).

Habits and routines:
18 I usually **eat** three meals a day.

We often use these **frequency expressions** with the simple present:

| | | |
|---|---|---|
| always | sometimes | every day / week / month… |
| usually | hardly ever | once / twice / three times a day / week / month… |
| often | never | |

For more information about adverbs of frequency and other frequency expressions, see Unit 3, pages 53 and 64.

### COMMON USES OF THE PRESENT PROGRESSIVE

Things happening right now (at the moment):
19 I'm **looking** for my keys.

Things happening now (these days):
20 Lisa **is taking** three classes this semester.

We often use these **time expressions** with the present progressive:

| | |
|---|---|
| now | today |
| right now | these days |
| at the moment | this week / month / semester / year… |

182

**🔊 23 | Identifying Simple Present and Present Progressive Verbs** Listen and complete the conversations with the missing words. Then check (✓) *simple present* or *present progressive* for each question or statement. **7.5 A**

|  | SIMPLE PRESENT | PRESENT PROGRESSIVE |
|---|---|---|
| 1. A: What ___is___ your dad ___watching___? |  | ✓ |
| B: The news. He always _____ the 7:00 news. | ☐ | ☐ |
| 2. A: _____ you _____ large bags of rice here? | ☐ | ☐ |
| B: No, we _____. Sorry! | ☐ | ☐ |
| 3. A: _____ you _____ notes? | ☐ | ☐ |
| B: No, I _____ just _____ a silly picture. | ☐ | ☐ |
| 4. A: Ouch! These bugs _____ me. | ☐ | ☐ |
| _____ they _____ you? | ☐ | ☐ |
| B: No, they _____. | ☐ | ☐ |
| Bugs never _____ me! | ☐ | ☐ |
| 5. A: What _____ Felix _____ here? | ☐ | ☐ |
| B: He _____ tickets. | ☐ | ☐ |
| He _____ a lot of money. | ☐ | ☐ |
| But he _____ a football game every weekend! | ☐ | ☐ |
| 6. A: Those children _____ their food now. | ☐ | ☐ |
| And their parents _____ anything! | ☐ | ☐ |
| B: Some parents _____ their children any manners¹⁰! | ☐ | ☐ |
| 7. A: How _____ you _____, Mrs. Paulson? | ☐ | ☐ |
| B: Pretty good. The diet _____! | ☐ | ☐ |
| I _____ weight. | ☐ | ☐ |
| 8. A: _____ you _____ that report now? | ☐ | ☐ |
| B: No, _____ still _____ on it. | ☐ | ☐ |
| These reports sometimes _____ a long time! | ☐ | ☐ |
| 9. A: _____ you _____ any evening classes this semester? | ☐ | ☐ |
| B: No, I _____. | ☐ | ☐ |
| I _____ my parents with their restaurant. | ☐ | ☐ |

**Talk about It** Talk with a partner. Where does each conversation above take place?

**Think about It** Underline the time expressions and frequency expressions in the conversations above.

*He <u>always</u> watches the 7:00 news.*

---

¹⁰**manners:** behavior that is acceptable or polite

**24 | Forming Simple Present and Present Progressive Statements and Questions** Complete the conversations with the simple present or the present progressive form of the verbs in parentheses. Use the verb form in the box. Use *do, does, is, am,* or *are* where necessary. `7.5 A`

1. A: _Do_ you _shop_ here often?
   (shop)

   B: Yes, all the time! It's my favorite store.

   | simple present |

2. A: What _____ you _____?
   (do)

   B: I _____ my friend. We _____ plans for this evening.
   (text)                      (make)

   | present progressive |

3. A: Dad, where _____ all these butterflies _____ in the fall?
   (go)

   B: They _____ from Canada all the way to Mexico!
   (fly)

   | simple present |

4. A: _____ prices _____ higher these days?
   (get)

   B: Probably. I _____ more money.
   (spend)

   | present progressive |

5. A: What _____ you _____?
   (do)

   B: I _____ in a law office. And sometimes I _____
   (work)                                    (teach)

   Spanish classes in the evenings.

   | simple present |

6. A: What _____ Ali _____ these days?
   (do)

   B: He _____ articles for a new website.
   (write)

   | present progressive |

7. A: _____ it _____ a lot in Miami?
   (rain)

   B: Yes, it _____ all the time, especially in the summer!
   (rain)

   | simple present |

8. A: Who _____ Petra _____ to?
   (talk)

   B. Someone from work. They _____ a project.
   (discuss)

   | present progressive |

**Think about It** Why do conversations 1, 3, 5, and 7 use the simple present? Why do conversations 2, 4, 6, and 8 use the present progressive?

**25 | Using the Simple Present and the Present Progressive** Complete the sentences with the simple present or present progressive form of the verbs in parentheses. `7.5 B`

# AN INTERVIEW WITH AN OCEANOGRAPHER

1. Q: What is oceanography? What do oceanographers study?

   A: Oceanographers _study_ the oceans and their plants and animals.
   (study)

2. Q: Where do you live?

   A: I usually _____ in San Diego, California. But this year I _____
   (live)                                              (live)

   on a ship! This month we _____ in the Pacific Ocean.
   (sail)

3. Q: Does it get lonely there?

   A: No. We often _____ with our friends and family. And right now
   (communicate)

   I _____ to you!
   (talk)

4. Q: Do you work long hours? What are you doing?

   A: We usually _____ for 12-hour periods. These days
                    (work)
      we _____ lots of samples[11] from the ocean.
              (collect)

5. Q: Why are oceans so important?

   A: Oceans _____ almost 75% of our planet!
                    (cover)
      So our planet always _____ healthy oceans.
                                  (need)
      These days human activities _____ our oceans.
                                          (change)
      So now we _____ more about these changes.
                      (learn)

an oceanographer

**Think about It**  Underline the adverbs of frequency and time expressions in the activity above. How do they help you decide between the simple present and the present progressive?

## 7.6 Action Verbs and Non-Action Verbs

**ACTION VERBS**

Many verbs are **action verbs**. They show the action of the subject. Here are some common action verbs:

| | | | | | | |
|---|---|---|---|---|---|---|
| ask | drink | go | plan | run | speak | tell |
| bring | drive | laugh | play | say | study | walk |
| buy | eat | learn | read | show | take | work |
| come | get | move | relax | sleep | talk | write |

We can use action verbs with the **simple present** or the **present progressive**.

**FACTS, HABITS, AND ROUTINES (SIMPLE PRESENT)**

1 We **drive** to school every day.

2 I usually **study** in the evening.

3 Abdul **speaks** English.

**THINGS HAPPENING NOW OR THESE DAYS (PRESENT PROGRESSIVE)**

4 We're **driving** to school now.

5 I'm **studying** a lot these days.

6 Abdul **is speaking** more English these days.

**NON-ACTION VERBS**

**A**  These verbs are often non-action verbs:

| FEELINGS | THOUGHTS | SENSES | NEEDS / PREFERENCES | POSSESSION | MEASUREMENTS | DESCRIPTIONS |
|---|---|---|---|---|---|---|
| dislike | believe | feel | need | belong | cost | be |
| feel* | know | hear | prefer | have | weigh | look |
| hate | think | see | want | own | | seem |
| like | understand | smell | | | | |
| love | | taste | | | | |

We usually use non-action verbs with the **simple present**. We rarely use them with the present progressive.

✓It **doesn't belong** to me.      ✗ It's **not belonging** to me.

✓I **want** some coffee.      ✗ I'm **wanting** some coffee.

*We sometimes use *feel* with the present progressive. The present progressive often means something is changing.

7 I'm **feeling** a little better today.

---

[11] **samples:**  a small amount of something that shows how the rest is

**26 | Listening for Action Verbs and Non-Action Verbs** Listen and complete the conversations with the verbs you hear. Then check *action verb* or *non-action verb*. Then practice the conversations with a partner. **7.6 A**

|  | | ACTION VERB | NON-ACTION VERB |
|---|---|:---:|:---:|
| 1. | A: Who is that? <br> B: That's Flora. She _____*speaks*_____ eight languages! | ☑ | ☐ |
| 2. | A: Oh, now I _____! <br> B: See? It's easy! | ☐ | ☑ |
| 3. | A: Young children always _____ rules. <br> B: You're right. But they always break the rules. | ☐ | ☐ |
| 4. | A: You _____ tired today. <br> B: I am tired. I'm working a lot this week. | ☐ | ☐ |
| 5. | A: Where's Javier? <br> B: He _____ an exam now. | ☐ | ☐ |
| 6. | A: You _____ great in that new dress! <br> B: Thanks! | ☐ | ☐ |
| 7. | A: I _____ lunch now. Can I call you back later? <br> B: OK. | ☐ | ☐ |
| 8. | A: Many people _____ broccoli. <br> B: Not me. I love it! | ☐ | ☐ |
| 9. | A: Are you sleeping well? <br> B: Yeah. I usually _____ for about 8 hours. | ☐ | ☐ |
| 10. | A: What do we need for dessert? <br> B: Let's get ice cream. Everyone _____ ice cream. | ☐ | ☐ |
| 11. | A: The sunset _____ beautiful tonight! <br> B: You're right. It's so colorful! | ☐ | ☐ |
| 12. | A: I _____ the winter. I _____ summer. <br> B: Not me. I like the cold! | ☐ | ☐ |
| 13. | A: We _____ to the beach every summer. <br> B: Where do you go? | ☐ | ☐ |
| 14. | A: My brother _____ video games every night. <br> B: Do you play with him? | ☐ | ☐ |
| 15. | A: What are you doing? <br> B: Right now we _____ the furniture. | ☐ | ☐ |
| 16. | A: I _____ your phone. It's under the table. <br> B: Oh, thanks! | ☐ | ☐ |
| 17. | A: Colin and Vika _____ across France now. <br> B: That sounds amazing! | ☐ | ☐ |
| 18. | A: Simone _____ a different email address now. <br> B: Can you give it to me? | ☐ | ☐ |

**Think about It**  Over each answer in Activity 26, write *SP* for simple present or *PP* for present progressive.

SP
*She speaks eight languages!*

## 27 | Using Action Verbs and Non-Action Verbs  Complete the conversations with the verbs in the box. Use the simple present or the present progressive. Use *do*, *does*, *am*, *is*, or *are* where necessary. Then label each main verb *A* (action) or *NA* (non-action).  `7.6 A`

1. A: It __'s__ (NA) late! Why __are__ you still __working__ (A)?

   B: I _____ for a test tomorrow morning.

   | be |
   | work |
   | study |

2. A: _____ Gina _____ a dessert today?

   B: I _____ so.

   | bring |
   | think |

3. A: What _____ you _____?

   It _____ good!

   B: It _____ the special sandwich. It _____ good!

   | eat |
   | look |
   | be |
   | taste |

4. A: How many languages _____ you _____?

   B: Two—Arabic and English. And I _____ French now.

   | know |
   | learn |

5. A: Where _____ you usually _____?

   B: In the library. It _____ quiet there!

   | study |
   | be |

6. A: I _____ your hat!

   B: Thanks!

   A: You always _____ interesting hats.

   Where _____ you _____ them?

   B: At that little store on 3ʳᵈ Street.

   | love |
   | have |
   | buy |

7. A: Why _____ you _____?

   B: I _____ sick. I _____ home.

   | leave |
   | feel |
   | go |

8. A: _____ you _____ your house?

   B: No, we don't. Houses here _____ a lot of money.

   | own |
   | cost |

**Think about It** In one of the conversations in Activity 27, there is one verb we can use with the simple present *or* the present progressive. Which verb is it?

🔊 **Talk about It** Listen and check your answers. Then practice the conversations with a partner.

**28 | Usage Note: *Think, Have,* and *Look*** Read the note. Then do Activity 29.

Some verbs like **think**, **have**, and **look** can be action verbs or non-action verbs.

**NON-ACTION MEANING**

When verbs have a **non-action meaning**, we usually use the **simple present**.

| 1 | I **think** he's nice. | = In my opinion, he's nice. |
| 2 | We **have** a car. | = We possess / own a car. |
| 3 | You **look** tired. | = I think you're tired. |

Notice: We can use **look** + an adjective.

**ACTION MEANING**

| THINK ABOUT | HAVE A GOOD / GREAT TIME | LOOK AT | LOOK FOR |
|---|---|---|---|
| **4** A: What are you **thinking** about? B: The test. | **5** I'm **having** a great time at the park! | **6** A: What are you **looking** at? B: There's a beautiful bird over there. | **7** A: What are you **looking** for? B: My keys. |

Notice: When these verbs have an **action meaning**, we can use them with the **present progressive** or the **simple present**.

**PRESENT PROGRESSIVE: HAPPENING NOW**

**8a** I'm **thinking** about my brother.

**9a** We're **having** a great time.

**10a** What is he **looking** at?

**SIMPLE PRESENT: HABITS AND ROUTINES**

**8b** I often **think** about my brother.

**9b** We always **have** a great time together.

**10b** You always **look** at your phone.

**29 | Understanding *Think, Have,* and *Look*** Read the conversations. Notice the form and the meaning of the **bold** verbs. Check (✓) the correct column.  `7.6 A`

| CONVERSATIONS AT SCHOOL | ACTION MEANING, PRESENT PROGRESSIVE | ACTION MEANING, SIMPLE PRESENT | NON-ACTION MEANING, SIMPLE PRESENT |
|---|---|---|---|
| 1. A: What **are** you **thinking** about? You look worried.<br>B: I don't know. Maybe about exams next week. | ✓ | ☐ | ☐ |
| 2. A: **Do** you **have** a smartphone?<br>B: No, I just **have** an old cellphone. | ☐ | ☐ | ☐ |
| 3. A: Is the new psychology teacher good?<br>B: Yeah, I really **think** so. | ☐ | ☐ | ☐ |
| 4. A: I'**m looking** for Smith Hall. Is it near here?<br>B: Sure! It's that big red brick building. | ☐ | ☐ | ☐ |
| 5. A: Your sneakers **look** old!<br>B: You're right! I need a new pair. | ☐ | ☐ | ☐ |
| 6. A: Do you usually stay in the city for the summer?<br>B: No. My parents always rent a house at the beach. My brothers and sisters and I all go. We **have** a great time! | ☐ | ☐ | ☐ |
| 7. A: Does Jason speak Spanish?<br>B: I **don't think** so. But I'm not sure. | ☐ | ☐ | ☐ |
| 8. A: What **are** you **looking** at?<br>B: A list of classes for next semester. I need a science class. | ☐ | ☐ | ☐ |
| 9. A: Why are you reading your essay again?<br>B: I always read my essays twice. The second time I **look** for grammar errors. | ☐ | ☐ | ☐ |
| 10. A: It's my mom … Hi, Mom!<br>B: How are you doing? We miss you!<br>A: I miss you and Dad too. I **think** about you every day! | ☐ | ☐ | ☐ |

**Write about It** Complete the sentences with your own ideas.

I'm having _____.

I have _____.

I'm thinking about _____.

I think _____.

**30 | Describing Actions and Feelings**  Look at the pictures. Write three sentences for each picture. Describe what the people are doing and how the people feel. Use the action verbs and non-action verbs from the box.  **7.6 A**

| | ACTION VERBS | | | NON-ACTION VERBS | |
|---|---|---|---|---|---|
| argue | have (a good time) | sit | think (about) | be | want |
| drink | help | smile | wear | love | see |
| eat | run | talk | | know | understand |

1.

2.

3.

4.

5.

6.

1. *The child is running to his mother.*

**Talk about It**  Find an interesting picture online or in a newspaper or magazine. Describe the picture with a partner.

## 31 | Error Correction  Find and correct the errors. (Some sentences may not have any errors.)

1. That pen is belong to Jamal.
2. We're having a new car.
3. Najati and I are eating lunch in the cafeteria.
4. I talk on the phone right now.
5. The children are seeming bored today.
6. I know the answer.
7. Who working late today?
8. He's feeling a little sick at the moment.
9. Annika studies a lot this week.
10. I make dinner now.

11. Are you believing him?
12. I always am eating three meals a day.
13. The temperature 32°F is equaling 0°C.
14. This shirt is costing a lot!
15. I'm thinking about my work now.
16. I call Joachim now.
17. Thanks, but I am not needing help.
18. I look at the questions now.
19. We always have a lot of fun here.
20. Alison is wanting a new car.

---

# WRAP-UP

**A | GRAMMAR IN READING**  Read the interview. Underline the present progressive verbs. Circle the simple present verbs.

## An Interview with Josh Neufeld

Q: Thanks for the interview, Josh. Tell me: What do you do?

A: I'm a comic book writer and artist. I write nonfiction[12] comic books.
I write and draw stories about real people in different parts of the world.

Q: What are you working on these days?

A: I'm working on an idea for a new book. I'm researching[13] the story.
It's an interesting story. But is it a good story for a comic book?
I don't know. I'm interviewing people and thinking about this question.

Q: What are you doing today? Are you working on the new story?

A: No, I'm drawing pictures for another writer's story. Sometimes I just
draw the pictures for a story.

Q: What's happening with comic books these days?

A: Comic books are changing a lot! Comics today aren't just for kids.
Many people are telling serious stories with comics. More adults are
buying and reading comics. Teachers are using comics in their classes.

A self-portrait of
Josh Neufeld

---

[12] **nonfiction:** writing that is about real people, events, and facts

[13] **researching:** studying something carefully to find out more about it

Q: Do you like your work? What do you like about it?

A: I love my work! It's really fun! I tell important stories and change people's ideas about comics.

Q: What is difficult about your work?

A: Well, some days I don't have good ideas. Sometimes I draw, and my drawings don't seem right.

**Write about It** Answer these questions about the interview. Write sentences with the simple present and the present progressive.

1. What work does Josh do?
2. What is Josh doing these days?
3. How does Josh feel about his work?
4. What are comic book writers doing differently these days?

**B | GRAMMAR IN SPEAKING** Interview someone (outside the class or in the class) about their job. Ask these questions and two questions of your own. Write the person's answers in the chart. Then tell the person's story to the class.

| An Interview with _____ | |
|---|---|
| **Questions** | **Answers** |
| 1. What do you do? | |
| 2. What are you doing in your work these days? | |
| 3. Is your work changing? How is it changing? | |
| 4. Are you working a lot these days? | |
| 5. Are you enjoying your work these days? | |
| 6. What do you like about your work? | |
| 7. What do you dislike about your work? | |
| 8. | |
| 9. | |

**USES**

We use the **present progressive** to talk about things happening now or continuing: this could be at the moment of speaking or over a longer time.

I'm **studying** math right now.

I'm **studying** a lot these days.

**POSITIVE STATEMENTS**

| | | |
|---|---|---|
| I | am<br>'m | waiting. |
| You<br>We<br>They | are<br>'re | |
| He<br>She<br>It | is<br>'s | |

**NEGATIVE STATEMENTS**

| | | |
|---|---|---|
| I | am not<br>'m not | waiting. |
| You<br>We<br>They | are not<br>'re not<br>aren't | |
| He<br>She<br>It | is not<br>'s not<br>isn't | |

*YES/NO* **QUESTIONS**

| | | |
|---|---|---|
| Am | I | helping? |
| Are | you | |
| Is | he<br>she<br>it | |

**SHORT ANSWERS**

| | | |
|---|---|---|
| Yes, | you<br>we<br>they | are. |
| No, | | aren't.<br>'re not. |
| Yes, | I | am. |
| No, | | 'm not. |
| Yes, | he<br>she<br>it | is. |
| No, | | isn't<br>'s not. |

*WH-* **QUESTIONS**

| | | | |
|---|---|---|---|
| **What** | am | I | doing? |
| **Who** | are | you<br>we<br>they | seeing? |
| **Where** | | | going? |
| **How** | is | he<br>she<br>it | doing? |
| **Why** | | | leaving? |

*WH-* **QUESTIONS ABOUT THE SUBJECT**

| | | |
|---|---|---|
| **What** | is | happening? |
| **Who** | | working? |

**ACTION VERBS AND NON-ACTION VERBS**

We can use the **simple present** or **present progressive** with action verbs.

I usually **drive** to school.     I'm **driving** to school now.

We usually use the **simple present** with non-action verbs.

✓ I **dislike** buses.     X I'm **disliking** buses.

# 8

# Simple Past

**GO ONLINE**

For the Unit Vocabulary Check, go to the Online Practice.

## IN THIS UNIT, WE USE the simple past to:

### Talk about past events and situations

1. We **cooked** dinner last night.

2. We **didn't do** the dishes.

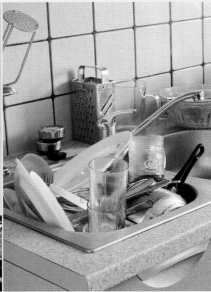

3. I **went** to a concert last weekend.

4. There **were** a lot of people there.

5. My parents **moved** to Seattle ten years ago.

6. They **opened** a restaurant in 2012.

7. I **was** a shy child.

8. My sister **had** a lot of books.

**Think about It** Read these sentences. Check (✓) *True* or *False*.

|  | TRUE | FALSE |
|---|---|---|
| 1. I cooked dinner last night. | ☐ | ☐ |
| 2. I did the dishes last night. | ☐ | ☐ |
| 3. I went to a concert last weekend. | ☐ | ☐ |
| 4. I moved to a new city a few years ago. | ☐ | ☐ |
| 5. I was a shy child. | ☐ | ☐ |

## 8.1 Positive Statements with the Simple Past

**A**

To form the **simple past**, we add **-ed** or **-d** to the base form of most verbs*.

1 I **worked** yesterday.

2 Jack **called** the doctor this morning.

3 We **enjoyed** the movie a lot.

4 You **exercised** three times last week.

| BASE FORM | SIMPLE PAST FORM |
|-----------|------------------|
| work | work**ed** |
| call | call**ed** |
| enjoy | enjoy**ed** |
| exercise | exercise**d** |

Notice: The simple past form is the same for all subjects (*I, he, they*, etc.).

*Simple past verbs that end in *-ed* are called **regular** simple past verbs. For irregular verbs, see Chart 8.2.

**B**

**TIME EXPRESSIONS**

We often use **time expressions** to refer to a specific time in the past.

| MON | TUE | WED | THU | FRI | SAT | SUN |
|-----|-----|-----|-----|-----|-----|-----|
| | | | **last** Thursday | a week **ago** | **last** weekend | |
| **on** Monday | | two days **ago** | **yesterday** **last** night | TODAY | | |

| | 6:00–11:00 a.m. | 1:00–5:00 p.m. | 6:00–9:00 p.m. | 10:00 p.m. |
|-----|-----|-----|-----|-----|
| TODAY | **this** morning | **this** afternoon | **this** evening **tonight** | NOW |

5 I **talked** to Leila **yesterday**.

6 She **applied** for the job **last week**.

7 They **replied** **this morning**.

8 I **worked** **on Saturday**.

9 My sister **arrived** **at noon**.

10 I **finished** my paper **around 10:00**.

11 Mark **moved** to Boston **three years ago**.

| yesterday | | |
|-----------|---|---|
| **last** | + | **night / week / Tuesday / weekend / month / year** |
| **this** | + | **morning / afternoon / evening** |
| **on** | + | **Wednesday / Friday / Saturday** |
| **at** | + | **8 a.m. / noon / 4:30** |
| **around** | + | **10:00 / noon / 6:45** |

| **two days / a week / five years** | + | **ago** |
|---|---|---|

GO ONLINE

**1 | Noticing the Simple Past of Regular Verbs** Underline the simple past verbs that end in *-ed*. Then complete each fact with the correct celebrity on page 197. **8.1 A**

BEFORE THEY WERE FAMOUS

1. _Madonna_____ <u>worked</u> at a donut shop. She started her singing career in the 1980s.

2. _____ dressed up as a chicken for a fast-food restaurant. Now he's an actor.

He performed¹ in the films *Fight Club* and *World War Z*.

¹ **perform (past form performed):** to be in something such as a play, movie, or other show

3. _____ served ice cream at an ice cream shop. Now he's a politician[2].

4. _____ performed for children at birthday parties. He was a clown. Now he's an actor. He played Wolverine in the *X-Men* movies.

5. _____ studied business at the London School of Economics. He also worked in a hospital. He earned about $7.80 per hour. Now he's a singer. He joined the Rolling Stones (the band) in 1962.

6. _____ fixed airplanes for the U.S. Air Force. Now he's an actor. He starred[3] in *Driving Miss Daisy* and the *Batman* movies.

7. _____ worked at her mother's hair salon. Now she's a very famous singer.

8. _____ worked in a hotel. He carried people's suitcases to their rooms. Now he's an actor. He starred in *Top Gun*, *Minority Report*, and the *Mission: Impossible* movies.

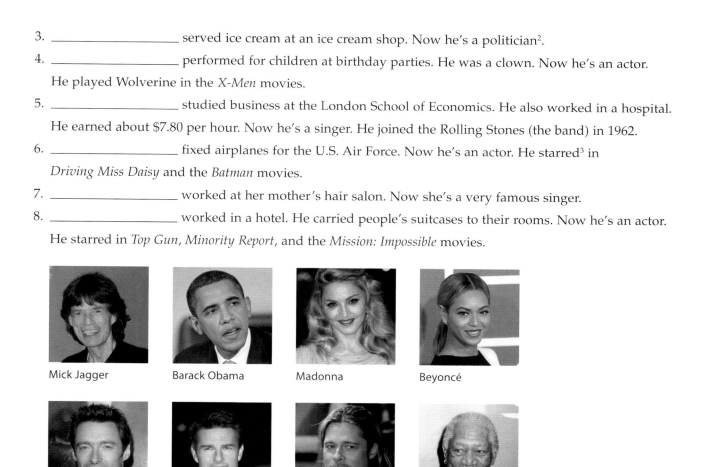

Mick Jagger   Barack Obama   Madonna   Beyoncé

Hugh Jackman   Tom Cruise   Brad Pitt   Morgan Freeman

**Talk about It**  Which facts in Activity 1 surprise you?

## 2 | Spelling Note: *-ed* Verb Endings  Read the note. Then do Activity 3.

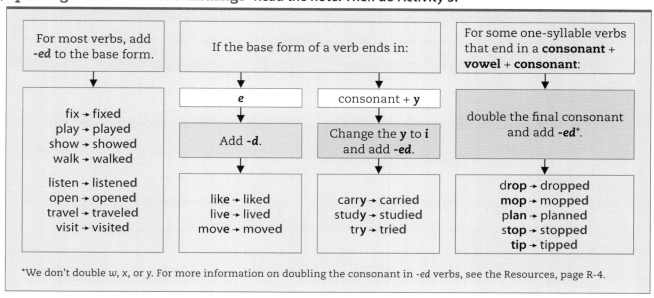

| For most verbs, add *-ed* to the base form. | If the base form of a verb ends in: | | For some one-syllable verbs that end in a **consonant** + **vowel** + **consonant**: |
|---|---|---|---|
| ↓ | *e* | consonant + *y* | ↓ |
| fix → fixed<br>play → played<br>show → showed<br>walk → walked | ↓<br>Add *-d*. | ↓<br>Change the *y* to *i* and add *-ed*. | double the final consonant and add *-ed\**. |
| listen → listened<br>open → opened<br>travel → traveled<br>visit → visited | ↓<br>like → liked<br>live → lived<br>move → moved | ↓<br>carry → carried<br>study → studied<br>try → tried | ↓<br>d**rop** → dropped<br>m**op** → mopped<br>pl**an** → planned<br>st**op** → stopped<br>t**ip** → tipped |

*We don't double *w*, *x*, or *y*. For more information on doubling the consonant in *-ed* verbs, see the Resources, page R-4.

[2] **politician:**  someone who works in politics (government)

[3] **star (past form *starred*):**  to be the main actor in a play or movie

**3 | Spelling Regular Simple Past Verbs** Write the simple past form of these verbs in the correct part of the chart below.

| | | | | | | | | | |
|---|---|---|---|---|---|---|---|---|---|
| add | call | drop | finish | hurry | need | shave | stop | tip | wait |
| apply | carry | dry | fix | learn | plan | smile | study | try | want |
| arrive | cry | enjoy | grade | live | practice | start | talk | visit | watch |
| ask | decide | explore | help | mop | reply | stay | taste | vote | work |

| Add -ed | Add -d | Change the *y* to *i* and add -ed | Double the final consonant and add -ed |
|---|---|---|---|
| *added* | | | |

**Write about It** Write three sentences about things you did recently. Use the verbs in the chart above and the time expressions in this box.

| | | |
|---|---|---|
| last night | this morning | yesterday |

*I called my parents last night.*

**4 | Using the Simple Past** Complete this email with the simple past form of the verbs in parentheses.

`8.1 A`

**To:** Stella

**Subject:** Thanks for everything!

Hi Stella,

Thanks for letting me stay here this weekend. I _____*spilled*_____ orange juice all over the carpet this
(1. spill)

morning. Sorry! I _____ to clean the carpet, but there's a stain⁴. I _____ the sofa
(2. try)                                                                (3. move)

to cover the stain.

I _____ the kitchen this morning. I _____ the dishes and _____
(4. clean)                          (5. wash)                          (6. mop)

the floor. I _____ breakfast for you, too! It's in the oven. I _____ some eggs
(7. cook)                                                      (8. drop)

behind the oven. Sorry! But I _____ the sink for you!
(9. fix)

I don't need a ride to the airport. I know you're tired. I _____ a taxi for 6 a.m. Oh, and I
(10. call)

_____ $40 from your wallet. I hope that's OK.
(11. borrow)

⁴**stain:** a spot or a mark

I really _____ the weekend! Let's do this again sometime soon!
(12. enjoy)

See you soon,

Samantha

P.S. Someone _____ you yesterday. I don't remember who. Your boss, maybe? Also, a
(13. call)
package _____ for you two days ago. It's in the kitchen.
(14. arrive)

**Talk about It** Do you think Stella wants Samantha to come to her house again soon? Why or why not?

**5 | Pronunciation Note: -ed Verb Endings** Listen to the note. Then do Activity 6.

Notice how we pronounce the **-ed** ending on simple past verbs.

| If the base form of a verb ends in the sound: | The **-ed** ending *sounds like:* |
|---|---|
| /f/ | coughed, laughed |
| /k/ | liked, talked |
| /p/ | ripped, stopped |
| /s/ | missed, passed |
| /ks/ | fixed, mixed |
| /tʃ/ | touched, watched |
| /ʃ/ | crashed, washed |

The **-ed** ending sounds like: **/t/**

| If the base form of a verb ends in the sound: | The **-ed** ending *sounds like:* |
|---|---|
| /b/ | grabbed, robbed |
| /g/ | bagged, jogged |
| /dʒ/ | aged, managed |
| /l/ | called, filed |
| /m/ | climbed, timed |
| /n/ | cleaned, signed |
| /r/ | cared, explored |
| /v/ | arrived, moved |
| /z/ | raised, realized |
| a vowel sound | carried, played |

The **-ed** ending sounds like: **/d/**

| | | |
|---|---|---|
| /d/ | decided, faded | /əd/ = "id" |
| /t/ | started, waited | |

**6 | Pronouncing Regular Simple Past Verbs** Underline the simple past verbs in these conversations. Check (✓) the correct pronunciation for each *-ed* ending. `8.1 A`

|  | /t/ | /d/ | /əd/ |
|---|---|---|---|
| 1. A: How's work? <br> B: Not great. I <u>applied</u> for a new job last week. <br> A: Oh, no! Why? <br> B: I don't feel comfortable there. The people are unfriendly. | ☐ | ☐ | ☐ |
| 2. A: Is Marcus OK? <br> B: I think so. Why? <br> A: He seemed sad this morning. | ☐ | ☐ | ☐ |

|  | /t/ | /d/ | /əd/ |
|---|---|---|---|

3. A: Are you ready for the history midterm?

   B: I think so. I studied all night long.

   A: Me too.

4. A: How are you?

   B: I'm really busy. I started school last week.

5. A: I'm so tired today.

   B: Why?

   A: I watched a movie until 3 a.m.

6. A: Where's your car?

   B: It's at home. I walked to work today.

7. A: Hey there. You're late.

   B: I know. I missed my bus this morning.

8. A: Are you sick?

   B: Yeah, I have a cold. I stayed home from work today.

9. A: I have good news. I passed my driving test!

   B: Oh, that's great! Congratulations!

10. A: You're a great guitar player.

    B: Thanks. Do you play any instruments?

    A: I played the guitar in high school. I don't really play it now.

11. A: The coffeemaker works!

    B: I know. I fixed it this morning.

12. A: You're home early. It's only 3:00.

    B: Yeah, our class ended early today.

**Talk about It** Listen and repeat the verbs from Activity 6. Check your answers.

**Talk about It** Now listen to the conversations in Activity 6. Practice the conversations with a partner. Use the correct pronunciation for -ed endings.

**7 | Understanding Time Expressions** Listen to these conversations. Underline the time expressions. Then match each conversation with the correct image on page 201. **8.1 B**

1. A: Do you want to watch this show with me?

   B: No, I watched it <u>last Monday</u>.

2. A: Do you want to go to the gym with me later?

   B: No, thanks. I worked out⁵ this morning.

3. A: You sound great! You're really good.

   B: Thanks! I practiced that song a lot yesterday.

4. A: Is your sister here?

   B: Yes, she arrived two days ago.

5. A: Do you want to work on our papers⁶ together?

   B: I finished my paper on Sunday night.

6. A: Are you hungry?

   B: No, my roommate cooked dinner for me tonight.

7. A: Oh, Kelly called me.

   B: When?

   A: Around 5:00.

8. A: Where do you live?

   B: I live in LA. I moved there two months ago.

---

⁵ **work out:** to do exercise, such as running, jogging, or lifting weights

⁶ **papers:** pieces of writing that you do for school

200

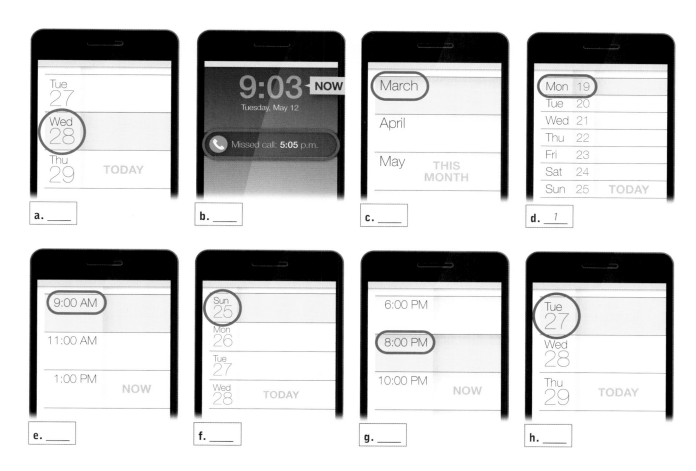

a. ____    b. ____    c. ____    d. _1_

e. ____    f. ____    g. ____    h. ____

**Talk about It** Tell a partner three interesting facts about your past. Use the phrases in this box or your own ideas. Use past time expressions.

| live in | move to | start English classes | study | travel to | work for |
|---------|---------|------------------------|-------|-----------|----------|

*"I lived in Dubai three years ago."*

## 8 | Using Past Time Expressions  Read these statements. Check (✓) *True* or *False*.  8.1 B

|  | TRUE | FALSE |
|--|------|-------|
| 1. I cleaned my bedroom yesterday. | ☐ | ☐ |
| 2. I studied for a test three days ago. | ☐ | ☐ |
| 3. I called a friend last night. | ☐ | ☐ |
| 4. I started English lessons in 2013. | ☐ | ☐ |
| 5. I visited a friend last weekend. | ☐ | ☐ |
| 6. I arrived at school around 9:00 this morning. | ☐ | ☐ |
| 7. I finished a book last month. | ☐ | ☐ |
| 8. I washed dishes this morning. | ☐ | ☐ |
| 9. I worked out on Monday. | ☐ | ☐ |
| 10. I ate lunch at noon yesterday. | ☐ | ☐ |

**Write about It** Rewrite the false statements above to make them true for you. Use different time expressions.

*I cleaned my bedroom two weeks ago.*

## 8.2 Simple Past Irregular Verbs

Many common verbs have **irregular simple past forms**. We don't add *-ed / -d* to these verbs.

A

| BASE FORM | SIMPLE PAST FORM |
|-----------|------------------|
| be* | was / were |
| buy | bought |
| choose | chose |
| come | came |
| do | did |
| drink | drank |
| eat | ate |

| BASE FORM | SIMPLE PAST FORM |
|-----------|------------------|
| get | got |
| give | gave |
| go | went |
| have | had |
| make | made |
| say | said |
| take | took |

| BASE FORM | SIMPLE PAST FORM |
|-----------|------------------|
| hurt | hurt |
| put | put |
| quit | quit |
| read | read** |

Notice: For some verbs, the simple past form is the same as the base form.

For more irregular verbs, see the Resources, page R-5.

*For more information about *was / were*, see Charts 8.5 and 8.6.
**The simple past form *read* is pronounced "red."

**9 | Learning Irregular Verbs** Listen and repeat the simple past verbs in Chart 8.2. 8.2 A

**Talk about It** Work with a partner. Close your book. Your partner reads a base form verb from Chart 8.2. You say and write the simple past form. Take turns. Practice all of the verbs.

A: *drink*
B: *drank*

**10 | Noticing Irregular Simple Past Forms** Underline the irregular simple past verbs in this article. Then write each of these verbs in the correct part of the chart on page 203. (Look on page R-5 for more irregular verbs.) 8.2 A

## iPad App Saves Kidnapped Boy

A car thief <u>stole</u> a car and kidnapped[7] a boy in Harris County, Texas, earlier this week. At 6 p.m., the boy's father drove to a local store. He parked his car, and he left his five-year-old son in the car. The father went inside the store for a few minutes. At 6:05, he came out of the store. His car was gone.

Police arrived quickly. The father was lucky: he had his iPad. His iPhone was in the car. The father used the iPad app "Find My iPhone." The app gave him the location of the iPhone, and the father gave the information to the police. The police quickly found the boy and the car. They arrested[8] the thief. An ambulance took the boy to the hospital. Luckily, the boy was OK.

> **FYI**
>
> When we tell a story, we often use a time expression at the beginning of a sentence.
>
> **At 6 p.m.,** the boy's father drove to a local store.

[7] **kidnap (past form *kidnapped*):** to take a person away and hide them

[8] **arrest (past form *arrested*):** to take a person away to ask them questions about a crime (and maybe take them to jail)

| Base form | Simple past form | Base form | Simple past form |
|---|---|---|---|
| 1. be | | 6. go | |
| 2. come | | 7. have | |
| 3. drive | | 8. leave | |
| 4. find | | 9. steal | *stole* |
| 5. give | | 10. take | |

**Think about It** Circle the regular simple past verbs in the article in Activity 10.

**Talk about It** Think about a news story you heard recently. Tell the story to a partner.

## 11 | Using Simple Past Forms Complete this story with the simple past form of the verbs in parentheses. Use regular and irregular past forms. `8.2 A`

### THE PERFECT GIFT

Michael and Jane _____*got*_____ married five years ago.
(1. get)
Yesterday was their anniversary. Last week, Michael _____
(2. go)
shopping. He _____ to buy a special anniversary gift for Jane.
(3. want)
A few months ago, Jane _____ a new surfboard. So Michael
(4. buy)
_____ the perfect gift: a beach vacation in Aruba. But the
(5. choose)
tickets were very expensive. He _____ more money, so
(6. need)
he _____ to sell his new skis. He _____ an
(7. decide)                                          (8. put)
advertisement online. Someone _____ his skis
(9. buy)
that day, and Michael _____ the plane tickets.
(10. buy)
Jane _____ to get a special anniversary gift for Michael,
(11. want)
too. Two weeks ago, she _____ Michael's brother Tom for
(12. ask)
ideas. Tom _____, "I know Michael wants to go skiing. He
(13. say)
bought new skis last month." Jane _____ the idea. So she
(14. like)
_____ the perfect gift: a skiing vacation in the Swiss Alps.
(15. choose)
But she _____ more money. . . .
(16. need)

a surfboard

skis

**Write about It** Write an ending to the story about Michael and Jane above. Write three to five sentences. Then share your ending with a partner. Use the verbs in this box or your own ideas.

| ask | buy | give | sell |
|---|---|---|---|

**Think about It** Put these events from Activity 11 in order. Add the time expressions from the box.

___ Michael sold his new skis _____.

___ Michael bought new skis _____.

_1_ Michael and Jane got married _____.

___ Jane asked Tom for ideas _____.

___ Jane bought a new surfboard _____.

last week
two weeks ago
last month
a few months ago
five years ago

---

## 8.3 Negative Statements with the Simple Past

**A**

For most verbs, we use *did not* (*didn't*) + the **base form of a verb** to form negative statements with the simple past.

| subject | *did + not* | base form verb |
|---|---|---|
| I<br>He<br>She<br>It<br>You<br>We<br>They | did not<br>didn't | go.<br>work.<br>start.<br>finish. |

*Didn't* is a **helping verb**.

This is the **main verb**.

**WARNING!** Don't use *didn't* + a past form of the main verb.

✓ I didn't work yesterday.

✗ I didn't **worked** yesterday.

---

**12 | Writing Negative Simple Past Statements** Listen and complete these conversations with the missing words. **8.3 A**

I DIDN'T DO IT!

1. A: Where's my soda? It was in the break room.

   B: I don't know. I _____*didn't drink*_____ it.

2. A: Someone left the TV on all night.

   B: Not me. I _____ TV last night.

3. A: Oh, no! My favorite mug is broken.

   B: I _____ it. I never use your mug.

4. A: There's a dent in the car door. What happened?

   B: We _____ the car! I think Dad drove it.

5. A: Someone ate my yogurt again! Where's Susan? She always eats my food.

   B: Susan _____ it. I think Sheila ate it. Go ask her.

6. A: Alex made a mess in the kitchen.

   B: He _____ it. He never cooks.

7. A: Someone used all my laundry detergent.

   B: I _____ it. I think José did laundry yesterday.

8. A: What happened to my shoes? They're really dirty.

   B: I don't know. I _____ them. They don't fit me.

FYI
We can use the negative simple past to **deny** things—to tell someone that we **didn't do** something bad.

a broken mug

a dent

laundry detergent

9. A: Where's my money? I'm missing $50.

   B: I _____ it! I promise.

10. A: Sam, there's a pizza delivery person at the door.

    B: I _____ a pizza. It was probably Jake. He's upstairs.

**Talk about It** Who are the people in the conversations in Activity 12—roommates, family members, or co-workers? Share your ideas with a partner.

**13 | Writing Positive and Negative Simple Past Statements** Look at the pictures. Complete the sentences with the positive or negative simple past form of the verbs in parentheses. **8.3 A**

WHAT HAPPENED YESTERDAY?

1. Alex ___*cleaned*___ the floor yesterday.
   (clean)
2. He _____ the laundry.
   (do)
3. He _____ the car.
   (wash)

4. Kylie _____ last night.
   (study)
5. She _____ asleep.
   (fall)
6. She _____ her homework.
   (finish)

7. Max _____ dinner last night.
   (cook)
8. He _____ chicken and rice.
   (make)
9. He _____ the dishes.
   (do)

**Write about It** Write three things that you did yesterday and three things that you didn't do yesterday. Use the verbs in this box or your own ideas. Then share your sentences with a partner.

| | | | | |
|---|---|---|---|---|
| call | cook | eat | see | talk to |
| clean | do | go | study | wash |

*I called my uncle. I didn't talk to my cousin.*

---

## 8.4 Questions with the Simple Past

For most verbs, we use **did** to form *yes/no* questions and short answers with the simple past.

**A**

**YES/NO QUESTIONS**

| | *did* | subject | base form verb | |
|---|---|---|---|---|
| 1 | | I | forget | something? |
| 2 | | you | work | last night? |
| 3 | | he | start | school this week? |
| 4 | Did | she | go | out last night? |
| 5 | | it | rain | yesterday? |
| 6 | | we | pass | the test? |
| 7 | | they | take | a vacation in June? |

**SHORT ANSWERS**

| | subject | *did* (+ *not*) |
|---|---|---|
| Yes, | you / I / he / she / it / you / we / they | did. |
| No, | | didn't. |

**OTHER WAYS TO ANSWER *YES/NO* QUESTIONS**

We often answer *yes/no* questions with more information.

**8** A: Did you go out last night?
B: **No, I stayed home.**

**9** A: Did she pass the test?
B: **Yes, she got an A!**

**WARNING!** Don't use *did* + a past form of the main verb.

✓ Did they go home?      ✗ Did they went home?

**B**

**WH- QUESTIONS**

| | *wh-* word | *did* | subject | base form verb | |
|---|---|---|---|---|---|
| 10 | What | | I | forget? | |
| 11 | Where | | you | go | last night? |
| 12 | When | did | he | come | home? |
| 13 | Why | | she | arrive | late? |
| 14 | How | | it | break? | |
| 15 | Who | | they | go | with? |

**16** A: **What did** you **do** last night?
B: I went out with friends.

**17** A: **When did** you **come** home?
B: Around midnight.

**18** A: **Who did** they **go** with?
B: They went with Mina and Kim.

**19** A: **How did** they **get** home?
B: They took a cab.

**WH- QUESTIONS ABOUT THE SUBJECT**

In these questions, *what* and *who* are the subject. We use just the **simple past form** of the main verb. We DON'T use *did*.

| | *wh-* word | simple past verb | |
|---|---|---|---|
| 20 | What | **happened?** | |
| 21 | Who | **ate** | the last cookie? |

**14 | Forming *Yes/No* Questions with the Simple Past** Complete these *yes/no* questions with the subject *you* and the verbs in parentheses. Use the simple past. `8.4 A`

**SOCIAL LIFE**

1. _Did you talk_ to your parents yesterday? (talk)
2. _____ your friends last night? (see)
3. _____ time with a friend last Saturday? (spend)

**FOOD**

4. _____ any vegetables today? (eat)
5. _____ coffee this morning? (drink)
6. _____ dinner last night? (cook)

**TRAVEL**

7. _____ the country last year? (leave)
8. _____ a vacation last summer? (take)
9. _____ a cousin last month? (visit)

**SCHOOL**

10. _____ any schoolwork last weekend? (do)
11. _____ something interesting last week? (learn)
12. _____ with a friend last week? (study)

**FREE TIME**

13. _____ a movie last weekend? (see)
14. _____ TV last night? (watch)
15. _____ something interesting yesterday? (read)

> **F Y I**
>
> Remember: Some questions and negative statements use a form of ***do*** as a **helping verb** and a **main verb**.
>
> A: **Did** you **do** your homework last night?
>
> B: No, I **didn't do** it yet.

**Talk about It** Ask and answer the questions above with a partner. Use short answers.

*1. A: Did you talk to your parents yesterday?     B: Yes, I did.*

**Write about It** Write positive and negative sentences about your partner.

*Anna called her parents yesterday. She didn't talk to her sister.*

**15 | Forming *Wh-* Questions with the Simple Past** Complete these conversations with the words in parentheses and the *wh-* words in the box. Then listen and check your answers. `8.4 B`

**A PARENT'S QUESTIONS**

1. A: _What did you do_ last night? (you/do)
   B: I went out with some friends.
2. A: _____? (you/go)
   B: We went downtown.
3. A: _____ there? (you/get)
   B: We took a taxi.

| how | where |
|-----|-------|
| what | who |
| when | why |

4. A: _____ out with? (you/go)

B: Marissa and Clara.

5. A: _____ a taxi? (you/take)

B: Because Marissa's car is in the shop⁹.

6. A: _____ home? (you/come)

B: Around 11:30.

7. A: _____ this morning? (call)

B: Clara called.

8. A: _____? (she/call)

B: Because she left her wallet in my backpack.

<table>
<tr><td>how</td><td>where</td></tr>
<tr><td>what</td><td>who</td></tr>
<tr><td>when</td><td>why</td></tr>
</table>

**F Y I**

In conversation, we can use prepositions like **with**, **to**, or **about** after the main verb in *wh-* questions.

Who did you go **with**?

Who did you talk **to**?

What did you talk **about**?

**Think about It**  Which question in Activity 15 is a question about the subject (the subject is *who* or *what*)?

🔊 **16 | Asking Questions with the Simple Past**  Use the words in each box to complete the questions in these conversations. Add *did* where necessary. Then listen and check your answers.  `8.4 A–B`

1. A: _Who did you call_____ this morning?

B: I called Gina. I didn't understand our homework.

2. A: _____ late last night?

B: Eric. He lost his keys.

3. A: _____ last night?

B: We went out with Sarah. We're exhausted!

what/you/do
who/called
who/you/call

4. A: _____ to Sam yesterday?

B: No. Why?

A: He has some interesting news.

5. A: _____ anywhere last weekend?

B: Yeah, we went to San Diego. It was a lot of fun.

6. A: _____ last weekend?

B: We went to the beach.

where/you/go
you/go
you/talk

7. A: I think I lost my phone.

B: _____ it last?

A: About an hour ago.

8. A: Are you OK?

B: No, I think I hurt my leg.

A: _____?

how/you/get
what/happened
when/you/have

9. A: Guess what? My car broke down¹⁰ again.

B: _____ to work?

A: A friend gave me a ride.

**Talk about It**  Continue conversations 7–9 above with a partner.

⁹**in the shop:** (for a car) getting fixed

¹⁰**break down (past form *broke down*):** to stop working

## 17 | Error Correction  Find and correct the errors. (Some sentences may not have any errors.)

*went*
1. I ~~go~~ home early yesterday.

2. Did you went to class yesterday?

3. Did Mike had fun?

4. How you do on your English test?

5. Marta didn't came to class this morning.

6. I didn't finish my homework.

7. Where did you get those shoes?

8. Stella buy a new car last week.

9. When did Stella arrive?

10. Why you get home so late?

11. We took Carla out to dinner last night.

12. Who gave you that book?

13. Did you finished your homework?

14. Who you study with?

15. What happen to David?

16. They didn't paid for their food.

---

## 8.5 Simple Past of *Be*: Positive and Negative Statements

The verb **be** in the simple past has two forms: **was** and **were**.

**POSITIVE STATEMENTS**

| | subject | was / were | |
|---|---|---|---|
| 1 | I | | a salesperson. |
| 2 | He | was | tired all the time. |
| 3 | She | | in class on Monday. |
| 4 | It | | really fun. |
| 5 | You | | lonely. |
| 6 | We | were | in New York. |
| 7 | They | | students here. |

15 The movie **was** great! I loved it.

16 We **were** out of town last week.
   We went to my mother's house.

**NEGATIVE STATEMENTS**

| | subject | was / were + not | |
|---|---|---|---|
| 8 | I | | a good swimmer. |
| 9 | He | was not | athletic. |
| 10 | She | wasn't | home often. |
| 11 | It | | very good. |
| 12 | You | | with your friends. |
| 13 | We | were not | in school. |
| 14 | They | weren't | happy. |

17 Sheila **wasn't** in class yesterday.
   She didn't feel well.

18 I called you, but you **weren't** home.

---

## 18 | Noticing the Past of *Be*  Read this passage. Underline the positive and negative forms of *was* and *were*. `8.5 A`

### Famous Artists of the Past

Andy Warhol <u>was</u> a popular American artist. He was born in 1928 and he died in 1987. His parents were immigrants[11] from Slovakia. As a child, Warhol wasn't very healthy. He was sick a lot. He learned to draw when he was sick in bed. Warhol's art became very popular in the 1960s. His paintings were fun and very colorful. He often painted cans of soup, soda bottles, and famous people like Marilyn Monroe.

> **FYI**
>
> We use the phrase **was born in** to talk about someone's place or year of birth.
>
> Jack was born **in Korea**.
> (*in* + place)
>
> He was born **in 1994**.
> (*in* + year)

[11] **immigrants:** people who come from another country to live in a new country

Frida Kahlo was a famous Mexican artist. She was born in Mexico City in 1907. In 1925, she was in a terrible bus accident. Before the accident, Kahlo wasn't an artist. She wanted to be a doctor. But after the accident, she didn't walk for a few months. She started to paint. Her husband, Diego Rivera, was also an artist. Many of Kahlo's paintings were self-portraits[12]. She once said, "I paint myself because I am so often alone. . . ." She died in 1954. She was 47.

Johannes Vermeer and Vincent Van Gogh were both Dutch[13] painters. Vermeer painted in the seventeenth century[14]. Many of his paintings show everyday activities. For example, in one painting, a woman is writing a letter. In another painting, a woman is pouring milk into a bowl. Van Gogh was a painter in the nineteenth century. His paintings were very colorful. He often painted flowers and fields. He also painted many self-portraits. He made more than 2,000 paintings and drawings, but his paintings weren't popular. He sold only a few paintings. Today people pay millions of dollars for paintings by Vermeer and Van Gogh. But Vermeer and Van Gogh weren't wealthy at all. They were both poor all their lives.

**Think about It** Read these statements about the artists in the reading in Activity 18. Check (✓) *True* or *False*. Then rewrite the false statements to make them true.

|  | TRUE | FALSE |
|---|---|---|
| 1. Andy Warhol's parents were from the United States. | ☐ | ✓ |
| 2. Warhol's paintings were popular in the 1940s. | ☐ | ☐ |
| 3. Kahlo was in a bus crash in 1925. | ☐ | ☐ |
| 4. Many of Kahlo's paintings were self-portraits. | ☐ | ☐ |
| 5. Van Gogh's work was popular in the nineteenth century. | ☐ | ☐ |
| 6. Van Gogh and Vermeer were wealthy artists. | ☐ | ☐ |

*1. Andy Warhol's parents were from Slovakia.*

**Talk about It** Go online. Find a painting by one of the artists in the reading in Activity 18. Describe the painting to a partner. Your partner tells you who made the painting.

*A: This painting has eight pictures of Elvis Presley on a silver background.*
*B: Andy Warhol painted that.*

**Write about It** Choose one the artists from this box. Go online to find information about the artist. Complete the sentences below. Share your information with the class.

| Mary Cassatt | Abidin Dino | Kim Hong-do | Jackson Pollock |
|---|---|---|---|
| Salvador Dali | Nicola Facchinetti | Edvard Munch | Qiu Ying |

1. _____ _____ born in _____ in _____.
   (artist's name)    (was / were)           (place)                    (year)

2. _____ parents _____ from _____.
   (his / her)    (was / were)              (place)

3. _____ often painted _____.
   (he / she)

4. _____ died in _____.
   (he / she)    (year)

[12] **self-portraits:** pictures of yourself that you draw or paint
[13] **Dutch:** from the Netherlands (Holland)

[14] **century:** a 100-year period of time (The seventeenth century is the time period of 1601 to 1700.)

**19 | Using the Simple Past of *Be*** Complete these paragraphs with the correct past form of *be* or *be + not*. **8.5 A**

## FAMOUS FIRSTS

The University of Al-Karouine and the University of Oxford

___*were*___ two of the first universities in the world. The University
(1. be)

of Al-Karouine is in Morocco. Fatima al-Fihri started the university in the

year 859. The University of Oxford _____ the first university
(2. be)

in England. Students started learning there almost a thousand years ago.

Orville and Wilbur Wright _____ brothers. They invented[15]
(3. be)

the first successful airplane. Their first flight _____ very
(4. be / not)

long—it only lasted 12 seconds! Their first flight didn't get a lot of

attention. People _____ very excited about the airplane.
(5. be / not)

But later, the Wright brothers became famous around the world.

Neil Armstrong and Buzz Aldrin _____ the first people
(6. be)

on the moon. They landed on the moon in July 1969. Armstrong stepped

onto the moon first. But Aldrin _____ the first person to eat
(7. be)

or drink on the moon. The 1969 flight _____ their first time in
(8. be / not)

space. Armstrong's first space flight happened in March 1966. Aldrin's first

flight _____ in November 1966.
(9. be)

the Wright brothers

Neil Armstrong and Buzz Aldrin

**Write about It** Think of another "famous first" from history. Write a sentence with *was/were*.

**20 | Pronunciation Note: *Were* vs. *Weren't*** Listen to the note. Then do Activity 21.

*Were* and *weren't* often sound similar. Notice:

| We usually DON'T stress *were*. | We usually stress *weren't*. |
|---|---|
| **1** They were in CLASS yesterday. | **3** They WEREN'T in class yesterday. |
| **2** We were LATE. | **4** We WEREN'T late. |

**21 | Pronouncing *Were* and *Weren't*** Listen to these sentences. Circle the word you hear. **8.5 A**

1. We (were / weren't) in Tokyo last spring.
2. You (were / weren't) in class on Monday.
3. Kim and I (were / weren't) roommates last year.
4. My brothers (were / weren't) born in Mexico.
5. The police (were / weren't) here this afternoon.
6. The stores (were / weren't) open on Sunday.

[15] **invent (past form *invented*):** to make or think of something for the first time

7. These shoes (were / weren't) very expensive.

8. Carl and Matthew (were / weren't) at soccer practice today.

9. My parents (were / weren't) born in China.

10. Eduardo and Josh (were / weren't) in my class last semester.

11. Alex and Jenna (were / weren't) here yesterday.

12. My classes (were / weren't) difficult this semester.

13. My neighbors (were / weren't) home this afternoon.

14. My roommates (were / weren't) really loud last night.

15. My family and I (were / weren't) in Asia last year.

16. My parents (were / weren't) on vacation last month.

**Talk about It** Listen to the sentences in Activity 21 again. Underline the stressed words in each sentence. Then practice the sentences with a partner.

*"We were in <u>Tokyo</u> last spring."*

**Write about It** Change sentences 9–16 above. Make them true for you. Then read your sentences to a partner.

*My parents were born in Egypt.*

**22 | Writing about Your Past** Think about your childhood. Complete these sentences with *was, wasn't, were,* or *weren't.* Then share your sentences with a partner. 8.5 A

AS A CHILD . . .

1. I _____ shy.

2. I _____ athletic[16].

3. I _____ a good student.

4. I _____ interested in languages.

5. I _____ in clubs at school.

6. My parents _____ home often.

7. My parents _____ strict[17].

8. My friends _____ similar to me.

9. My neighborhood _____ safe.

10. My school _____ close to my home.

**Write about It** Write four more simple past sentences about your childhood. Use subjects and verbs from these boxes or your own ideas. Write two sentences with *be* and two sentences with other verbs.

| SUBJECT | VERB |
|---|---|
| My home | be (+ not) |
| My best friend(s) | |

| SUBJECT | VERB |
|---|---|
| I | (not +) like |
| | (not +) have |

*My best friends were Lisa and Ira.*     *I didn't like bugs.*

**Think about it** In the sentences you wrote above, underline *not*. Where does *not* go in sentences with *be*? Where does *not* go in sentences with other verbs?

[16] **athletic:** good at sports        [17] **strict:** making people follow certain rules

## 8.6 Simple Past Questions with *Be*

**A**

**YES/NO QUESTIONS**

*was / were* subject

| | | | |
|---|---|---|---|
| **1** | Was | I<br>he<br>she<br>it | late? |
| **2** | Were | you<br>we<br>they | |

**SHORT ANSWERS**

*yes / no* subject *was / were (+ not)*

| | | | |
|---|---|---|---|
| **3** | Yes, | I<br>he<br>she<br>it | was. |
| **4** | No, | | wasn't. |
| **5** | Yes, | you<br>we<br>they | were. |
| **6** | No, | | weren't. |

**7** A: **Was** the movie good?
B: Yes, it was. It was really funny!

**8** A: **Were** your friends angry?
B: No, they weren't.

**OTHER WAYS TO ANSWER *YES/NO* QUESTIONS**

Remember: We often answer *yes/no* questions with more information. We can use *be* or other verbs in the answers.

**9** A: Was Jack in class today?
B: **No, he was sick.**

**10** A: Were you late this morning?
B: **No, I got here on time.**

**B**

**WH- QUESTIONS**

*wh-* word *was / were* subject

| | | | | |
|---|---|---|---|---|
| **11** | Where | was | Jim | yesterday? |
| **12** | When | were | you | in Tokyo? |

**13** A: **Where** was Jim yesterday?
B: He was at work.

**14** A: **How** was the movie?
B: It was really good.

**15** A: **What** was your favorite class last semester?
B: Psychology.

**16** A: **How much** were the tickets?
B: They were $30 each.

**17** A: **Why** were Karen and Will so late?
B: They got lost.

**18** A: **Who** were they with?
B: They came with their parents.

**WH- QUESTIONS ABOUT THE SUBJECT**

> In these questions, the word *who* or *what* is the subject.
> In questions like these, we usually use the singular form *was*.

**19** A: **Who** was there?      X Who were there?
B: Luis and Carlos.

**20** A: **What** was in the mail?
B: Just some bills.

**C**

**PAST OF *BE* VS. OTHER VERBS**

Remember: We often use *did* in questions with other verbs. We DON'T use *did* when the main verb is *be*.

**BE**

✓**Was** she late?      X Did she late?

✓Where **were** you?      X Where **did** you?

**OTHER VERBS**

✓**Did** she **arrive**?

✓Where **did** you **go**?

**23 | Asking *Yes/No* Questions with *Was/Were*** Write questions with *was* and *were* and the words in parentheses. Then listen and check your answers. `8.6 A`

1. A: Hi. _Were you asleep?_ _____
   (you / asleep)

   B: What? Uh, no. I wasn't asleep.

2. A: _____
   (your sister / here / last weekend)

   B: Yes, she just left.

   A: She's really messy!

3. A: _____
   (the test / hard)

   B: No, it was easy! I think I got an A!

4. A: Hi. Sorry I missed your call. I was at a movie.

   B: That's OK. _____
   (the movie / good)

   A: Yeah, I loved it!

5. A: You look worried.

   B: I forgot to pay the electric bill again.

   A: Oh, no! _____
   (your roommates / angry)

   B: Yes, they were. We have to pay a late fee.

6. A: Hi, Jackie. _____
   (you / in class / today)

   B: Yes, I was. Why?

   A: I missed class. I'm sick in bed. Can I borrow your notes?

7. A: Hey! You found your wallet!

   B: Yes, finally.

   A: _____
   (it / at / Gina's house)

   B: No, it was in my backpack. I just didn't see it!

8. A: _____
   (dinner / good)

   B: Yeah, it was great. I really like that new restaurant.

   A: What did you have?

   B: I had chicken. Here, I brought you some.

**24 | Asking Questions with *Was/Were*** Complete these conversations with simple past questions. Use *was/were* or a *wh-* word (*what, where, why, who,* or *how much*) + *was/were*. Then listen and check your answers. `8.6 A–B`

AT A JOB INTERVIEW

1. A: _Were_ _____ you a manager at your last company?

   B: Yes, I was.

2. A: _____ your work responsibilities?

   B: I worked at the front desk of the hotel. I helped guests check in, and I answered their questions.

3. A: _____ you unemployed[18] for two years?

   B: I was in school.

check in

**TALKING TO A FRIEND**

4. A: _____ you last weekend?

   B: I was at the beach.

5. A: _____ there with you?

   B: James and Rico and a few other people.

6. A: _____ it fun?

   B: Yes, it was great!

**TALKING TO A ROOMMATE**

7. A: _____ the electric bill?

   B: It was $200! We need to use less electricity.

8. A: _____ the problem with the door?

   B: The lock was broken. But it's working now.

9. A: _____ the landlord here?

   B: He needed to fix the sink.

**Talk about It** Choose three of the questions in Activity 24. Give a different answer.

**25 | Questions with *Did* and *Was/Were*** Complete these questions with *did* or *was/were*. Think about your life at ages 5, 10, and 13. Write your answers in the chart. 8.6 C

**THE WAY YOU WERE**

|  | At age 5 | At age 10 | At age 13 |
|---|---|---|---|
| 1. What ___*did*___ you do for fun? |  |  |  |
| 2. What _____ your three favorite foods? |  |  |  |
| 3. What food _____ you hate? |  |  |  |
| 4. Who _____ your best friends? |  |  |  |
| 5. What _____ your favorite hobbies? |  |  |  |
| 6. What _____ your favorite song? |  |  |  |
| 7. What _____ your favorite book? |  |  |  |
| 8. What _____ you afraid of? |  |  |  |

[18] **unemployed:** without a job

| | At age 5 | At age 10 | At age 13 |
|---|---|---|---|
| 9. Where _____ you go on vacation? | | | |
| 10. What _____ you do on the weekends? | | | |
| 11. What _____ you do in the summer? | | | |
| 12. _____ you like vegetables? | | | |
| 13. _____ you a picky eater[19]? | | | |
| 14. _____ you quiet? | | | |
| 15. _____ you have a pet? | | | |
| 16. _____ you ride a bike? | | | |

**Talk about It** Ask and answer the questions in Activity 25 with a partner. Which answers change from age 5 to 10 and 13? Which answers stay the same?

*A: What did you do for fun at age 5?*
*B: I played with my cousins a lot.*

**Write about It** Compare your life in the past with your life now. Change the questions in Activity 25 to **simple present** questions. Ask and answer your questions with a partner.

*What do you do for fun?*

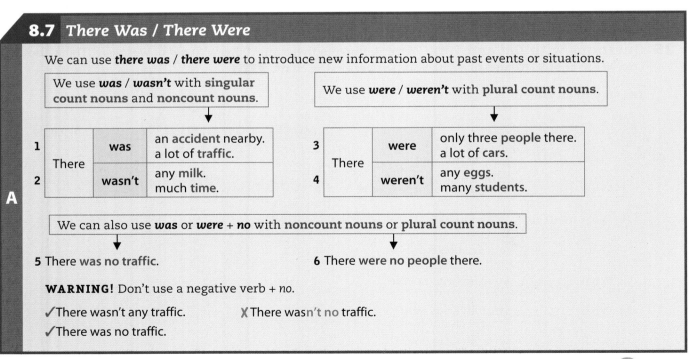

**8.7** *There Was / There Were*

We can use **there was / there were** to introduce new information about past events or situations.

We use **was / wasn't** with **singular count nouns** and **noncount nouns**.

| | | |
|---|---|---|
| 1 | There **was** | an **accident** nearby. a lot of **traffic**. |
| 2 | **wasn't** | any **milk**. much **time**. |

We use **were / weren't** with **plural count nouns**.

| | | |
|---|---|---|
| 3 | There **were** | only three **people** there. a lot of **cars**. |
| 4 | **weren't** | any **eggs**. many **students**. |

We can also use **was** or **were** + **no** with **noncount nouns** or **plural count nouns**.

**5** There **was no traffic**.

**6** There **were no people** there.

**WARNING!** Don't use a negative verb + *no*.

✓There wasn't any traffic.      ✗There wasn't no traffic.
✓There was no traffic.

A

GO ONLINE

---

[19]**picky eater:** someone who doesn't like many foods

**◀)) 26 | Using *There Was* and *There Were*** Complete these conversations with *there was, there wasn't, there were*, or *there weren't*. Then listen and check your answers. **8.7 A**

TALKING ABOUT EVENTS

1.  A: __There was_____ a great event at the museum last weekend.

    B: I know. I tried to go to it.

    A: You didn't go?

    B: No, I got there too late. _____ any tickets left.

2.  A: Did you go to the free concert?

    B: Yeah.

    A: How was it?

    B: It was really crowded. I think _____ about 20,000 people there.

    _____ no seats!

3.  A: Where were you tonight?

    B: I was at a restaurant opening. My friend John opened a new restaurant.

    A: Oh, that's cool. How was it?

    B: It was great. _____ a lot of delicious food. _____

    a band, too.

4.  A: Hey, did you do anything last weekend?

    B: Yeah, _____ an arts and crafts fair[20] downtown.

    A: How was it?

    B: It was really fun. _____ over 100 vendors[21]. I bought some homemade

    soap and a handmade sweater.

5.  A: How was your sister's wedding?

    B: It was beautiful. It was in a garden, so _____ flowers everywhere.

    My sister was really happy. How was your dinner?

    A: It was terrible. My oven broke, so _____ much food. Everyone left early.

6.  A: Did you enjoy your trip to France?

    B: Not really. We don't speak any French, so we decided to take a bus tour.

    A: What happened? Did you have a bad tour guide?

    B: No, _____ no tour guide! _____ just a bus driver!

    _____ also a lot of angry tourists.

**Write about It** Think about an event you went to recently. Write two sentences with *there was/were* or *there wasn't/weren't.*

*I went to a wedding. There was a lot of food. There wasn't a band.*

---

[20] **arts and crafts fair:** an event where people show and sell the things they make

[21] **vendors:** people who sell things, but not in stores

**A | GRAMMAR IN READING** Read these passages. Underline the simple past verbs.

# DR. MARTIN LUTHER KING, JR. AND ROSA PARKS

Dr. Martin Luther King, Jr. <u>was</u> born in Atlanta, Georgia in 1929. He grew up in Atlanta, and later he got his PhD at Boston University. He became a famous civil rights[22] leader. His fight for civil rights began in 1955 in Montgomery, Alabama. There were segregation laws[23] in Alabama—African-American people did not have the same rights as white people. One day in 1955, an African-American woman named Rosa Parks got on a bus and sat down. A white man got on the bus, and the bus driver asked Ms. Parks to give her seat to the white man. She said no. The police arrested her.

That night, Dr. King and other African-American leaders decided to boycott[24] the Montgomery buses. The boycott continued for 381 days. Then the U.S. Supreme Court ended the segregation laws in Alabama. Dr. King continued to fight for equal rights[25]. In 1968, someone shot and killed Dr. King in Memphis, Tennessee. Today people everywhere still remember his important work and his powerful words.

Dr. Martin Luther King, Jr.

# NELSON MANDELA

Nelson Mandela was born on July 18, 1918 in Mvezo, South Africa. Mandela grew up in Mvezo. He studied at the University of South Africa. In South Africa, non-whites did not have the same rights as white people. As a young man, Mandela fought for equal rights for non-whites. He fought for their right to vote[26]. Because of his work, he went to prison in 1962 for 27 years. He got out of prison in 1990. In 1994, non-whites got the right to vote. Nelson Mandela ran for president in 1994, and he won. People around the world loved Mandela. He died on December 5, 2013 after a long illness. He was 95 years old. Nelson Mandela is gone, but he continues to be a symbol of peace.

Rosa Parks

Nelson Mandela

**Write about It** Write five questions about the people and events in the reading above. Then trade books with a partner. Write answers to your partner's questions.

*1. When was Dr. King born?*

**Write about It** How were Martin Luther King, Jr. and Nelson Mandela similar? How were they different? Copy this Venn diagram in your notebook. Write two sentences in each part of the diagram. Use the simple past form of the words and phrases in the box or your own ideas.

**DR. MARTIN LUTHER KING, JR.**
Dr. King . . .

Both men . . .

**NELSON MANDELA**
Mandela . . .

| | |
|---|---|
| be born in/on | fight for equal rights |
| become | go to prison |
| boycott | grow up in |
| die | |

---

[22] **civil rights:** things that every person should be allowed to do or have
[23] **segregation laws:** laws that separated people because of their race
[24] **boycott:** to stop using or buying something until changes happen

[25] **equal rights:** the same rights for all people (so everyone is allowed to do or have the same things)
[26] **vote:** to officially choose someone, such as a government leader (If you have the **right to vote**, you are allowed to vote by law.)

**B | GRAMMAR IN SPEAKING** Think of someone famous from the past. Go online and find answers to these questions. Then find two more facts. Tell your information to a partner, but don't say the person's name. Your partner will guess the person.

Where and when was the person born? _____

What did the person do? _____

Two more facts: _____

_____

## 8.8 Summary of the Simple Past

We use the simple past to talk about past events and situations.

**POSITIVE STATEMENTS**

| I / You / We / He / She / It | arrived came | yesterday. |
|---|---|---|

**NEGATIVE STATEMENTS**

| I / You / We / He / She / It | did not didn't | arrive come | yesterday. |
|---|---|---|---|

**YES/NO QUESTIONS**

| Did | I / you / we / he / she / it | go | out? |
|---|---|---|---|

**SHORT ANSWERS**

| Yes, | you / I / we / he / she / it | did. |
|---|---|---|
| No, | | didn't. |

**WH- QUESTIONS**

| When Where Why | did | I / you / we / he / she / it | leave? |
|---|---|---|---|

**WH- QUESTIONS ABOUT THE SUBJECT**

| Who | called? |
|---|---|
| What | happened? |

### THE SIMPLE PAST OF THE VERB *BE*

**POSITIVE STATEMENTS**

| I / He / She / It | was | at home. |
|---|---|---|
| You / We / They | were | at home. |

**NEGATIVE STATEMENTS**

| I / He / She / It | was not wasn't | at work. |
|---|---|---|
| You / We / They | were not weren't | at work. |

**YES/NO QUESTIONS**

| Was | I / he / she / it | late? |
|---|---|---|
| Were | you / we / they | |

**SHORT ANSWERS**

| Yes, | I he she it | was. |
|---|---|---|
| No, | | wasn't. |
| Yes, | you we they | were. |
| No, | | weren't. |

**WH- QUESTIONS**

| Where How | was | I / he / she / it? | |
|---|---|---|---|
| When Who | were | you / we / they | in class? with? |

**WH- QUESTIONS ABOUT THE SUBJECT**

| Who | was | there? |
|---|---|---|
| What | was | on TV? |

### STATEMENTS WITH *THERE WAS / THERE WERE*

**POSITIVE STATEMENTS**

| There | was | a band. |
|---|---|---|
| | were | a lot of people. |

**NEGATIVE STATEMENTS**

| There | wasn't | a cake. |
|---|---|---|
| | weren't | many seats. |

# 9

# Adjectives

**For the Unit Vocabulary Check, go to the Online Practice.**

## IN THIS UNIT, WE USE adjectives to:

### Describe nouns

1. My friend Kate is very **funny** and **friendly**.

2. That ride looks too **scary**!

3. Lake Hillier is a **pink** lake on an **Australian** island.

4. I love the ocean on **cold**, **windy** days!

**Think about It** Complete these sentences. You can circle more than one answer.

1. My friend _____ is (funny / friendly / interesting).

2. I like (funny / exciting / scary) movies.

3. I like (cold / snowy / warm / sunny) days.

4. I live in (a boring / an interesting) place.

## Make comparisons

5. The Burj Khalifa is **taller** than the Empire State Building.

2,722 feet = 829.7 meters    1,250 feet = 381 meters

6. A peacock is **more colorful** than a pigeon.

7. Mount Everest is **the tallest** mountain in the world.

**Think about It**  Do you agree with these statements? Check (✓) *True* or *False*.

|  | TRUE | FALSE |
|---|---|---|
| 1. Dubai is more interesting than New York. | ☐ | ☐ |
| 2. Paris is the most beautiful city in the world. | ☐ | ☐ |
| 3. Peacocks are more beautiful than pigeons. | ☐ | ☐ |
| 4. The beach is more relaxing than the mountains. | ☐ | ☐ |

**Adjectives** describe and give more information about **nouns** (people, places, and things). We often place adjectives:

| before the **noun** they describe | | after *be*\* |

**A**

1 The **new students** are from Dubai.
2 This **cheap phone** doesn't work well.
3 That was a **delicious dinner**!
4 Can I please have a **large coffee**?
5 I bought a **black wool coat**.

6 The **weather** today **is perfect**.
7 **Weekends are** too **short**!
8 I love your **boots**! **They're awesome**!
9 **That test was** really **hard**!
10 Our **conversation was short** but **interesting**.

Notice: We can use more than one adjective to describe a noun.

\*In these sentences, *be* is a **linking verb**. A linking verb links, or joins, the subject noun (or pronoun) and the adjective(s).

Remember: We use *a* when the next word begins with a consonant sound. We use *an* when the next word begins with a vowel sound.

11 This is **an old car** with a **new engine**.

**LINKING VERB + ADJECTIVE**

We can use an adjective after a **linking verb**. *Be* is the most common linking verb. Here are some other common linking verbs:

**B**

| seem | 12 So far my new boss **seems nice**. | taste | 19 The soup **tastes delicious**! |
|------|----------------------------------------|-------|------------------------------------|
| feel | 13 Oof! Why does this box **feel** so **heavy**? | smell | 20 Those roses **smell great**! |
|      | 14 I **feel sorry** for Jason. He's having a hard time. | | |
| look | 15 You **look** really **good** in that new dress. | get\* | 21 The trip was long, and the children **got tired**. |
|      | 16 Your book **looks interesting**. What is it about? | | |
| sound | 17 This music **sounds sad**. What is it? | | |
|       | 18 The price **sounds good**. Let's buy it. | | |

\*As a linking verb, *get* means "become."

For more linking verbs, see the Resources, page R-6.

**ONLINE**

**1 | Noticing Adjectives and Nouns** Look at the **bold** adjectives in these sentences. Underline the nouns that the adjectives describe. Then check (✓) the placement of the adjectives in each sentence. `9.1 A`

| AMAZING ANIMALS | BEFORE THE NOUN | AFTER BE |
|-----------------|:---------------:|:--------:|
| 1. Aye-ayes live in the **tall** <u>trees</u> of Madagascar. | ✓ | ☐ |
| 2. Their <u>ears</u> are **big**. | ☐ | ✓ |
| 3. Their teeth are **sharp**. | ☐ | ☐ |
| 4. They have a very **long**, **thin** finger. | ☐ | ☐ |

an aye-aye in a tree

| | BEFORE THE NOUN | AFTER BE |
|---|---|---|
| 5. Aye-ayes eat **small** insects in trees. | ☐ | ☐ |
| 6. They use their **big** ears to hear insects inside the trees. | ☐ | ☐ |
| 7. They use their **sharp** teeth to make a **small** hole in a tree. | ☐ | ☐ |
| 8. They use their **long**, **thin** finger to reach into the hole and get the insects. | ☐ | ☐ |

**Now look at the <u>underlined</u> nouns. Circle the adjectives that describe these nouns. Then check (✓) the placement of the adjectives in each sentence.**

| | BEFORE THE NOUN | AFTER BE |
|---|---|---|
| 9. Sand puppies live in the (hot) <u>deserts</u> of East Africa. They live under the ground. | ☐ | ☐ |
| 10. Sand puppies have no hair. They have short <u>legs</u> and tiny <u>eyes</u>. | ☐ | ☐ |
| 11. They have two very long, thin <u>teeth</u>. | ☐ | ☐ |
| 12. They dig long <u>tunnels</u> (sometimes over a kilometer long). | ☐ | ☐ |
| 13. Many people think <u>sand puppies</u> are ugly. | ☐ | ☐ |
| 14. <u>Axolotls</u> are often black or brown. | ☐ | ☐ |
| 15. Sometimes <u>they</u> are gold or pink. | ☐ | ☐ |
| 16. Axolotls have a special <u>ability</u>. Sometimes a leg falls off, and the axolotl grows a new <u>leg</u>! | ☐ | ☐ |

a sand puppy in a tunnel

an axolotl (pronounced "ax-o-lottle")

**Write about It** Look at these pictures of two more animals. Write two sentences about each animal: one with adjective + noun and one with *be* + adjective. Use the adjectives in the box below or your own ideas.

an alpaca

an Angora rabbit

| big | brown | cute | long | round | short | small | ugly |
|---|---|---|---|---|---|---|---|

*The alpaca is brown. It has short legs.*

**2 | Identifying Linking Verbs + Adjectives** Read the article below. Underline the uses of linking verb + adjective. Look for forms of the linking verbs in the box. `9.1 B`

| be | feel | get | look | seem | sound | taste |

## CAN YOU *FEEL* THE MUSIC?

Synesthesia (pronounced "si-nəs-THEE-zhə") means "combined senses[1]." About 4 percent of people have synesthesia. There are many types of synesthesia. For example:

**Letters and numbers → Color**

Carol is an artist. For her, the letter *A* looks pink, *E* looks red, and *G* looks green. This type of synesthesia is common.

**Letters and numbers → Personality**

For a few people, letters and numbers have personalities. For example, one person says *J* always seems strong and *K* always seems quiet.

**Sound → Feeling**

Jennifer has this kind of synesthesia. For her, guitar music sounds beautiful. It also feels soft on her skin.

**Taste → Color**

For Sean, steak tastes delicious. It also tastes blue.

How does synesthesia feel? For some people, synesthesia gets tiring[2]. But for most people it feels normal and interesting.

For some people with synesthesia, letters and numbers have colors.

**Talk about It** Do you think life is very different for people with synesthesia? Does synesthesia seem like a good or bad experience? Why?

**3 | Using Linking Verbs + Adjectives** Look at the pictures below. Write a sentence about each picture with a linking verb + adjective(s). Use the words in parentheses and adjectives from the box. `9.1 B`

| angry | beautiful | delicious | funny | interesting | sad |
| bad | dangerous | exciting | great | OK | scary |

1. (she/feel)

   *She feels angry and sad.*

   _____

2. (the food/taste)

   _____

   _____

3. (the music/sound)

   _____

   _____

[1] **senses:** the power to see, hear, smell, taste, and feel          [2] **tiring (adjective):** making you feel tired

4. (that/look)

_____

_____

5. (the movie/seem)

_____

_____

6. (the book/look)

_____

_____

**4 | Forming Sentences with Adjectives** Complete these conversations with the words in parentheses. Put the words in order to form sentences with adjective + noun or linking verb + adjective.  9.1 A–B

ASKING FOR AN OPINION

1. A: Do you want to see that Korean movie?

   B: Yeah, _____*it sounds interesting*_____.
   (it / interesting / sounds)

2. A: _____?
   (this shirt / tight / does / look)

   B: Not at all. It looks great on you.

3. A: _____ in here?
   (does / it / hot / feel)

   B: Maybe a bit. _____ in the living room.
   (open / window / big / the)

4. A: Can you taste the soup for me? Is the seasoning³ OK? _____.
   (I / new / used / a / recipe)

   B: Yes, the seasoning is perfect. _____.
   (the / delicious / soup / tastes)

5. A: _____ near here?
   (is there / pizza place / a / good)

   B: Try Marino's. _____.
   (pizza / excellent / they / make)

6. A: Which set of plates do you like?

   B: I like both. _____. But the blue ones are pretty!
   (seem / white / the / plates / useful)

7. A: I think _____.
   (is / this class / confusing)

   B: Yeah, me too. _____.
   (hard / the material / is)

8. A: _____?
   (is / good / your / French teacher / new)

   B: Yeah, _____.
   (seems / she / great)

9. A: How was your winter vacation? _____?
   (did / good / time / you / have / a)

   B: _____! I worked at the store six days a week.
   (was / tiring / my vacation)

> **FYI**
>
> Many common adjectives end in **-ing**. These words come from verb forms, but we use them as adjectives.
>
> That was a really **interesting** movie!

🔊 **Talk about It** Listen and check your answers above. Then practice the conversations with a partner.

**Think about It** Look at the sentences you wrote above. Answer these questions.

1. Which sentences have an adjective + noun?
2. Which sentences have a linking verb + adjective? (*be* or other linking verb)
3. Which sentences have an adjective + noun AND a linking verb + adjective?

³ **seasoning:** things we use to add flavor to food (salt, pepper, spices, etc.)

**Talk about It** Work with a partner. Ask your partner for an opinion. Ask about one of these topics or another idea.

| a class | a movie | a product | a restaurant | a store |

A: *Are the stores on Fifth Avenue good?*
B: *They're nice, but they're expensive.*

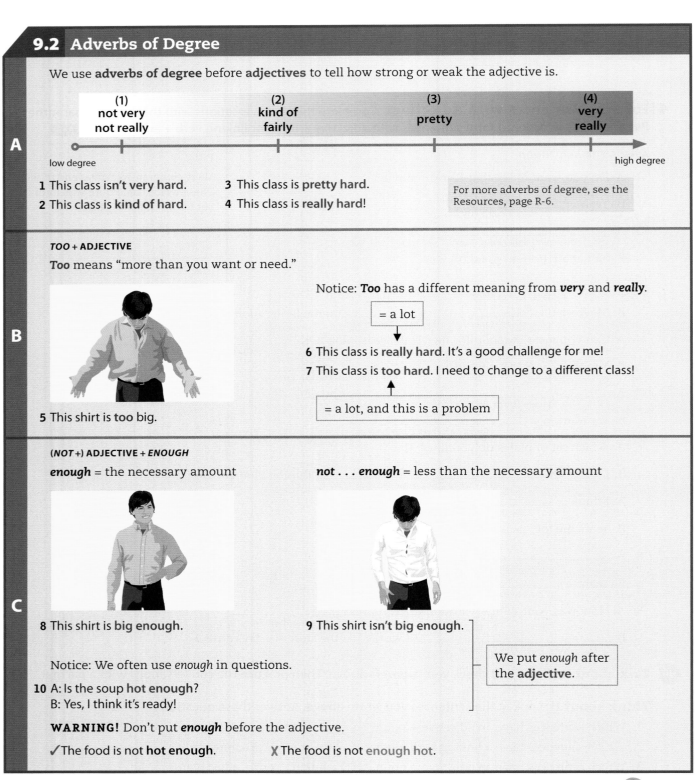

**9.2 Adverbs of Degree**

We use **adverbs of degree** before **adjectives** to tell how strong or weak the adjective is.

**A**

| (1) not very not really | (2) kind of fairly | (3) pretty | (4) very really |

low degree → high degree

**1** This class isn't **very hard**.
**2** This class is **kind of hard**.

**3** This class is **pretty hard**.
**4** This class is **really hard**!

For more adverbs of degree, see the Resources, page R-6.

**B**

**TOO + ADJECTIVE**

**Too** means "more than you want or need."

**5** This shirt is **too big**.

Notice: **Too** has a different meaning from **very** and **really**.

= a lot
↓
**6** This class is **really hard**. It's a good challenge for me!
**7** This class is **too hard**. I need to change to a different class!
↑
= a lot, and this is a problem

**C**

**(NOT +) ADJECTIVE + ENOUGH**

**enough** = the necessary amount

**not ... enough** = less than the necessary amount

**8** This shirt is **big enough**.

**9** This shirt isn't **big enough**.

We put *enough* after the **adjective**.

Notice: We often use *enough* in questions.

**10** A: Is the soup **hot enough**?
B: Yes, I think it's ready!

**WARNING!** Don't put **enough** before the adjective.

✓ The food is not **hot enough**.          ✗ The food is not enough hot.

GO ONLINE

**5 | Understanding Adverbs of Degree** Listen and write the adverbs you hear. Then underline the adjective that each adverb describes. **9.2 A**

CONVERSATIONS AT SCHOOL

1. A: I'm _____*really*_____ <u>nervous</u> about the exam. Are you?

   B: I'm actually _____ calm. I studied a lot. I know this stuff.

2. A: How late is the library open?

   B: I'm not sure. It's usually open _____ late.

3. A: I'm confused. Is the whole paper due on Monday or just

      the introduction?

   B: Hmm. It's _____ clear to me either.

4. A: I wanted to register for the child psychology class, but there's already

      a waiting list.

   B: I'm not surprised. That class is _____ popular.

5. A: Are we on time for the meeting?

   B: Actually, we're _____ early. No one's here yet.

6. A: It's lunchtime, but I'm _____ hungry. What about you?

   B: I'm not hungry either. Let's have lunch after class.

7. A: How's your economics class?

   B: It's _____ disappointing. We're just doing stuff from last

      semester again.

8. A: You look _____ tired today.

   B: I am! Some of my friends came over, and I stayed up _____ late.

9. A: Do you like your new adviser?

   B: I do! She's _____ helpful. She gave me some great advice

      about my class schedule.

10. A: Did you read the book for our English class?

    B: Not yet. Why?

    A: I don't understand it. It's _____ confusing!

> **RESEARCH SAYS...**
>
> The adverbs **pretty** and **kind of** are much more common in conversation than in writing. **Fairly** is more common in writing.
>
> CORPUS

> **FYI**
>
> Notice that the adverb **pretty** and the adjective **pretty** have different meanings.
>
> He's **pretty** smart.
> (adverb = softer than *really*)
>
> That's a **pretty** dress.
> (adjective = looks nice)

**Talk about It** Talk to a partner about the topics in this box. Use adverbs of degree and adjectives.

| your breakfast/lunch today | your last exam |
|---|---|
| your classes this semester | your last vacation |

*"My lunch today was pretty good."*
*"My classes this semester are really interesting."*

**Think about It** In conversation 7 above, there is one adjective that ends in *-ing* and one verb that ends in *-ing*. Label the adjective *A* and label the verb *V*.

**6 | Using Adverbs of Degree** Look at the personal qualities below. Do these qualities describe you? Write sentences about yourself with each adjective and an adverb of degree from the box. (Use a dictionary to look up any adjectives you don't know.) **9.2 A**

PERSONAL QUALITIES SURVEY

| not very      pretty      very | *I'm pretty calm.* |

1. calm _____
2. careful _____
3. confident _____
4. creative _____
5. curious⁴ _____
6. helpful _____

7. honest _____
8. independent⁵ _____
9. organized _____
10. outgoing⁶ _____
11. polite _____
12. responsible _____

**Talk about It** Think about the qualities of a good manager. Which of the qualities above are the most important? Discuss your ideas as a class.

*"Good managers are very confident. They are also very creative. . . ."*

**7 | Using *Too* and *Really*** Complete each conversation with *too* or *really*. Then listen and check your answers. **9.2 B**

AN EVENING AT HOME

1. A: Can we park there?

   B: I don't think so. That space is _____*too*_____ small for my car.

2. A: Did you finish your paper?

   B: Yes and no. I finished it, but it's _____ short. The assignment says 500 words, and I only have 400. I can't think of anything else to say.

3. A: Is the soup hot now? Does it seem ready?

   B: Yeah. It's _____ hot. And it smells delicious.

4. A: Where did you buy those new coffee cups? They're nice!

   B: At SaveCo. I liked them a lot, and they were _____ cheap.

5. A: What's wrong with the cake?

   B: I usually like sweet desserts, but this is _____ sweet. I can't eat it.

6. A: The hot water is working again. Is it OK now?

   B: Ouch! No, now it's _____ hot!

7. A: How are the new neighbors? Do they seem nice?

   B: Yeah, I like them. They're _____ friendly.

8. A: How was the movie?

   B: It was _____ interesting! I liked it a lot.

9. A: Did you find an apartment?

   B: Yes, I chose one yesterday! It's _____ big and sunny.

---

⁴**curious:** interested in learning about things
⁵**independent:** not needing help

⁶**outgoing:** friendly and interested in other people

**8 | Using *Enough*** Look at the pictures. Complete the sentences below with the words in parentheses. Use the verb *be* and *enough* or *not . . . enough*. **9.2 C**

1. _This office isn't big enough_ for all of us!
    (this office / big)

2. A: _____ now?
    (the ice cream / soft)

   B: Not yet! It needs a few more minutes!

3. A: _____?
    (that coat / warm)

   B: Not really. I'm pretty cold!

4. A: Do you need more sugar?

   B: No, thanks. _____.
    (the tea / sweet)

5. A: What do you think?

   B: _____!
    (the door / wide)

6. _____ now?
    (my room / clean)

7. _____ for your things.
   (this box / big)

8. A: Do you need help?

   B: Yes, please. Can you get me that box?

   _____.
                                    (I / tall)

**9 | Using Adverbs of Degree** Read these reviews. Complete the sentences with the phrases in each box. You will not use all of the phrases. **9.2 A–C**

○ ○ ○

## Maria's Tacos
**Reviews**

Evan ★★★★★

The food at Maria's is _____*very good*_____. My wife and I love it! The portions[7] are

_____. You get a lot of food! And the owner and waiters make you

feel comfortable. It's a _____ place.

| really big |
| too friendly |
| too small |
| very friendly |
| very good |

Brad ★

The food is _____. Actually, it's terrible. And that's not the only

problem. The service[8] is _____. Last night my friends and I waited

almost an hour for our tacos! The tacos were probably in the kitchen all that time.

My tacos were _____, and my friends' tacos were cold.

| fast enough |
| hot enough |
| not hot enough |
| not very good |
| too slow |

Leonel ★★★

This is not a special restaurant, but everything is OK. Not great, not bad. The food is

_____. The service is _____. The waiter brought us

our food in about 15 minutes—not bad, but not great. Try the chicken and mushroom

tacos. The prices are OK.

| fast enough |
| good enough |
| really good |
| very fast |

[7] **portions:** amounts of food for each person

[8] **service:** the work people do for customers in a restaurant or other business

Tamara ★★

Where were the chilies? Mexican food is usually spicy. But at Maria's our food was

_____. We didn't finish our food because the portions were

_____. And Maria's is also _____—maybe because

you pay for all that extra food.

big enough
cheap enough
not very spicy
too big
too expensive

Rosa ★★★★

This restaurant has interesting and tasty food. There is only one problem: too

many people like Maria's! The restaurant is _____—there are

only about seven tables, so there's not a lot of space. For this reason, it is often

_____. I waited almost an hour for a seat! Don't go to Maria's for

an evening of quiet conversation—it's _____.

noisy enough
not very small
really small
too crowded
too noisy

**Talk about It** Work with a partner. Read the reviews in Activity 9 again. Do you want to eat at Maria's Tacos? Why or why not?

**Write about It** Write a short review (three to four sentences) of a restaurant you went to recently. Include answers to these questions. Use adjectives and adverbs of degree.

Is the food good?
Is the service fast?
Is the food expensive?

## 9.3 Questions with *How* + Adjective

We use **how** + an **adjective** to ask about the degree of the adjective:

| | QUESTION | POSSIBLE ANSWERS |
|---|---|---|
| 1 | **How hot** is it today? | It's not very hot.<br>It's about 80 degrees. (80°F = 27°C) |
| 2 | **How hungry** are you? | I'm starving!<br>I'm not very hungry. |
| 3 | **How big** is your school? | It's pretty big.<br>There are about 15,000 students. |
| 4 | **How far** is your house from here? | It's just a few blocks away.<br>About 3 miles (4.8 km) from here. |
| 5 | **How tall** is your brother? | He's about 6 feet tall.<br>He's 5'11". ("five-eleven" =<br>5 feet, 11 inches = 1.9 m) |
| 6 | **How high** is that hill? | It's pretty high!<br>It's about 300 feet. (91 m) |
| 7 | **How long** is the trip? | Usually a couple of hours.<br>It's not very long. |
| 8 | **How old** are your children? | They're 2 and 5 years old. |

A

**10 | Asking and Answering Questions with *How* + Adjective** Complete the questions below. Use *how* + an adjective from the box. Then guess the answers to the questions. `9.3 A`

| cold | deep | far | heavy | high | long | old | tall |
|------|------|-----|-------|------|------|-----|------|

---

## Did You Know?

1. ___How high___ is Mount Everest?

   a. 26,105 feet      b. 29,029 feet      c. 30,230 feet
   (7,957 meters)      (8,848 meters)      (9,214 meters)

2. _____ is a flight from Auckland, New Zealand to New York City?

   a. 6 hours      b. 13 hours      c. 18 hours

   lightning

3. _____ is the average⁹ professional basketball player?

   a. about 6'3" (1.91 meters)      b. about 6'7" (2.01 meters)      c. about 6'11" (2.11 meters)

4. _____ are the Egyptian pyramids at Giza?

   a. about 2,500 years old      b. about 3,500 years old      c. about 4,500 years old

5. _____ is a new baby elephant?

   a. about 100 pounds      b. about 150 pounds      c. about 200 pounds
   (45 kilograms)      (68 kilograms)      (91 kilograms)

6. You see lightning. Five seconds later you hear thunder. _____ is the lightning from you?

   a. about 1 mile      b. about 5 miles      c. about 10 miles
   (1.6 kilometers)      (8 kilometers)      (16 kilometers)

7. _____ is the ocean on average?

   a. 5,500 feet (1,700 meters)      b. 9,000 feet (2,743 meters)      c. 14,000 feet (4,267 meters)

8. _____ is an average January day in New Delhi, India?

   a. about 55°F (13°C)      b. about 65°F (18°C)      c. about 70°F (21°C)

Answers: 1. b; 2. c; 3. b; 4. c; 5. c; 6. a; 7. c; 8. a

---

**Talk about It** Ask and answer these questions with a partner.

1. Do you have siblings? How old are they?
2. How big is your immediate family (mother, father, and siblings)?
   How big is your extended family (cousins, aunts, uncles, and grandparents)?
3. How far is your home from school? How long is your trip to school?
4. How big is your home? (How many rooms does it have?)
5. How tall are you?

---

⁹ **average:** normal or usual

## 9.4 Adjectives with -er and More

We can use adjectives to **compare** (describe differences between) people or things. Adjectives that compare have two forms:

**A**

| With some adjectives, we use the **adjective** + -er. | With some adjectives, we use *more* + the **adjective**. |

**TONY'S**
PIZZA

**1** Tony's is **smaller** than Il Pranzo.

**2** Il Pranzo is **more expensive**.

**GRAMMAR TERM:** These kinds of adjectives are also called **comparative forms**.

**B**

**FORMING ADJECTIVES WITH -ER AND MORE**

| ONE-SYLLABLE ADJECTIVES | TWO-SYLLABLE ADJECTIVES ENDING IN Y* |
|---|---|
| cheap → **cheap**er<br>hard → **hard**er<br>strong → **strong**er | hap·py → **happier**<br>heav·y → **heavier**<br>la·zy → **lazier** |

| TWO-SYLLABLE ADJECTIVES | THREE-SYLLABLE ADJECTIVES |
|---|---|
| bor·ing → **more boring**<br>care·ful → **more careful**<br>po·lite → **more polite** | ex·cit·ing → **more exciting**<br>im·por·tant → **more important**<br>prac·ti·cal → **more practical** |

**USE WITH -ER OR MORE**

| narrow → **narrower** OR **more narrow**<br>quiet → **quieter** OR **more quiet** |

**IRREGULAR FORMS**

| bad → **worse** | good → **better** | far → **farther** |

*For more information on spelling -er adjectives, see the Spelling Note on page 234.

We usually use **-er** with:
- most one-syllable adjectives
- some two-syllable adjectives (for example, words that end in y)

We use *more* with:
- other two-syllable adjectives
- adjectives with more than two syllables

For some adjectives, we can use either **-er** or **more**.

Some adjectives like **bad**, **good**, and **far** have irregular comparative forms.

GO ONLINE

---

**11 | Identifying Adjectives with -er and More** Underline the adjectives with -er and *more* in these trivia questions. Then write the answers to the questions. **9.4 A**

## World Trivia

**GEOGRAPHY**[10]

1. Which continent is <u>larger</u>, Europe or South America? _____

2. Which continent is <u>more populated</u>[11], Africa or Europe? _____

3. Which ocean is deeper, the Atlantic Ocean or the Pacific Ocean? _____

4. Which city is more expensive, London or Paris? _____

> **FYI**
> We can use the *wh*- word **which** to ask about a choice between things.
>
> Which color looks better, red or blue?

[10] **geography:** the study of the earth, including its land and people

[11] **more populated:** having more people

**ANIMALS**

5. Which animals are faster, lions or giraffes?  _____

6. Which animals are bigger, lions or tigers?  _____

7. Which whales are heavier, blue whales or gray whales?  _____

8. Which insects are more dangerous to humans, mosquitoes or bees?  _____

**LANGUAGES**

9. Which sound is more common in the world's languages, the /l/ sound or the /p/ sound?  _____

10. Which alphabet is shorter, the English alphabet or the Russian alphabet?  _____

11. Which English word is newer, *cell phone* or *blog*?  _____

12. Which language is more similar to English, Russian or Swedish?  _____

a giraffe

a mosquito

Look on page 249 for the answers.

**Think about It** For each adjective form you underlined in Activity 11, write the simple adjective (without *-er* or *more*). How many syllables does the simple adjective have?

1. *large* = 1 syllable
2. *populated* = 4 syllables

**12 | Spelling Note: Adjectives + *-er*** Read the note. Then do Activity 13.

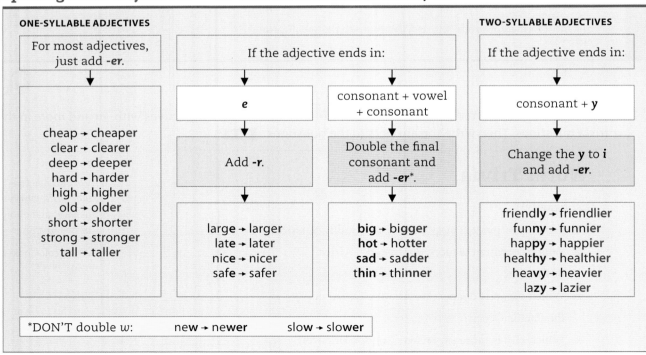

| ONE-SYLLABLE ADJECTIVES | | | TWO-SYLLABLE ADJECTIVES |
|---|---|---|---|
| For most adjectives, just add *-er*. | If the adjective ends in: | | If the adjective ends in: |
| | *e* | consonant + vowel + consonant | consonant + **y** |
| | Add *-r*. | Double the final consonant and add *-er*\*. | Change the **y** to **i** and add *-er*. |
| cheap → cheaper<br>clear → clearer<br>deep → deeper<br>hard → harder<br>high → higher<br>old → older<br>short → shorter<br>strong → stronger<br>tall → taller | large → larger<br>late → later<br>nice → nicer<br>safe → safer | big → bigger<br>hot → hotter<br>sad → sadder<br>thin → thinner | friendly → friendlier<br>funny → funnier<br>happy → happier<br>healthy → healthier<br>heavy → heavier<br>lazy → lazier |

\*DON'T double *w*:      new → newer      slow → slower

## 13 | Spelling -er Adjectives

Write the -er form of each adjective in the box in the correct column of the chart below. **9.4 B**

| big | close | early | hungry | loud | nice | sad | sunny |
|---|---|---|---|---|---|---|---|
| busy | cool | heavy | large | neat | noisy | safe | thin |
| cheap | deep | hot | late | new | old | slow | wet |

| ONE-SYLLABLE ADJECTIVES | | | TWO-SYLLABLE ADJECTIVES |
|---|---|---|---|
| Ending in e | Ending in consonant + vowel + consonant (not w) | All other one-syllable adjectives | Ending in consonant + y |
| | *bigger* | | |

## 14 | Forming Adjectives with -er and More

Complete these conversations with the correct form of the adjective(s) in parentheses. **9.4 B**

DECISIONS

1. A: Liam and Zach both seem good. Who do you want to hire?

   B: It's a difficult choice. . . . But maybe Liam. He seems

   _____*more outgoing*_____ (outgoing).

2. A: Are you taking Biology II?

   B: No, it was too hard for me. I switched to Environmental Science.

   It's a little _____ (easy).

3. A: Did you fly to Zurich?

   B: No, I took the train. It's a _____ (slow) trip, but it's

   _____ (cheap).

4. A: Which apartment did you choose?

   B: The apartment on the top floor. It's a little _____ (small)

   than the first-floor apartment, but it's a lot _____ (sunny).

5. A: Which supermarket do you go to—the ShopBest or the FoodPlace?

   B: I usually go to the ShopBest. It's a little _____ (far)

   for me, but the fruits and vegetables there are really good.

6. A: My friends want to go to an Ethiopian restaurant. Where can I take

   them? Maybe to Gojo?

   B: What about Kokeb? The food there is _____ (expensive),

   but it's also _____ (interesting).

7. A: We can take the red trail or the green trail. What do you think?

   B: Let's take the red trail. It's _____ (long), and it looks

   _____ (challenging).

**F Y I**

We can use **much** and **a lot** before adjectives with -er/more to show a big difference between the two things in the comparison.

My new apartment is **a lot** bigger than my old one. (My new apartment is very big, and my old apartment was very small.)

We can use **a little** to show a small difference.

The apartment is **a little** farther from school, but that's OK.

8. A: What schools did you get accepted to?

   B: Florida State University and the University of Chicago.

   A: Wow! The University of Chicago is a really good school!

   B: Yeah, but Florida State is a _____ (good) school for music.

**Write about It** Look again at the conversations in Activity 14. Complete the sentences below about the other thing or person in each conversation. Use an adjective from the box with *-er* or *more*.

| bad | boring | dark | expensive | hard | quiet |
|-----|--------|------|-----------|------|-------|
| big | cheap | easy | fast | near | short |

1. Zach is _____*quieter*_____.

2. Biology II is _____.

3. The flight to Zurich is _____
   _____.

4. The first-floor apartment is _____.

5. The FoodPlace is _____.

6. The food at Gojo is _____.

7. The green trail is _____.

8. The music department at the University of Chicago is _____.

## 9.5 Using Adjectives to Compare

We can use an **adjective with *-er* or *more* + *than*** in sentences that compare two people or things.

**A**

| | | be | adjective + *-er* or *more* | than | |
|---|---|----|-----------------------------|------|---|
| **1** | The bus | is | **cheaper** | **than** | the train. |
| **2** | Zack | is | **older** | **than** | his brother. |
| **3** | Tests | are | **more important** | **than** | quizzes. |

We can also use the adjective alone (without *than*). We do this when the listener understands which nouns we mean.

**4** A: Are the sandwiches here good?
B: Yeah, but the hamburgers are **better**. (= The hamburgers are better than the sandwiches.)

**B**

**USING PRONOUNS AFTER *THAN***

We can use a **subject pronoun** + *be* after *than*. This structure is common in writing.

↓

**5a** Sarah is older than | **he is.**
(= Sarah is older than John is.)

**6a** My roommate was neater than | **I was.**

In speaking or very informal writing, we often use an **object pronoun*** after *than*.

↓

**5b** Sarah is older than | **him.**

**6b** My roommate was neater than | **me.**

**7** The green dress is prettier than | the black **one.** ◄—

**8** Your phone is better than | **mine.** ◄—

We can also use:
• a phrase with *one*

• a **possessive pronoun*** or noun (*mine, yours, his, hers, ours, theirs, Karen's*)

These structures are common in both speaking and writing.

*For more information on object pronouns and possessive pronouns, see Unit 6, pages 153 and 157.

236

## 15 | Noticing Comparisons Read this online discussion. Circle the adjectives with *-er/more*. Underline *than* + the words after *than*. Then complete the instructions below. 9.5 A–B

9.5 A–B

# How are you different from your brother or sister?

**Max:** My brother and I look really similar, so people think we are similar in other ways. But we're actually very different. I am much (more athletic) than he is. In school I was better at sports. I was usually on the soccer and basketball teams. My brother was never on a team. But my brother is smarter than me. His grades in school were a lot better than mine. Our parents were always proud of his grades and angry about mine.

**Karen:** My sister is taller and thinner than I am. She's also a lot more energetic[12]. I like to sit in the park or in a café and read a book. My sister never sits still[13]. After two minutes, she jumps up and wants to go somewhere. We take a walk, and she talks to everyone! She is much more outgoing than I am. I love my sister, but after a visit from her, I'm happy to sit down and relax!

**Diego:** My brother is more practical[14] than me, and I'm more artistic[15] than him. He has a wife and child, and he spends most of his free time with them. I live alone, and I travel a lot. He's probably more responsible than me. We have very different ideas about the world, but that's OK. We just don't talk about politics!

**Ahmed:** My brother's handwriting is much worse than mine! No one can read his handwriting. But in many ways we are very similar. The differences between us are small. For example, I'm pretty funny, but my brother is even funnier. We're both friendly and happy people. We always have a great time together.

**FYI**

In informal writing like online posts, you might see a mix of formal (written) and informal (spoken) language.

I'm older than **he is**. (more formal)

I'm older than **him**. (informal)

### INSTRUCTIONS

1. Which sentences above have an *-er/more* adjective but DON'T have *than*? Write **X** above these adjectives.
2. Which sentences have *than* + **object pronoun** (*me, him, her*)? Write **O** above the object pronouns.
3. Which sentences have *than* + **possessive pronoun** (*mine, his, hers*)? Write **P** above the possessive pronouns.
4. Which sentences have *than* + **subject pronoun** + *am/is/are*? Write **S** above the subject pronouns.

---

[12] **energetic:** full of energy so you can do a lot of things
[13] **still:** without moving
[14] **practical:** good at dealing with problems and making decisions

[15] **artistic:** good at making things connected with art (such as painting or music)

**Think about It** Look at the sentences you labeled *O* (sentences with *than* + object pronoun) in Activity 15. Rewrite these sentences with *than* + subject pronoun + *am/is/are*.

*But my brother is smarter than me. = But my brother is smarter than I am.*

**Talk about It** Think of a family member or a friend. How are you different from him or her? Complete these sentences with *-er/more* adjectives. Discuss your answers with a partner.

1. I am _____ than my _____.
2. My _____ is _____ than me.

**16 | Writing Comparisons** Use each group of words to make a sentence. Use the **bold** adjective + *-er* or *more* + *than*. Keep the words in the same order. Do you agree with the sentence? Check (✓) *Agree* or *Disagree*. `9.5 A`

| | AGREE | DISAGREE |
|---|---|---|
| **COMPARING VACATIONS** | | |
| 1. *The beach is more relaxing than the mountains.* <br> (the beach / **relaxing** / the mountains) | ☐ | ☐ |
| 2. _____ <br> (a long vacation / **good** / a short vacation) | ☐ | ☐ |
| **COMPARING AGES** | | |
| 3. _____ <br> (old people / **wise**[16] / young people) | ☐ | ☐ |
| 4. _____ <br> (old people / **responsible** / young people) | ☐ | ☐ |
| **COMPARING UNIVERSITY CHOICES** | | |
| 5. _____ <br> (a face-to-face[17] course / **good** / an online course) | ☐ | ☐ |
| 6. _____ <br> (small schools / **friendly** / large schools) | ☐ | ☐ |
| **COMPARING PLACES TO LIVE** | | |
| 7. _____ <br> (life in a small town / **easy** / life in the city) | ☐ | ☐ |
| 8. _____ <br> (life in the country[18] / **healthy** / life in the city) | ☐ | ☐ |
| **COMPARING ENTERTAINMENT** | | |
| 9. _____ <br> (basketball / **exciting** / soccer) | ☐ | ☐ |
| 10. _____ <br> (movies / **interesting** / TV shows) | ☐ | ☐ |

**Talk about It** Discuss your ideas as a class. Which sentences above do most students agree with?

---

[16] **wise:** knowing and understanding a lot about many things
[17] **face-to-face:** in a classroom with other students and a teacher
[18] **the country:** land that is away from towns and cities

**17 | Using Pronouns in Comparisons** Complete these conversations with the words in parentheses. Use the adjective with *-er* or *more + than.* **9.5 B**

1. A: How is the new computer system?

   B: I'm not sure. In some ways, the old system was _____*easier than the new one*_____.
      (easy / the new one)

2. A: We can take my car.

   B: Let's go in my car. It's _____.
      (big / yours)

3. A: Is your cousin Alfie our age?

   B: No, he's _____.
      (young / us)

4. A: Can you help me with this paragraph in French?

   B: I can try. But your French is _____.
      (good / mine)

5. A: Let's buy one of these photos. Which one do you like?

   B: Hmm. I think the little photo is _____.
      (interesting / the big one)

6. A: Which math teacher is better, Ms. Alvarez or Mr. Tyson?

   B: They're both good. Ms. Alvarez's class is hard. Maybe Mr. Tyson's class is a little

      _____.
      (easy / hers)

7. A: Do you need any help?

   B: Maybe you can open this jar. You're _____.
      (strong / me)

8. A: Do you think we can win? Are we good enough?

   B: Sure. We're _____.
      (good / them)

**Talk about It** Listen and check your answers above. Then practice the conversations with a partner.

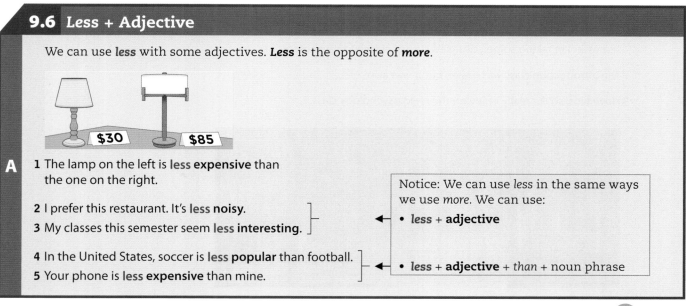

**9.6 Less + Adjective**

We can use **less** with some adjectives. **Less** is the opposite of **more**.

**A**

**1** The lamp on the left is **less expensive** than the one on the right.

**2** I prefer this restaurant. It's **less noisy**.
**3** My classes this semester seem **less interesting**.

**4** In the United States, soccer is **less popular** than football.
**5** Your phone is **less expensive** than mine.

Notice: We can use *less* in the same ways we use *more*. We can use:

• **less + adjective**

• **less + adjective** + *than* + noun phrase

**18 | Using *Less* + Adjective** Complete the blog entries below with *less* and an adjective from the box. **9.6 A**

| difficult | expensive | fattening | hungry | interesting | lonely | worried |

## First Year, Second Semester

**February 2**

This semester I'm living on campus. I liked my apartment in town

last semester. But I didn't meet many people at school. So over the

vacation I moved to a dorm. This was the right decision! I feel a lot

_____*less lonely*_____ . And the dorm is _____ than
     1                                                        2

the apartment, so I'm also saving money.

**February 8**

The food in the cafeteria here is so fattening[19]. I gained 20 pounds last

semester! But now I'm on a diet and it's really working. I cook all my meals

and just make healthy stuff, so the food is _____ .
                                                             3

I'm eating less, but I actually feel _____ .
                                                    4

**February 25**

School is a lot better these days. I'm getting used to[20] the work, so my classes

seem _____ . I'm feeling _____ about
           5                                        6

my grades.

Last semester I took an introduction to psychology class, but this

semester I'm taking some advanced classes like child psychology.

The introduction class was easier, but it was also _____ .
                                                                   7

I love kids, so I'm really enjoying the child psychology class.

**RESEARCH SAYS...**

Comparisons with *less* are less common than comparisons with *more*.

CORPUS

---

[19]**fattening:** likely to make you fat

[20]**get used to:** to become more familiar with something because you are doing it a lot

**19 | Using *More/-er* and *Less*** Complete the sentences below. Use the adjectives in each box + *-er*, *more*, or *less*. (See Chart 9.4 for help with *-er/more*.) `9.6 A`

WHICH IS BETTER—THE SUBURBS²¹ OR THE CITY?

**A. Advantages²² of the suburbs:**
People in the suburbs say . . .

**B. Advantages of the city:**
People in cities say . . .

| 1. interesting    safe |
| --- |

1a. People here don't worry about crime. The neighborhoods seem _____*safer*_____.

1b. Streets in the suburbs all look the same. They're boring. City streets are _____.

| 2. friendly    similar |
| --- |

2a. People here are _____. Everyone says hello.

2b. People in the suburbs all seem the same. In cities, people are much _____. You meet many different and interesting people!

| 3. interesting    quiet |
| --- |

3a. It's _____ here. Some days I just hear the birds.

3b. Some people think city life is too stressful. But I disagree. Life in the city is fun, and fun activities make my life _____.

| 4. crowded    far |
| --- |

4a. It's much _____ here. People have a lot of space. I have my own house and yard.

4b. I can walk everywhere, and there are lots of stores nearby. In the suburbs, the stores are _____ away, and you need a car.

| 5. exciting    expensive |
| --- |

5a. Homes are _____ here. For the same money, you can buy a tiny apartment in the city or a huge house in my neighborhood!

5b. Concerts, plays, movies, art—things are happening all the time. Life is _____ _____ here.

²¹ **suburbs:** areas where people live that are outside the central part of a city

²² **advantages:** things that are good or useful

| 6. difficult | healthy |
|---|---|

6a. Our kids have clean, fresh air and lots of places for exercise. The suburbs are _____ places for kids.

6b. There are more jobs in the city. In the suburbs, good jobs are often _____ to find.

**Write about It** Look at the sentences in Activity 19 again. How can we use *too* and *not . . . enough* to talk about these ideas? Write two sentences about problems with life in the suburbs and two sentences about problems with life in cities. Use *too* and *not . . . enough* and the adjectives in Activity 19. (Review Chart 9.2 for help.)

*Cities aren't safe enough.*

**Talk about It** Where do you prefer to live: in a suburb or in a city? Why?

---

## 9.7 Adjectives with -est and Most

We can use adjectives to compare one member of a group to the rest of the group. We form these adjectives in two ways:

**A**

With some adjectives, we use **the** + **adjective** + **-est**.

**1** That's **the nic**est watch in the store.

With some adjectives, we use **the most** + **adjective**.

**2** It's also **the most expensive** one.

**GRAMMAR TERM:** These kinds of adjectives are also called **superlative forms**.

$500    $4000    $250

**B**

**FORMING ADJECTIVES WITH -EST AND MOST**

| ONE-SYLLABLE ADJECTIVES | TWO-SYLLABLE ADJECTIVES ENDING IN Y* |
|---|---|
| cheap → **the cheapest**<br>hard → **the hardest**<br>strong → **the strongest**<br>tall → **the tallest** | hap·py → **the happiest**<br>heav·y → **the heaviest**<br>la·zy → **the laziest** |

| TWO-SYLLABLE ADJECTIVES | THREE-SYLLABLE ADJECTIVES |
|---|---|
| bor·ing → **the most boring**<br>care·ful → **the most careful**<br>po·lite → **the most polite** | ex·cit·ing → **the most exciting**<br>im·por·tant → **the most important**<br>prac·ti·cal → **the most practical** |

**USE WITH -EST OR MOST**

narrow → **the narrowest** OR **the most narrow**
quiet → **the quietest** OR **the most quiet**

**IRREGULAR FORMS**

| bad → **the worst** | good → **the best** | far → **the farthest** |
|---|---|---|

*For more information on spelling *-est* adjectives, see the Spelling Note on page 244.

We usually use **the** + **-est** with:
• most one-syllable adjectives
• some two-syllable adjectives (for example, words that end in y)

We use **the most** with:
• other two-syllable adjectives
• adjectives with more than two syllables

For some adjectives, we can use either **-est** or **most**.

Some adjectives like **bad**, **good**, and **far** have irregular superlative forms.

## 20 | Identifying Adjectives with -est and Most

Read this article. Underline the adjectives with -est and most. **9.7 A**

### Oldest Child and Youngest Child: Birth Order and Personality

Does birth order influence[23] personality? Many psychologists think so. Some personality qualities are more common in the oldest child in a family. Other qualities are more common in the youngest child. For example:

**The oldest child** in a family is often the most successful. In many families, this child is the smartest, the most confident, and the most responsible. As an adult, the oldest child often has a more important job than the other children.

**The youngest child** is often the most artistic and the most creative. This child is often the funniest and the most outgoing child in the family. He or she often has a bold[24] personality.

What explains these differences? Here are some possibilities:

The oldest child is often the only child for many years. Many parents pay a lot of attention[25] to their first child. This makes the child feel very confident. In many families, the oldest child also helps with younger siblings. This helps the child feel more responsible.

Many parents are less strict[26] with their youngest child. Maybe, with less strict parents, the child feels bolder.

**Think about It** Complete this chart with the forms from the article above.

| ADJECTIVE + -EST | | THE MOST + ADJECTIVE | |
|---|---|---|---|
| *The +* -est form | Adjective | *The most* form | Adjective |
| the oldest | old | | |
| | | | |
| | | | |
| | | | |
| | | | |

**Talk about It** Do you agree with the article above? Think about people you know who are the oldest or youngest in their family. Do these people have the qualities described above?

---

[23] **influence:** to change or shape in some way
[24] **bold:** brave and not afraid

[25] **pay a lot of attention:** to look or listen carefully very often
[26] **strict:** not allowing children to behave badly

**21 | Spelling Note: Adjectives + -est** Read the note. Then do Activity 22.

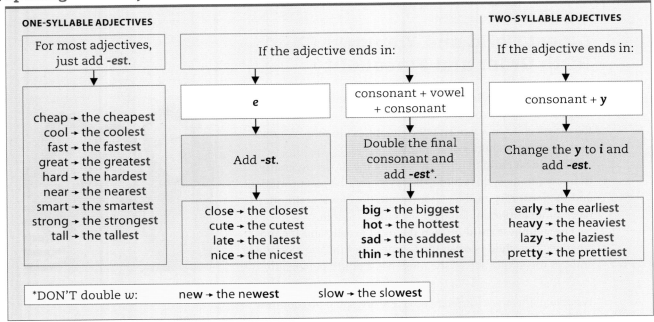

| ONE-SYLLABLE ADJECTIVES | | | | TWO-SYLLABLE ADJECTIVES |

For most adjectives, just add **-est**.

cheap → the cheapest
cool → the coolest
fast → the fastest
great → the greatest
hard → the hardest
near → the nearest
smart → the smartest
strong → the strongest
tall → the tallest

If the adjective ends in:

*e*

Add **-st**.

close → the closest
cute → the cutest
late → the latest
nice → the nicest

consonant + vowel + consonant

Double the final consonant and add **-est***.

**big** → the biggest
**hot** → the hottest
**sad** → the saddest
**thin** → the thinnest

If the adjective ends in:

consonant + **y**

Change the **y** to **i** and add **-est**.

**early** → the earliest
**heavy** → the heaviest
**lazy** → the laziest
**pretty** → the prettiest

*DON'T double *w*:     **new** → the ne**west**     **slow** → the slo**west**

**22 | Spelling -est Adjectives** Write the *-est* form of each adjective in the box in the correct column of the chart below. Include *the*.   9.7 B

| big | fast | late | messy | rich | thin |
| brave | happy | lazy | near | rude | warm |
| cheap | healthy | loud | new | safe | wet |
| easy | hot | low | quick | scary | wide |

| ONE-SYLLABLE ADJECTIVES | | | TWO-SYLLABLE ADJECTIVES |
|---|---|---|---|
| **Ending in *e*** | **Ending in consonant + vowel + consonant (not *w*)** | **All other one-syllable adjectives** | **Ending in consonant + *y*** |
| | *the biggest* | | |

**23 | Forming Adjectives with -est and Most** Look at this chart that compares three tablets. Then complete the sentences below with the adjectives in parentheses and the information in the chart. Use *the* + adjective + *-est* or *the* + *most* + adjective. **9.7 B**

| A COMPARISON OF THREE BEST-SELLING TABLETS | | | |
| --- | --- | --- | --- |
| Features | Tablet A | Tablet B | Tablet C |
| | | | |
| Overall[27] score (1–10) | 9 | 8 | 5 |
| Battery life (hours) | 9 hours | 11 hours | 8 hours |
| Speed | 2.5 GHz | 1.8 GHz | 1.5 GHz |
| Storage space[28] | 32 GB | 64 GB | 16 GB |
| Screen size (inches) | 7.87 inches (20 centimeters) | 10 inches (25.4 centimeters) | 13 inches (33 centimeters) |
| Weight (pounds) | 0.73 pounds (331 grams) | 1.6 pounds (726 grams) | 2 pounds (907 grams) |
| Picture quality (1–10) | 8 | 9 | 7 |
| Ease of use (1–5 stars) | ★★★★★ | ★★★★ | ★★★★ |
| Quality of customer service (1–5 stars) | ★★★★ | ★★★★★ | ★★★★ |
| Cost | $399 | $499 | $219 |

1. Of the three tablets, Tablet __A__ gets _____the best_____ overall score.
   (good)

   Tablet ____ gets _____ overall score.
   (bad)

2. Tablet ____ has _____ battery life.
   (long)

3. Tablet ____ is _____. Tablet ____ has _____ price.
   (expensive)                                    (low)

4. Tablet ____ is _____ tablet. Tablet ____ is _____.
   (heavy)                                      (light)

5. The tablet with _____ speed is Tablet ____.
   (fast)

6. The tablet with _____ amount of storage space is Tablet ____.
   (large)

7. Tablet ____ is _____ tablet for people to use.
   (easy)

8. Tablet ____ has _____ screen.
   (big)

9. Tablet ____ has _____ picture quality.
   (good)

   Tablet ____ has _____ picture quality.
   (bad)

10. People with Tablet ____ can expect _____ customer service.
    (helpful)

[27] **overall:** including everything

[28] **storage space:** (electronics) space for information such as photos, music, videos, etc.

**Write about It** Choose a kind of product from this box or use your own idea. Think about some popular brands for the product. Write sentences with *-est/most* about the different brands.

| cars | makeup | shoes | smartphones | TVs |

## 24 | Usage Note: Prepositional Phrases after *-est/Most* Forms  Read the note. Then do Activity 25.

Sometimes we include a **prepositional phrase** after adjectives with *-est / most*. This prepositional phrase describes the group.

**1** Reina is the best runner **on the team.**

**2** Breakfast is the most important meal **of the day.**

**3** Mount Everest is the tallest mountain **in the world.**

We often don't use a prepositional phrase because the meaning is clear to the listener.

**4** This store has **the lowest** prices.

**5** He makes **the best** sandwiches.

## 25 | Writing Sentences with *-est* and *Most*  Complete the questions with the words in parentheses. Use *the + -est* or *most* with the adjective. Then circle the correct answers.  `9.7 B`

### Geography Quiz

1. What is _____ *the longest river in Europe* _____?
   (long / river / in Europe)

   a. the Danube          b. the Dnieper          c. the Ural          d. the Volga

2. Which continent has _____?
   (tall / mountains)

   a. Africa          b. Asia          c. North America          d. South America

3. What is _____?
   (long / border / in the world)

   a. the border between   b. the border between   c. the border between   d. the border between
   China and India          China and                the United States       the United States
                            Mongolia                 and Canada              and Mexico

4. What is _____?
   (expensive / country / in the world)

   a. Japan          b. New Zealand          c. Norway          d. the United Kingdom

5. What is _____?
   (popular / country / for tourists)

   a. China          b. France          c. Spain          d. the United States

6. Which is _____?
   (large / island)

   a. Greenland          b. Iceland          c. Madagascar          d. New Guinea

7. What is _____?
   (large / country / in the world)

   a. Canada          b. China          c. Russia          d. the United States

8. What is _____?
   (populated / city / in the world)

   a. Buenos Aires    b. Moscow         c. Mumbai          d. Shanghai

9. What is _____?
   (small / country / in the world)

   a. San Marino      b. Vatican City   c. Monaco          d. Tuvalu

10. What is _____?
    (deep / ocean)

    a. the Arctic Ocean   b. the Atlantic Ocean   c. the Indian Ocean   d. the Pacific Ocean

Answers: 1. d; 2. b; 3. c; 4. c; 5. b; 6. a; 7. c; 8. c; 9. d; 10. d

**Think about It** Circle the prepositional phrases in the questions in Activity 25. Which questions DON'T have a prepositional phrase?

**Write about It** Work with a partner. Write three sentences with adjectives with -*est* or *most* about places you know. Use the phrases in this box or other adjectives.

| the best | the biggest | the most beautiful | the most interesting | the worst |
|---|---|---|---|---|

*The University of Toronto is the biggest university in Ontario, Canada.*

## 26 | Error Correction  Find and correct the errors. (Some sentences might not have any errors.)

1. Languages are more harder for me than math or science.
2. In my opinion, Machu Picchu is the beautiful place in the world.
3. The suitcase isn't enough big for all those things.
4. The library is too quiet, so we study there.
5. Michael's new job is more bad than his last one.
6. All the children in the group are good, but Tanya is probably the most good child.
7. Jelani lives farther from school now.
8. This apartment is the larger one in the building.
9. Ayisha is the amazingest worker!
10. This apartment seems too small for us.
11. I live the most far from school, so I have the longest ride.
12. Lee is the tallest in his family.
13. Your smartphone is newer from mine.
14. My nephew is six years old.
15. This is the more large TV in the store.
16. Laurent is the most smartest person in the class.

**A | GRAMMAR IN READING** Read this article about two vacation spots. Underline the adjectives with -er, more, less, -est, or most. Circle the other adjectives.

# Mexico's Best Resorts[29]

**Acapulco: "The queen of Mexican beach resorts"**

Acapulco is a city and resort on the Pacific Ocean. It is the largest resort in Mexico, and it is probably also the most exciting resort. For many tourists, Acapulco offers the perfect combination—amazing excitement and natural beauty.

Acapulco

REVIEWS

"We come here every year and stay at the beach all day. The water is a beautiful blue color. The sand on the beach looks gold. My children love Acapulco. It's a fun place for families!"—Sean H.

"Acapulco is a great place for shopping! The malls here are better and less expensive than the malls at home. And the markets have interesting Mexican art."—Maria S.

"Evenings in Acapulco are special. The restaurants have excellent food. You can hear some great music. The streets are full of people. Everyone's having a good time."—Katie R.

**Tulum: Ancient, beautiful, and peaceful**

Tulum is on the Caribbean. It is on top of a tall cliff[30] over the water. The Mayas[31] lived at Tulum, and visitors today can see their buildings from the years 1200 to 1500. They can see amazing Mayan art and learn about Mayan life. Tulum is also a beach resort. Visitors can walk down the cliff to a beautiful beach.

Tulum

REVIEWS

"Tulum is less crowded than other resorts. There aren't so many hotels or tourists. I come here to relax!"—Tom D.

"My best photos are from Tulum. You see the tall cliff, the old buildings, and the bright blue sea. It's amazing!"—Alexis G.

"Tulum is my favorite place for a vacation. The area has strange old buildings, interesting plants and animals, quiet and beautiful beaches, and good yoga classes!"—Irina J.

---

[29] **resorts:** places where a lot of people go on vacation
[30] **cliff:** a high area of rock by the ocean, with a side that goes down very quickly

[31] **Mayas (noun), Mayan (adjective):** a group of Indian people, mainly from Mexico and Guatemala, that goes back several thousand years

**Talk about It** Where do you want to go on vacation: Acapulco or Tulum? Explain your reasons to a partner.

*"I want to go to Tulum. It seems more relaxing. . . ."*

**B | GRAMMAR IN WRITING** Write a short paragraph (about five to six sentences) about your favorite vacation place. Follow these guidelines:

1. In the first sentence, answer these questions:
   • What kind of place is it? (for example: a beach, a place in the mountains, a city, etc.)
   • Where is it?

2. In the other sentences, answer these questions:
   • Why is the place special? What do you and other visitors like about it?
   • What do visitors see and do there?
   • How is this place different from other vacation places?

3. Use adjectives in your paragraph. Use at least one adjective with *-er/more*, *less*, or *-est/most*. You can use some of these adjectives or your own ideas:

| amazing | exciting | good | interesting | relaxing |
|---------|----------|------|-------------|----------|
| beautiful | fun | great | popular | special |

*Bangkok is the capital of Thailand, and it is the biggest city in Thailand. It is a popular place for visitors because . . .*

## 9.8 Summary of Adjectives

**Adjectives** describe or give more information about **nouns**. Adjectives can go:

| Before the **noun** they describe | After *be* or another **linking verb** |
|---|---|
| I need some **large boxes**.<br>My **new apartment** is just a few blocks from school. | Your **friends are** really **nice**.<br>That **class seems interesting**. |

**COMPARISONS WITH ADJECTIVES**

• We can use an **adjective** + **-er**, **more**, or **less** to describe differences between nouns.

• Sometimes we use a phrase with **than** after the adjective.

> Both restaurants are good, but I think Mitchell's pizza is **better**.
> My brother is much **taller than I am**. / My brother is much **taller than me**.
> Your apartment is **more expensive than mine**.
> This movie seems **more interesting**.
> New York is **less crowded than Beijing**.

• We can use **the** + **adjective** + **-est** or **the** + **most** + **adjective** to describe differences between one member of a group and the rest of the group.

> The python is **the longest** snake in the world.
> Mexico has **the most beautiful** beaches!
> Mitchell's pizza is **the best**.

---

**Answers to Activity 11 on pages 233–234:**

| 1. South America | 3. Pacific Ocean | 5. lions | 7. blue whales | 9. the /p/ sound | 11. *blog* |
|---|---|---|---|---|---|
| 2. Africa | 4. London | 6. tigers | 8. mosquitoes | 10. the English alphabet | 12. Swedish |

# 10

# Future Forms

**GO ONLINE**

For the Unit Vocabulary Check, go to the Online Practice.

## IN THIS UNIT, WE USE future forms to:

### Talk about plans

1. **I'm going to travel** to London this summer.

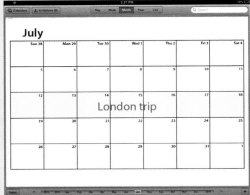

2. I **might go** to Dublin, too.

3. **I'm buying** my ticket this weekend.

**Think about It**  Complete these sentences with your own information.

1. I'm going to travel to _____ this summer.
   (place)

2. I might buy _____ next week.
   (thing)

3. I'm going to see _____ this weekend.
   (person)

## Make predictions

4. It **might rain** later.

5. I**'m going to miss** my train!

6. In the future, people **will drive** flying cars.

7. A person **will land** on Mars.

## Make offers and promises

8. I**'ll help** you with that.

9. Don't worry. I**'ll drive** carefully.

**Think about It** Think about your future. Check (✓) *Likely* (probably yes) or *Unlikely* (probably no).

|  | LIKELY | UNLIKELY |
|---|---|---|
| 1. I'll eat a healthy dinner tonight. | ☐ | ☐ |
| 2. I'll exercise two times this week. | ☐ | ☐ |
| 3. I'm going to get a new job soon. | ☐ | ☐ |
| 4. I might move to a different country someday. | ☐ | ☐ |

## 10.1 Positive and Negative Statements with *Be Going To*

We can use **be going to** to talk about the future.

**POSITIVE STATEMENTS**

**A**

| | subject | be | going to | base form verb | |
|---|---|---|---|---|---|
| 1 | I | am<br>'m | | stay. | |
| 2 | We<br>You<br>They | are<br>'re | going to | be | late. |
| 3 | He<br>She<br>It | is<br>'s | | work | this week. |

> **Notice:**
> *Be going to* is a kind of **helping verb** in this form. The base form verb is the **main verb**.

**NEGATIVE STATEMENTS**

**B**

| | subject | be + not | going to | base form verb | |
|---|---|---|---|---|---|
| 4 | I | am not<br>'m not | | leave | now. |
| 5 | We<br>You<br>They | are not<br>'re not<br>aren't | going to | be | here tomorrow. |
| 6 | He<br>She<br>It | is not<br>'s not<br>isn't | | work | next week. |

**GO ONLINE**

**1 | Noticing *Be Going To* in Predictions**  Underline the forms of *be going to* + the main verb. Then check (✓) *Yes*, *No*, or *Maybe*. **10.1 A**

| TEN YEARS FROM NOW . . . | YES | NO | MAYBE |
|---|---|---|---|
| 1. I'm going to live in a different town or city. | ☐ | ☐ | ☐ |
| 2. I'm going to have a job. | ☐ | ☐ | ☐ |
| 3. I'm going to have a lot of money. | ☐ | ☐ | ☐ |
| 4. I'm going to have the same friends. | ☐ | ☐ | ☐ |
| 5. My parents are going to live near me. | ☐ | ☐ | ☐ |
| 6. I'm going to speak English very well. | ☐ | ☐ | ☐ |
| 7. I'm going to travel a lot. | ☐ | ☐ | ☐ |
| 8. My personality is going to change. | ☐ | ☐ | ☐ |
| 9. My appearance[1] is going to change. | ☐ | ☐ | ☐ |
| 10. My life is going to be more fun. | ☐ | ☐ | ☐ |

> **FYI**
>
> Notice: We can use the main verb **go** after *am/is/are going to.*
>
> We**'re going to go** to London next month.
>
> When the main verb is *be*, we use the base form *be* after *am/is/are going to.*
>
> I**'m going to be** at work at noon.

**Talk about It**  Compare your answers above as a class.

---

[1] **appearance:** the way someone looks

## 2 | Pronunciation Note: *Gonna*   Listen to the note. Then do Activity 3.

We often pronounce **going to** as "gonna."

1 I'm **going to** go home soon.      *sounds like*      "I'm **gonna** go home soon."

2 She's **going to** call me back.      *sounds like*      "She's **gonna** call me back."

**WARNING!** We don't usually use "gonna" in writing.

## 3 | Using *Be Going To* for Predictions   Look at the television scenes below. Complete the sentence under each scene with the correct form of *be going to* and a verb from the box. Then listen and check your answers.   `10.1 A`

| drive | hit | make | trip² |
|-------|-----|------|-------|
| get | jump | take | win |

WHAT'S GOING TO HAPPEN NEXT?

1. That bike is _____ her!

2. They _____ lost.

3. He _____!

4. They _____ into the river!

5. He _____ the key!

6. She _____!

² **trip:** to hit your foot against something so that you fall

7. They _____!

8. She _____ an omelet.

**Talk about It** Take turns saying the sentences in Activity 3 to a partner. Pronounce *going to* as *gonna*. Your partner points to the correct photo.

**Write about It** Choose five of the scenes in Activity 3. Imagine what is going to happen next. Write a sentence about each scene.

1. *She's going to fall and break her phone.*

**4 | Using *Be + Not + Going To*** Complete each sentence below with the negative form of *be going to* and the verb in parentheses. Then match each picture with a sentence. `10.1 B`

a. ____

b. ____

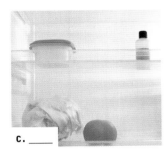
c. ____

d. ____

e. ____

f. _1_

g. ____

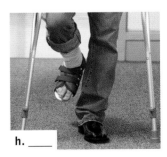
h. ____

**CHANGE OF PLANS**

1. I don't feel well. I _'m not going to go_ _____ to work today. (go)

2. Susanna has to study. She _____ with us. (come)

3. It's raining. We _____ soccer today. (play)

4. We _____ tonight. We don't have any food! (cook)

5. I _____ these boots. They're too expensive. (buy)

6. We _____ this exercise machine. Let's sell it. (use)

7. Jack _____ today. He hurt his foot. (run)

8. I _____ my sandwich. Do you want it? (eat)

**5 | Usage Note: *There Is/There Are Going to Be*** Read the note. Then do Activity 6.

We can make statements about the future with **there is / there are** (+ **not**) + **going to be**.

**1** A: Do you want to go out later?
B: I don't think so. **There's going to be** a storm tonight.

**2** A: Are there any cookies in the kitchen?
B: Yeah, there are a few. But go get one now. **There aren't going to be** any left later today.

| There | is<br>'s<br>are | going to | be | a storm | tonight. |
|---|---|---|---|---|---|
| | | | | a lot of people | at the concert. |

| There | isn't<br>'s not<br>aren't | going to | be | anyone* | at work tomorrow. |
|---|---|---|---|---|---|
| | | | | a lot of people | next week. |

For more information about *there is / there are*, see Unit 6.

*Anyone* is a singular pronoun. It means "a person."

**6 | Using *There Is/There Are Going to Be*** Complete conversations 1–5 with *there is/there are going to be*. Complete conversations 6–10 with *there is/there are not* going to be. Then listen and check your answers. `10.1 A–B`

1. A: The movie is at 7. What time do you want to leave?
   B: Let's leave early. _____ a lot of traffic.

2. A: _____ ten people here for dinner. Do we have enough food?
   B: Yeah, I went shopping this afternoon. We have a lot of food.

3. A: Do you want to play basketball tomorrow?
   B: Not tomorrow. _____ a big storm.

4. A: Why are you making cupcakes?
   B: I'm making them for school. _____ a study group after class.

5. A: Why is the break room³ closed?
   B: _____ a meeting in there at noon.

6. A: We can buy our tickets at the theater.
   B: No, let's buy them online. _____ any tickets left at 7:30.

7. A: Do you want to bring food to the park?
   B: Yeah, let's bring some sandwiches. _____ any food there.

8. A: These cookies are delicious.
   B: Don't eat them all. _____ any left for dessert!

9. A: Do you want to have lunch before the meeting?
   B: _____ time for lunch. Our appointment is at 12:30.

10. A: I want to return your sweater. Can I bring it over tonight?
    B: _____ anyone home tonight. How about tomorrow night?

> **F Y I**
>
> We can use **enough** before a noun.
>
> We're not going to have **enough food**.
>
> Do we have **enough money**?
>
> For more information about *enough*, see Unit 9, page 226.

cupcakes

³ **break room:** a room at a business that people use for coffee breaks, lunches, or other activities that are not work

## 10.2 Future Time Expressions

We use certain **time expressions** to refer to a specific time in the future.

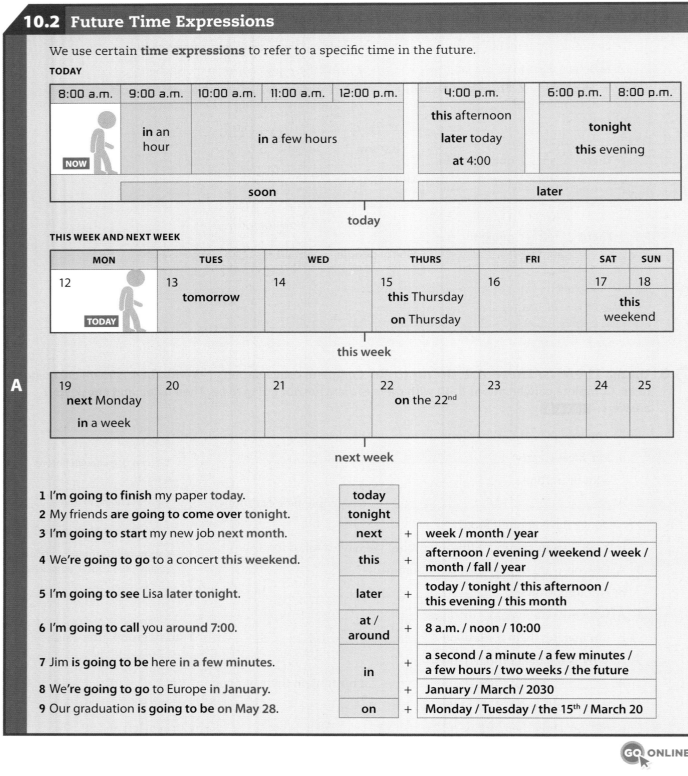

**TODAY**

| 8:00 a.m. | 9:00 a.m. | 10:00 a.m. | 11:00 a.m. | 12:00 p.m. | | 4:00 p.m. | | 6:00 p.m. | 8:00 p.m. |
|---|---|---|---|---|---|---|---|---|---|

- **in** an hour
- **in** a few hours
- **this** afternoon / **later** today / **at** 4:00
- **tonight** / **this** evening
- soon
- later

today

**THIS WEEK AND NEXT WEEK**

| MON | TUES | WED | THURS | FRI | SAT | SUN |
|---|---|---|---|---|---|---|
| 12 TODAY | 13 **tomorrow** | 14 | 15 **this** Thursday / **on** Thursday | 16 | 17 | 18 **this** weekend |

this week

**A**

| 19 **next** Monday / **in** a week | 20 | 21 | 22 **on** the 22^nd | 23 | 24 | 25 |
|---|---|---|---|---|---|---|

next week

1 I**'m going to finish** my paper **today**.
2 My friends **are going to come over** **tonight**.
3 I**'m going to start** my new job **next month**.
4 We**'re going to go** to a concert **this weekend**.
5 I**'m going to see** Lisa **later tonight**.
6 I**'m going to call** you **around 7:00**.
7 Jim **is going to be** here **in a few minutes**.
8 We**'re going to go** to Europe **in January**.
9 Our graduation **is going to be** **on May 28**.

| today | | |
|---|---|---|
| tonight | | |
| next | + | week / month / year |
| this | + | afternoon / evening / weekend / week / month / fall / year |
| later | + | today / tonight / this afternoon / this evening / this month |
| at / around | + | 8 a.m. / noon / 10:00 |
| in | + | a second / a minute / a few minutes / a few hours / two weeks / the future |
| | + | January / March / 2030 |
| on | + | Monday / Tuesday / the 15^th / March 20 |

GO ONLINE

**7 | Using *Be Going To* with Future Time Expressions** Underline the time expressions in these sentences. Then complete the sentences with *be (not) going to* and the verbs in parentheses. Make true statements about your plans. **10.2 A**

MY PLANS

1. I _____ dinner with friends on Friday. (have)

2. I _____ a vacation next month. (take)

3. I _____ tonight. (study)

4. I _____ later today. (work out)

5. I _____ home in a few hours. (go)

6. I _____ late for class on Friday. (be)

7. My cousins _____ me next week. (visit)

8. My friends and I _____ tomorrow. (hang out⁴)

9. I _____ a new job soon. (get)

10. I _____ a new class in two months. (start)

11. I _____ to a new city in a few years. (move)

12. My friends and I _____ a movie this weekend. (see)

F Y I

We say **this evening** or **tonight**. We don't say ~~this night~~.

**Talk about It** Compare your answers in Activity 7 with a partner. Are your plans similar or different?

**Write about It** Change your negative sentences in Activity 7 to positive sentences. Use different time expressions. Share your answers with a partner.

*1. I'm going to have dinner with friends tonight.*

## 8 | Using Time Expressions to Talk about Future Plans Alicia is a journalist for a magazine. Look at her calendar. Then check (✓) *True* or *False* for each statement on page 258. `10.2 A`

A JOURNALIST'S SCHEDULE

| MON | TUES | WED | THURS | FRI | SAT | SUN |
|---|---|---|---|---|---|---|
| 1 | 2 TODAY | 3 have dinner with Mom | 4 | 5 fly to Tokyo | 6 go to the symphony with Akira | 7 meet Japanese film directors |
| 8 interview the prime minister⁵ | 9 | 10 return to LA from Tokyo | 11 fly to New York | 12 visit the *New York Times* office | 13 have lunch with Mark and Lana | 14 return to LA from New York |
| 15 visit movie studio | 16 interview Bradley Cooper | 17 | 18 interview Jennifer Lawrence | 19 | 20 fly to Buenos Aires | 21 |
| 22 interview Spike Jonze | 23 | 24 return to LA from Buenos Aires | 25 | 26 start vacation: drive to Santa Barbara | 27 | 28 |
| 29 | 30 | | | | | |

⁴**hang out:** (informal) to spend time with people

⁵**prime minister:** the leader of the government in some countries, for example, in Japan

|   | TRUE | FALSE |
|---|---|---|
| 1. Alicia is going to fly to Tokyo next week. | ☐ | ☐ |
| 2. Alicia and Akira are going to go to the symphony this Sunday. | ☐ | ☐ |
| 3. Alicia is going to interview the prime minister next Monday. | ☐ | ☐ |
| 4. She's going to have dinner with her mom tomorrow. | ☐ | ☐ |
| 5. Later this week, she's going to meet some Japanese film directors. | ☐ | ☐ |
| 6. Mark, Lana, and Alicia are going to have lunch this weekend. | ☐ | ☐ |
| 7. Alicia is going to interview Jennifer Lawrence on the 21st. | ☐ | ☐ |
| 8. She's going to visit a movie studio in two days. | ☐ | ☐ |
| 9. In three weeks, she is going to interview Bradley Cooper. | ☐ | ☐ |
| 10. Later this month, Alicia is going to take a vacation. | ☐ | ☐ |

**Write about It** Correct the false statements in Activity 8. Use the correct time expressions.

   *1.  Alicia is going to fly to Tokyo on Friday.*

**9 | Usage Note: *I Think* and *Probably*** Read the note. Then do Activity 10.

When we're not sure about a plan or a prediction, we can use *probably* or *I think*.

1  It's **going to** rain all day tomorrow.

UNCERTAIN — CERTAIN

2  It's probably **going to** rain tomorrow.

3  I think it's **going to** rain tomorrow.

UNCERTAIN — CERTAIN

Use *probably* or *probably not* between *is / am / are* and *going to*.

4  I'm probably going to stay home tonight.
5  It's probably going to rain.

6  I'm probably not going to go out.
7  It's probably not going to snow.

Use *I think* or *I don't think* at the beginning of a sentence.

8  I think I'm going to stay home tonight.
9  I think it's going to rain.

10  I don't think I'm going to go out.
11  I don't think it's going to snow.

**10 | Using *I Think* and *Probably*** Write predictions about the weather in your area. Use *be going to* and *I think/I don't think* or *probably/probably not*. Use the time expressions in parentheses. Use the weather words and phrases in the box or your own ideas.  `10.2 A`

PREDICTING THE WEATHER

1.  *I think it's going to rain tonight.* _____ (tonight)
2.  _____ (tomorrow)
3.  _____ (this weekend)
4.  _____ (next week)
5.  _____ (this summer)
6.  _____ (this winter)
7.  _____ (next month)

| |
|---|
| be cloudy |
| be hot |
| be nice |
| be sunny |
| be windy |
| rain |
| snow |

**Write about It** Write predictions about the weather this weekend in these cities around the world. Use *be going to* and *I think* or *probably*. Then go online and check your predictions.

THIS WEEKEND . . .

1. In Seoul, South Korea: _It's probably going to be cold._ _____

2. In London, England: _____

3. In Santiago, Chile: _____

4. In Sydney, Australia: _____

5. In Riyadh, Saudi Arabia: _____

---

## 10.3 Yes/No Questions and Short Answers with *Be Going To*

**YES/NO QUESTIONS**

| | *be* | subject | *going to* | base form verb | |
|---|---|---|---|---|---|
| 1 | Are | you we they | going to | **move** | next month? |
| 2 | Am | I | | **go** | with you? |
| 3 | Is | he she it | | **be** | there tonight? |

**SHORT ANSWERS**

| | | subject | *be* |
|---|---|---|---|
| 4 | Yes, | I | am. |
| | | you we they | are. |
| | | he she it | is. |

| | | | |
|---|---|---|---|
| 5 | No, | I | am not. 'm not. |
| | | you we they | are not. 're not. aren't. |
| | | he she it | is not. 's not. isn't. |

**A**

**OTHER WAYS TO ANSWER *YES/NO* QUESTIONS**

| ANSWER *YES* | ANSWER *I DON'T KNOW* | ANSWER *NO* |
|---|---|---|
| Probably. I think so. I hope so. Yes, . . . (more information) | Maybe. I don't know. I'm not sure. | Probably not. I don't think so. I hope not. No, . . . (more information) |

6 A: **Are** you **going to get** a new job?
   B: I hope so. I have an interview next week.

7 A: **Are** you **going to drive** to school?
   B: No, I'm going to take the subway.

8 A: **Are** you **going to be** here tomorrow?
   B: Probably.

9 A: **Am** I **going to be** late?
   B: I don't think so.

GO ONLINE

---

🔊 **11 | Asking *Yes/No* Questions with *Be Going To*** Complete these conversations with the correct form of *be going to* and the verb in parentheses. Then listen and check your answers. `10.3 A`

ASKING ABOUT WEEKEND PLANS

1. A: _____ Carl _____ over tonight? (come)

   B: No, he's busy.

2. A: _____ you _____ shopping tomorrow? (go)

   B: No, why?

   A: I need to buy a gift for my mom.

3. A: _____ you and Karen _____ out this weekend? (go)

   B: Yeah, I think we're going to see a concert.

RESEARCH SAYS...

*Be going to* is more common in conversation than in writing.

CORPUS

4. A: _____ you _____ your free movie ticket tonight? (use)

   B: No, do you want it?

5. A: _____ Elisa _____ with us this weekend? (stay)

   B: Probably not. I think she's going to stay with Sandra.

6. A: _____ we _____ anyone this weekend? (see)

   B: Yeah, we're going to have dinner with Joe and Mike.

7. A: Where's Jose?

   B: He went home.

   A: _____ he _____ back to the beach this weekend? (come)

   B: I don't think so. He's getting ready to start school next week.

8. A: How's Jackie?

   B: She's great. She and Elena are going to go to Portland this weekend.

   A: _____ they _____? (fly)

   B: No, they're going to drive.

9. A: _____ you _____ home this weekend? (be)

   B: Yeah, are you?

   A: Yeah, I am. Do you want to see a movie or something?

   B: Sure. That sounds great.

10. A: Who was that on the phone?

    B: It was Karen.

    A: _____ she _____ us at the restaurant? (meet)

    B: No, she wants us to pick her up.

**Talk about It** Work with a partner. Ask about your partner's plans. Use the phrases and time expressions in this box or your own ideas. Answer with short answers or with more information.

| PHRASES | | | | TIME EXPRESSIONS | |
|---|---|---|---|---|---|
| go out to dinner | go to a movie | read a book | study | on Saturday | tomorrow |
| go shopping | hang out with friends | stay home | watch TV | this weekend | tonight |

*A: Are you going to go out to dinner this weekend?*
*B: No, I'm not. / No, I'm going to stay home.*

## 12 | Asking and Answering Questions about Future Plans Write *yes/no* questions with the words in parentheses and *be going to*. Then write two more questions. `10.3 A`

WHAT ARE YOU GOING TO DO THIS YEAR?

| | Questions | Answered *yes* |
|---|---|---|
| 1. (take music lessons) | *Are you going to take music lessons this year?* | |
| 2. (move to a new city) | | |
| 3. (get a job) | | |

| Questions | Answered *yes* |
|---|---|
| 4. (get in shape[6]) | |
| 5. (learn a new sport) | |
| 6. (go to a wedding) | |
| 7. (leave the country) | |
| 8. (learn a new language) | |
| 9. | |
| 10. | |

**Talk about It**  Ask your classmates your questions. Write the number of people who answer *yes* in the chart in Activity 12.

A:  *Are you going to take music lessons this year?*
B:  *No, I'm not.*

A:  *Are you going to take music lessons this year?*
C:  *Yes, I'm going to take guitar lessons.*

**Talk about It**  Tell the class about the results of your survey.

*"Two students are going to take music lessons this year: Eduardo and Maria."*

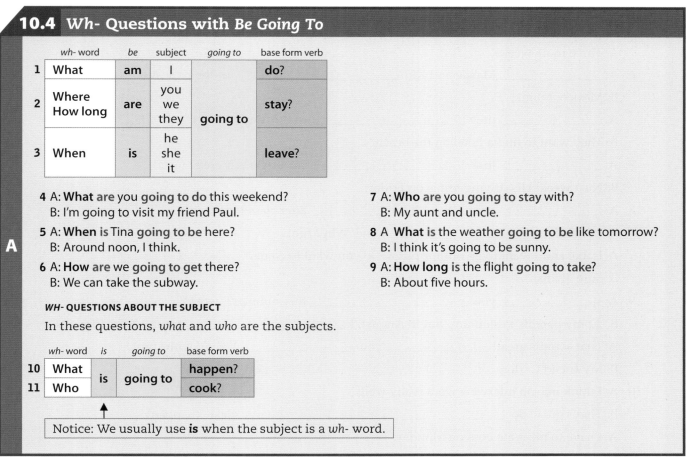

## 10.4 *Wh-* Questions with *Be Going To*

**A**

| | *wh-* word | *be* | subject | *going to* | base form verb |
|---|---|---|---|---|---|
| 1 | What | am | I | | do? |
| 2 | Where / How long | are | you we they | going to | stay? |
| 3 | When | is | he she it | | leave? |

4 A: **What are** you **going to do** this weekend?
 B: I'm going to visit my friend Paul.

5 A: **When is** Tina **going to be** here?
 B: Around noon, I think.

6 A: **How are** we **going to get** there?
 B: We can take the subway.

7 A: **Who are** you **going to stay** with?
 B: My aunt and uncle.

8 A **What is** the weather **going to be** like tomorrow?
 B: I think it's going to be sunny.

9 A: **How long is** the flight **going to take**?
 B: About five hours.

**WH- QUESTIONS ABOUT THE SUBJECT**

In these questions, *what* and *who* are the subjects.

| | *wh-* word | *is* | *going to* | base form verb |
|---|---|---|---|---|
| 10 | What | is | going to | happen? |
| 11 | Who | | | cook? |

Notice: We usually use **is** when the subject is a *wh-* word.

[6] **get in shape:** to become healthy and physically fit (often by exercising and eating healthy food)

**13 | Asking and Answering *Wh-* Questions with *Be Going To*** Complete the conversations below with the correct form of *be going to*. Use the *wh-* words in the box and the verbs in parentheses. Then listen and check your answers. **10.4 A**

| how long | what | when | where | who |
|----------|------|------|-------|-----|

1. A: Are you going to travel this summer?

   B: Yeah! I can't wait.

   A: _____*Where are*_____ you _____*going to go*_____? (go)

   B: Probably Los Angeles or San Diego.

2. A: Is everyone ready? Let's go.

   B: We're ready. _____ _____? (drive)

   A: Pam—she has the biggest car.

3. A: Are you still watching that movie?

   B: Yeah, it's really long.

   A: _____ it _____? (end)

   B: Soon, I hope!

4. A: _____ the weather _____ like this weekend? (be)

   B: I think it _____ really hot. (be)

   A: Oh, let's go to the beach!

5. A: There's construction on my street. It wakes me up at 7 every morning!

   B: _____ the work _____? (last)

   A: Three more weeks!

6. A: _____ Marcie and Kim _____ for their vacation? (go)

   B: Mexico, I think.

   A: _____ they _____ stay? (stay)

   B: They want to find a hotel on the beach.

7. A: _____ Jose _____ his driver's license? (get)

   B: Next week! His driving test is on Friday.

8. A: _____ you _____ after class today? (do)

   B: I think I _____ home. Why? (go)

   A: Isabel and I want to go out for pizza. Do you want to come?

   B: Sure, thanks!

9. A: _____ you _____ this summer? (work)

   B: At my parents' restaurant. But in August, I _____ around Asia. (travel)

   A: That sounds great! _____ you _____ with? (go)

   B: My friend Carlos.

10. A: I think my job interview went really well!

    B: That's great! So, _____ _____ next? (happen)

    A: I have to meet the boss on Monday.

construction

**Think about It** Which questions above are questions about the subject?

262

**Talk about It** Write questions with these words and *be going to*. Then ask and answer your questions with a partner.

YOUR NEXT VACATION

1. (where/you/go/on your next vacation) _____
2. (what/you/do/there) _____
3. (when/you/go) _____
4. (how/you/get there) _____
5. (who/go/with you) _____
6. (where/you/stay) _____
7. (who/make/the reservations) _____

1. A: *Where are you going to go on your next vacation?*
   B: *I think I'm going to go to Thailand.*

## 14 | Error Correction  Find and correct the errors. (Some sentences may not have any errors.)

1. Where you going to go tonight?
2. I going to call Marisol later.
3. What she going to do?
4. You going to stay with Joanna?
5. Is Sonya going cook dinner tonight?
6. They no going be here tomorrow.
7. Sarah is going to come over tonight.
8. We're going to leaving in a few minutes.
9. When they're going to arrive?
10. Are we going have a test tomorrow?
11. They going to be here soon?
12. Who going to come with us?
13. Is she going to make a cake?
14. What's going be on TV tonight?

---

## 10.5 Using the Present Progressive to Talk about Future Plans

We sometimes use the **present progressive** to talk about future plans (when the plans are already decided). We often use **future time expressions** to show future meaning.

Remember: We form the present progressive with **be** (+ **not**) + the **-ing form of a verb**.

**POSITIVE STATEMENTS**

1 I'm **leaving** tomorrow.
2 She's **starting** school **next week**.

**NEGATIVE STATEMENTS**

3 Ken **isn't coming this weekend**.
4 We're **not going** out **tonight**.

**YES/NO QUESTIONS**

5 Are you **cooking** dinner **tonight**?
6 Is Gina **staying** with us **this weekend**?

**WH- QUESTIONS**

7 What **are** you **doing on Friday**?
8 Who's **coming tomorrow**?

---

**PRESENT MEANING VS. FUTURE MEANING**

Notice:

**PRESENT MEANING**

9 I can't talk now. I'm **working**.
10 What **are** you **doing** these days?

**FUTURE MEANING**

11 I'm **working** this weekend.
12 What **are** you **doing** tomorrow?

For more information about the present progressive, see Unit 7.

**15 | Using the Present Progressive for Present and Future Meaning** Complete these conversations with the present progressive form of the verbs in parentheses. Then check (✓) *Present Meaning* or *Future Meaning*. Practice the conversations with a partner. `10.5 A`

|  | PRESENT MEANING | FUTURE MEANING |
|---|---|---|
| 1. A: Is Erica here?<br>B: No, she __'s working__. (work) | ✓ | ☐ |
| 2. A: _____ Alice and Jay _____ over for dinner tomorrow? (come)<br>B: Yes, they are. | ☐ | ☐ |
| 3. A: Hi, are you busy?<br>B: No, I _____ anything right now. What's up? (not do) | ☐ | ☐ |
| 4. A: What _____ Lucas _____? (do)<br>B: I think he's writing an email. | ☐ | ☐ |
| 5. A: _____ you _____ out tonight? (go)<br>B: No, we can't. Ken has a really bad cold. | ☐ | ☐ |
| 6. A: Katie _____ any classes next semester. (not take)<br>B: Why not?<br>A: She wants to work more hours. | ☐ | ☐ |
| 7. A: Who _____ you _____ to? (talk)<br>B: Stephen. He's in New York. | ☐ | ☐ |
| 8. A: What _____ you _____ this weekend? (do)<br>B: I'm not sure. | ☐ | ☐ |
| 9. A: Can I ask you a question?<br>B: I can't talk right now. I'm late.<br>A: Where _____ you _____? (go)<br>B: To class. | ☐ | ☐ |
| 10. A: Do you want to see a movie on Friday?<br>B: I can't. I _____ on Friday night. (work) | ☐ | ☐ |
| 11. A: What time is your guitar lesson tonight?<br>B: I _____ a lesson tonight. My teacher is sick. (not have) | ☐ | ☐ |
| 12. A: _____ Sam _____ at the library? (study)<br>B: No, he's at Ken's house. | ☐ | ☐ |

**Think about It** Underline the future time expressions in the sentences above.

**Talk about It** Talk with a partner. Tell your partner your plans for this week. Use the present progressive.

*"Tomorrow, I'm going to the movies with my friend Sarah. On Thursday, I'm working in the morning and going to class in the evening...."*

TALKING ABOUT PLANS

1. A: _____Are_____ you _____*leaving*_____ soon? __PP__

   B: No, we _____ for a while. _____

   How about you?

   A: We _____ around 8. _____

2. A: What _____ you _____ this summer? _____

   B: I _____ some classes. How about you? _____

   A: I _____ to Europe for the summer. _____

3. A: I _____ a new job next Monday. _____

   B: Congratulations! Where _____ you _____? _____

   A: At the new mall downtown.

4. A: _____ you _____ anything

   this weekend? _____

   B: Yeah, we _____ to the street fair

   on Saturday. _____

   A: Oh, I _____ to the fair, too! _____

5. A: What _____ you _____? _____

   B: I _____ a plane ticket online. _____

   A: Oh, where _____ you _____? _____

   B: To Mexico.

6. A. Hey, how are you?

   B: I'm great, but really busy.

   A: How many classes _____ you _____ this semester? _____

   B: Five! Next semester, I _____ three classes. _____

7. A: Is Misha home?

   B: No, she _____ at the library. _____

   A: OK. _____ she _____ home soon? _____

   B: I'm not sure. I can tell her to call you.

   A: Great. Thanks.

8. A: Do you have plans for this weekend?

   B: No, I think I _____ home. How about you? _____

   A: Sarah and I _____ to the beach on Saturday. Do you want to come? _____

   B: Hmm. OK. Thanks.

9. A: Can you email me your salmon recipe? I _____ dinner for my parents

   tonight. _____

   B: Of course. No problem.

a street fair

**FYI**

When we use the present progressive for personal plans, it means our plans are already decided.

**I'm taking** a class this summer.
(= I already made plans to take a class this summer.)

**Think about It** Look at the present progressive sentences in the conversations above. Which sentences have a future meaning? Which have a present meaning?

# 10.6 May and Might for Future Possibility

We can use **may** or **might** + the **base form of a verb** to talk about possible future events.

**A**

**POSITIVE STATEMENTS**

| | subject | *may / might* | base form verb | |
|---|---|---|---|---|
| 1 | I You We They He She It | **may might** | **be** | late tomorrow. |

2 It **may rain** on Friday.

3 We **might go** out tonight.

4 They **might come** with us.

**NEGATIVE STATEMENTS**

| | subject | *may / might + not* | base form verb | |
|---|---|---|---|---|
| 5 | I You We They He She It | **may not might not** | **be** | late tomorrow. |

6 He **may not be** home tonight.

7 She **might not pass** the test.

8 I **may not play** tennis next year.

**WARNING!** Use the **base form of a verb** after *may* or *might*.

✓ We may **go** out tonight.

✓ I might not **take** this class next semester.

✗ We **may to go** out tonight.

✗ I might not **taking** this class next semester.

**GRAMMAR TERM:** *May* and *might* are **modals**. For more information about modals, see Units 11 and 12.

**B**

**May** and **might** show a weaker certainty than other future forms.

| | |
|---|---|
| *BE GOING TO* | We**'re going to go** out tonight. |
| PRESENT PROGRESSIVE | We**'re going** out tonight. |

UNCERTAIN        CERTAIN

| | |
|---|---|
| *MAY* | We **may go** out tonight. |
| *MIGHT* | We **might go** out tonight. |

UNCERTAIN        CERTAIN

GO ONLINE

---

**17 | Using *Might* and *Might Not*** Complete conversations 1–4 with *might* and a verb from the box. Then complete conversations 5–8 with *might not* and a verb from the box. `10.6 A–B`

MAKING, ACCEPTING, AND DECLINING[7] INVITATIONS

1. A: What are you doing tonight?

   B: I'm not sure. I _____*might see*_____ a movie later. How about you?

   A: I'm going to an art show. Do you want to come with me?

   B: Hmm. OK. Sure.

2. A: Do you want to do something this weekend?

   B: Thanks, but I can't. My brother is getting married this weekend.

   A: Oh, that's great! Have fun!

   B: What are you going to do this weekend?

   A: I don't know. I _____ skiing with my cousins.

| go |
|----|
| see |

**RESEARCH SAYS...**

*Might* is more common in conversation. *May* is more common in academic writing.

We **might** go out tonight.

The population **may** increase by 50 percent.

CORPU

[7]**declining:** saying no

266

3. A: Do you want to come to a concert in the park tonight?

   My friends have an extra ticket.

   B: I don't think so. Look at the sky. It _____.

   A: You're right.

like
rain

4. A: I'm going to a jazz show tonight. Do you want to come?

   B: Maybe. I don't really know jazz music.

   A: Just try it. You _____ it.

   B: OK.

5. A: I'm hungry! Do you want to go out for lunch after class?

   B: Yeah, but I _____ enough time.

   I have a meeting with my advisor at 1.

   A: Oh, OK. Maybe tomorrow!

go
have

6. A: Do you want a ride to school tomorrow?

   B: I don't know. I _____ to school tomorrow.

   I don't feel very well.

   A: Oh, no. There's a really bad cold going around right now.

7. A: Where are you going to go for vacation this summer?

   B: I _____ a vacation this summer.

   I don't think I have enough money.

   A: Kelly and I are going to go to my uncle's beach house in July.

   It's free. Do you want to come with us?

   B: Sure! Thanks!

be
take

8. A: Do you want to come over for dinner tonight? I'm making spaghetti with shrimp.

   B: That sounds delicious, but I _____ hungry for dinner.

   I ate a really big lunch.

   A: Come over anyway. Stacey is going to be there.

   B: OK.

**Talk about It** Listen and check your answers. Then practice the conversations in Activity 17 with a partner.

**Think about It** In the conversations in Activity 17, underline the forms of *be going to* and the present progressive with a future meaning. In each conversation, which speaker is talking about certain events? Which speaker is talking about possible events?

*In conversation 1, Speaker A is talking about certain events.*
*Speaker B is talking about possible events.*

**18 | Writing Sentences with *May* and *Might***  Look at these photos. For each photo, write one positive sentence and one negative sentence with *may* or *might*. Use verbs in the boxes below or your own ideas.

`10.6 A`

MAKING PREDICTIONS

1

| go | rain | stay |

*It might rain later.*

2

| go | play | stay |

3

| be | get | miss |

4

| make | miss | score |

**19 | Writing Sentences with *Be Going To, May,* and *Might***  Write sentences about your plans. Complete the sentences below with the ideas in the box or your own ideas. Use the forms in parentheses. (Look at Charts 10.1–10.2 for help with *be going to*.)  `10.6 A–B`

DEFINITE PLANS AND POSSIBLE PLANS

| be in school | buy a car | go on vacation | live in (city) | move |
|---|---|---|---|---|
| be in this city | get a pet | have my dream job | live in my dream house | take classes |

1. (be going to) _____ next year.

2. (be not going to) _____ next year.

3. (might) _____ next year.

4. (might not) _____ next year.

5. (be going to) _____ in five years.

6. (be not going to) _____ in five years.

7. (may) _____ in five years.

8. (may not) _____ in five years.

9. (be going to) _____ in ten years.

10. (be not going to) _____ in ten years.

11. (might) _____ in ten years.

12. (may not) _____ in ten years.

## 10.7 Statements with *Will*

Another form we use to talk about the future is *will*. We use *will* + the **base form of a verb**.

**POSITIVE STATEMENTS**

**A** **1**

| subject | *will* | base form verb | |
|---|---|---|---|
| I / You / We / They / He / She / It | **will** **'ll** | **be** | there in five minutes. |

In speaking and informal writing, we usually use the contraction *'ll*.

**2** I**'ll pick** you up after work.

**3** Scientists **will discover** another planet soon.

**4** The weather **will be** nice next week.

**NEGATIVE STATEMENTS**

**B** **5**

| subject | *will + not* | base form verb | |
|---|---|---|---|
| I / You / We / They / He / She / It | **will not** **won't** | **leave** | without you. |

In speaking and informal writing, we usually use the contraction *won't*.

**6** We **won't stay** very long.

**7** I promise I **won't leave**!

**8** We **won't get** there on time.

**20 | Forming Statements with *Will*** Complete these sentences with *will* and the verbs in parentheses. Do you think the predictions will happen? Check (✓) *Likely* or *Not Likely*.  **10.7 A**

# Predictions in Science and Technology

**Here are some predictions from scientists and technology experts[8]:**

| | | LIKELY | NOT LIKELY |
|---|---|---|---|
| 1. Computers _____ a sense of smell. (have) | | ☐ | ☐ |
| 2. People _____ their thoughts into a computer. (upload[9]) | | ☐ | ☐ |
| 3. People _____ all of their conversations. (record) | | ☐ | ☐ |
| 4. We _____ to computers directly from our brains. (connect) | | ☐ | ☐ |
| 5. People _____ on vacations in space. (go) | | ☐ | ☐ |
| 6. Cars _____ without human drivers. (drive) | | ☐ | ☐ |
| 7. Many people _____ for 150 years or more. (live) | | ☐ | ☐ |
| 8. Airplanes _____ without pilots. (fly) | | ☐ | ☐ |
| 9. Some buildings _____ ten kilometers high. (be) | | ☐ | ☐ |
| 10. An astronaut _____ on Mars. (land) | | ☐ | ☐ |

[8] **experts:** people who know a lot about something

[9] **upload:** to copy or transfer information from one computer to another

**Talk about It** Compare your answers in Activity 20 as a class. Which predictions do most students believe?

🔊 **21 | Making Offers with *I'll*** Listen and complete these conversations with the words you hear (*I'll* + a main verb). Then practice the conversations with a partner. ██ 10.7 A

MAKING OFFERS

1. A: What's wrong?

   B: My taxi isn't here. I have to get to the airport soon.

   A: _I'll take_____ you.

   B: Really? Thanks so much!

2. A: Do you need some help?

   B: Yeah. I can't reach that book.

   A: _____ it for you.

3. A: Are you lost?

   B: Yeah, I'm looking for the museum. Is it near here?

   A: Yeah, let me see your map. _____ you.

   B: Thank you. I appreciate it.

4. A: What's wrong?

   B: I left my wallet at home.

   A: _____ this time. You can pay next time.

   B: It's a deal.

5. A: Did you do the math homework?

   B: Yeah, I did. Did you?

   A: Not yet. I don't understand it at all.

   B: _____ you with it.

6. A: Oh, are you baking cookies?

   B: Well, I wanted to, but I can't. We don't have any eggs.

   A: _____ some. I have to go to the store anyway.

   B: Great. Thanks.

7. A: Is Sarah here yet?

   B: No, she isn't. I don't know where she is.

   A: _____ her.

   B: Good idea.

8. A: Welcome! I'm so excited to see you!

   B: I'm excited to be here!

   A: Was it a long drive?

   B: Yeah, I'm really tired.

   A: Well, come in and sit down. _____ your suitcase in from the car.

I can't reach that book.

In conversation, we usually use the contraction **'ll** with pronouns. Sometimes the **'ll** is difficult to hear. Notice the difference between sentences with **'ll** and sentences with the simple present.

| FUTURE WITH '*LL* | SIMPLE PRESENT |
|---|---|
| **1** I'll call you tomorrow. | **3** I call my mother every weekend. |
| **2** She'll make dinner tonight. | **4** She makes dinner on Tuesdays. |

Time expressions and other clues can help you decide if the sentence describes the present or future.

◁)) **23 | Listening for '*ll*** Listen and write the words you hear. Check (✓) *Future with 'll* or *Simple Present*. Then practice the conversations with a partner. **10.7 A**

|  | FUTURE WITH '*LL* | SIMPLE PRESENT |
|---|:---:|:---:|
| 1. A: I'm going to be home late. Can you order a pizza for dinner?<br>B: _____ dinner. I'm going to be home early. | ☐ | ☐ |
| 2. A: Mom, I can't reach the cereal.<br>B: _____ it for you. | ☐ | ☐ |
| 3. A: The faucet is dripping again.<br>B: The plumber[10] is coming tomorrow. _____ it. | ☐ | ☐ |
| 4. A: Oh, no. We're out of milk.<br>B: I'm going to the store today. _____ some. | ☐ | ☐ |
| 5. A: Do your parents like this show?<br>B: Yeah, they love it. _____ it every week. | ☐ | ☐ |
| 6. A: Are you going to play tennis tonight?<br>B: Yeah, _____ every Wednesday. | ☐ | ☐ |
| 7. A: What do you do on the weekends?<br>B: _____ at a sandwich shop. | ☐ | ☐ |
| 8. A: These bags are so heavy.<br>B: _____ one of them. | ☐ | ☐ |
| 9. A: Oh, no! I'm late. I'm going to miss the bus.<br>B: I'm not busy. _____ you a ride. | ☐ | ☐ |
| 10. A: We need more towels. Also, there's no soap in the bathroom.<br>B: _____ the front desk. | ☐ | ☐ |

The faucet is dripping.

**Think about It** What words in the conversations above helped you choose *'ll* or the simple present?

[10] **plumber:** a person who repairs things like water pipes and toilets

**24 | Using _Won't_** Complete each sentence with _won't_ and the verb in parentheses. When are these predictions going to happen? Check (✓) a time period for each statement. **10.7 B**

## SOME PREDICTIONS ABOUT THE FUTURE

| | 10 YEARS FROM NOW | 50 YEARS FROM NOW | 100 YEARS FROM NOW |
|---|:---:|:---:|:---:|
| 1. We _____ books on paper. (read) | ☐ | ☐ | ☐ |
| 2. Cars _____ gasoline. (use) | ☐ | ☐ | ☐ |
| 3. We _____ any gasoline left. (have) | ☐ | ☐ | ☐ |
| 4. People _____ regular mail anymore. (send) | ☐ | ☐ | ☐ |
| 5. Young children _____ handwriting. (learn) | ☐ | ☐ | ☐ |
| 6. In big cities, the air _____ safe to breathe. (be) | ☐ | ☐ | ☐ |
| 7. We _____ on paper anymore. (write) | ☐ | ☐ | ☐ |
| 8. People _____ for things with cash anymore. (pay) | ☐ | ☐ | ☐ |
| 9. In big cities, the tap water[11] _____ safe to drink. (be) | ☐ | ☐ | ☐ |
| 10. People _____ a time without smartphones. (remember) | ☐ | ☐ | ☐ |

**Talk about It** Compare your answers above as a class. Did you make the same predictions?

**Write about It** Write two more predictions about the future. Write one sentence with _will_ and one sentence with _won't_. Share your predictions with a partner.

_In the future, scientists will control the weather._
_People won't worry about hurricanes or tsunamis._

**25 | Using _'ll_ and _Won't_** Complete these conversations with _'ll_ or _won't_ and the verbs in parentheses. Then listen and check your answers. **10.7 A–B**

PROMISES AND REASSURANCES[12]

1. A: I need to pick up my car from the shop[13]. What bus is around here?

   B: I ___'ll drive___ you there. It's on my way.
   (drive)

   A: Oh, thank you!

---

[11] **tap water:** water that comes from a faucet
[12] **reassurances:** things you say to make people feel better

[13] **the shop:** a place where cars get fixed

2. A: My taxi is going to be here in ten minutes and I'm not ready!

   B: Don't worry. The driver _____ without you.
   (leave)

   A: I don't want to miss my flight.

   B: You _____ your flight. You're probably going to get to the airport
   (miss)

   three hours early.

3. A: How's Karen doing?

   B: Not great. She's probably going to stay in the hospital for another week.

   A: Don't worry. She _____ OK.
   (be)

4. A: What are you studying?

   B: Geometry. I can't understand anything! I think I'm going to fail the test.

   A: You _____. I _____ you study.
   (fail)          (help)

   B: Are you sure? You're so busy.

   A: Yeah, I don't mind at all. I really like geometry.

5. A: Are you excited about your interview tomorrow?

   B: No, I'm so nervous.

   A: Don't worry. You _____ fine. You're perfect for the job.
   (be)

   They _____ you.
   (love)

   B: Thanks. I hope so!

6. A: Hi. Are you busy? I have a question for you.

   B: I'm cooking dinner. Can I call you back in half an hour?

   A: I _____ home in half an hour. I'm leaving in a few minutes.
   (be)

   B: OK. Then I _____ you later tonight.
   (call)

   A: Don't forget, OK?

   B: I _____, I promise.
   (forget)

7. A: How do you like your new apartment?

   B: It's great! You're going to help me paint the living room this weekend, right? Don't forget!

   A: I _____, I promise. I _____ over at 10 on Saturday.
   (remember)          (come)

8. A: Hello?

   B: Hi, Mark. This is Sam. Sorry, but I _____ late for work this morning.
   (be)

   My car isn't starting.

   A: OK. Are you going to miss the meeting?

   B: No, I _____ the meeting. I _____ there by 11.
   (miss)          (be)

## A

**YES/NO QUESTIONS**

| | will | subject | base form verb | |
|---|---|---|---|---|
| 1 | | I | **miss** | my flight? |
| 2 | | you | **meet** | me tomorrow? |
| 3 | | we | **get** | there on time? |
| 4 | Will | they | **help** | us? |
| 5 | | he | **pass** | his class? |
| 6 | | she | **be** | here tomorrow? |
| 7 | | it | **leave** | on time? |

**SHORT ANSWERS**

| | | | |
|---|---|---|---|
| 8 | Yes, | you I we they he she it | **will.** |
| 9 | No, | | **won't.** |

**OTHER WAYS TO ANSWER *YES/NO* QUESTIONS**

| ANSWER *YES* | ANSWER *I DON'T KNOW* | ANSWER *NO* |
|---|---|---|
| Probably.<br>I think so.<br>I hope so.<br>Yes, . . . (more information) | Maybe.<br>I don't know.<br>I'm not sure. | Probably not.<br>I don't think so.<br>I hope not.<br>No, . . . (more information) |

**10** A: Will you live in the city next year?
B: **Yes**, I'm going to move in the fall.

**11** A: Will you be here tomorrow?
B: **No**, I'll be out of town.

## B

**WH- QUESTIONS**

| | wh- word | will | subject | base form verb | |
|---|---|---|---|---|---|
| 12 | When | | I | **see** | you? |
| 13 | Who | | you we | **hire?** | |
| 14 | How | will | they | **get** | here? |
| 15 | How long | | he she | **stay** | with you? |
| 16 | What time | | it | **start?** | |

**WH- QUESTIONS ABOUT THE SUBJECT**

In these questions, *what* and *who* are the subjects.

| | wh- word | will | base form verb | |
|---|---|---|---|---|
| 17 | What | will | **happen** | to Sandra? |
| 18 | Who | | **be** | there tonight? |

**26 | Asking Questions with *Will*** Put the words in the correct order to write *yes/no* and *wh-* questions with *will*. Circle the best answer for each question.  `10.8 A–B`

1. (get/up tomorrow morning/when/you/will)

   *When will you get up tomorrow morning?*
   _____

   a. Yes, I will.          b. At 6.          c. I'll take the train.

2. (see/will/your friends tomorrow/you)

   _____

   a. No, I won't.          b. In the morning.          c. At school.

3. (you/get/home today/when/will)

   _____

   a. Yes, I will.          b. At 5:30.          c. I think so.

4. (you/be/tomorrow/will/in class)

   _____

   a. In Mexico.          b. Next month.          c. Probably.

5. (do/what/on your next vacation/will/you)

_____

    a. Go to San Diego.    b. Probably.             c. No, I won't.

6. (have/more information/when/will/you)

_____

    a. Next week.        b. I don't think so.    c. Probably not.

7. (will/what/your next job/be)

_____

    a. In the summer.     b. Yes, I will.       c. I don't know.

8. (be/who/will/at your house tonight)

_____

    a. No, I won't.       b. My roommate Jane.    c. I don't think so.

**Talk about It** Work with a partner. Ask the questions in Activity 26. Answer with your own ideas.

*A: When will you get up tomorrow morning?*
*B: At 8.*

**27 | Asking and Answering Questions with *Will*** Use the words in parentheses to write *yes/no* and *wh-* questions with *will*. 10.8 A–B

## What will your life be like in the future?

Imagine your life in 5 years and in 20 years. Think about these questions.

1. (you/own a house)
    *Will you own a house?*

2. (where/you/live)

_____

3. (who/you/live/with)

_____

4. (what/job/you/have)

_____

5. (you/have/children)

_____

6. (how many/children/you/have)

_____

7. (what/you/do/for fun)

_____

8. (you/have/a pet)

_____

9. (you/be/in school)

_____

10. (what/you/look like)

_____

**Talk about It** Ask and answer the questions above with a partner. Ask each question twice. Add "in 5 years" and "in 20 years."

*A: Will you own a house in 5 years?*    *A: Will you own a house in 20 years?*
*B: Probably not.*                   *B: I hope so!*

**Write about It** Write predictions about your life in 60 years.

*In 60 years, I will live with my grandchildren.*

**A | GRAMMAR IN READING** Read this article. Underline the verbs that refer to future time. Then check (✓) *True* or *False* for each statement below.

## Is the World's Population Growing or Shrinking?

There are now more than 7 billion people on Earth. The population grew from 6 billion to 7 billion in only 12 years (from 1999 to 2011). In comparison, the population grew from 1 billion to 2 billion from 1804 to 1927—that's 123 years. The recent growth rate[14] is almost ten times faster.

Today the growth rate is a little slower than it was in the 1990s. In the past, people had a lot of children. Now, couples in many countries have just one or two children. But the growth rate may rise again. The United Nations estimates[15] that we will reach 8 billion people by 2024 and 10 billion people by 2064. Some environmentalists[16] are worried about faster population growth. They say we are going to run out of[17] clean water and oil.

Some experts disagree about the problem. Warren Sanderson is an expert on population growth. He's a professor of economics, and he does research at Austria's International Institute for Applied Systems Analysis (IIASA). He believes the world's population may never reach 10 billion. He says the population will reach 9 billion in 2050—then it will get smaller: "After 2050, we're going to reach a state of . . . zero population growth." That means the population won't get bigger or smaller. Then the growth rate will go down. The IIASA believes the population will fall to 3.5 billion by 2200. By 2300, there may be only 1 billion people on Earth.

| THE UNITED NATIONS AND ENVIRONMENTALISTS SAY . . . | TRUE | FALSE |
|---|---|---|
| 1. The world's population won't reach 10 billion by 2064. | ☐ | ☐ |
| 2. The growth rate will continue to fall. | ☐ | ☐ |
| 3. We're going to run out of oil. | ☐ | ☐ |

| WARREN SANDERSON AND THE IIASA SAY . . . | TRUE | FALSE |
|---|---|---|
| 4. The population will reach 10 billion. | ☐ | ☐ |
| 5. The population is going to grow after 2050. | ☐ | ☐ |
| 6. There will be 3.5 billion people on Earth in 2200. | ☐ | ☐ |
| 7. There may be only 1 billion people on Earth in 2300. | ☐ | ☐ |

**Write about It** Correct the false statements above.

**B | GRAMMAR IN WRITING** According to the reading above, environmentalists predict that we will run out of clean water or oil. Predict more possible problems. Write six sentences with *will, won't, may,* and *may not*. Use the ideas in the box or your own ideas.

| apartments/be smaller | have enough food | there/be enough houses |
|---|---|---|
| food/be more expensive | have enough water | there/be too many cars |

*We may have more violent weather in the future.*     *The sea level will rise a lot more in the next 20 years.*

[14] **growth rate:** the measurement of how fast something grows
[15] **estimate:** to guess or predict the size of something
[16] **environmentalists:** people who try to protect the environment
[17] **run out of:** to not have any left

**Talk about It** Imagine that it's the year 2050 and your predictions happened. What are you going to do? Write four ideas with *be going to*. Compare your ideas with a partner.

*I'm not going to build a house near the ocean!*
*I'm going to plant a big garden and share the food with other people.*

---

## 10.9 Summary of Future Forms

### *BE GOING TO*

**POSITIVE STATEMENTS**

| | | | |
|---|---|---|---|
| I | am | | |
| You / We / They | are | going to | leave. |
| He / She / It | is | | |

**NEGATIVE STATEMENTS**

| | | | |
|---|---|---|---|
| I | am not / 'm not | | |
| You / We / They | are not / 're not / aren't | going to | stay. |
| He / She / It | is not / 's not / isn't | | |

**YES/NO QUESTIONS**

| | | | |
|---|---|---|---|
| Am | I | | |
| Are | you / we / they | going to | come? |
| Is | he / she / it | | |

**SHORT ANSWERS**

| | | | | | | |
|---|---|---|---|---|---|---|
| | you / we / they | are. | | | you / we / they | are not. / 're not. / aren't. |
| Yes, | I | am. | | No, | I | am not. / 'm not. |
| | he / she / it | is. | | | he / she / it | is not. / 's not. / isn't. |

**WH- QUESTIONS**

| | | | | |
|---|---|---|---|---|
| What | am | I | | do? |
| Where | are | you / we / they | going to | go? |
| When | is | he / she / it | | arrive? |

**QUESTIONS ABOUT THE SUBJECT**

| | | | |
|---|---|---|---|
| Who | is | going to | drive? |
| What | | | happen? |

---

### *MAY, MIGHT,* AND *WILL*

**POSITIVE STATEMENTS**

| | | | |
|---|---|---|---|
| I / You / We / They / He / She / It | may might / will / 'll | arrive | on Friday. |

**NEGATIVE STATEMENTS**

| | | | |
|---|---|---|---|
| I / You / We / They / He / She / It | may not might not / will not won't | be | here tomorrow. |

### QUESTIONS WITH *WILL*

**YES/NO QUESTIONS**

| | | | |
|---|---|---|---|
| Will | I / you / we / they / he / she / it | be | at the office on Monday? |

**SHORT ANSWERS**

| | | |
|---|---|---|
| Yes, | you / I / we / they / he / she / it | will. |
| No, | | won't. |

**WH- QUESTIONS**

| | | | |
|---|---|---|---|
| What | | I / you / we / they / he / she / it | do? |
| Where | will | | go? |
| When | | | arrive? |

**WH- QUESTIONS ABOUT THE SUBJECT**

| | | |
|---|---|---|
| Who | will | be there? |
| What | | happen? |

# 11

# Modals I

**GO ONLINE**

For the Unit Vocabulary Check, go to the Online Practice.

## IN THIS UNIT, WE USE modals to talk about:

### Ability and possibility

1. I **can** play the piano.

2. My great-grandfather **could** fix cars.

3. We **won't be able to** go swimming today.

4. She **can't** see the board.

**Think about It** Read these sentences. Check (✓) *True* or *False*.

| | TRUE | FALSE |
|---|---|---|
| 1. I can play the piano. | ☐ | ☐ |
| 2. I can fix cars. | ☐ | ☐ |
| 3. I'll be able to go swimming tomorrow. | ☐ | ☐ |
| 4. I can see the board right now. | ☐ | ☐ |
| 5. I will be able to come to class tomorrow. | ☐ | ☐ |
| 6. I was able to finish my homework last night. | ☐ | ☐ |

## Requests and permission

5. A: **Can** you call back later?
   B: Sure.

6. A: **Could** I use your computer for a minute?
   B: Sorry. I need it right now.

## Offers and invitations

7. A: **May** I help you?
   B: I'm looking for a formal shirt.

8. A: **Would you like to** sit down?
   B: Thank you.

**Think about It** Read the conversations above. Underline the word before the subject in each question. Does each question ask about the past, the present, or the future?

## 11.1 Can for Ability and Possibility

**A**

We can use **can** to talk about ability and possibility in the present.

**POSITIVE STATEMENTS**

| | subject | can | base form verb | |
|---|---|---|---|---|
| 1 | I<br>He<br>She<br>We<br>You<br>They | can | work | today. |

**NEGATIVE STATEMENTS**

| | subject | can + not | base form verb | |
|---|---|---|---|---|
| 2 | I<br>He<br>She<br>We<br>You<br>They | cannot*<br>can't | work | today. |

> The modal **can** (+ **not**) is a **helping verb**. The **base form verb** is the **main verb**.

*The full negative form is **cannot**. In speaking and informal writing, we usually use the contraction **can't**.

Notice: Sometimes **can** has a future meaning.

3 I **can call** you after 3:00.

4 She **can come** to work early tomorrow.

5 I'm sorry I **can't come** to dinner tonight.

6 We **can't get** to the airport on time.

 ONLINE

## 1 | Using *Can*  Complete the sentences below with *can* + a base form verb from the box.  `11.1 A`

**OLYMPIC ATHLETES**

a ski jumper

a weightlifter

a shot putter

a downhill skier

a speed skater

an archer

a luge racer

a figure skater

1. Olympic runners _____*can run*_____ a marathon[1] in 2 hours and 18 minutes.

2. Olympic swimmers _____ 100 meters (109.4 yards) in 48.82 seconds.

3. Olympic ski jumpers _____ over 200 meters (218.7 yards).

4. Some Olympic weightlifters _____ over 200 kilograms (440 pounds).

| |
|---|
| jump |
| lift |
| run |
| swim |

[1] **marathon:** a long-distance race of about 26 miles

5. Olympic shot putters _____ a shot put over 20 meters (65.6 feet).

6. Downhill skiers _____ down a mountain at over 120 kilometers (74.6 miles) per hour.

7. Speed skaters _____ 1000 meters (1093.6 yards) in just over a minute.

| skate |
| ski |
| throw |

8. Archers _____ a 12.2-centimeter (4.8-inch) bull's-eye[2] from 70 meters (76.6 yards) away.

9. Luge racers _____ 140 kilometers (87 miles) an hour.

10. A figure skater _____ 30 or 40 times without falling down.

| go |
| hit |
| spin[3] |

**Talk about It** Go online and look up information about Olympic athletes. Take notes. Then tell a partner what three different athletes can do.

*"Apolo Ohno can skate 40 miles an hour!"*

**2 | Usage Note: *Very Well*, *Pretty Well*, and *Not at All*** Read the note. Then do Activity 3.

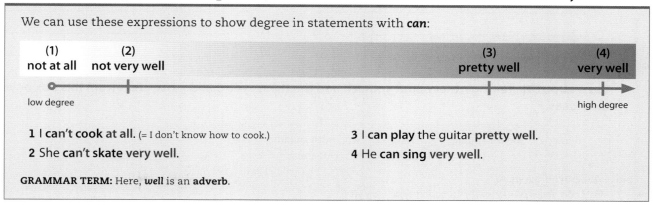

We can use these expressions to show degree in statements with *can*:

| (1) not at all | (2) not very well | | (3) pretty well | (4) very well |

low degree ————————————————————————→ high degree

**1** I **can't cook at all.** (= I don't know how to cook.)     **3** I **can play** the guitar **pretty well.**
**2** She **can't skate very well.**     **4** He **can sing very well.**

**GRAMMAR TERM:** Here, *well* is an **adverb**.

**3 | Using *Can* and *Can't*** How well can you do the things in this chart? Check (✓) the box that describes your ability. Then write a sentence on page 282 for each item. **11.1 A**

## JOB SKILLS SURVEY

| | VERY WELL | PRETTY WELL | NOT VERY WELL | NOT AT ALL |
|---|---|---|---|---|
| 1. work with others | | | | |
| 2. work independently | | | | |
| 3. learn new things | | | | |
| 4. solve problems | | | | |
| 5. accept criticism[4] | | | | |
| 6. lead others | | | | |
| 7. speak English | | | | |

[2] **bull's-eye:** the center of a target     [4] **criticism:** a description of someone's bad points
[3] **spin:** to turn around quickly

| | VERY WELL | PRETTY WELL | NOT VERY WELL | NOT AT ALL |
|---|---|---|---|---|
| 8. do basic math | | | | |
| 9. use common software programs | | | | |
| 10. use tools and building equipment⁵ | | | | |
| 11. drive | | | | |
| 12. cook | | | | |

*I can work with others very well.*

1. _____
2. _____
3. _____
4. _____
5. _____
6. _____
7. _____

8. _____
9. _____
_____
10. _____
_____
11. _____
12. _____

**Talk about It** Tell a partner about yourself and the things you can do. Use ideas from this box or your own ideas.

| draw | speak in public⁶ | type | work with children |
|---|---|---|---|

*A: I can't draw at all.*
*B: I can draw pretty well, but I can't type very well.*

**Write about It** Choose three of the jobs from this box. Write about what people with those jobs can do well.

| astronomer | counselor | engineer | manager | server |
|---|---|---|---|---|
| cashier | designer | journalist | nurse | teacher |

*A nurse can read a medical chart.*

🔊 **4 | Pronunciation Note: *Can* vs. *Can't*** Listen to the note. Then do Activity 5.

We usually do not stress *can*. We stress the **main verb**, and we pronounce *can* as /kn/.

**1** I can **WORK** tomorrow.    **2** We can **HELP** you with that.

In sentences with *can't*, we often stress both **can't** and the **main verb**. We pronounce *can't* with a clear "a" sound (/æ/) , as in *man*.

**3** I **CAN'T WORK** tomorrow.    **4** We **CAN'T HELP** you with that.

Sometimes we stress the word *can* to disagree or show a contrast.

**5** A: Did you say you **CAN** or you **CAN'T** help me?
B: I **CAN** help you. I'm happy to do that.

⁵**equipment:** things that are needed for a particular activity    ⁶**in public:** when other people are there

**5 | Listening for *Can* and *Can't*** Listen to these sentences. Circle the word you hear. Then listen again and repeat the sentences. **11.1 A**

SCHEDULES

1. I (can / can't) get to school early tomorrow.
2. I (can / can't) go out to dinner tonight.
3. I (can / can't) meet at lunchtime tomorrow.
4. I (can / can't) pick you up from the airport on Wednesday.
5. I (can / can't) go home before 4:00.
6. I (can / can't) call you in the morning.
7. I (can / can't) come to class next week.

8. I (can / can't) study over the weekend.
9. I (can / can't) stay late today.
10. I (can / can't) watch TV tonight.
11. I (can / can't) study in the library tonight.
12. I (can / can't) take some time off this week.
13. I (can / can't) go to a movie tomorrow night.
14. I (can /can't) sleep late tomorrow morning.

**Talk about It** Read the sentences above to a partner. Use *can* or *can't* to make each sentence true for you. Your partner listens for the correct form.

*1. A: I can't get to school early tomorrow.*
*B: You said can't.*

**Talk about It** Make a lunch date with your partner. Talk about when you can and can't go to lunch. Your partner listens for *can* or *can't*. Check your understanding.

*A: I can't meet you tomorrow.*
*B: Did you say can't?*
*A: That's right. I can't meet you tomorrow. I can meet you on Tuesday.*

## 11.2 Questions with *Can*

**YES/NO QUESTIONS**

| | | can | subject | base form verb | |
|---|---|---|---|---|---|
| **A** | **1** | **Can** | I you he she it we they | **finish** | today? |

**SHORT ANSWERS**

| | | subject | can / can't |
|---|---|---|---|
| **2** | Yes, | you I he she it we they | **can.** |
| **3** | No, | | **can't.** |

**WH- QUESTIONS**

| | | wh- word | can | subject | base form verb | |
|---|---|---|---|---|---|---|
| **B** | **4** | What | | I | **eat?** | |
| | **5** | Where | | he | **meet** | us? |
| | **6** | When | | she | **get** | here? |
| | **7** | How fast | can | it | **go?** | |
| | **8** | Why | | we | **hear** | your neighbor? |
| | **9** | Who | | you | **ask** | about the schedule? |
| | **10** | How | | they | **swim** | so fast? |

**ANSWERS**

| |
|---|
| There's some leftover pizza. |
| At the station. |
| In a couple of hours. |
| About 50 miles per hour. |
| He speaks very loudly. |
| I'm not sure. Maybe Mr. Potter? |
| They practice every day. |

GO ONLINE

**6 | Asking *Yes/No* Questions with *Can*** Write *yes/no* questions with *can you* and the phrases in this chart. Add two questions of your own. Then ask and answer the questions with a partner. `11.2 A`

| Abilities | |
|---|---|
| 1. ride a motorcycle | *Can you ride a motorcycle?* |
| 2. make a cake | |
| 3. say a poem from memory | |
| 4. wiggle⁷ your ears | |
| 5. raise one eyebrow | |
| 6. remember your first teacher's name | |
| 7. run 12 miles | |
| 8. sing well | |
| 9. count to ten in French | |
| 10. play a musical instrument | |
| 11. add two-digit numbers in your head⁸ | |
| 12. name the seven continents in English | |
| 13. [your own question] | |
| 14. [your own question] | |

**F Y I**

In short answers, we stress *can*. We pronounce it /kæn/, not /kn/.

Yes, I **CAN**.

Yes, she **CAN**.

raise one eyebrow

$$\begin{array}{r} 83 \\ + 54 \\ \hline 137 \end{array}$$

add two-digit numbers in your head

1. A: *Can you ride a motorcycle?*
   B: *Yes, I can. / No, I can't.*

**7 | Understanding Questions and Statements with *Can*** Look at these photos and captions. Then listen and complete the statements and *yes/no* questions on page 285. Add punctuation. `11.2 A`

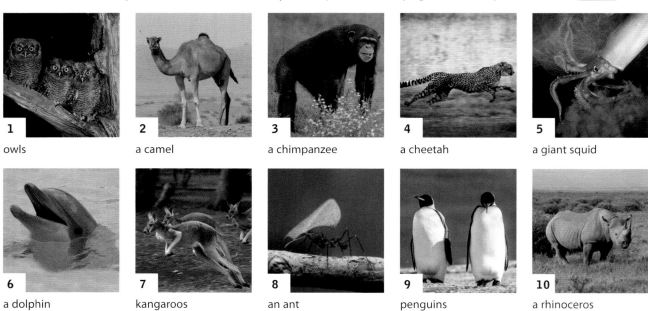

| 1 | 2 | 3 | 4 | 5 |
|---|---|---|---|---|
| owls | a camel | a chimpanzee | a cheetah | a giant squid |

| 6 | 7 | 8 | 9 | 10 |
|---|---|---|---|---|
| a dolphin | kangaroos | an ant | penguins | a rhinoceros |

⁷**wiggle:** to move back and forth          ⁸**in [your] head:** without writing

**ANIMAL FACTS**

1. _Can owls see_ _____ in the dark?
2. _____ for more than a week without water
3. _____ swim
4. _____ over 60 miles per hour
5. _____ to over 40 feet long
6. _____ underwater
7. _____ 30 feet
8. _____ more than three times its own weight
9. _____ fly
10. _____ jump

**Talk about It** Ask a partner the questions in Activity 7. Go online to find any answers that you and your partner don't know.

1. *A: Can owls see in the dark?*
   *B: Yes, they can.*

**Write about It** Write three more questions with *can* about animals. If you don't know the answers, look them up online.

**8 | Asking and Answering Questions with *Can*** Complete these questions using the words in parentheses and *can*. `11.2 A–B`

**MAKING PLANS**

1. A: _____ after class today?
   (how long / you / stay)
   B: I can stay until 1. I have to work at 1:30.

2. A: _____?
   (when / we / meet)
   B: I'm not sure. Maybe next week.

3. A: _____ to lunch with us?
   (your brother / come)
   B: I don't know. I'll ask him.

4. A: _____ you?
   (when / I / call)
   B: After 6 tonight.

5. A: _____ together?
   (when / we / get)
   B: Hmm. I'm busy this week. How about next weekend?

6. A: _____ here at 3?
   (you / be)
   B: I think so. I'll hurry.

7. A: _____ batteries?
   (where / I / find)
   B: They're next to the cash register.

8. A: _____ the doctor?
   (when / I / see)
   B: Are you free this afternoon? The doctor is available around 3.

9. A: _____ a good meal around here?
        (where / I / get)
  B: Smythe's. The food is good and it's cheap.

10. A: _____ me with my computer?
        (who / help)
   B: Ask Barry.

11. A: _____ more days this week?
        (I / work)
   B: Maybe, but I'm not sure yet.

12. A: _____ to about my class schedule?
        (who / I / talk)
   B: Dr. Andrews can help you with that.

**Talk about It** Choose three of the questions in Activity 8. Ask a partner the questions. Give your own answers.

---

## 11.3 *Could* for Past Ability

We sometimes use *could* and *could not* to talk about past ability.

**A**

**POSITIVE STATEMENTS**

| | subject | *could* | base form verb | |
|---|---|---|---|---|
| **1** | I / You He / She / It / We / They | **could** | **run** | very well. |

**NEGATIVE STATEMENTS**

| | subject | *could + not* | base form verb |
|---|---|---|---|
| **2** | I / You He / She / It / We / They | **could not couldn't** | **swim.** |

In speaking, we usually use the contraction ***couldn't***.

Notice: When we talk about ability, **could** refers to past time. **Can** refers to present or future time.

| PAST ABILITY (*COULD*) | PRESENT OR FUTURE ABILITY (*CAN*) |
|---|---|
| **3a** My grandmother **could sew** beautiful clothing. | **3b** I **can sew** pretty well. I learned from my grandmother. |
| **4a** As a young girl, I **could run** really fast. | **4b** I **can run** short distances. |
| **5a** My parents **couldn't speak** English. | **5b** I **can't speak** Spanish well, but I'm taking classes. |

**B**

We can use **can**, **can't**, and ***couldn't*** to talk about specific actions and possibilities.

| | PAST MEANING (*COULD*) | PRESENT OR FUTURE MEANING (*CAN*) |
|---|---|---|
| **POSITIVE** | – | **6** I **can study** with you next week. <br> **7** I **can hear** you now. |
| **NEGATIVE** | **8a** I **couldn't study** in the library yesterday. It was closed. | **8b** Sorry, I **can't study** with you tomorrow. |
| | **9a** We called them, but they **couldn't hear** us. | **9b** I **can't hear** you. Can you speak louder? |
| | **10a** I tried to talk to her last night, but I **couldn't find** her. | **10b** I **can't find** my keys. Do you have them? |

**WARNING!** We don't usually use the positive form *could* for specific past actions.

X I could study in the library yesterday.

GO ONLINE

**9 | Using *Could* and *Couldn't* for Past Ability** Think about your life at age seven. Complete these sentences with *could* or *couldn't*. Underline the main verb in each sentence. Then compare your sentences with a partner. ▎11.3 A

WHEN I WAS SEVEN YEARS OLD . . .

1. I _____ <u>stand</u> on my head.
2. I _____ do a cartwheel.
3. I _____ swim across a pool.
4. I _____ run a mile.
5. I _____ draw well.
6. I _____ multiply large numbers.
7. I _____ speak two languages.
8. I _____ ride a bicycle.
9. I _____ make my own dinner.
10. I _____ tie my own shoes.

stand on my head

do a cartwheel

987
× 652
643,524

multiply large numbers

**Talk about It** Talk to a partner. Compare the past with the present. Which of the things above can you do now? Which things *can't* you do now?

*"When I was seven years old, I could do a cartwheel. I can't do a cartwheel now."*

**10 | Writing Sentences with *Could* and *Couldn't*** Complete the sentences below. Use *could* or *couldn't* and the verbs in parentheses. ▎11.3 A

THE OLD DAYS

1. In the 1600s, people _____*could eat*_____ (eat) fresh vegetables only in the summer. They _____ (freeze) their food for later.

2. In the 1700s, many people _____ (ride) horses, but they _____ (travel) very fast.

3. In the 1800s, most people

_____ (buy) new

clothing very often, but many women

_____ (sew) their

own clothes.

4. In the 1950s, some people

_____ (watch) TV

in their living room, but most people

_____ (afford⁹) a television.

5. In the 1960s, people _____

(talk) to each other on the phone, but they

_____ (text) their friends.

6. In the 1980s, people _____

(type) on a computer, but they

_____ (search) for

information on the Internet.

**Write about It** Choose one of the time periods from Activity 10. Write two more sentences about what people could or couldn't do at that time. Use the verbs in this box or your own ideas.

| buy | drive | make | travel |
|-----|-------|------|--------|
| call | fly | see | work |

*In the 1700s, people could see a lot of stars at night.*
*They couldn't make telephone calls.*

⁹ **afford:** to have enough money to pay for something

## 11 | Using *Couldn't* and *Can't* Complete these sentences with *couldn't* or *can't*. Then listen and check your answers.  `11.3 B`

**EXPLANATIONS AND EXCUSES**

1. A: Where's your book?

   B: I don't know. I looked for it last night, but I _____ find it.

2. A: Did you ask your brother about the car?

   B: He wasn't home, so I _____ ask him.

3. A: What did she say?

   B: I don't know. I _____ hear her.

4. A: Did you like the dinner?

   B: It was good, but I _____ finish my food. I wasn't very hungry.

5. A: Do you want to come to dinner tonight?

   B: I really want to, but I _____. I have to work.

6. A: I _____ hear the radio. Can you turn it up a little?

   B: Sure.

7. A: How was the movie last night?

   B: I'm not sure. I didn't see the end. I _____ stay awake.

8. A: Do you know him?

   B: I know his face, but I _____ remember his name.

9. A: You look bored.

   B: I'm not bored; I'm frustrated[10]. I _____ understand this article.

10. A: Where were you last week?

    B: I was home sick. I _____ get out of bed.

11. A: I want to visit my family, but I _____ afford it.

    B: Yeah, flights are really expensive now.

12. A: What did you do last summer?

    B: I wanted to take a vacation, but I _____ take time off work.

**Think about It** How did you choose *can't* or *couldn't* above? What other words in the conversations helped you decide?

**Write about It** Complete these sentences. Use *can't* or *couldn't* and your own ideas.

1. I wanted to _____, but I _____.

2. I want to _____, but I _____.

## 12 | Error Correction Find and correct the errors. (Some sentences may not have any errors.)

1. We can to leave at 6 p.m.
2. Do you can come over next week?
3. My brother can't swim very well.
4. I looked for you at school, but I can't find you.
5. When I can call you?
6. She can't decided where to go.
7. I couldn't hear you. The children were very noisy.
8. He can very well play the piano.
9. I asked him, but he couldn't to answer my question.
10. Where I can get a good deal[11]?

[10]**frustrated:** angry or not satisfied

[11]**a good deal:** a good price on something

## 11.4 Be Able To

Sometimes we use **be able to** to talk about ability in the present, past, and future.

**POSITIVE STATEMENTS**

| | | subject | be | able to | base form verb | |
|---|---|---|---|---|---|---|
| **PRESENT** | **1** | I | am<br>'m | able to | **spend** | more time at home now. |
| | **2** | He / She / It | is<br>'s | | **add** | numbers quickly. |
| | **3** | We / You / They | are<br>'re | | **see** | the stars at night. |

| | | subject | be | able to | base form verb | |
|---|---|---|---|---|---|---|
| **PAST*** | **4** | I / He / She / It | was | able to | **fly.** | |
| | **5** | We / You / They | were | | **attend** | the meeting. |

| | | subject | *will + be* | able to | base form verb | |
|---|---|---|---|---|---|---|
| **FUTURE** | **6** | I / He / She / It /<br>We / You / They | will be<br>'ll be | able to | **complete** | the task. |

The **base form verb** is the **main verb**.

Notice: *Be able to* often has a meaning similar to *can / could*.

*We can use *was / were able to* to talk about specific abilities in the past. We don't use *could* in these situations.

✓ I **was able to** finish the project yesterday.        ✗ I **could** finish the project yesterday.

**GRAMMAR TERM:** *Be able to* is a **phrasal modal**. Phrasal modals are different from simple modals (like *can* and *could*) because they must agree with the subject.

**NEGATIVE STATEMENTS**

| | | subject | be + not | able to | base form verb | |
|---|---|---|---|---|---|---|
| **PRESENT** | **7** | I | am not<br>'m not | able to | **come** | home now. |
| | **8** | He / She / It | is not<br>'s not<br>isn't | | **add** | numbers quickly. |
| | **9** | We / You / They | are not<br>'re not<br>aren't | | **see** | the stars at night. |

| | | subject | be + not | able to | base form verb | |
|---|---|---|---|---|---|---|
| **PAST** | **10** | I / He / She / It | was not<br>wasn't | able to | **fly.** | |
| | **11** | We / You / They | were not<br>weren't | | **attend** | the meeting. |

| | | subject | *will + not + be* | able to | base form verb | |
|---|---|---|---|---|---|---|
| **FUTURE** | **12** | I / He / She / It /<br>We / You / They | will not be<br>won't be | able to | **complete** | the task. |

**WARNING!**

✓ We **will not be able** to go.        ✗ We **will be not able** to go.

**13 | Noticing Forms of *Be Able To*** Read these texts. Underline *be (not) able to* + the main verb. Label the forms *PA* (past), *PR* (present), or *F* (future). `11.4 A–B`

### Is there a black rose?

Roses grow all around the world—from China to Egypt, and from Australia to

Alaska. People <u>are able to grow</u> *(PR)* roses in hundreds of colors. There is no black

rose, but growers keep trying to make one. They can grow very dark purple

and red roses. Maybe someday they will be able to grow a black rose.

a dark purple rose

### Who is Stephen Hawking?

Stephen Hawking is a famous physicist[12]. He is not able to walk or speak.

He uses a wheelchair and communicates through a computer. He first

became ill when he was 21 years old. Doctors said he might only live for

two more years. But Hawking was able to finish graduate school, and he

became a university professor. He gives lectures[13] and writes popular books

about science.

Stephen Hawking

### What is Halley's Comet?

Most comets pass by Earth very rarely—for example, every 200 years or every

1,000 years. You usually need a telescope[14] to see most comets. But every

75–76 years, people are able to look up at the sky and see Halley's Comet.

People described the comet thousands of years ago. In 1705, the astronomer

Edmond Halley studied the comet. Now we have more information about it.

People were able to see Halley's Comet in February 1986. We will be able to

see it again in 2061.

a comet

**14 | Using *Be Able To* for Past, Present, and Future Ability** Read these conversations. Look at the **bold** words. Check (✓) *Past*, *Present*, or *Future* for each conversation. Then complete the conversations with the correct form of *be able to*. Use positive forms for 1–5. Use negative forms for 6–10. `11.4 A–B`

COMPUTER PROBLEMS

Use *be able to*

| | PAST | PRESENT | FUTURE |
|---|---|---|---|
| 1. A: What's the problem? | ☐ | ✓ | ☐ |
| B: I ___'m able to___ log in, but I **can't see** my information. | | | |
| 2. A: Is there a problem with the file? | ☐ | ☐ | ☐ |
| B: Yes. I _____ open it, but it **doesn't look** right. | | | |

---

[12]**physicist:** a person who studies or knows a lot about physics
(the scientific study of things like heat, light, and sound)
[13]**lectures:** talks to groups of people to teach them about
something

[14]**telescope:** a long tool that you look through to make things
that are far away look bigger

|         | PAST | PRESENT | FUTURE |
|---------|------|---------|--------|

3.  A: Is your computer working?
    B: Yeah. The tech[15] _____ fix it **yesterday**.

4.  A: I don't know what to do!
    B: I'm busy right now. I _____ help you
    **in a few minutes**.

5.  A: What happened?
    B: My computer **crashed**[16], but the tech _____
    save my files.

**Use** *be not able to*

6.  A: What**'s** the problem?
    B: I _____ hear anything through the headset.

7.  A: I need my computer back tomorrow!
    B: I'm sorry. I _____ return it **tomorrow**.
    It will be ready next week.

8.  A: Did the tech look at your computer?
    B: Yeah, he **came yesterday**. But he _____ fix it.

9.  A: Sorry for the mistakes. My "e" key **is** broken, so
    I _____ type very well.
    B: That's OK. Do you need to buy a new keyboard?

10. A: What**'s** wrong with your mother's computer?
    B: I don't know. We _____ start it up.
    A: Is it plugged in[17]?

**Talk about It** Practice conversations 6–10 above with a partner. Use *can't* or *couldn't* instead of *be* (*not*) *able to.*

6.  A: What's the problem?
    B: I can't hear anything through the headset.

## 15 | Using *Be Able To* + *Not* Rewrite these sentences with a negative form of *be able to*. `11.4 B`

APOLOGIES

1.  I'm sorry I can't come to your dinner next week.
    *I'm sorry I won't be able to come to your dinner next week.*

2.  I'm sorry I couldn't help with the cooking last night.
3.  He's very sorry, but he can't help you right now.
4.  We apologize. We couldn't respond to your email yesterday. Our office was very busy.
5.  I'm sorry, but Mr. Wong can't come to the phone right now.

6.  I'm sorry I can't come to class tomorrow.
7.  I'm sorry I couldn't call you last night.
8.  We're sorry we cannot complete your order at this time.
9.  John is sorry, but he can't come to the office this morning.
10. Gina sends her apologies, but she can't attend the meeting next month.

---

[15] **tech (technician):** a person who helps fix computer problems
[16] **crash:** to stop working (computer)

[17] **plugged in:** connected to the electrical supply with a plug

**Think about It** How did you know which form of *be able to* to use in Activity 15? Underline the words that tell you the sentence is past, present, or future.

**Talk about It** Work with a partner. Your partner reads a question or statement from this box. You respond with an apology. Use a form of *be not able to* in your apology.

1. Can you come over to our place tomorrow evening?
2. You missed the meeting yesterday!
3. Can you pay me back now?
4. Did you call Mr. Thompson?
5. Can you work on Tuesday?
6. Can you help me with this?

A: *Can you come over to our place tomorrow evening?*
B: *Sorry, but we won't be able to. We'll be out of town.*

---

## 11.5 Permission with *Can, Could,* and *May* + *I / We*

**A**

We often use **can** and **could** to ask for permission.

**1** A: **Can we have** dessert now?
B: Finish your dinner first.

**2** A: **Could I use** your pencil?
B: Sorry. I need it.

> **Could** usually sounds a little more formal and polite than **can**.
>
> Notice: **Could** describes the present or future in these questions. It does NOT describe the past.

**B**

Sometimes we use **may** to ask for permission. **May** is more formal. It is much less common than *can* or *could.*

**3** A: **May I ask** you a question?
B: Of course.

**4** A: **May we sit** down?
B: Yes, of course.

---

**16 | Asking for Permission with *Can* and *Could*** Complete these questions. Put the words in parentheses in the correct order. Then match each question with the speaker. Compare your answers with a partner. `11.5 A`

WHO'S TALKING?

1. A: _Could I sit_____ near the board, please? (could/sit/I) __b__
   B: Sure. There's an empty seat right here.

2. A: _____ with you for a minute about my work schedule?
   (I/could/speak) ____
   B: Of course.

3. A: _____ dinner at Tim's house? (can/eat/we) ____
   B: No. I want you both home tonight.

a. child to parent
b. student to teacher
c. employee to employer
d. classmate to classmate
e. customer to store clerk

4. A: _____ your dictionary for a minute? (use/I/can) ____

   B: Sure.

5. A: _____ TV now? (we/can/watch) ____

   B: Did you clean your rooms?

6. A: _____ yesterday's homework back? (have/could/I) ____

   B: Of course. And please look at my comments about your writing.

7. A: _____ your notes? (can/copy/we) ____

   B: Yeah, sure.

8. A: _____ a different color? (see/we/can) ____

   B: Yes. We have it in blue and brown.

9. A: _____ your office for the sales meeting tomorrow morning? (could/use/we) ____

   B: Good idea. There's lots of space.

10. A: _____ these shoes? (I/can/try on[18]) ____

   B: Of course. What size do you need?

a. child to parent
b. student to teacher
c. employee to employer
d. classmate to classmate
e. customer to store clerk

**Write about It**  Choose three of the speakers in Activity 16. Write a different request for permission for each one.

*Child:  Can I go outside?*          *Parent:  OK. But don't play in the street.*

**17 | Using *May I***  Look at the pictures below. Complete each question with *may I* + a verb from the box.  `11.5 B`

| ask | buy | come | take |

1. A: _____ in?

   B: Of course. And please sit down.

2. A: _____ this chair?

   B: Go ahead. I'm not using it.

3. A: _____ a question?

   B: Of course.

4. A: _____ that cake?

   B: Certainly.

[18] **try on:**  to put on clothes to see if they fit

| help | look at | sit | speak |
|------|---------|-----|-------|

5. A: Excuse me. _____ to you
    for a minute?

    B: OK, just a second.

6. A: _____ that?

    B: Sure!

7. A: _____ you?

    B: No, thanks. I'm just looking.

8. A: _____ here?

    B: Yeah, sure.

---

## 11.6 Requests with *Can*, *Could*, and *Would* + *You*

**A**

We can use *can*, *could*, and *would* with the subject **you** to ask someone to do something.

**1** A: **Can you call** back later?
B: Sure.

**2** A: **Can you hand** me that glass?
B: I can't reach it.

**3** A: **Could you hold** this for a minute?
B: Of course.

**4** A: **Would you save** my seat?
B: Sure. No problem.

> *Could* and *would* are a little more formal and polite than *can*.

**B**

We can make requests more polite with **please**. We can put **please** between the subject and the main verb.

| | modal | subject | *please* | main verb | |
|---|-------|---------|----------|-----------|---|
| **5** | Can | | | speak | a little louder? |
| **6** | Could | **you** | **please** | repeat | the question? |
| **7** | Would | | | sit | in the front? |

We can also put *please* at the end of the question:

**8** Could you wait a moment, **please**?

**9** Can you pick up the kids today, **please**?

**WARNING!** Don't put *please* before *can*, *could*, or *would*.

✓Can you **please** speak a little louder?     ✗ **Please can** you speak a little louder?

**18 | Making Requests with *Can, Could,* and *Would*** Listen and complete these requests with the words you hear. `11.6 A–B`

1. A: *Could you clean* _____ your room? It looks terrible.

   B: Now?

2. A: _____ your chair a little? I can't see the board.

   B: Sure.

3. A: _____ dinner? I'm tired.

   B: Of course.

4. A: _____ that book? I can't reach up there.

   B: No problem.

5. A: _____ the homework? I don't understand it.

   B: Yeah, sure.

6. A: _____ this box into my office? It's too heavy for me.

   B: Of course.

7. A: _____ a message?

   B: Sure. Let me get my pencil.

8. A: _____ that? I didn't hear you.

   B: No problem.

9. A: _____ the door? It's cold in here!

   B: OK.

10. A: _____ back tomorrow? I can't talk right now.

    B: OK.

11. A: _____ a few more minutes? I'm almost ready.

    B: No problem.

12. A: _____ over? I want to sit down.

    B: Uh-huh.

13. A: _____ a picture of us? Here's my camera.

    B: Sure. No problem.

14. A: _____ off the light? I have a headache.

    B: Oh, of course. I'm sorry.

**Think about It** Listen to the requests above again. Which people do you think are talking to a friend or family member? Why?

**Talk about It** Practice the conversations above with a partner. Use *please.*

> 1. A: *Could you please clean your room? It looks terrible.*
>    B: *Now?*

**Talk about It** Write four new requests. Use *can, would, could,* and four of the verbs from the activity above. Ask and answer your requests with a partner. Use *please.*

> A: *Could you please move your backpack?*
> B: *OK.*

**18 | Making Requests with *Can, Could,* and *Would***

## 19 | Making Requests and Asking for Permission

Complete these conversations. Use the verb in parentheses and *you* or *I* as the subject. Then practice the conversations with a partner. (See Chart 11.5 for help with permission with *I*.) **11.6 A**

**ON AN AIRPLANE**

1. A: _____ me another blanket? (could/bring)

   B: Of course. I'll be right back.

2. A: _____ some water? (can/have)

   B: Sure!

3. A: _____ me a new pair of headphones? (would/get)

   B: OK. I'll be right back.

**AT A BANK**

4. A: _____ four twenties and two tens? (could/have)

   B: Yes, of course.

5. A: _____ my balance[19], please? (would/check)

   B: Can I see your ID?

6. A: _____ my sister's check? (can/deposit[20])

   B: I'm sorry. Your sister needs to sign it.

**AT A CLOTHING STORE**

7. A: _____ this in a larger size? (could/see)

   B: I'll check.

8. A: _____ this for me until tomorrow? (would/hold)

   B: I'm sorry. I can't do that.

9. A: _____ this shirt? (can/try on)

   B: Of course. The fitting room[21] is over there.

**AT A CAFETERIA**

10. A: _____ a table? (could/look for)

    B: Uh-huh.

11. A: _____ in front of you? (could/go) I'm in a hurry.

    B: No problem.

12. A: _____ some more sugar? (could/have)

    B: Sure. How many packets?

**Think about It**  In the questions above, which speakers are asking for permission? Which speakers are making a request (asking someone else to do something)?

**Talk about It**  Work with a partner. Write another question and answer for each location above. Use *can*, *could*, and *would*. Use the ideas in this box or your own ideas.

| bring me a pillow | have some salad dressing | open a new account |
| get a fork | help me find . . . | speak to a manager |

*A: Can I open a new account, please?*
*B: Of course. Let me help you with that.*

---

[19] **balance:** the amount of money in someone's bank account
[20] **deposit:** to put money in the bank

[21] **fitting room:** a room in a store where people try on clothes

**20 | Usage Note:** *Borrow, Have, Lend,* and *Give*  Read the note. Then do Activity 21.

We often make requests with **borrow**, **have**, **lend**, and **give**.

We can use **borrow*** or **have** in questions with **I** (permission questions).

| 1 | Can<br>Could | I | borrow | your eraser? |
|---|---|---|---|---|
| | | | have | a glass of water? |

We can use **lend**** or **give** in questions with **you** (requests).

| 2 | Can<br>Could<br>Would | you | lend | me | your book? |
|---|---|---|---|---|---|
| | | | give | | a glass of water? |

Notice: We use an **object** after **lend** and **give**. This is often an object pronoun (*me, you, him, her, us,* or *them*).

*When you **borrow** something, you do not keep it. You return it.
**When someone **lends** you something, you do not keep it. You return it.

**WARNING!** Do not confuse *borrow* and *lend*.

✓ Could you **lend** me a pen?          ✗ Could you borrow me a pen?

---

**21 | Using** *Borrow, Have, Lend,* **and** *Give* **for Permission and Requests**  Complete the questions with *can, could,* or *would + I* or *you.*

LENDING AND BORROWING

1. A: _Could I_____ have that eraser?

   B: Sure.

2. A: _____ give me a ride to school?

   B: Sure.

3. A: _____ lend me some money for lunch? I'll pay you back.

   B: Sorry. I'm broke.[22]

4. A: _____ give me some paper? I forgot my notebook.

   B: No problem.

5. A: _____ borrow your phone? Mine is dead.

   B: I'm sorry. I left mine in the car.

6. A: _____ give me a different laptop? This one doesn't work.

   B: I'm sorry. We don't have any extras.

7. A: _____ borrow your keys?

   B: Why?

8. A: _____ have your phone number?

   B: Sure. Give me your phone. I'll add my number.

9. A: _____ have the scissors?

   B: Sure. Don't forget to put them back.

10. A: _____ borrow your calculator tonight?

    B: Sorry. I need it for my homework.

FYI
Remember:
✗ Would I . . .

[22] **broke:** having no money

**Talk about It** Work with a partner. Ask and answer the questions below. Use the items in this box or your own ideas. Use the subjects *I* or *you*.

| some money | some paper | your car | your laptop | your notes | your phone |

1. Can ___ borrow ___?
2. Would ___ lend me ___?
3. Could ___ have ___?
4. Would ___ give me ___?

*A: Can I borrow your car?*     *B: Sorry. I don't have a car!*

**22 | Error Correction** Find and correct the errors. (Some sentences may not have any errors.)

1. May you ask a question?
2. Could I can use the computer?
3. Would you borrow me your dictionary?
4. Can I call you tomorrow?
5. Please can you repeat that?
6. Could you take a number.
7. You could wait here a minute?
8. Can I have a cup of coffee?
9. Can I lend me a few dollars?
10. Would I please have another sandwich?
11. Would you can answer a question for me?
12. Could I have another cup of coffee.

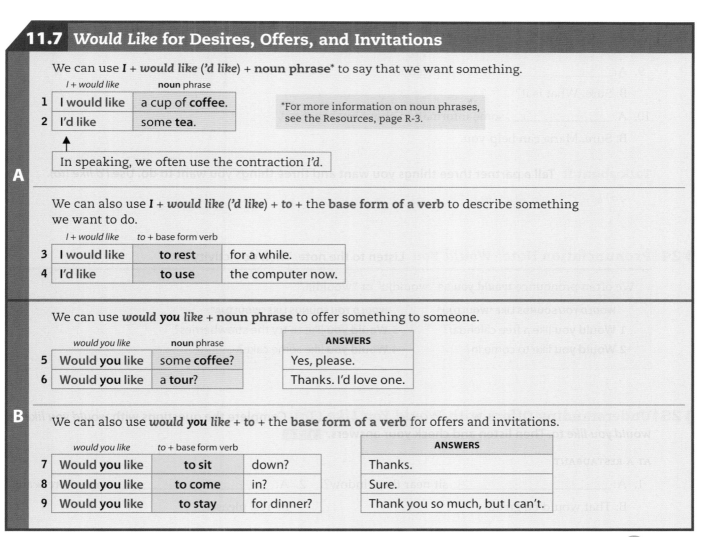

## 11.7 *Would Like* for Desires, Offers, and Invitations

**A**

We can use **I** + ***would like*** (***'d like***) + **noun phrase*** to say that we want something.

| *I + would like* | **noun** phrase |
|---|---|
| **1** | I would like | a cup of **coffee.** |
| **2** | I'd like | some **tea.** |

*For more information on noun phrases, see the Resources, page R-3.

↑ In speaking, we often use the contraction *I'd*.

We can also use **I** + ***would like*** (***'d like***) + **to** + the **base form of a verb** to describe something we want to do.

| *I + would like* | *to* + base form verb | |
|---|---|---|
| **3** | I would like | **to rest** | for a while. |
| **4** | I'd like | **to use** | the computer now. |

**B**

We can use ***would you like*** + **noun phrase** to offer something to someone.

| *would you like* | **noun** phrase | | **ANSWERS** |
|---|---|---|---|
| **5** | Would **you** like | some **coffee?** | Yes, please. |
| **6** | Would **you** like | a **tour?** | Thanks. I'd love one. |

We can also use ***would you like*** + **to** + the **base form of a verb** for offers and invitations.

| *would you like* | *to* + base form verb | | **ANSWERS** |
|---|---|---|---|
| **7** | Would **you** like | **to sit** | down? | Thanks. |
| **8** | Would **you** like | **to come** | in? | Sure. |
| **9** | Would **you** like | **to stay** | for dinner? | Thank you so much, but I can't. |

🔊 **23 | Using** *I'd Like (To)* **Complete the statements with** *I'd like* **or** *I'd like to.* **Then listen and check your answers.** `11.7 A`

AT WORK

1. A: _____ go home early today.

   B: OK.

2. A: _____ some more time to finish this project.

   B: OK. You can have another day.

3. A: _____ work some overtime this week.

   B: That might be possible. I'll check the schedule.

4. A: _____ take Thursday off.

   B: That's fine.

5. A: _____ get a new chair. Mine is broken.

   B: No problem. Talk to Alan about that.

6. A: _____ the morning shift[23].

   B: I'm sorry. The morning shift is full.

7. A: My computer isn't working very well. _____ get a new one.

   B: Let's try to fix it first.

8. A: _____ some help with this project.

   B: OK. Could you ask Celine?

9. A: _____ ask you a question.

   B: Sure. What is it?

10. A: _____ some information about my benefits[24].

    B: Sure. Maria can help you.

**Talk about It** Tell a partner three things you want and three things you want to do. Use *I'd like* (to).

   *"I'd like . . ."*          *"I'd like to . . ."*

🔊 **24 | Pronunciation Note:** *Would You* **Listen to the note. Then do Activity 25.**

> We often pronounce **would you** as "wouldju" or "wouldja."
>
> ***WOULD YOU* SOUNDS LIKE "WOULDJU"**          ***WOULD YOU* SOUNDS LIKE "WOULDJA"**
>
> **1 Would you** like a free calendar?          **3 Would you** like to try the strawberries?
>
> **2 Would you** like to come in?          **4 Would you** like some cake?

🔊 **25 | Understanding Offers with** *Would You Like* **(To) Complete the questions with** *would you like* **or** *would you like to.* **Then listen and check your answers.** `11.7 B`

AT A RESTAURANT

1. A: _____ sit near the window?     2. A: _____ some more water?

   B: That would be great.                         B: Yes, please.

---

[23] **shift:** a group of workers who work together during a specific period of time

[24] **benefits:** money or other advantages that you get from your job (for example, health care)

3. A: _____ something to drink?

   B: I'll have some tea.

4. A: _____ see the

   dessert menu?

   B: No, I think we're finished. Thanks.

5. A: _____ hear about

   our specials?

   B: Sure.

6. A: _____ a few more minutes?

   B: That's OK. We're ready.

7. A: _____ another soda?

   B: No, that's OK.

8. A: _____ order now?

   B: Yes, we're ready.

9. A: _____ a box for

   your leftovers[25]?

   B: No, thanks.

10. A: _____ your check now?

    B: Yes, please.

11. A: _____ join our

    diners' club?

    B: Not today, thanks.

12. A: _____ anything else?

    B: No, we're good. Thanks.

**Talk about It** Practice the conversations in Activity 25 with a partner. Pronounce *would you* as *wouldju* or *wouldja*.

**Think about It** In the questions in Activity 25, underline the noun or pronoun after *would you like*. Circle the verb after *would you like to*.

1. *Would you like to* (sit) *near the window?*
2. *Would you like some more* water?

**Talk about It** Add two more items to each list. Ask and answer the questions with a partner.

WOULD YOU LIKE . . .

a salad?

dessert?

some coffee?

_____

_____

WOULD YOU LIKE TO . . .

get some dessert?

have lunch now?

order anything else?

_____

_____

**26 | Using *Would You Like* and *Would You Like To*** Complete these conversations with *would you like* or *would you like to*. Then read the questions and answers with a partner. `11.7 B`

TALKING TO GUESTS

1. A: _____ come over for dinner?

   B: I'd love to.

2. A: _____ sit down?

   B: Thanks.

3. A: _____ give me your coat?

   B: Sure. Thanks.

4. A: _____ see the house?

   B: Yes, please.

5. A: _____ a pillow?

   B: That's OK.

> FYI
>
> We often use these words and phrases to say yes to offers and invitations:
>
> | | |
> |---|---|
> | Sure. | That sounds great. |
> | Yes, please. | I'd love to. |
> | Thanks. | |
>
> We often use these phrases to say no:
>
> | | |
> |---|---|
> | No, thank you. | It's all right. |
> | That's OK. | I'm sorry. I can't. |
> | Not right now. | |

[25]**leftovers:** food that is left after the meal

6. A: _____ cream or sugar?

    B: No, thank you.

7. A: _____ play a game?

    B: That sounds great.

8. A: _____ watch a movie?

    B: Sure.

9. A: _____ another cookie?

    B: Yes, thank you.

10. A: _____ a ride home?

    B: That's OK. Thanks. I enjoy taking the bus.

11. A: _____ some ice?

    B: No, thank you.

12. A: _____ sit outside

    on the patio?

    B: That sounds great.

13. A: _____ come back

    next week?

    B: I'm sorry. I can't.

14. A: _____ something to eat?

    B: That's OK. Thank you.

**Talk about It** Write four more offers or invitations for a guest in your home. Practice asking and answering the questions with a partner.

Would you like to _____?

Would you like _____?

Would you like to _____?

Would you like _____?

*A: Would you like to take a walk?*
*B: That sounds great.*

**27 | Usage Note: *Would Like* vs. *Want*** Read this note and the Pronunciation Note below. Then do Activity 29.

> We can use **would like** or **want** to make offers and invitations. *Would like* is more formal and polite than *want*.
>
> **WANT + NOUN PHRASE**
> **1** Do you **want** some coffee?
>
> **WANT + TO + VERB**
> **2** Do you **want to** have lunch?
>
> **WOULD YOU LIKE + NOUN PHRASE**
> **3** Would you like some coffee?
>
> **WOULD YOU LIKE + TO + VERB**
> **4** Would you like to see a menu?

**28 | Pronunciation Note: *D'you Wanna*** Read the note. Then do Activity 29.

> We often pronounce **do you** as "d'you" or "do ya" and **want to** as "wanna."
>
> | | | |
> |---|---|---|
> | **1 Do you want to** go? | *sounds like* | "**D'you wanna** go?" |
> | **2 Do you want to** try again? | *sounds like* | "**D'you wanna** try again?" |
> | **3 Do you want to** come over? | *sounds like* | "**Do ya wanna** come over?" |
> | **4 Do you want to** watch TV? | *sounds like* | "**Do ya wanna** watch TV?" |
>
> In informal speaking, we sometimes omit *do you*.
>
> **5** Want to come over after class? (= <u>Do you</u> want to come over after class?)
>
> **6** Want to get some coffee? (= <u>Do you</u> want to get some coffee?)

**◀)) 29 | Using *Would Like* and *Want*** Listen and complete these conversations. Are the speakers using formal or informal language? Check (✓) the correct column.

| OFFERS AND INVITATIONS | FORMAL | INFORMAL |
|---|---|---|
| 1. A: _____ sleep for a little while? <br> B: No, I'm OK. | ☐ | ☐ |
| 2. A: _____ a cough drop? <br> B: Thanks. | ☐ | ☐ |
| 3. A: _____ wait for Mr. Burns in his office? <br> B: Yes, please. | ☐ | ☐ |
| 4. A: _____ hear my poem? <br> B: Yeah, sure. | ☐ | ☐ |
| 5. A: _____ see the red one? <br> B: Please. | ☐ | ☐ |
| 6. A: _____ work some extra hours next week? <br> B: Yes, please. | ☐ | ☐ |
| 7. A: _____ meet at the library? <br> B: Can't today. Maybe tomorrow. | ☐ | ☐ |
| 8. A: _____ a bag for that? <br> B: Yes, thank you. | ☐ | ☐ |
| 9. A: _____ call Tony? <br> B: Mm. Not really. | ☐ | ☐ |
| 10. A: _____ take a walk? <br> B: Yeah, sure. | ☐ | ☐ |
| 11. A: _____ speak to the secretary? <br> B: Yes, please. | ☐ | ☐ |
| 12: A: _____ go out tonight? <br> B: Maybe. I'll call you. | ☐ | ☐ |

**Talk about It** Practice the conversations above with a partner. Pronounce *want to* as *wanna* and *would you* as *wouldju* or *wouldja*.

**Talk about It** Talk to a partner. Use the words in this box to make offers and invitations. Use *do you want* and *would you like*.

| | | |
|---|---|---|
| a piece of candy | have lunch together | study with me |
| an eraser | some help | use my phone |

*A: Do you want to have lunch together?*
*B: Sorry, I can't today. How about tomorrow?*

## WRAP-UP

**A | GRAMMAR IN READING** Read this article. Underline the forms of *can, could, would like,* and *be able to.*

# LA's Favorite Food Truck

<u>Would you like</u> to eat food from a truck? Go to downtown Los Angeles at lunchtime, and you will see food trucks everywhere. You can get Mexican food, Chinese food, Indian food, or Korean food. You can get gourmet[26] food or hamburgers and hot dogs. Nowadays, food trucks sell just about everything. Can't find your favorite truck? Just check online! Many trucks post their locations on blogs or other websites.

Korean tacos from the Kogi food truck

In 2008, food trucks were not so popular in Los Angeles. Many trucks sold tacos or sandwiches, but there wasn't much variety[27]. You couldn't find gourmet or unusual food at a truck. Then a man named Roy Choi helped to change that. Choi could cook Korean food and Mexican food, so he decided to put them together. He made Mexican tacos and quesadillas with Korean ingredients and spices. He started a food truck company called Kogi. Soon his food trucks became very popular.

People loved Choi's food, but they often weren't able to find the Kogi trucks. So Choi started to use social media (websites like Facebook) to communicate with customers. He had thousands of followers online. Sometimes more than 600 people came to his truck and waited in line for an hour.

Choi became famous. He was able to open two restaurants, and now he is writing a book about his life. These days, there are gourmet food trucks all over the U.S. Thousands of people follow food trucks on social media. Go to any big American city, and you will be able to buy interesting food from a truck!

**Think about It** Which modals above describe the past? Which describe the present? Which describes the future? Write *PA* above the past forms, *PR* above the present forms, and *F* above the future form.

**B | GRAMMAR IN SPEAKING** Interview a classmate. Use these questions and two questions of your own.

**NOW**

1. Can you find food trucks in your city? Where?
2. What kinds of food can you get near here?
3. Would you like to try Roy Choi's Mexican-Korean food?
4. Would you like to have lunch from a food truck?
5. Can you cook well?
6. What is one thing you can't cook?

**WHEN YOU WERE 12 YEARS OLD**

7. Could you cook your own dinner?
8. What kinds of food were you able to prepare?
9. Were there any foods you couldn't eat?

**Write about It** Write your partner's answers to questions 5–9 above.

5. *Suma can cook very well.*

[26] **gourmet food:** very good or special food          [27] **variety:** different kinds

## 11.8 Summary of Modals I

**OVERVIEW OF MODAL USES**

|  |  | CAN | COULD | BE ABLE TO | MAY | WOULD | WOULD LIKE |
|---|---|---|---|---|---|---|---|
| ABILITY / POSSIBILITY | PAST | — | ✓ | ✓ | — | — | — |
|  | PRESENT | ✓ | — | ✓ | — | — | — |
|  | FUTURE | ✓ | — | ✓ | — | — | — |
| ASKING PERMISSION | | ✓ | ✓ | — | ✓ | — | — |
| REQUESTS | | ✓ | ✓ | — | — | ✓ | — |
| DESIRES, OFFERS, AND INVITATIONS | | — | — | — | — | — | ✓ |

You will learn more uses of modals in Unit 12.

| MODALS | USES | EXAMPLES |
|---|---|---|
| CAN | Ability / Possibility | Can you swim?<br>I can't see you.<br>She can visit tomorrow. |
|  | Asking Permission | Can I sit here? |
|  | Requests | Can you call me later?<br>Can they take me home?<br>Can she bring her parents? |
| COULD | Past Ability | My grandfather could play the piano.<br>Could you hear him?<br>I couldn't come to class yesterday. |
|  | Asking Permission | Could I have the car keys? |
|  | Requests | Could you help me with this? |
| MAY | Asking Permission | May I ask a question? |
| WOULD | Requests | Would you say that again? |
| WOULD YOU LIKE (TO) | Offers and Invitations | Would you like a cup of tea?<br>Would you like to call back later? |
| BE ABLE TO | Present Ability | I'm able to open my files.<br>She's able to understand me.<br>They're able to attend the meetings.<br>He isn't able to be here.<br>We aren't able to help you. |
|  | Past Ability | He was able to fix my car.<br>They were able to finish on time.<br>I wasn't able to call you.<br>We weren't able to start. |
|  | Future Ability | I'll be able to do this later.<br>He'll be able to talk to you.<br>They won't be able to work on Tuesday. |

# 12

# Modals II

## IN THIS UNIT, WE USE modals to:

### Give our opinion

1. He **should** go to bed.

2. They **shouldn't** drive now. It's dangerous.

### Give advice and make suggestions

3. You **should** call the IT department.

4. **Why don't you** rest for a few minutes?

**Think about It** Read these sentences. Check (✓) *True* or *False*.

| TODAY . . . | TRUE | FALSE |
|---|---|---|
| 1. I should go to bed early. | ☐ | ☐ |
| 2. I shouldn't go outside. | ☐ | ☐ |
| 3. I should rest for a while before dinner. | ☐ | ☐ |
| 4. I should do the laundry. | ☐ | ☐ |
| 5. I should finish my homework. | ☐ | ☐ |

**GO ONLINE**

For the Unit Vocabulary Check, go to the Online Practice.

## Talk about necessity and prohibition

5. The students here **have to** wear uniforms.

6. He **has to** study for the exam.

7. Employees **must** wear safety glasses.

8. Visitors **must not** touch the art.

**Think about It** Read these sentences. Check (✓) *True* or *False*.

|  | TRUE | FALSE |
|---|---|---|
| 1. I have to study for a test tonight. | ☐ | ☐ |
| 2. I need to bring a laptop to class. | ☐ | ☐ |
| 3. Students at my school have to do a lot of homework. | ☐ | ☐ |
| 4. I need to take a math class next semester. | ☐ | ☐ |

**Check (✓) the rules that are true at your school.**

5. ☐ Students must not chew gum.

6. ☐ Students must not use cell phones during class.

7. ☐ Students must not eat or drink in class.

8. ☐ Visitors must report to the office.

## 12.1 Advice and Opinions with *Should* and *Shouldn't*

We can use **should** or **shouldn't** to give advice or to give our opinion about the right or wrong thing to do.

**1** It's late. You **should go** to bed soon. (The speaker is giving advice TO someone.)

**2** Children **should respect** their parents. (The speaker is giving an opinion ABOUT someone or something.)

**A**

**POSITIVE STATEMENTS**

| | subject | should | base form verb | |
|---|---|---|---|---|
| **3** | I / You / He / She / We / They / Teenagers | should | **study** | for the test. |
| **4** | | | **see** | a doctor once a year. |
| **5** | | | **exercise** | more. |

**NEGATIVE STATEMENTS**

| | subject | should + not | base form verb | |
|---|---|---|---|---|
| **6** | I / You / He / She / Bob / We / They | should not shouldn't | **leave** | too late. |
| **7** | | | **worry** | about it. |

**1 | Pronunciation Note: Stress with *Should* and *Shouldn't*** Listen to the note. Then do Activity 2.

> We do not usually stress **should**. We stress the main verb.
>
> **1** Students should **BRING** a pen and a notebook.     **2** You should **CALL** him.
>
> In sentences with **shouldn't**, we often stress both *shouldn't* and the main verb.
>
> **3** We **SHOULDN'T PAY** for this.
>
> **4** Teenagers **SHOULDN'T SPEND** too much time online.

**2 | Noticing *Should* and *Shouldn't*** Listen and complete these statements with *should* or *shouldn't* + the main verb. Then check (✓) *Always Agree*, *Sometimes Agree*, or *Disagree*. **12.1 A**

| OPINIONS | ALWAYS AGREE | SOMETIMES AGREE | DISAGREE |
|---|---|---|---|
| 1. Rich people _____ money to charity[1]. | ☐ | ☐ | ☐ |
| 2. Everyone _____ children. | ☐ | ☐ | ☐ |
| 3. Students _____ each other with homework. | ☐ | ☐ | ☐ |
| 4. People _____ kind to animals. | ☐ | ☐ | ☐ |
| 5. Parents _____ their children. | ☐ | ☐ | ☐ |
| 6. Stores _____ on holidays. | ☐ | ☐ | ☐ |
| 7. Everyone _____ married. | ☐ | ☐ | ☐ |
| 8. Children _____ to their parents. | ☐ | ☐ | ☐ |
| 9. The government _____ health care[2]. | ☐ | ☐ | ☐ |
| 10. Employees _____ six weeks of paid vacation every year. | ☐ | ☐ | ☐ |
| 11. Teenagers _____ violent[3] video games. | ☐ | ☐ | ☐ |

---

[1] **charity:** organizations that collect money to help people who need it

[2] **health care:** medical care

[3] **violent:** showing harm and destruction

|                                                  | ALWAYS AGREE | SOMETIMES AGREE | DISAGREE |
|--------------------------------------------------|:---:|:---:|:---:|
| 12. Universities _____ free.         | ☐ | ☐ | ☐ |
| 13. A ten-year-old child _____ a cell phone. | ☐ | ☐ | ☐ |
| 14. Governments _____ money to the arts. | ☐ | ☐ | ☐ |

🔊 **Talk about It** Listen again and repeat the sentences in Activity 2. Pay attention to the stressed words.

**Talk about It** Discuss your answers for Activity 2 as a class. Which statements do most students agree with?

**3 | Using *Should* and *Shouldn't*** Read these sentences about the average American. Then complete the advice with *should* or *shouldn't* and a main verb. 12.1 A

ADVICE FOR AMERICANS

1. Americans spend 34 hours a week watching television.

   They _____*should watch*_____ less television.

2. Twenty percent of Americans sleep less than 6 hours a night.

   They _____ for 8 hours a night.

3. Americans use credit cards very often. Many families have over $15,000 in credit card debt[4].

   They _____ credit cards so often.

4. About 48 percent of Americans drink soda every day.

   They _____ soda every day.

5. Many American children play video games for over 13 hours a week.

   They _____ video games so much.

6. Eighty percent of Americans don't exercise enough.

   They _____ more.

7. Most American high school students do not study calculus.

   More students _____ calculus.

8. Many Americans don't save money. Half of Americans don't have enough savings to pay their bills for three months.

   They _____ more money.

9. Many Americans do not learn a second language.

   More people _____ a second language.

calculus

10. Most Americans eat too many calories every day.

    They _____ so many calories.

**Talk about It** Tell a partner about your habits. Explain which things you should or shouldn't do, and which are OK.

*"I watch television for about five hours a week. I think that's OK."*
*"I only study two hours a day. I should study for four or five hours a day."*

---

[4] **debt:** money that you need to pay

**4 | Usage Note:** *I (Don't) Think* **and** *Maybe* **in Statements with** *Should* **Read the note. Then do Activity 5.**

We can use **I think** or **maybe** in sentences with **should** to make our opinions softer (less strong).

*I THINK...SHOULD*

**1** I think you should talk to your teacher.

*I DON'T THINK...SHOULD*

**3** I don't think you should give him the answers.

**4** I don't think she should come in tomorrow.

*MAYBE...SHOULD*

**2** Maybe he should wait for a couple of days.

*MAYBE...SHOULDN'T*

**5** Maybe we shouldn't eat here.

**6** Maybe we shouldn't leave now.

Sometimes we use **I think** and **maybe** together.

**7** I think maybe we should leave.

**5 | Using** *I (Don't) Think* **or** *Maybe + Should* **Read each situation. Choose two of the phrases in the box. Write advice with** *I (don't) think* **or** *maybe*. `12.1 A`

WHAT SHOULD THEY DO?

1. John's co-worker steals office supplies.

   *I think John should tell his boss.*
   *Maybe he shouldn't tell his other co-workers.*

   | | |
   |---|---|
   | tell his boss | talk to his co-worker |
   | tell his other co-workers | ignore[5] it |

2. Someone hit a parked car and drove away. Marta saw him.

   | | |
   |---|---|
   | call the police | ignore it |
   | chase the car | |

3. Sara's classmate cheated[6] on a test.

   | | |
   |---|---|
   | tell the teacher | talk to the classmate |
   | tell other students | ignore it |

4. An old woman stole fruit from the grocery store. Tom saw her.

   | | |
   |---|---|
   | call the police | tell the store owner |
   | talk to the woman | ignore it |

5. Ana found $100 cash in the street.

   | | |
   |---|---|
   | keep it | tell people nearby |
   | take it to the police | |

6. Rita is driving at night. She sees a car broken down[7] by the side of the road.

   | | |
   |---|---|
   | call the police | stop and help |
   | keep driving | |

7. There is a suspicious-looking person[8] in front of Sean's neighbor's house. His neighbor isn't home.

   | | |
   |---|---|
   | call the police | keep watching |
   | go talk to the person | |

---

[5] **ignore:** to not pay attention to
[6] **cheat:** to do something that is not honest (for example, copy another student's answers)

[7] **broken down:** not working
[8] **suspicious-looking person:** a person who looks like they might commit a crime

8. The teacher missed some of Teruko's mistakes on the test and gave her a high score.

| | |
|---|---|
| tell her friends | ignore it |
| tell the teacher | |

9. The cashier at the grocery store gave George too much change. George is already home.

| | |
|---|---|
| go back to the store and return the money | |
| call the store | keep the money |
| go back the next day | |

10. Anita's friend has bad breath[9].

| | |
|---|---|
| give her friend some mouthwash | ignore it |
| tell her friend | |

**Write about It** Write a new piece of advice for each of these situations. Use your own ideas.

1. Ann's sister has a new dress. Ann thinks it's ugly.
2. There's an important football game on TV. Jim doesn't want to go to work.
3. Carol has a new employee. He's very nice, but he's not very good at his job.

*1. I think Ann should tell her sister the truth.*

**Talk about It** Work with a partner. Write two more problems. Give each other advice with *should* or *shouldn't*.

*A: I'm angry at my best friend.*
*B: I think you should talk to her.*

## 12.2 Questions with *Should*

**A**

**YES/NO QUESTIONS**

| | should | subject | base form verb | |
|---|---|---|---|---|
| 1 | Should | I / you / he / she / we / they | **buy** | this? |
| 2 | | | **take** | the job? |

**SHORT ANSWERS**

| | yes / no | subject | should (+ not) |
|---|---|---|---|
| 3 | Yes, | you / I / he / she / we / they | **should.** |
| 4 | No, | | **shouldn't.** |

**OTHER WAYS TO ANSWER *YES/NO* QUESTIONS**

| ANSWER *YES* | ANSWER *NO* |
|---|---|
| 5 A: Should I take the job? <br> B: **Definitely!** It sounds great. | 7 A: Should we wait for you? <br> B: **No**, you can start eating. We'll be there later. |
| 6 A: Should I buy this watch? <br> B: **Why not?** | 8 A: Should I call Robert? <br> B: **I don't think so.** He's really busy. |

**B**

**WH- QUESTIONS**

| | wh- word | should | subject | base form verb | |
|---|---|---|---|---|---|
| 9 | Where | | I / you / he / she / we / they / Aunt Karen | **have** | dinner? |
| 10 | When | should | | **arrive?** | |
| 11 | How long | | | **wait?** | |

[9] **bad breath:** when the air that comes out of your mouth has a bad smell

## 6 | Asking and Answering *Yes/No* Questions with *Should*  Write each question for Speaker A under the correct picture. Then practice the conversations with a partner.  `12.2 A`

| | | |
|---|---|---|
| Should I bring an umbrella? | Should I invite Karen? | Should we get dessert? |
| Should I buy this? | Should I throw it away? | Should we go to Tahiti? |
| Should I call the doctor? | Should we call the police? | |

1. A: _____

   B: I don't think so.

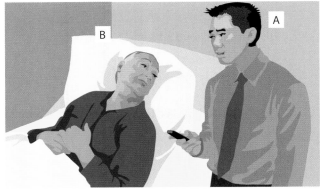

2. A: _____

   B: No, I'll be fine.

3. A: _____

   B: Oh, yes. She's really fun.

4. A: _____

   B: Oh, I don't think so. I'm too full!

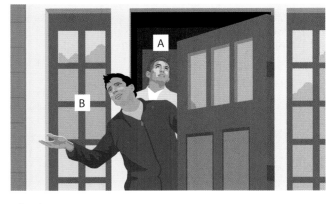

5. A: _____

   B: Good idea. It's pretty cloudy out there.

6. A: _____

   B: Yes, I think we should.

7. A: _____

B: Maybe. Or maybe we should go to Hawaii!

8. A: _____

B: Nah. I can fix that for you.

**Talk about It** Choose three of the pictures in Activity 6 and write a new question with *should* for each. Then ask and answer your questions with a partner.

*Picture 1*
A: *Should I try a different size?*
B: *Yes—and maybe a different color, too.*

**7 | Asking for and Giving Advice with *Should*** Complete these questions and answers. Use the words in parentheses and *should* or *shouldn't*. 12.2 A–B

---

## Making a Good Impression[10]: FAQ

**I have a job interview tomorrow.**

1. Q: _____?
   (what / I / wear)
   A: Wear professional clothes. It's OK to be a little too formal, but it's not OK to be too casual.

2. Q: _____ about the salary[11]?
   (when / I / ask)
   A: Don't ask at the interview. Ask when they offer you the job.

3. Q: _____ after the interview?
   (what / I / do)
   A: Send a thank-you note right away, but don't call about the job right away.

   _____ them time to interview other people and make a decision.
   (you / give)

**I'm having dinner with my boss tomorrow.**

4. Q: My boss invited me to a restaurant. _____ for dinner?
   (I / pay)
   A: Your boss won't expect you to pay for dinner. He or she will pay.

5. Q: _____?
   (what / I / order)
   A: Order something you like, but _____ the most expensive thing
   (you / not get)

   on the menu.

---

[10] **making a good impression:** making other people have positive thoughts or feelings about you

[11] **salary:** money that you receive for the work you do

**My co-worker is having a potluck dinner[12].**

6. Q: How much food _____ ?
   (I / bring)
   A: Bring a small serving for everyone.

7. Q: _____ right on time?
   (I / arrive)
   A: It's OK to be 10 or 15 minutes late, but not much later than that.

   And _____ early!
   (you / not arrive)

8. Q: _____ my wife/husband?
   (I / bring)
   A: _____ the host. At casual events, people sometimes bring their spouses.
   (you / ask)

**My co-workers are exchanging gifts.**

9. Q: _____ my presents?
   (when / I / open)
   A: This can be different for different people. Thank them for the gift.

   Then ask, "_____ it now?"
   (I / open)

10. Q: _____ a thank-you card to everyone?
    (I / send)
    A: Everyone likes a thank-you card. For a small group of co-workers, _____
    (you / send)
    one to each person. For a large group, you can post one thank-you note for the whole group.

**Talk about It** Write two questions with *should* for each of these situations. Write one *yes/no* question and one *wh-* question. Ask and answer the questions with a partner.

1. You are attending a friend's wedding.

   *What should I wear?*

2. You are attending an important meeting at your new job.

---

## 12.3 Suggestions with *Why Don't You / We*

**A**

We can use *why don't you* or *why don't we* to make a suggestion.

| | base form verb | |
|---|---|---|
| 1 | **Why don't you** | **sit** | down? |
| 2 | **Why don't we** | **go** | somewhere? |

3 A: You look tired. **Why don't you sit** down?
  B: Good idea. I think I will.

4 A: I'm bored. **Why don't we go** somewhere?
  B: Sure. Where should we go?

Notice: The meaning of *why don't we* is similar to *let's*. For more information on *let's*, see Unit 1, page 19.

**B**

*Why don't you* has a softer meaning than *should*.

STRONGER, MORE DIRECT MEANING

5 A: I want to go out, but I have a test tomorrow.
  B: You **should stay** home and study. You can go out tomorrow.

SOFTER, LESS DIRECT MEANING

6 A: **Why don't you get** some rest? You'll feel better.
  B: Thanks. That's a good idea.

---

[12] **potluck dinner:** a dinner where each guest brings some of the food

**8 | Making Suggestions with *Why Don't You* and *Why Don't We*** Complete these conversations with the suggestions in the box. Then listen and check your answers. Practice the conversations with a partner. `12.3 A`

GOING OUT

1. A: Well, we can't go to the zoo now. It's raining.

   B: _____

   A: That's a good idea. I think there's a Picasso exhibit

      this month. And it's free today.

2. A: I need to get some exercise.

   B: Me too. _____

   A: OK. I'll change my shoes.

3. A: I'm bored.

   B: _____

   A: He's working today.

4. A: Oh, no! The show is sold out[13] this weekend.

   B: _____

   A: OK. I'm free next Saturday. I'll get the tickets now.

5. A: What should we do today?

   B: _____

   A: No, it's not hot enough. And the water is too cold.

6. A: _____ There are a lot of good sales.

   B: I can't. I'm broke[14].

7. A: Ugh. I'm so tired of pizza.

   B: _____

   A: That's a good idea. Want to come?

8. A: _____ You're really good.

   B: I want to, but I don't have time to play every weekend.

> Why don't we go next weekend?
> Why don't we go shopping tomorrow?
> Why don't we go to a museum?
> Why don't we go to the beach?
> Why don't we take a walk?
> Why don't you call Tomas?
> Why don't you join the baseball team?
> Why don't you try the new Chinese place?

**Talk about It** Choose three of the conversations above. Write a different suggestion with *why don't you* or *why don't we*. Practice the new conversations with a partner.

*A: I'm bored.*
*B: Why don't we go to a movie?*
*A: OK. What's playing?*

**9 | Using *Why Don't You* and *Why Don't We*** Write a suggestion for each problem. Use *why don't you* or *why don't we*. Use the phrases in each box. `12.3 A`

SCHOOL PROBLEMS

1. A: You look tired.

   B: I am. I can't finish this homework tonight.

   A: *Why don't you sleep for a while?* _____

> get a tutor
> go to the library
> sleep for a while

---

[13] **sold out:** there are no more tickets                    [14] **broke:** having no money

2. A: Should we study in your room?

   B: We can't. My roommate makes too much noise.

   A: _____

3. A: What's wrong?

   B: My chemistry class is really difficult.

   A: _____

get a tutor
go to the library
sleep for a while

4. A: I'm hungry.

   B: Me too, but the cafeteria is closed.

   A: _____

5. A: I didn't understand the class today. Did you?

   B: No, I didn't. _____

6. A: I'm thinking about changing my major.

   B: _____

go off-campus today
go see the teacher
talk to your adviser first

7. A: Oh, no! I lost my homework.

   B: _____

8. A: I have three tests next week.

   B: Me too. _____

9. A: I'm tired of eating the same food.

   B: _____

ask for some extra time
study together
try something new

10. A: Want to study with me?

    B: Sure, but I think the library is closed.

    A: _____

11. A: I really want to take that class, but it's full.

    B: _____

12. A: The textbook is really expensive.

    B: _____

buy a used one
email the professor
go to a café

**Talk about It** Continue the conversations in Activity 9 with a partner. Respond to each suggestion with one of the answers from this box. If your partner gives a negative answer, make another suggestion.

| | |
|---|---|
| OK. | I want to, but I can't. |
| Good idea. | I don't have enough money. |
| Sure. | I don't have time. |

A: *You look tired.*
B: *I am. I can't finish this homework tonight.*
A: *Why don't you sleep for a while?*
B: *I want to, but I can't. I'm too worried about my homework!*
A: *OK. Why don't you watch TV for a while? Then maybe you'll be able to sleep.*

**10 | Using *Why Don't You* or *You Should*** Listen and complete the suggestions with the words you hear. `12.3 B`

**AT HOME**

1. A: _You should leave_____ soon. You'll be late for the bus.

   B: Oh, you're right! I didn't notice the time! Thanks.

2. A: Ugh. I feel horrible.

   B: You look really sick. _____ home?

   A: I want to, but I can't. I have a meeting with my boss this morning.

   B: She'll understand. Just call her.

3. A: Can I borrow the car?

   B: I'm not sure. _____ your dad. He might need it.

**AT A RESTAURANT**

4. A: I can't eat spicy food.

   B: Well, _____ the noodles? They're not spicy.

   A: OK. I'll have those.

5. A: What do you recommend?

   B: _____ the hot and sour soup. It's delicious.

   A: OK. I'll try it.

**AT A POST OFFICE**

6. A: This needs to get to Seoul by tomorrow.

   B: _____ it Overnight Express.

7. A: I need to send this bracelet to Buenos Aires.

   B: _____ insurance[15] for that.

8. A: The line is so long! I just need to buy some stamps.

   B: _____ them from the machine?

**AT A LIBRARY**

9. A: Can you recommend a book for me? I like mysteries[16].

   B: _____ Agatha Christie? She's a very famous

      English mystery writer.

10. A: I'd like to reserve a study room for Wednesday.

    B: How many people are in your group?

    A: Eight.

    B: _____ Room C. It's the biggest one.

**Talk about It** Write a new conversation for each location above: home, a restaurant, a post office, and a library. Practice your conversations with a partner. Include suggestions with *why don't you* and *you should*.

---

[15] **insurance:** an agreement where you pay money to a company so that it will give you money if something bad happens

[16] **mysteries:** (literature) stories about something strange that you cannot understand or explain (for example, a strange crime)

## 12.4 Necessity with *Have To* and *Need To*

### A

**POSITIVE STATEMENTS**

We can use **have to** or **need to** to say that something is necessary or required.

**1** There's no food in the house.
I **have to go** shopping.

**2** School is starting next month.
Julie **needs to register** for classes.

**3**

| subject | have to / need to | base form verb | |
|---|---|---|---|
| I You We They | have to need to | do | the laundry. |

**4**

| subject | has to / needs to | base form verb | |
|---|---|---|---|
| He She Julie | has to needs to | buy | the course book. |

Notice: *Have to* is a **phrasal modal**. It must agree with the subject. We often use *need to* like we use *have to*.

### B

**NEGATIVE STATEMENTS**

We can use **do / does** + **not** + **have to / need to** to say that something is NOT necessary or required.

**5** There's a lot of food in the house.
We **don't have to go** shopping.

**6** Paul **doesn't need to work** today.
It's his day off.

**7**

| subject | do + not | have to / need to | base form verb | |
|---|---|---|---|---|
| I You We They | do not don't | have to need to | leave. | |

**8**

| subject | does + not | has to / needs to | base form verb | |
|---|---|---|---|---|
| He She Julie | does not doesn't | have to need to | work | today. |

We usually use the contractions **don't** and **doesn't** in conversation.

Notice:

✓ We **don't have** to come today.
✓ He **doesn't have** to come today.

✗ We **no have** to come today.
✗ He **don't** have to come today.
✗ He **doesn't has** to come today.

## 11 | Using *Have To* and *Need To*  Complete excerpts 1–3 with *have to/has to* and excerpts 4–5 with *need to/needs to*. Underline the main verb.  `12.4 A`

PREPARING FOR CAREERS

### Medical doctor

1. Medical doctors go to school for a long time. Medical students ____*have to*____ take

    a lot of biology courses. They also _____ get a medical license[17].

### Commercial pilot

2. Some pilots get a private license first. Other pilots start in the military[18].

    A commercial pilot _____ complete many hours of flying time.

    Many pilots also _____ pass a medical exam every year.

a commercial pilot

---

[17] **license:** an official piece of paper that shows you are allowed to do or have something

[18] **military:** a country's soldiers who fight on land, in the air, or on water

**Police officer**

3. In many places, police officers _____ have a high school
   diploma. They usually also _____ take written tests and
   physical tests.

**Lawyer**

4. Lawyers _____ attend law school. Then they
   _____ get a license to practice law. In some places,
   it's very hard to get the license. They _____ take
   a very long, difficult test.

**Teacher**

5. A teacher _____ have a college degree and take special
   courses in education. Student teachers[19] usually _____
   practice in a classroom.

**Talk about It** Think of another career. Talk with a partner about things
that people have to do to prepare for the career. Use the ideas in this box
or your own ideas.

> be a good speaker
> be a good writer
> be in good physical health
> get a college degree
> get a license
> take a difficult exam
> take a lot of science courses

**F Y I**

Notice: We can use the main verb **have** after **have to**.

A truck driver **has to have** a special license.

Nurses **have to have** a license.

🔊 **12 | Pronunciation Note: *Have To* and *Need To*** Listen to the note. Then do Activity 13.

Notice how we usually pronounce **have to** and **need to**. The **to** sounds like /tə/.

| | | | |
|---|---|---|---|
| **1 have to** | *sounds like* | "hafta" | I **have to** go. |
| **2 has to** | *sounds like* | "hasta" | He **has to** try again. |
| **3 need to** | *sounds like* | "need-ta" | I **need to** get up early. |
| **4 needs to** | *sounds like* | "needs-ta" | She **needs to** come back tomorrow. |

Notice: We also use **have/need** + noun phrase*. There is no to before the noun phrase.

**5 I have a class** today.

**6 A:** Do you **need the car** today?
   **B:** No, I **need it** tomorrow.

*For more information on noun phrases, see the Resources, page R-3.

[19] **student teachers:** people who are studying to become teachers

**13 | Listening for *Have To* and *Need To*** Listen and complete these conversations. Are the speakers saying *have to/need to* + verb or *have/need* + noun phrase? Check (✓) the correct column. Then practice the conversations with a partner. **12.4 A**

| EXCUSES | HAVE TO / NEED TO + VERB | HAVE / NEED + NOUN PHRASE |
|---|---|---|
| 1. A: Why don't we go out tonight?<br>B: I can't. I _____. | ☐ | ☐ |
| 2. A: Do you want to have breakfast tomorrow?<br>B: I can't. I _____ in the morning. | ☐ | ☐ |
| 3. A: Do you want to come over?<br>B: Thanks, but I _____ home. My father | ☐ | ☐ |
| _____ with something. | ☐ | ☐ |
| 4. A: Can you stay a little longer today?<br>B: I'm sorry. I can't. I _____ in about ten minutes. | ☐ | ☐ |
| 5. A: Did you get my message?<br>B: No, I didn't, sorry. I _____. | ☐ | ☐ |
| 6. A: Where is Karla?<br>B: She _____ late on Tuesdays. She'll be here later. | ☐ | ☐ |
| 7. A: Can we talk at 12?<br>B: Not today. I _____ Brad a ride home after class. | ☐ | ☐ |
| 8. A: Did you just wake up?<br>B: Yeah, sorry. I _____. | ☐ | ☐ |
| 9. A: Can you help me move this weekend?<br>B: Sorry. I _____ a paper. | ☐ | ☐ |
| 10. A: Call me tomorrow!<br>B: I _____ all day. I'll call you on Saturday. | ☐ | ☐ |
| 11. A: Want to go to the movie?<br>B: I can't. I _____ early tomorrow. | ☐ | ☐ |
| 12. A: Can I borrow your book?<br>B: Sorry. I _____ tonight. | ☐ | ☐ |

**14 | Using *Not Have To* and *Not Need To*** Complete conversations 1–5 with a form of *not have to* and conversations 6–10 with a form of *not need to*. Use the verbs in parentheses. Then listen and check your answers. **12.4 B**

GETTING READY FOR GUESTS

1. A: I ordered pizza tonight, so we _____. (cook)

   B: Oh, good. I'm exhausted[20].

2. A: Ana will bring coffee and soda.

   B: She _____ coffee. Max is bringing some. (bring)

RESEARCH SAYS...

We use *have to* more often in conversation than in writing.

CORPU

---

[20]**exhausted:** very tired

3. A: I'll call you before we come.

   B: You _____. Just come! (call)

4. A: I hope you can come to the city with us.

   B: Oh, I can. I just talked to my boss. I _____ that day. (work)

5. A: Mick wants to help us get ready.

   B: He _____. But that's nice of him. (help)

6. A: I'll order some flowers.

   B  Thanks, but you _____ that. My uncle is a florist. He'll bring some flowers. (do)

7. A: The dinner might get pretty loud. Should we tell the neighbors?

   B: No, we _____ them anything. They'll be out of town. (tell)

8. A: My oven isn't very big.

   B: Why don't you barbecue[21]? Then you _____ the oven. (use)

9. A: Ana wants to make dessert.

   B: She _____ dessert! She made it last time. (make)

10. A: How much is the salad dressing?

    B: You _____ for it. It comes with the salad. (pay)

**Talk about It** Imagine ten people are coming to your home for dinner. What do you have to do? What do you not have to do? Use the ideas in this box or your own ideas. Tell a partner.

| borrow furniture | buy paper plates | cook | order food | warn your neighbors |
|---|---|---|---|---|

*"I have to cook all the food."*
*"I don't have to make dessert. My friend is making a cake."*

**Talk about It** Compare your answers in Activity 14 as a class. How are your ideas different?

## 12.5 Questions with *Have To* and *Need To*

**YES/NO QUESTIONS**

| | | do / does | subject | have to / need to | base form verb | |
|---|---|---|---|---|---|---|
| **A** | 1 | Do | I / you / we / they | **have to** | leave | now? |
| | 2 | Does | he / she / Maria | **need to** | work | today? |

**SHORT ANSWERS**

| | | |
|---|---|---|
| Yes, | you / I / we / they | do. |
| No, | | don't. |
| Yes, | he / she | does. |
| No, | | doesn't. |

**WH- QUESTIONS**

| | | wh- word | do / does | subject | have to / need to | base form verb | |
|---|---|---|---|---|---|---|---|
| **B** | 3 | What time / When | do | we | **need to** | get | there? |
| | 4 | How long / Why / Where | does | he | **have to** | wait? | |

---

[21] **barbecue:** to cook food on a fire outside

**15 | Asking Questions with *Have To* or *Need To*** Complete these questions with *have to* or *need to* and the words in parentheses. Use the subject *you*. `12.5 A–B`

CHORES

1. _What do you have to do_ _____ next weekend? (what/do)
2. _____ tonight? (study)
3. _____ today? (when/leave)
4. _____ the floors today? (clean)
5. _____ tomorrow morning?
   (what time/get up)
6. _____ any emails tonight? (send)
7. _____ your rent? (when/pay)
8. _____ the dishes every day? (wash)
9. _____ to class? (what time/get)
10. _____ grocery shopping
    tomorrow? (go)
11. _____ today? (how long/work)
12. _____ dinner tonight? (cook)

> **F Y I**
>
> Remember: **Have to** is a phrasal modal. We use *do/does* in negative statements and questions with *have to*, like we do with other **simple present verbs**.
>
> **Do** you **have to work** today?
> You **don't have to work** today.
> (*have to* + main verb *work*)
>
> **Do** you **have** a job?
> We **don't have** any homework today.
> (main verb *have*; simple present)

**Talk about It** Ask and answer the questions above with a partner.

*A: What do you have to do next weekend?*
*B: I have to do laundry and clean my apartment.*

**Talk about It** Work with a new partner. What do you remember about your classmates? Quiz your partner. Use *does . . . have to/need to.*

*"What does Jin have to do next weekend?"*

**Write about It** Write about three differences between yourself and your partner.

*Jamal has to study tonight, but I don't. I don't have any homework.*
*I have to pay my rent on the first of the month. Jamal doesn't need to pay rent. He lives at home with his parents.*

**16 | Error Correction** Find and correct the errors. (Some sentences may not have any errors.)

1. He don't have to wear a uniform.
2. She need to come on time every day.
3. What time does he should call you?
4. I'm not have to study for this test.
5. What time are you have to be at work?
6. When he has to finish the essay?
7. I think I should to study a little more.
8. I don't need get up early tomorrow.
9. How long do we have to wait?
10. When do he have to arrive?
11. I have to homework tonight.
12. Does she has to pay for the tickets?

## 12.6 Necessity and Prohibition with *Must*

**A**

**POSITIVE STATEMENTS**

We can use *must* to talk about things that are necessary.

1 All students **must take** an English exam at the beginning of the semester.

2

| subject | must | base form verb | |
|---|---|---|---|
| I / You / He / She / Carlos / We / They | **must** | **follow** | the directions. |

> *Must* is similar in meaning to **have to** and **need to**, but it is more formal. We don't usually use *must* to express necessity in conversation.

**WARNING!** Don't add *to* after *must*.

✓Employees **must arrive** on time.    ✗ Employees must to arrive on time.

**B**

**NEGATIVE STATEMENTS**

We use *must not* to express **prohibition**: to say that something is forbidden (not permitted).

3 Students **must not smoke** on campus. (= Smoking is not permitted on campus.)

4

| subject | must + not | base form verb | |
|---|---|---|---|
| I / You / He / She / Lisa / We / They | **must not** | **enter** | the construction area. |

**17 | Noticing *Must* and *Must Not*** Complete these signs with *must* or *must not*. Underline the main verb.
`12.6 A–B`

1.

2.

3.

4.

**5.**

**6.**

**7.**

**8.**

**Talk about It**  Where might you see each of the signs in Activity 17?

**Write about It**  Choose two locations from this box. Write two rules with *must* and *must not*. Write complete sentences.

| | |
|---|---|
| an apartment building | a library |
| a beach | a park |
| a gym | a public swimming pool |

*A public swimming pool*
*Swimmers must not run near the pool.*
*You must bring your own towel.*

**18 | Usage Note:** *Must Not* **vs.** *Not Have To*  Read the note. Then do Activity 19.

The negative forms **not have to** and **must not** have very different meanings.

| ***NOT HAVE TO* = NOT NECESSARY; NOT REQUIRED** | ***MUST NOT* = FORBIDDEN; NOT PERMITTED** |
|---|---|
| **1** Students **don't have to bring** a laptop to school. (It's not required.) | **3** Students **must not smoke** on campus. (It's not permitted.) |
| **2** Maria **doesn't have to wake** up early today. It's a holiday. (It's not necessary.) | |

## 19 | Using *Not Have To* and *Must Not*  Complete these sentences with *must not* or *don't/doesn't have to.*

`12.6 B`

STATEMENTS FROM A HOTEL MANAGER

### To guests

1. Welcome to the Oaks Hotel! We provide daily housekeeping, so you ____don't have to____ clean up.

2. You _____ leave your room for meals. We have a full room service[22] menu.

3. This is a smoke-free hotel. You _____ smoke in the rooms, bathrooms, or lobby.

4. Checkout time is 12:00. You _____ notify[23] the front desk if you leave on time.

5. We offer automatic checkout. You _____ check out at the front desk. Just leave the key in your room.

a hotel guest

### To housekeepers

6. Your job is to keep the rooms clean for our guests. You will make the beds, vacuum, pick up trash, and clean the bathrooms every day. Usually, you _____ change the sheets every day for the same guest. You can change them every other day.

7. Guests _____ take towels or pillows from the room. Please notify the front desk if items are missing.

8. You _____ look through the guests' suitcases or personal items.

9. You _____ provide extra services to guests, like carrying suitcases. Guests should contact the front desk for extra help.

a housekeeper

### To desk clerks

10. You _____ wear a uniform, but please wear a black or gray jacket.

11. The privacy of our guests is very important. You _____ give guests' names or room numbers to other people.

a desk clerk

**Write about It**  Work with a partner. Write six sentences with *don't have to* and *must not* about people at a restaurant. You can write about customers, servers, cooks, or hosts.

*1. Customers don't have to clean the tables.*

---

[22] **room service:** food that comes to your hotel room          [23] **notify:** to tell

## 12.7 Comparing Modals: *Can* vs. *Should* vs. *Have To*

**A**

### STATEMENTS

| We use *can* for ability, possibility, and permission*. | We use *should* for advice, opinions, and suggestions. | We use *have to* for necessity. |
|---|---|---|
| **1** She **can type** 90 words per minute. **2** You **can't use** your phone here. **3** We **can be** there at 5:00. | **4** He looks cold. He **should go** inside. **5** You **shouldn't bother** her. She's busy. | **6** You **have to throw** away old food. It can make you sick. **7** You **don't have to wear** a suit. This is an informal meeting. |

### QUESTIONS

| We use *can* for permission*. | We use *should* to ask for advice or an opinion. | We use *do / does* . . . *have to* to ask if something is necessary. |
|---|---|---|
| **8** Can I have a glass of water? | **9** Should I call him? | **10** Does he have to stay home from school? |

*For more information on *can*, see Unit 11, pages 280 and 283.

**20 | Noticing *Can*, *Should*, and *Have To*** Listen and complete these conversations with the words you hear. Then match each conversation with a place in the box. Practice the conversations with a partner. **12.7 A**

___c___ 1. A: My son wants to study engineering.

B: That's a difficult major. He _____has to_____ get very high scores in math.

A: Oh, he does.

____ 2. A: What time is my appointment?

B: It's at 3:00, but you _____ try to get here at 2:45.

A: Why?

B: You _____ complete some paperwork[24] before your appointment.

____ 3. A: First, you _____ take the written test. Then you can take the driving test.

B: OK. _____ I make an appointment for the driving test?

A: Of course.

____ 4. A: Oh, it's too crowded here. We _____ go somewhere else.

B: But I really want fried chicken!

A: Well, we _____ find another place.

> a. at a doctor's office
> b. at a restaurant
> c. at a school counselor's office
> d. at an amusement park
> e. at the Department of Motor Vehicles (DMV)

Department of Motor Vehicles (DMV)

---

[24] **paperwork:** written work that you have to do, such as completing forms

____ 5. A: You _____ go on the

   Scream Machine! It's so much fun!

   B: No, thanks. I don't like scary rides.

   A: Really? Oh, that's too bad. . . . But you

   _____ try it anyway! It's fun.

   B: Nope.

____ 6. A: Do I _____ take any medication?

   B: No, you don't. But you _____

   change your diet.

   A: I know, I know.

____ 7. A: You _____ take a history class

   next semester.

   B: Next semester? Why?

   A: It's a graduation requirement.

____ 8. A: Where _____ I go now?

   B: Stand in that line over there. We _____ take your picture.

   A: OK.

____ 9. A: I'm sorry. Your son _____ go on this ride.

   B: But he's nine years old.

   A: Passengers _____ be five feet tall.

   B: Oh, I didn't see that.

____10. A: I _____ eat any of this food! I _____ watch my diet.

   B: You _____ order a salad.

   A: I guess.

an amusement park

**Think about It** Look at each example of *have to* in Activity 20. Why do you think the speaker chose *have to* instead of *should*?

**Write about It** Choose two places from Activity 20. Write new conversations with *can*, *should*, or *have to*. Practice your conversations with a partner.

*Doctor's office*
*A: When should I come back?*
*B: Sometime next week. We have to do a few more tests.*

**21 | Using *Can*, *Should*, and *Have To*** Complete these conversations with the correct modal in parentheses. Then practice the conversations with a partner. `12.7 A`

1. A: Do you want to see a movie or go dancing?

   B: Hmm. I think we _____*should*_____ go dancing.
   <br>(should / have to)

2. A: Can you come over tomorrow?

   B: I can't. I _____ go to work.
   <br>(should / have to)

3. A: Ron is applying for a job in Mexico.

   B: _____ he speak Spanish?
      (can / should)

   A: Yes, he speaks it very well.

4. A: I have a headache.

   B: You _____ drink some tea.
      (should / have to)

   A: Good idea.

5. A: Do you want some peanuts?

   B: No, thanks. I _____ eat nuts. I'm allergic[25] to them.
      (don't have to / can't)

6. A: Why is Tina wearing that cap?

   B: It's part of her uniform. She _____ wear it.
      (has to / can)

7. A: Can I buy one of these?

   B: You _____ buy them. They're free.
      (don't have to / shouldn't)

8. A: Are you coming to the show?

   B: No, I'm not. Sorry. I _____ work from 9 a.m. to 9 p.m. that day.
      (have to / can)

9. A: I can't go out tonight.

   B: _____ study?
      (should you / do you have to)

   A: Yep. Big test tomorrow.

10. A: I don't think I like this color.

    B: _____ show you a different color?
       (do I have to / should I)

    A: Yes, please.

**Write about It** Write a response for each of these statements and questions. Use *can*, *should*, or *have to*.

1. A: Why are you working so late?

   B: *I have to make some extra money.* _____

2. A: The store is closed.

   B: _____

3. A: My phone isn't working.

   B: _____

4. A: What's the matter?

   B: _____

5. A: Uh-oh. My car won't start.

   B: _____

[25] **allergic:** having a medical condition that makes you sick when you eat something

# WRAP-UP

**A | GRAMMAR IN READING** Read this article. Underline the forms of *should, have to, need to, can,* and *must.*

## Tips for Travelers

### 1. Packing

Are you traveling to several places? You don't want to carry a heavy suitcase around, so you should plan your trip carefully. Maybe you don't really have to take that winter coat. Sometimes it's better to take two sweaters. Do you really need that fancy dress? Maybe you can just bring a simple dress and a nice piece of jewelry. And you definitely don't have to carry your heavy guidebook[26]. Read it *before* you go. Then photocopy the important pages.

### 2. Airplane comfort

Airplanes are noisy, crowded, and uncomfortable, but you don't have to suffer[27] on your trip. A pair of good headphones will reduce the noise so you can enjoy your music and videos.

You don't have to eat the terrible airplane food. Bring your own food. Or order the vegetarian choice. It won't be as heavy, and you'll feel better. You should wear comfortable shoes, but don't wear sandals on the plane. They won't protect your feet.

### 3. Travel apps

Do you need to take public transportation[28] in a strange city? There are apps to help you plan routes in most major cities. Apps can also give you information about interesting places to visit. Most of the apps are very cheap. But on some phone plans, customers must pay high fees for international Internet service. You should download the apps before you leave. Use free Wi-Fi as much as possible.

### 4. Making friends

You don't have to speak the language in a foreign country. You can still make friends. Smile, be polite, and communicate with your hands—people will be happy to help you! You should try to learn a few words in the local language. People love that. And you shouldn't shout[29] at them in English. That doesn't help.

Maybe you want to travel, but you don't have anyone to go with. Don't worry—you don't have to travel alone. You can join a tour group and make new friends!

Have a nice trip!

---

[26] **guidebook:** a book that tells you about a place you are visiting
[27] **suffer:** to feel pain, sadness, or another unpleasant feeling

[28] **public transportation:** buses, trains, subways, etc.
[29] **shout:** to speak very loudly

**Write about It** Complete these statements about the article on page 329. There are many possible answers. Compare your sentences with a partner.

ACCORDING TO THE WRITER . . .

1. Sometimes travelers have to  *take public transportation in a strange city* _____ .

2. Travelers shouldn't _____ .

3. Travelers don't have to _____ .

4. Travelers should _____ .

**B | GRAMMAR IN SPEAKING** Work with a partner. Complete this chart with your partner's responses.

| TRAVEL ADVICE | |
| --- | --- |
| **When I travel . . .** | **My partner's name:** _____ |
| 1. What should I bring on the airplane? | |
| 2. What should I always pack? | |
| 3. What shouldn't I bring? | |
| 4. What should I do in a new city? | |
| **Complete these sentences about your native country.** | **Native country:** _____ |
| 5. Visitors should . . . | |
| 6. Foreign visitors have to . . . | |
| 7. Visitors don't have to . . . | |
| 8. I don't think visitors should . . . | |
| 9. Visitors can . . . | |
| 10. Visitors shouldn't . . . | |
| 11. Foreign visitors must not . . . | |
| 12. Visitors must . . . | |

**Write about It** Write a list of tips for travelers. Use your partner's ideas and/or your own ideas. Write about traveling in general, visiting your own country, or visiting another country.

*You should bring a tablet on the plane.*

| USES | | EXAMPLES |
|---|---|---|
| Advice / Suggestions / Opinions | should<br>should not | You **should do** your homework. |
| | | He **should study** more. |
| | | **Should** we **take** the bus? |
| | | Jack **shouldn't stay** up so late. |
| Suggestions | why don't you / we | **Why don't we have** a salad? |
| | | **Why don't you take** a break? |
| Necessity | have to | I **have to clean** the house. |
| | | She **has to pay** her bills. |
| | | **Do** you **have to work** tomorrow? |
| | | **Does** he **have to take** this class? |
| | need to | You **need to call** the doctor. |
| | | He **needs to go** home. |
| | | **Do** you **need to borrow** a pen? |
| | | **Does** she **need to work** late? |
| | must | Everyone **must report** to the manager. |
| No Necessity | not have to | We **don't have to go** to school on Saturday. |
| | | He **doesn't have to buy** a new book. |
| | not need to | We **don't need to read** page 43. |
| | | She **doesn't need to call** me. |
| Prohibition (something forbidden; not permitted) | must not | Children **must not play** in this area. |

For more modals, see Chart 11.8 on page 305.

# 13

# Types of Verbs

**GO ONLINE**

For the Unit Vocabulary Check, go to the Online Practice.

## IN THIS UNIT, WE STUDY verbs.

### Past, present, and future verb forms

1. In the 1800s, people **rode** in carriages. (past)

2. Today many people **drive** cars. (present)

3. In many cities, bicycles **are becoming** popular. (present)

4. In the future, there **will be** new kinds of transportation. (future)

**Think about It** Read these sentences. Check (✓) *True* or *False*.

| | TRUE | FALSE |
|---|---|---|
| 1. In my childhood, I traveled a lot. | ☐ | ☐ |
| 2. Most years I go somewhere on vacation. | ☐ | ☐ |
| 3. I usually fly one or more times a year. | ☐ | ☐ |
| 4. I'm planning a vacation this year. | ☐ | ☐ |
| 5. In the future, I'll probably travel a lot. | ☐ | ☐ |

## WE USE different types of verbs in different ways.

5. I **bought some vegetables** for dinner.
(verb + object)

6. I **slept** a lot last night.
(verb with no object)

7. I**'m sick** today. I **feel terrible**.
(linking verb + adjective)

8. My sister **is** in Colorado. She**'s** a ski instructor.
(*be*)

9. My friend Gina and I **talk about** everything.
(multi-word verb)

10. I'll **pick** you **up** at 6:00.
(multi-word verb)

**Think about It** Choose all the answers that are correct for you.

1. I bought ____ last weekend.
   ☐ food  ☐ clothes  ☐ music  ☐ other: _____

2. I ____ a lot yesterday.
   ☐ worked  ☐ slept  ☐ laughed  ☐ walked  ☐ studied  ☐ other: _____

3. Today I feel ____.
   ☐ sick  ☐ relaxed  ☐ excited  ☐ bored  ☐ happy  ☐ tired  ☐ other: _____

4. My friends and I often talk about ____.
   ☐ movies  ☐ books  ☐ sports  ☐ politics  ☐ other: _____

## 13.1 Overview of Past, Present, and Future Verb Forms

We studied these **past**, **present**, and **future** verb forms in this book.

Notice that some verb forms have **helping verbs** and **main verbs**.

**STATEMENTS**

### A

| | | POSITIVE STATEMENTS | NEGATIVE STATEMENTS | COMMON TIME EXPRESSIONS |
|---|---|---|---|---|
| **PAST** | **SIMPLE PAST\*** | We **worked** last week.<br>I **came** to class yesterday. | They **didn't work** yesterday.<br>You **didn't come** to class. | yesterday<br>last week<br>five years ago<br>in 2010 |
| | **BE** | She **was** angry.<br>We **were** here yesterday. | He **wasn't** angry.<br>Our friends **weren't** here. | |
| **PRESENT** | **SIMPLE PRESENT** | We often **work** there.<br>He **works** twice a week. | They **don't work** there.<br>She **doesn't work** with me. | always, usually<br>every day<br>twice a week |
| | **BE** | I'**m** a student.<br>We'**re** never late for class.<br>She'**s** here today. | I'**m not** the teacher.<br>They'**re not** late.<br>He'**s not** here. | |
| | **PRESENT PROGRESSIVE** | I'**m working** on my paper.<br>We'**re working** together.<br>It'**s working** now. | I'**m not working** right now.<br>We'**re not working** now.<br>This **isn't working**. | (right) now<br>these days<br>this semester |
| **FUTURE** | **FUTURE WITH BE GOING TO** | I'**m going to go** soon.<br>They'**re going to go** later.<br>She'**s going to go** at 6:00. | I'**m not going to go** to class.<br>We'**re not going to go**.<br>He'**s not going to go** tomorrow. | soon, later<br>tomorrow<br>next week<br>in two weeks |
| | **FUTURE WITH WILL** | I'**ll go** with you. | They **won't go** next week. | |
| | **FUTURE WITH PRESENT PROGRESSIVE** | We'**re leaving** tomorrow. | We'**re not leaving** tomorrow. | |
| **IMPERATIVE** | | **Do** your homework now.<br>**Call** me tonight! | **Don't forget** your keys! | |

\*For a list of irregular simple past verbs, see the Resources, page R-5.

**QUESTIONS**

### B

| | | *YES/NO* QUESTIONS AND SHORT ANSWERS | | *WH-* QUESTIONS AND *WH-* QUESTIONS ABOUT THE SUBJECT |
|---|---|---|---|---|
| **PAST** | **SIMPLE PAST** | **Did** he **fall**? | Yes, he **did**.<br>No, he **didn't**. | **When did** he **fall**?<br>**What fell**? |
| | **BE** | **Was** he angry?<br>**Were** they angry? | Yes, he **was**.<br>No, they **weren't**. | **Why was** he angry?<br>**Who was** angry? |
| **PRESENT** | **SIMPLE PRESENT** | **Do** you **work**?<br>**Does** she **work**? | Yes, I **do**.<br>No, she **doesn't**. | **Where do** they **work**?<br>**Who works** here? |
| | **BE** | **Is** he a student?<br>**Are** you hungry? | Yes, he **is**.<br>No, I'**m not**. | **Where is** it?<br>**Who is** at the door? |
| | **PRESENT PROGRESSIVE** | **Am** I **working**?<br>**Are** they **working**?<br>**Is** it **working**? | Yes, you **are**.<br>No, they **aren't**.<br>No, it **isn't**. | **Why are** you **working**?<br>**What's happening**? |
| **FUTURE** | **FUTURE WITH BE GOING TO** | **Am** I **going to drive**?<br>**Is** she **going to drive**?<br>**Are** they **going to drive**? | Yes, you **are**.<br>No, she **isn't**.<br>No, they **aren't**. | **Where are** you **going to go**?<br>**Who's going to drive**? |
| | **FUTURE WITH WILL** | **Will** you **stay** here? | Yes, I **will**.<br>No, I **won't**. | **Where will** you **stay**?<br>**Who will stay** here? |
| | **FUTURE WITH PRESENT PROGRESSIVE** | **Are** you **working** this weekend? | No, I'**m not**. | **Why are** you **working** tomorrow?<br>**Who is coming** this weekend? |

**1 | Identifying Past, Present, and Future Verb Forms** Listen and write the words you hear. Are the verbs past, present, or future forms? Label the verbs *PA* (past), *PR* (present), or *F* (future). (For present progressive verbs with future meaning, write *F*.) `13.1 A-B`

TALKING ABOUT PLANS

**F Y I**

We can use some **time expressions** with **present**, **past**, or **future** forms.

I'**m working** at the office **this morning**. (I'm at the office, and it's before noon.)

I **saw** Jim **this morning**. (I saw Jim today before noon.)

I'**m going to see** Jim **this morning**. (I'm going to see Jim today before noon.)

These time expressions include *today, tonight,* and *this + morning/ afternoon/week.*

1. A: What _____*are you doing* [PR]_____ these days? Are you still in school?

   B: No, _____ last semester. A friend and I started a business.

   A: What kind of business is it?

   B: We design and _____ jewelry. Next month _____ a little store.

2. A: _____ yet?

   B: No, _____ so. But it's going to start soon. _____ almost two feet of snow!

   A: We'll be OK. _____ lots of groceries this morning.

3. A: Sure, _____ your cats next week. No problem.

   B: Thanks. I really appreciate it. _____ for Kenya on Monday.

   A: That _____ exciting! _____ on a safari?

   B: No, _____ for my friend Danielle's wedding. Danielle _____ my first roommate in college. She's from Nairobi.

4. A: Where _____ for graduate school?

   B: I don't know. MIT was my first choice. But _____ in[1].

   A: That's too bad!

   B: Yeah. So right now _____ for decisions from the other schools. _____ probably _____ from them this week.

5. A: How was your weekend?

   B: Crazy! My friend Erin _____ over with all her stuff around midnight on Friday. She and her roommates _____ a huge fight.

   A: What's she going to do now?

   B: _____ back. She's going to look for a new place.

6. A: _____ cream and sugar in your coffee?

   B: No, thanks. I usually _____ lots of cream and three spoons of sugar. But these days _____ on a strict diet. So now _____ my coffee black.

   A: A strict diet—that's great!

   B: Yeah. My goal[2] is to lose 20 pounds by summer.

---

[1] **get in:** to be accepted      [2] **goal:** something you want to do very much

**Think about It** Circle the time expressions in Activity 1. Which verb forms are used with each time expression?

**Think about It** Which sentences in Activity 1 use the present progressive? Which sentences use the present progressive to talk about the future?

**2 | Usage Note: Action Verbs and Non-Action Verbs with Present Forms** Read the note. Then do the tasks below.

Remember: We often use verbs like *be*, *feel*, *have*, *like*, *need*, *own*, *seem*, *think*, and *want* as **non-action verbs**.

With **non-action verbs** in present time, we usually use the **simple present**, even if the action is happening now.

With **action verbs**, we often use the **simple present** or the **present progressive**.

| | FACTS, HABITS, AND ROUTINES<br>Use the **simple present** for all verbs. | THINGS HAPPENING NOW<br>Use the **present progressive** for action verbs.<br>Use the **simple present** for non-action verbs. |
|---|---|---|
| **ACTION VERBS** | The kids often **drink** hot chocolate. | The kids **are drinking** hot chocolate now. |
| **NON-ACTION VERBS** | The kids often **want** hot chocolate. | The kids **want** hot chocolate now. |

For more information about action verbs and non-action verbs, see Unit 7, pages 185 and 188.
For a list of non-action verbs, see the Resources, page R-5.

**Think about It** Look at conversation 6 in Activity 1. Which verbs are action verbs and which are non-action verbs? Do they use the simple present or the present progressive? Why?

**Talk about It** What is your life like these days? Tell a partner. Use some of the verbs from each box.

| ACTION VERBS | | | | NON-ACTION VERBS | | | |
|---|---|---|---|---|---|---|---|
| drink | go | study | wear | be | have | need | seem |
| eat | sleep | take | work | feel | like | own | want |

*"These days I'm not sleeping enough. I often feel tired. I need to sleep more."*
*"This semester I really like school. My classes all seem interesting."*

**3 | Forming Statements with Past, Present, and Future Forms** Underline the time expressions in these sentences. Then complete the sentences with the correct form of the verbs in parentheses. (More than one verb form may be possible.) **13.1 A**

BICYCLES: PAST, PRESENT, AND FUTURE

1. In 1817, Baron von Drais _____invented_____ (invent) a bicycle.

   The bicycle _____ (not/be) very useful.

   It _____ (not/have) any pedals. People used their

   feet to push the bicycle.

2. The French _____ (introduce) the word *bicycle*

   (*bicyclette*, or "two wheel") in the 1860s.

the first "bicycle" from 1817

3. By 1865, bicycles had pedals on the front wheel. In the 1870s and 1880s, the front wheel _____ (become) larger and larger. Bicycles _____ (be) more useful and more popular. But they were expensive, and they _____ (not/be) very safe. Many riders got hurt.

4. By the 1890s, new designs _____ (make) bicycles cheaper and more useful. Workers _____ (buy) bicycles and _____ (ride) their bikes to work. After the 1890s, bicycles _____ (not/change) very much.

5. Today there _____ (be) more than 1 billion bicycles in the world! Every year factories _____ (make) more than 100 million new bicycles.

6. People in China _____ (own) more than half of the bicycles in the world.

7. These days, even in China, people _____ (drive) cars more than before, and they _____ (not/use) bicycles as much.

8. Will bicycles have a place in our future? According to some experts, bicycles _____ (become) even more important in the future, for several reasons.

9. These days more people _____ (move) to cities. Bicycles are very useful in cities.

10. Bicycles are better for the environment than cars. These days many cities _____ (build) more bicycle paths. Amsterdam and Copenhagen are two examples.

11. In Amsterdam and Copenhagen, many people _____ (ride) their bicycles to work every day. In these cities, many people _____ (not/own) cars.

12. New designs may make bicycles even more popular in the future. In a few years, your new bicycle _____ probably _____ (have) a special design. For example, maybe you _____ (not/need) a lock for your bike. Your bike _____ (fold) into a backpack!

pedals

a bicycle from 1875

a bicycle of the future

**Think about It** Look at the verb forms you added to the sentences in Activity 3. Which of these forms use the helping verbs *be*, *do*, or *will*? Circle the helping verbs.

**Talk about It** Ask a partner these questions. Share your partner's answers with the class.

BICYCLE SURVEY

1. Can you ride a bicycle? (If YES, go to #2. If NO, go to #5.)
2. When did you learn to ride a bicycle? How old were you?
3. Do you own a bicycle now?
4. Do you ride a bicycle to school and/or work? Do you ride a bicycle for fun?

5. In your opinion, does your city/town have enough bicycle paths?

6. In the future, will you own and ride a bicycle?

7. In your opinion, will bicycles become more important in the future? Why or why not?

**4 | Understanding Questions with Past, Present, and Future Forms** Listen and write the questions you hear. Circle the best response to each question. **13.1 B**

1. _Did the 12:00 bus come?_

   a. No, it didn't.      b. No, it doesn't.      c. No, it won't.

2. _____

   a. No, I didn't. Sorry!    b. No, I don't. Sorry!    c. No, I won't. Sorry!

3. _____

   a. No, I probably didn't.   b. No, I probably don't.   c. No, I probably won't.

4. _____ We need a ride home.

   a. Yes, I was.      b. Yes, I am.      c. Yes, I will.

5. Excuse me. _____

   a. Yes, it did.      b. Yes, it does.      c. Yes, it will.

6. _____

   a. Yes, I did.      b. Yes, I do.      c. Yes, I will.

7. _____

   a. Yes, you were.      b. Yes, you do.      c. Yes, you are.

8. _____

   a. No, there probably weren't.   b. No, there aren't any now.   c. No, there probably won't.

9. _____

   a. Yes, earlier today.   b. Yes, I'm on the last paragraph.   c. Yes, maybe next week.

10. _____

    a. He graduated from UCLA.   b. He's studying at UCLA.   c. He'll go to UCLA.

11. _____

    a. A few days ago.      b. These days.      c. Next week.

12. _____

    a. I enjoyed it.      b. I enjoy it.      c. I'll enjoy it.

13. _____

    a. I didn't do much, but I relaxed a lot!   b. I'm not doing much, but I'm relaxing a lot!   c. I probably won't do much, but I'll relax a lot!

14. _____

    a. Last Saturday.      b. On Saturdays.      c. Next Saturday.

**Talk about It** Practice the conversations above with a partner. Give your own answers.

1. A: Did the 12:00 bus come?
   B: Yes, it came five minutes ago.

## 5 | Forming Questions with Past, Present, and Future Forms  Use the words in parentheses to write *yes/no* and *wh-* questions. Put the **bold** verbs in the correct form. Add the helping verbs *do*, *be*, or *will* where necessary. More than one verb form may be possible.  `13.1 B`

# Soccer and the World Cup: FAQ

1. Q: _Is soccer the most popular sport in the world?_
   (**be** / soccer / the most popular sport in the world)
   A: Yes, it is. Soccer is the most popular sport—both to watch and to play.

2. Q: _____
   (how many people / **play** / soccer)
   A: About 300 million people around the world play soccer!

3. Q: _____
   (how often / the World Cup / **take** place³)
   A: It happens every four years.

4. Q: _____
   (when / **be** / the first World Cup)
   _____
   (where / **be** / it)
   A: It was in 1930, in Uruguay. Uruguay beat Argentina 4–2 in the final.

5. Q: _____
   (**be** / there / a World Cup for women)
   A: Yes, there is.

6. Q: _____
   (when / the Women's World Cup / **begin**)
   A: It began in 1991. The first Women's World Cup was in China. The United States beat Norway 2–1 in the final.

7. Q: _____
   (how many teams / **play** / in the World Cup)
   A: Thirty-two teams usually play. There are eight groups, each with four teams.

8. Q: _____
   (the number of teams / **increase** / in the future)
   A: It might increase to 40 teams.

9. Q: _____
   (the host country⁴ / always / **play** / in the World Cup)
   A: Yes, it does. The host country always has a team.

10. Q: _____
    (soccer / **become** / more popular / in the United States)
    A: Yes, it probably will. Americans are more interested in soccer today than in the past.

11. Q: _____
    (**be** / the World Cup / on TV in every country)
    A: Yes, it is. You can even watch it in Antarctica!

12. Q: _____
    (how many people / **watch** / the 2014 World Cup)
    A: About 1 billion people!

13. Q: _____
    (when / **be** / the first World Cup in Asia)
    A: In 2002. This was also the first World Cup with two host countries— Japan and South Korea.

³**take place:** to happen          ⁴**host country:** the country that has the games

## 6 | Error Correction  Find and correct the errors. (Some sentences may not have any errors.)

1. Yuki talks to her brother right now.
2. Who did they got the keys from?
3. Meera and Anna are leaving tonight.
4. That hat was on sale and only cost $10.
5. We're not really knowing the neighborhood yet.
6. I have my own business in ten years.
7. Who going to take the kids to school tomorrow?
8. Aisha is usually studying on the weekends.
9. We finally finish the homework!
10. Felipe didn't came to class yesterday.
11. Our study group is meeting this morning.
12. I take you to the mall this weekend.
13. Look! It snows now!
14. Did you ate dinner already?
15. There won't be any more tickets tomorrow.
16. The bus never more than a few minutes late.

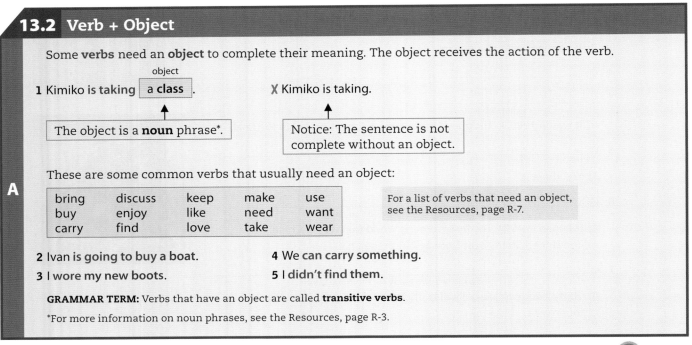

### 13.2 Verb + Object

Some **verbs** need an **object** to complete their meaning. The object receives the action of the verb.

        object

**1** Kimiko is taking  [ a class ] .      **X** Kimiko is taking.

   The object is a **noun** phrase*.      Notice: The sentence is not complete without an object.

**A**

These are some common verbs that usually need an object:

| bring | discuss | keep | make | use |
|-------|---------|------|------|-----|
| buy | enjoy | like | need | want |
| carry | find | love | take | wear |

For a list of verbs that need an object, see the Resources, page R-7.

**2** Ivan is going to buy a boat.    **4** We can carry something.
**3** I wore my new boots.    **5** I didn't find them.

**GRAMMAR TERM:** Verbs that have an object are called **transitive verbs**.

*For more information on noun phrases, see the Resources, page R-3.

 **GO ONLINE**

## 7 | Noticing Verb + Object  Underline the main verbs in these conversations. Then listen and complete the conversations with the object that follows each verb.  **13.2 A**

**TRAVELING**

1. A: Did you <u>find</u> _____*your passport*_____ ?
   B: Not yet. But I will.

2. A: Do you need _____?
   B: No, thanks. I'm OK.

3. A: Should I bring _____?
   B: You won't need _____.
      A light jacket should be enough.

4. A: Can I bring _____
      on the plane?
   B: I'm sorry. It's too large.

5. A: Are we forgetting _____?
   B: Oh! Bug spray[5]!

6. A: Can I take _____?
   B: No. It's not going to fit in the car.

[5] **bug spray:**  a liquid you put on your body to keep bugs away

7. A: I can carry _____ in
   my backpack.

   B: Thanks. Mine is really full.

8. A: I think we can take _____ to
   San Francisco.

   B: Let's do it. I love _____.

9. A: Can I use _____?

   B: Sure. There's just a little left. Keep
   _____.

10. A: I love _____! Where did
    you buy _____?

    B: Thanks. I bought them at Athletic World.

**Talk about It** Discuss the conversations in Activity 7 with a partner. Where are the speakers or where are they going?

## 8 | Writing Sentences with Verb + Object Complete each sentence with an object. Share your answers with a partner. 13.2 A

SOME INTERESTING FACTS ABOUT ME

1. On a trip, I always take _a comfortable jacket with lots of pockets._____.

2. My friends and I often discuss _____.

3. My friends and I really like _____.

4. In school, I enjoy _____.

5. In (cold/warm) weather, I often wear _____.

6. In the grocery store, I usually buy _____.

7. In the morning, I often want _____.

8. After a long day, I need _____.

## 9 | Usage Note: Common Phrases with *Make* and *Take* Read the note. Then do Activity 10.

We often use *make* and *take* with certain objects.

**MAKE +**

| an appointment | I'd like to make an appointment with the doctor. |
|---|---|
| plans | They're making plans for their summer vacation. |
| a decision | Jack finally made his decision. |
| a mess | You kids are making a mess! |
| a mistake | You're making a big mistake! |
| a good / bad impression | Dress nicely. You want to make a good impression.[6] |

**TAKE +**

| a picture | John took beautiful pictures on his trip. |
|---|---|
| a long time | This train ride is taking a long time. |
| a minute a few minutes an hour / all day . . . | This is going to take a few minutes. |
| a taxi / bus / train . . . | Did you take the train here? |
| a walk | Let's take a walk. We can go through the park. |
| a break | Let's take a break. We'll come back in ten minutes. |
| a class / a course | How many classes are you taking? |

[6]**impression:** feelings or thoughts you have about someone or something

**10 | Using Objects with *Take* and *Make*** Complete the sentences below with the form of *make* or *take* in parentheses and a word or phrase from the box. **13.2 A**

| an appointment | classes | a plan | a picture |
|---|---|---|---|

1. A: Alice is _____taking_____ four _____classes_____ next semester. What about you?
      (making / taking)

   B: I don't know yet. I have to _____ _____ with my adviser.
      (make / take)

2. A: What should we do this weekend?

   B: I don't know. Let's _____ _____!
      (make / take)

3. A: Can you _____ _____ of us?
      (make / take)

   B: Sure!

| a break | a decision | a long time | a mess |
|---|---|---|---|

4. A: Which apartment are you going to rent?

   B: I don't know. I really like them both. I have to _____ _____.
      (make / take)

5. A: Did you finish your paper?

   B: No. It's _____ _____. I'm exhausted. I can't think anymore.
      (making / taking)

   A: Then you should _____ _____. Let's watch a movie.
      (make / take)

6. A: Did you fix the kitchen sink⁷?

   B: Yeah. The sink is OK now. But I _____ _____ in the kitchen.
      (made / took)

| a good impression | a mistake | a taxi |
|---|---|---|

7. A: How did you do on the quiz?

   B: I don't know. I think I _____ _____ on the last question,
      (made / took)
      and it's worth a lot of points.

8. A: Is this a good outfit⁸ for a job interview?

   B: Yeah, you look great.

   A: Are you sure? I have to _____ _____.
      (make / take)

9. A: How did you get here so fast?

   B: I _____ _____.
      (made / took)

---

⁷**kitchen sink:** a large container in a kitchen where you wash dishes

⁸**outfit:** a set of clothes you wear together

## 13.3 Verbs with No Object

Some **verbs** are complete without an object.

**A**

**1** Diego **is waiting**.    X Diego **is waiting** me.

> Notice: It is incorrect to use an object here in this way. ↑

These are some common verbs that usually do not take an object:

| | | | | | |
|---|---|---|---|---|---|
| arrive | fall | happen | sit | stay | walk |
| come | go | laugh | sleep | wait | work |

For a list of verbs that do not take an object, see the Resources, page R-7.

**2** The children **are sleeping**.    **4** I can't **work** this evening.

**3** Your package **arrived** yesterday.    **5** Jennifer **will go** with you.

> Notice: We can use a **prepositional phrase** or **time expression** after these verbs. ↓ ↓

**6** Diego **is waiting for** me.    **7** We're **leaving tomorrow**.

**GRAMMAR TERM:** Verbs that do not have an object are called **intransitive** verbs.

GO ONLINE

**11 | Using Verbs with No Object** Underline the main verbs in this survey. Then check (✓) your answers to the survey. `13.3 A`

---

## Time Survey

1. When do you usually <u>arrive</u> . . .

   . . . for class?  ☐ on time  ☐ early  ☐ late

   . . . for a doctor's appointment?  ☐ on time  ☐ early  ☐ late

   . . . for dinner with a friend?  ☐ on time  ☐ early  ☐ late

2. During the semester, how often do you work in the library?

   ☐ almost every day    ☐ about once a week    ☐ less than once a week

3. On the night before a test, do you usually sleep a lot or study late?

   ☐ I sleep a lot.    ☐ I study late.

4. You are waiting in a long line for tickets. You'll probably wait for an hour or more. Do you wait patiently[9] or impatiently?

   ☐ I wait patiently.    ☐ I wait impatiently.

5. You are waiting for your friend at a restaurant. After 30 minutes, your friend doesn't come. Do you stay and wait? Or do you go home?

   ☐ I stay and wait.    ☐ I don't wait any longer. I go home.

6. You are sitting at your desk and studying for a test tomorrow. Some friends come to your door. They're all going out to dinner. What happens?

   ☐ I go with my friends.    ☐ I stay at my desk and work.

waiting impatiently

---

**Talk about It**  Ask and answer the survey questions above with a partner. Compare your answers.

[9]**patiently:** staying calm and not getting angry while waiting

**12 | Usage Note: Verb + Object vs. No Object** Read the note. Then do Activity 13.

We can use many **verbs** with an **object** OR without an object. Some of these verbs include:

| begin | break | leave | move | study |

| **VERB + OBJECT** | **VERB WITH NO OBJECT** |
|---|---|
| **1a** Noor **studies** law at my school. | **1b** Noor **studies** at my school. |
| **2a** We **began** our project today. | **2b** Classes **began** today. |
| **3a** I **broke** something. | **3b** Something **broke**. |
| **4a** Daniel **left his phone** in your car. | **4b** Daniel **left** yesterday. |

For more verbs that can be used with or without an object, see the Resources, page R-7.

**13 | Noticing Verb + Object or No Object** Look at the **bold** main verbs. Which verbs are followed by an object? Which are NOT followed by an object? Check (✓) the correct column. If there is an object, underline the object. `13.3 A`

| | VERB + OBJECT | NO OBJECT |
|---|:---:|:---:|
| 1. A: Is Dillon still at school? <br> B: No, he's here. But he's **studying**. | ☐ | ✓ |
| 2. A: I'll help you clear the table¹⁰. <br> B: It's OK. **Leave** <u>the dishes</u>. I'll take care of them later. | ✓ | ☐ |
| 3. A: What's wrong? <br> B: My printer **broke** again. This time I'm getting a new one! | ☐ | ☐ |
| 4. A: What's for lunch? <br> B: Ramen noodles. I'm **boiling** the water now. | ☐ | ☐ |
| 5. A: Is your son **studying** law? <br> B: Either law or political science. He's not sure yet. | ☐ | ☐ |
| 6. A: Do you want to go out for lunch? <br> B: Unfortunately, I can't. I have to **leave**. | ☐ | ☐ |
| 7. A: Can you **move** your things? I need to put these boxes here. <br> B: Sure. Sorry about that! | ☐ | ☐ |
| 8. A: Did you **begin** the new project yet? <br> B: No, we're still waiting for some information. | ☐ | ☐ |
| 9. A: What did the doctor say? <br> B: Good news! I didn't **break** my wrist¹¹. It will be better soon. | ☐ | ☐ |
| 10. A: Do you go to the gym a lot? <br> B: No, not really. But I **run** every day. | ☐ | ☐ |
| 11. A: When are you **moving**? <br> B: In just a couple of weeks. I'm so excited! | ☐ | ☐ |
| 12. A: When do classes **begin**? <br> B: A week from Monday. | ☐ | ☐ |

**Talk about It** Listen to the conversations above. Then practice them with a partner.

¹⁰ **clear the table:** to remove the dirty dishes from the table  ¹¹ **wrist:** the part of your body where your arm joins your hand

## 13.4 Be and Other Linking Verbs

We do not use objects after **linking verbs**. We use other words and phrases. **Be** is the most common linking verb.

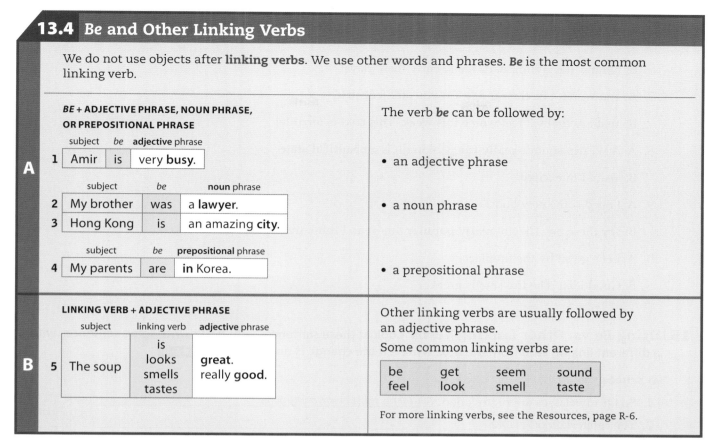

**A**

**BE + ADJECTIVE PHRASE, NOUN PHRASE, OR PREPOSITIONAL PHRASE**

|  | subject | be | adjective phrase |
|---|---|---|---|
| 1 | Amir | is | very **busy.** |

|  | subject | be | noun phrase |
|---|---|---|---|
| 2 | My brother | was | a **lawyer.** |
| 3 | Hong Kong | is | an amazing **city.** |

|  | subject | be | prepositional phrase |
|---|---|---|---|
| 4 | My parents | are | **in** Korea. |

The verb **be** can be followed by:

- an adjective phrase

- a noun phrase

- a prepositional phrase

**B**

**LINKING VERB + ADJECTIVE PHRASE**

|  | subject | linking verb | adjective phrase |
|---|---|---|---|
| 5 | The soup | is / looks / smells / tastes | **great.** really **good.** |

Other linking verbs are usually followed by an adjective phrase.

Some common linking verbs are:

| be | get | seem | sound |
|---|---|---|---|
| feel | look | smell | taste |

For more linking verbs, see the Resources, page R-6.

 **GO ONLINE**

**14 | Identifying Linking Verbs** Underline the linking verbs before the **bold** phrases. Then label the **bold** phrases *A* (adjective phrase), *N* (noun phrase), or *P* (prepositional phrase). **13.4 A–B**

CONVERSATIONS IN SUMMER

1. A: These chairs <u>are</u> **so comfortable**. And the sun <u>feels</u> **wonderful**!

   B: Yeah. We're in a perfect place. And it's a perfect day.

2. A: These are **for you**. They're **from my garden**.

   B: Lilies! They're **my favorite flower**. They smell **amazing**!

3. A: Come in the water!

   B: No, it's **too cold**!

   A: It's not **cold**. It's **perfect**!

4. A: Did the kids finish school yet?

   B: Yeah, they finished last week. They're **at home**. They're **really bored**,

   but their summer camp will start next Monday.

5. A: Should we go to the outdoor concert tonight?

   B: That sounds **lovely**. It seems **so hot** right now, but it will be **nice and cool** this evening.

lilies

6. A: It's **so dark** and it's only 5:00!

   B: I know. It's getting **dark** really early these days!

7. A: You weren't **in class** today. Do you still feel **sick**?

   B: Yeah. Actually, I feel **worse** this week. This cold is **terrible**!

8. A: A ski trip sounds **really fun**. Colorado is **a beautiful state**.

   B: Yeah. I'm **excited**!

9. A: I need some new boots.

   B: Try these on. They're **really popular** this year. I think they'll look **good** on you.

10. A: Let's go sit by the fireplace.

    B: Good idea. The fire smells **great**.

## 15 | Using *Be* vs. Other Linking Verbs Look at these sentences with *be*. Rewrite some sentences with a different linking verb from the box. Write *X* if the change is not possible. [13.4 A–B]

AT SCHOOL

1. So far my classes are pretty good. *So far my classes seem pretty good.*

2. The cafeteria food is OK. _____

3. My new roommate is interesting. _____

4. She's from Mexico. _____

5. We're in the best dorm. _____

6. We decorated our room, and it's beautiful now. _____

7. My friend Lisa is across the hall. _____

| |
|---|
| look |
| seem |
| sound |
| taste |

## 13.5 Comparing Different Types of Verbs

We use different words and phrases after different types of **verbs**. Review Charts 13.2, 13.3, and 13.4 for more information about types of verbs.

**A**

**VERB + OBJECT**

| | | object (**noun** phrase) |
|---|---|---|
| 1 | He wants | some **ice cream**. |
| 2 | I bought | a new **sofa**. |

X He wants.

**VERB WITH NO OBJECT**

| | | |
|---|---|---|
| 3 | The package **arrived**. | |
| 4 | The package arrived | **at** 3:00. (prepositional phrase) |
| 5 | | yesterday. (time expression) |

X The package arrived us.

**BE + ADJECTIVE PHRASE, NOUN PHRASE, OR PREPOSITIONAL PHRASE**

| | | |
|---|---|---|
| 6 | | really **beautiful**. (adjective phrase) |
| 7 | Shanghai is | a big **city**. (noun phrase) |
| 8 | | **in** China. (prepositional phrase) |

X Shanghai is.

**OTHER LINKING VERB + ADJECTIVE PHRASE**

| | | **adjective** phrase |
|---|---|---|
| 9 | The music sounds | **beautiful**. |
| 10 | You seem | really **tired**. |

X That music sounds.

**16 | Noticing Different Types of Verbs** Read this interview. Underline the main verbs in the **bold** phrases. Then write the verbs in the chart below. `13.5 A`

○ ○ ○

# Interview with a Restaurant Reviewer

1. Q: Your job **sounds fun**. Do you **enjoy it**?
   A: Yes, but it's hard work, too. My job **seems easy**, so I always explain this.
2. Q: How do you **do your job**?
   A: Well, first, I **find some friends**. We **go to a restaurant**. I don't say my name.
3. Q: But do people **recognize**[12] **you**? You probably **look familiar**.
   A: That *is* a problem. I change my look—sometimes I **have a beard**, but sometimes I don't have a beard. I even wear disguises[13]. . . . Anyway, we all **order different things**. And we each try everything.
4. Q: What's your usual experience?
   A: There is no usual experience. Anything **can happen**. Sometimes food **looks great** and **smells great**, but it **doesn't taste very good**. Or it **looks terrible** but **tastes great**.
5. Q: After a meal, do you write your review?
   A: No. I return to the restaurant two or three more times, always with other people. This way, I **try many things** on the restaurant's menu. Then I **stay in my office** all day and write my reviews.
6. Q: And on your days off[14]—do you go to restaurants?
   A: Almost never. Restaurants **are great**, but I **get tired** of them. And on my days off I usually **don't feel very hungry**!

**F Y I**
Prepositions include:

**at       in       to**
**for      on**

Remember: A prepositional phrase is NOT an object.

| Verbs followed by an object | Verbs with no object | Linking verbs |
|---|---|---|
| *enjoy* | | *sounds* |

**17 | Forming Sentences with Different Types of Verbs** Use words from each box to form sentences. Write five sentences for each group of words. (Ø means no words.) `13.5 A`

| 1. | Bob | is<br>seems<br>works | a lawyer.<br>every day.<br>in Chicago. | really nice.<br>tired these days.<br>Ø. |
|---|---|---|---|---|

*Bob works every day.      Bob works.*

| 2. | The students | discussed<br>sounded<br>worked | a little bored today.<br>at their desks.<br>in the library. | the questions.<br>their plans for the semester.<br>Ø. |
|---|---|---|---|---|

[12] **recognize:** to know who someone is because you saw them before
[13] **disguises:** things you wear so people don't know who you are
[14] **days off:** days when you don't go to work

| 3. | This car | is<br>looks<br>uses | a Fiat Panda.<br>a lot of gas.<br>kind of dirty. | mine.<br>really new.<br>Ø. |
|---|---|---|---|---|

| 4. | The children | got<br>seemed<br>slept | a lot of attention from everyone.<br>dessert after dinner.<br>every afternoon. | for a long time.<br>tired at the end of the day.<br>Ø. |
|---|---|---|---|---|

**Write about It** Write six sentences about yourself or events in your life. Use two verbs from each of these groups. Use past, present, or future forms of the verbs.

| GROUP 1 | | GROUP 2 | | GROUP 3 | |
|---|---|---|---|---|---|
| buy | take | go | stay | be | look |
| enjoy | wear | sleep | work | feel | seem |

*I bought a new car a few years ago.*

## 13.6 *Be* + Adjective Phrase + Preposition

We often use *be* + **adjective phrase** + **preposition**. We use certain prepositions after certain adjectives.

| | *be (+ not)* | adjective phrase | preposition | noun phrase |
|---|---|---|---|---|
| **1** | I | **'m** | **nervous** | **about** | the test. |
| **2** | They | **'re not** | **very good** | **at** | tennis. |

Here are some common adjective + preposition combinations:

| | | |
|---|---|---|
| **ADJECTIVE + *ABOUT*** | **angry about (something)*** | **3** He was **angry about** the bill. |
| | **excited about** | **4** We're **excited about** our trip to China. |
| | **nervous about** | **5** She's **nervous about** the test. |
| **ADJECTIVE + *AT*** | **angry at (someone)*** | **6** I'm **angry at** my roommate. |
| | **bad at** | **7** My brother is **bad at** math. |
| | **good at*** | **8** He's really **good at** chess. |
| **ADJECTIVE + *FOR*** | **bad for** | **9** Too much sugar is **bad for** you. |
| | **good for*** | **10** Water is **good for** you. |
| | **easy for** | **11** Languages are **easy for** some people. |
| | **hard for** | **12** Languages are **very hard for** me. |
| **ADJECTIVE + *IN*** | **interested in** | **13** He's **interested in** sports, especially soccer. |
| **ADJECTIVE + *OF*** | **afraid of** | **14** I'm **afraid of** spiders. |
| | **proud of** | **15** Your parents **are so proud of** you. |

*Notice: With some adjectives, we use different prepositions for different meanings.

**16a** My sister **is good at** math. (She can do math well.)

**16b** Vegetables **are good for** you.
    (Vegetables have a good effect.)

**17a** Lisa **is angry at** me. (*angry at* + person)

**17b** Lisa **is angry about** the bill.
    (*angry about* + thing or situation)

For more adjective + preposition combinations, see the Resources, page R-6.

A

**18 | Noticing *Be* + Adjective Phrase + Preposition** Listen and complete the sentences with the words you hear. Then practice the conversations with a partner. `13.6 A`

1. A: _____Are_____ you _____*angry about*_____ something?

   B: No, I'm just in a bad mood[15] today. Sorry!

2. A: Are you starting your new job tomorrow?

   B: Yeah. _____ _____ it now, but I'll be fine in the morning.

3. A: How are your son's swimming lessons going?

   B: Great! A month ago he _____ the water. Now I can't get him out of the pool.

4. A: I heard your new album[16]. Congratulations!

   B: Thanks. _____ _____ it.

5. A: I'm going to the Indian music festival next weekend. Do you want to come?

   B: Definitely! _____ _____ Indian music.

6. A: _____ coffee _____ you?

   B: I'm not sure. I think maybe one or two cups a day are OK.

7. A: Why _____ those customers _____ you?

   B: They wanted to return some stuff. But they didn't have a receipt[17].

8. A: My classes this semester seem hard.

   B: Hard classes _____ you. You'll learn more.

9. A: How can you do those problems? They seem impossible!

   B: They _____ me. I love math!

10. A: Thanks for the ride. I really appreciate it.

    B: Sure. _____ us. We go right by your house.

**Think about It** Look at the sentences you completed above. Do they use past, present, or future verb forms?

---

**19 | Using *Be* + Adjective Phrase + Preposition in Sentences** Look at these pictures. Complete the sentences below with *is/are* + an adjective from the box + *about*, *at*, *for*, *in*, or *of*. `13.6 A`

1.

Julio     Juan

a. Julio _____ _____ sports.

b. Juan _____ _____ sports.

| good |
|------|
| not interested |

2.

Nadia     Berta

a. Nadia _____ the trip to New Zealand.

b. Berta _____ the trip to New Zealand.

| excited |
|---------|
| nervous |

---

[15] **in a bad mood:** feeling bad at a particular time

[16] **album:** a collection of songs on one CD, etc.

[17] **receipt:** a piece of paper that shows you paid for something

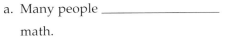

**3.**

a. Many people _____ math.

b. Math _____ Jeanine.

bad
easy

**4.**

a. Soda _____ you.

b. Water _____ you.

bad
good

**5.**

a. Marta _____ her son.

b. She _____ the broken lamp.

angry
angry

**6.**

a. Nighttime _____ Ethan.

b. He _____ the dark.

afraid
hard

**20 | Using *Be* + Adjective Phrase + Preposition** Compare your life in the past with your life today. Ask and answer these questions with a partner. Write down your partner's answers. **13.6 A**

| | When you were a child . . . | Today . . . |
|---|---|---|
| **Your interests** | 1a. What school subjects were you interested in?<br>2a. What other activities were you interested in? | 1b. What academic subjects are you interested in today?<br>2b. What other activities are you interested in? |
| **Your skills** | 3a. What were you good at?<br>4a. What were you bad at?<br>5a. What subjects or activities were easy for you?<br>6a. What subjects or activities were hard for you? | 3b. What are you good at now?<br>4b. What are you bad at?<br>5b. What subjects or activities are easy for you?<br>6b. What subjects or activities are hard for you? |
| **Your passions**[18] | 7a. What were you often excited about? | 7b. What are you excited about now? |

A: *What school subjects were you interested in?*
B: *I was interested in art and music.*

[18] **passions:** things you like a lot or are very interested in

**Talk about It** Tell the class about your partner's present interests, skills, and passions.

*"Alexa is interested in birds and animals. At school she's really interested in biology and other science classes. She goes on hikes and looks for unusual birds."*

## 13.7 Multi-Word Verbs (Part 1)

Sometimes verbs have two or more words. They can include a verb + a preposition. These are some common **verb** + **preposition** combinations:

**A**

| VERB + PREPOSITION | EXAMPLE |
|---|---|
| look at | 1 We're **looking at** some pictures of Mika's family. |
| look for | 2 I'm **looking for** a one-bedroom apartment. |
| look like | 3 You really **look like** your brother. |
| talk to (someone) | 4 I **talked to** Sylvie yesterday. |
| talk about (something) | 5 We **talked about** our plans for the summer. |
| listen to | 6 We're **listening to** some new music. |
| write to | 7 Who are you **writing to**? |
| think about | 8 I'm **thinking about** my interview. |
| know about | 9 Did you **know about** Ted's problems at work? |
| worry about | 10 Don't **worry about** the dishes. I'll wash them later. |
| pay for | 11 Where can I **pay for** this shirt? |
| wait for | 12 **Wait for** Eduardo. He's coming, too. |

For more multi-word verbs, see the Resources, page R-6.

**GO ONLINE**

**21 | Identifying Verb + Preposition Combinations** Read this article. Underline the verb + preposition combinations from Chart 13.7. **13.7 A**

# THE GREATEST ART THEFT[19]

On Tuesday, August 22, 1911, Louis Beróud went to the Louvre museum in Paris, France to see the *Mona Lisa*. He looked for the painting in its usual place, but it wasn't there. Beróud immediately told the museum guards. They didn't know about the disappearance of the painting. But they didn't worry about it. Probably the museum's photographers had the painting.

The photographers did not have the painting. Soon the police arrived and closed the Louvre. For a week they looked for the *Mona Lisa* everywhere in the museum. They didn't find it. They talked to all the museum's workers. One thing became clear: The theft happened on Monday morning. On Mondays the museum was closed. Did a worker steal the *Mona Lisa*? The police investigated[20] and thought about the possibilities.

Time passed. The police waited for more information. There was none.

Then, one day in 1913 (almost two years later), a man named Vincenzo Peruggia went to Florence, Italy and wrote to the owner of an art store there. He had the *Mona Lisa* for sale.

[19]**theft:** the crime of stealing something          [20]**investigate:** to try to find out about something

Was this painting real or just a copy? The owner of the art store met with Peruggia and looked at the painting. It looked like the *Mona Lisa*. After a closer look, he was sure: It *was* the *Mona Lisa*.

How did Peruggia steal the *Mona Lisa*? He hid in the Louvre on Sunday, and he stayed in the museum overnight. On Monday the museum was closed. He took the painting and left the museum.

Why did Peruggia steal the *Mona Lisa*? There were two reasons. First, Peruggia wanted this Italian painting for an Italian museum. Second, he wanted money for the painting. The art store owner did not pay for the *Mona Lisa*. Instead, Peruggia went to jail for six months.

The *Mona Lisa* traveled to museums around Italy for a year, and then it returned to the Louvre. Every year millions of visitors look at the *Mona Lisa*.

**22 | Using Verb + Preposition Combinations** Complete the conversations below with the correct preposition from the box. Then listen and check your answers. **13.7 A**

| about | at | for | like | to |
|---|---|---|---|---|

1. A: I'll pay _____*for*_____ it.
   B: No, you paid last time. It's my turn.

2. A: Who are you looking _____?
   B: That guy in the brown jacket. Do you know him? He looks really familiar.

3. A: I'm sorry. I can't help you.
   B: Maybe someone else can help me. Can I talk _____ your supervisor, please?

4. A: There's still lots of time. We'll wait _____ you.
   B: It's OK. You don't have to wait. I can meet you there.

5. A: You worry _____ everything!
   B: There's a reason for that: You don't worry _____ anything!

6. A: I can't believe you're not her. You really look _____ her!
   B: I know. People always ask me for an autograph[21].

7. A: Did you know _____ the missing[22] money?
   B: No. No one said anything to me.

8. A: What are you thinking _____?
   B: Our plans for the summer. I'm really excited!

9. A: I'm sorry. I looked _____ it everywhere. I asked everyone. But no one found it.
   B: OK. Thanks for looking.

10. A: What did you and Sam talk _____?
    B: The usual. He still feels homesick.

**Talk about It** Who are the speakers in each conversation above? What are they talking about? Discuss your ideas with a partner.

*"In conversation 1, I think two friends are having lunch together at a restaurant."*

**Talk about It** Ask and answer these questions with a partner.

1. Who in your family do you look like? Do you look like any famous people?
2. What topics do you know a lot about?
3. What things do you often think about?
4. What things do you sometimes worry about?
5. What do you and your friends often talk about? What do you and your family often talk about?
6. Who do you talk to often? Who do you talk to about problems or important decisions?

[21] **autograph:** a famous person's name, which they themselves write

[22] **missing:** lost, or not in the usual place

**23 | Error Correction** Find and correct the errors. (Some sentences may not have any errors.) More than one correction may be possible for some sentences.

1. My younger brother Davi is afraid from bees.
2. I worry of my children all the time.
3. We're flying tonight, and I'm very nervous for it.
4. Don't be angry about me. I'm really sorry!
5. Gabriel is very interested at modern art.
6. We're looking at pictures from our vacation.
7. My friend Valeria is really good for chess.
8. Don't rush! We can wait to you.
9. Children should listen their parents and obey them.
10. I didn't pay the concert tickets. My friend bought them.
11. What are you listening to?
12. I'm easy at math.

## 13.8 Multi-Word Verbs (Part 2)

**A**

Some multi-word verbs include a verb + another small word like *along, back, down, off, on, out, over,* and *up.* The two words work together to form a new meaning.

**MULTI-WORD VERBS WITH NO OBJECT**

| MULTI-WORD VERB | MEANING | EXAMPLE |
|---|---|---|
| come back | return | 1 We'll **come back** after the appointment. |
| come over | visit someone in their house | 2 **Come over** anytime! |
| get along | behave in a friendly way | 3 Everyone in our group **gets along**. |
| get up | move to a standing position | 4 **Don't get up**. I'll answer the door. |
| | get out of bed | 5 We **got up** late this morning. |
| sit down | move to a sitting position | 6 Grab a chair and **sit down**. |
| wake up | stop sleeping | 7 I **woke up** in the middle of the night. |
| work out | exercise | 8 She **works out** at the gym every day. |
| | have a good result | 9 We had some problems at the meeting, but everything **worked out**. |

**MULTI-WORD VERBS + OBJECT**

Some multi-word verbs need an **object** to complete their meaning.

| MULTI-WORD VERB | MEANING | EXAMPLE |
|---|---|---|
| figure out | understand how to do something after trying | 10 I finally **figured out** the answer. |
| fill out | complete a form | 11 He's **filling out** the application. |
| look up | look for information | 12 Let's **look up** the directions. |
| pick up | take something and lift it up | 13 I can't **pick up** this box. It's too heavy. |
| | go get something or someone, especially in a car | 14 We'll **pick up** the children after school. |
| turn down | make something lower, for example, in loudness | 15 Can you please **turn down** the music? |
| turn on | make something start | 16 Did you **turn on** the TV? |
| turn off | make something stop | 17 Can I **turn off** the TV? |

For more multi-word verbs, see the Resources, page R-6.

**GRAMMAR TERM:** some multi-word verbs are also called **phrasal verbs**.

**◀))** **24 | Understanding Multi-Word Verbs** Listen and complete these conversations with the words you hear. Then practice the conversations with a partner. `13.8 A`

1. A: Can I _____*turn on*_____ the light? Or will it bother you?

   B: Go ahead. It won't bother me at all.

2. A: I can't _____ the answer.

   B: I can't either. Let's _____ it _____ online.

3. A: I had a great time. Thanks for everything.

   B: We did, too. _____ and visit us again soon.

4. A: Can you _____ the TV? It's too loud.

   B: I can _____ it _____. I'm not really watching it.

5. A: Please _____ these forms. The doctor will be with you shortly.

   B: OK. Thanks very much.

6. A: How's your day going?

   B: Really good so far. I actually _____ early this morning and _____.

7. A: What time is your plane tomorrow?

   B: Ugh. It leaves at 6 in the morning. I have to _____ really early.

8. A: Are you still vacuuming?

   B: Yeah. Can you _____ for a minute? I need to vacuum under the couch.

9. A: Did you register for classes yet?

   B: Yeah, I did. There were some schedule problems, but in the end everything _____.

10. A: Do you live here in London?

    B: Not anymore. But I studied here, and I often _____ to visit people.

> **F Y I**
>
> Sometimes we use an **object pronoun** with a multi-word verb. We put the pronoun between the **verb** and the **small word**.
>
> Let's **look it up**.
> I'll **pick you up** at 6:00.

**25 | Using Multi-Word Verbs** Complete these conversations with the multi-word verbs from each box. Change the form of the verb if necessary. `13.8 A`

1. A: You're home already.

   B: Yeah. The game was boring. So we _____*came back*_____ early.

2. A: _____! It's 9:00.

   B: Oh, no! I didn't hear my alarm!

3. A: What did you do last night?

   B: Some friends _____ and we made dinner together.

4. A: I'm worried about my schedule. I won't have much time between classes.

   B: Don't worry. It will _____. You'll see.

> come back
> come over
> wake up
> work out

5. A: Would you like to _____?

   B: Thanks very much, but it's OK. I'm getting off at the next stop.

6. A: How often do you _____?

   B: Almost every day. I ride my bike or run in the park.

7. A: I'm hungry.

   B: Me too. Let's _____ some Chinese food.

8. A: How's your new job?

   B: I really like it. The people are great. Everyone _____ really well.

> get along
> pick up
> sit down
> work out

9. A: Can you give me a ride to the airport tomorrow?

   B: OK. What time should I _____ you _____?

10. A: Can you _____ the music? I'm trying to do my homework.

    B: OK. . . . Is that better?

11. A: Can you please _____ this form and then bring it back to me?

    B: Sure.

12. A: Are you leaving?

    B: Yeah, it's getting late. I have to _____ early tomorrow.

fill out
get up
pick up
turn down

**Write about It**  Work with a partner. Choose two of these situations. Write a short conversation for each. Use one of the multi-word verbs from Chart 13.8 in each conversation.

1. Your friends stayed with you for a week. Now they are leaving.
2. You're going to the gym. You want your friend to go with you.
3. You want to invite a friend to your apartment for dinner.
4. You are talking to friends. It's very late. Tomorrow you have an early morning class.

*Situation 1*
*A: It was great to see you. Come back soon!*
*B: Thanks. We will!*

# WRAP-UP

**A** | **GRAMMAR IN READING**  Read the graduate school application essay below. Label the **bold** verbs with the verb forms in this box. Then answer the questions on page 356.

| Simple present: *SPr* | Present progressive: *PP* | Simple past: *SPa* | Future with *will*: *F* | Imperative: *I* |
| --- | --- | --- | --- | --- |

## Graduate School Application Essay

### Marcus Johnson

*PP*

Why **am** I **applying** for the master's program in Emergency and Disaster Management[23]? The answer **is**

a long story, and here it is.

Six years ago, I **graduated** from college with a degree in film studies. I **had** a plan: I wanted to make

movies and become a famous director. Well, that **didn't happen**.

After college I **went** to New York City, and soon I began to work on movies. I'm still working on movies

today. This **sounds** perfect for me, but it's not. These days I**'m writing** schedules and **planning** budgets.

Am I making art? No, I**'m making** phone calls and giving advice to actors. "Don't **get** nervous," I tell the

actors. "And, remember, **get** a good night's sleep before work!"

[23]**emergency and disaster management:**  the field that helps people plan for and deal with dangerous situations (emergencies) and disasters (bad events that can hurt many people)

I may not be happy with my work, but I **am** good at my job. I can organize and plan projects. I can help people feel better about themselves and their situations. I don't want to be in the film business, but I do want to use those skills. A year ago, I **volunteered**[24] for the American Red Cross. They **trained** me in disaster response[25]. I'm still doing this volunteer work, and I love it. I like to help people. A family's house burned down, and we **found** a hotel room for them. They **thanked** me again and again. I **felt** good.

disaster relief after a hurricane

I want to continue in disaster response. This master's program **will give** me important skills and knowledge. Through my studies in the program, I **will become** a better disaster responder. Disasters like hurricanes and tornadoes **are** big challenges. To save people's lives, we need to plan before, during, and after disasters. This planning **takes** a lot of skills. I want to learn these skills and save lives.

**Circle all the answers that are correct.**

1. What did Marcus study in college?
   a. film
   b. painting
   c. business
   d. emergency and disaster management

2. What is Marcus doing now?
   a. He's in a film studies program.
   b. He's in an emergency and disaster management program.
   c. He's working on movies.
   d. He's doing volunteer work for the Red Cross.

3. When did Marcus become interested in emergency and disaster management?
   a. in college
   b. after graduation, six years ago
   c. during the last year
   d. after a tornado

4. What work does Marcus do for movies?
   a. He writes schedules.
   b. He plans budgets.
   c. He is an actor.
   d. He films with a camera.

5. Why does Marcus want to study emergency and disaster management?
   a. He wants to help people.
   b. He wants to work for the Red Cross.
   c. He wants to use his planning skills.
   d. He wants to film hurricanes and tornadoes.

**Think about It** Look again at the **bold** verbs in the reading. Why did the writer use these verb forms? What other words in the sentences tell you about past, present, or future meaning?

**Think about It** Which **bold** verbs in the reading are followed by an object? Which verbs are followed by an adjective phrase?

[24] **volunteer:** to do work without pay          [25] **disaster response:** helping people after a disaster

**B | GRAMMAR IN WRITING** Write a paragraph of about five or six sentences. Imagine that you are applying for a program of study or a job that interests you. In your paragraph, answer some of these questions.

- What program or job are you applying for?
- What are you interested in?
- What things in your past led to this interest?

- What related things are you doing now?
- What will you do in the future?

*I am applying for the master's program in architecture. I am interested in the design of apartment buildings. In high school, I learned about the history of art and architecture. This was always my interest. Now I am studying for a bachelor's degree in engineering. In the future, I'll design interesting and comfortable buildings for people.*

## 13.9 Summary of Types of Verbs

### VERB FORMS

**SIMPLE PRESENT**

| |
|---|
| I work here. / We work here. / He works here. |
| They don't work here. / She doesn't work here. |
| Do you work here? / When do you work? Does he work here? / Where does he work? Who works here? |

**FUTURE WITH *BE GOING TO***

| |
|---|
| I'm going to leave. / He's going to leave. / They're going to leave. |
| I'm not going to leave. / She's not going to leave. / They're not going to leave. |
| Am I going to leave? / Is she going to leave? / Are they going to leave? Where am I going to work? / Where is he going to work? / Where are they going to work? Who is going to work? |

**PRESENT PROGRESSIVE**

| |
|---|
| I'm working. / She's working. / We're working. |
| I'm not working. / She's not working. / We're not working. |
| Are you working? / Why are you working? Who is working? |

**FUTURE WITH *WILL***

| |
|---|
| I'll work. |
| He won't work. |
| Will it work? Where will you work? Who will work here? |

**SIMPLE PAST**

| |
|---|
| We worked. / She left. |
| We didn't work. / She didn't leave. |
| Did you work? / Did she leave? What happened? |

**IMPERATIVE**

| |
|---|
| Come here. |
| Don't forget your lunch! |
| |

### TYPES OF VERBS

| VERB + OBJECT | |
|---|---|
| Mina often wears | red sneakers. (object) |
| We bought | a new car. (object) |

| VERB WITH NO OBJECT | |
|---|---|
| Tina is sleeping. | |
| Tina is sleeping | on the couch. (prepositional phrase) |
| James is going to arrive | this evening. (time expression) |

| LINKING VERBS | | | |
|---|---|---|---|
| Abel | is | really nice. (adjective phrase) | be |
| | | a good friend. (noun phrase) | |
| | | in the kitchen. (prepositional phrase) | |
| Abel | looks seems | really nice. (adjective phrase) | other linking verbs |

# 14

# Sentence Patterns

**GO ONLINE**

For the Unit Vocabulary Check, go to the Online Practice.

**IN THIS UNIT, WE STUDY** sentence patterns.

1. I bought some fruit at the market.

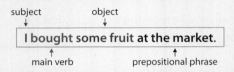

subject · object

**I bought some fruit at the market.**

main verb · prepositional phrase

2. Did you cook breakfast this morning?

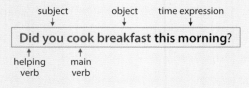

subject · object · time expression

**Did you cook breakfast this morning?**

helping verb · main verb

3. It's a cold day, but the sun is shining.

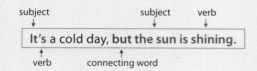

4. I always wear a hat when it's cold outside.

I always wear a hat | when it's cold outside | .

time clause

**Think about It** Read these sentences. What is true about you? Check (✓) *True* or *False*.

|  | TRUE | FALSE |
|---|---|---|
| 1. I bought some fruit yesterday. | ☐ | ☐ |
| 2. I cooked breakfast this morning. | ☐ | ☐ |
| 3. It's cold out now, but the sun is shining. | ☐ | ☐ |
| 4. I usually wear a hat when it's cold outside. | ☐ | ☐ |
| 5. I often watch TV when I get home. | ☐ | ☐ |
| 6. I usually read before I go to bed. | ☐ | ☐ |

## 14.1 What Is a Sentence?

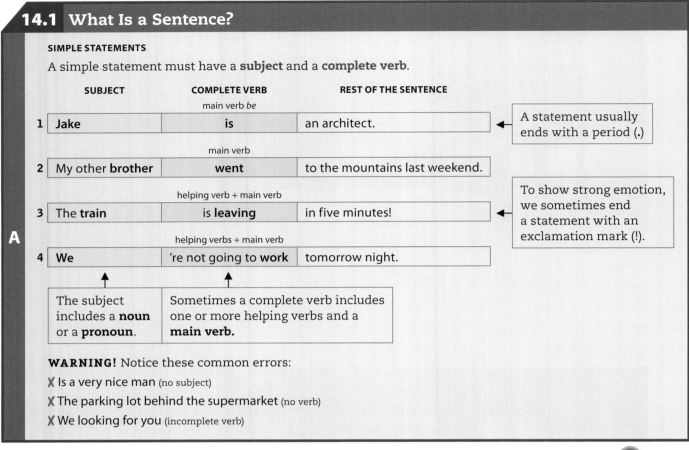

**A**

**SIMPLE STATEMENTS**

A simple statement must have a **subject** and a **complete verb**.

| SUBJECT | COMPLETE VERB | REST OF THE SENTENCE |
|---|---|---|
| | main verb *be* | |
| 1  Jake | is | an architect. |
| | main verb | |
| 2  My other **brother** | went | to the mountains last weekend. |
| | helping verb + main verb | |
| 3  The **train** | is **leaving** | in five minutes! |
| | helping verbs + main verb | |
| 4  We | 're not going to **work** | tomorrow night. |

A statement usually ends with a period (.)

To show strong emotion, we sometimes end a statement with an exclamation mark (!).

The subject includes a **noun** or a **pronoun**.

Sometimes a complete verb includes one or more helping verbs and a **main verb.**

**WARNING!** Notice these common errors:

✗ Is a very nice man (no subject)

✗ The parking lot behind the supermarket (no verb)

✗ We looking for you (incomplete verb)

**1 | Noticing Subjects and Verbs** Circle the subject in these sentences. Underline the complete verb.

**14.1 A**

ABOUT ME

1.  (My best friend) <u>is studying</u> English.

2.  I'm living on campus this year.

3.  Yesterday was an excellent day.

4.  I watched TV for several hours last night.

5.  My classes started in September.

6.  I'll get home around 9 p.m. tonight.

7.  My hometown is a large city.

8.  My family is going to take a vacation next summer.

9.  My parents live in another country.

10.  History is my favorite subject.

11.  I can play the guitar.

12.  I have an interesting job.

**Write about It** Rewrite the sentences above to make them true for you. Change the subject and/or the verb in each sentence. Don't change the other parts of the sentence.

*1.  **My sister** is studying English.*

*2.  I'm **not living** on campus this year.*

**2 | Error Correction** Some of these sentences are not complete. Label the incomplete sentences *NS* (no subject), *NV* (no verb), or *IV* (incomplete verb). If the sentence is correct, write a checkmark (✓) on the line and add a period (.) or exclamation mark (!) to the sentence. 14.1 A

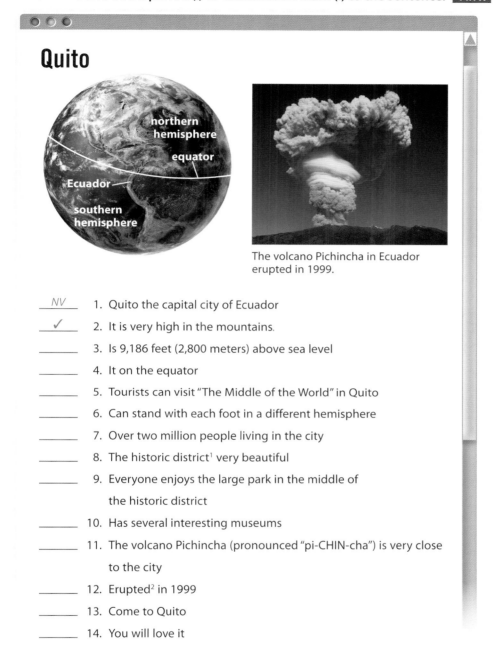

## Quito

northern hemisphere

equator

Ecuador

southern hemisphere

The volcano Pichincha in Ecuador erupted in 1999.

**F Y I**

In imperative sentences, the subject (*you*) is invisible.

(You) **Come** back next week.
(You) **Stop** that!

For more information about imperative sentences, see page 19.

___NV___ 1. Quito the capital city of Ecuador

___✓___ 2. It is very high in the mountains.

_____ 3. Is 9,186 feet (2,800 meters) above sea level

_____ 4. It on the equator

_____ 5. Tourists can visit "The Middle of the World" in Quito

_____ 6. Can stand with each foot in a different hemisphere

_____ 7. Over two million people living in the city

_____ 8. The historic district[1] very beautiful

_____ 9. Everyone enjoys the large park in the middle of the historic district

_____ 10. Has several interesting museums

_____ 11. The volcano Pichincha (pronounced "pi-CHIN-cha") is very close to the city

_____ 12. Erupted[2] in 1999

_____ 13. Come to Quito

_____ 14. You will love it

**Write about It** Correct the incomplete sentences above. Add a period (.) or an exclamation mark (!).

1. *Quito is the capital city of Ecuador.*

**Think about It** Compare your answers with a partner. Did you use an exclamation point (!) in any of the sentences above? Why?

---

[1] **historic district:** an area in a city with old structures or buildings that are important in history

[2] **erupt:** When a volcano **erupts**, smoke, hot rocks, or liquid rock (called lava) suddenly come out.

## 14.2 Subjects and Verbs in Questions

A

In most questions, the **subject** is after the **first helping verb** or the **main verb _be_**.

| | wh- word | be / first helping verb | subject | (other helping verbs +) main verb | rest of the question |
|---|---|---|---|---|---|
| 1 | - | **Were** | the questions | - | difficult? |
| 2 | - | **Are** | your computer classes | continuing | in the summer? |
| 3 | - | **Can** | Thomas | hear | me? |
| 4 | When | **did** | the eye doctor | call? | |
| 5 | Where | **are** | your parents | going to go | on vacation? |

A question ends with a question mark (?).

In some questions with _who_ and _what_, the _wh-_ word is the subject. It comes before the complete verb.

| | wh- word (= subject) | complete verb | rest of the question |
|---|---|---|---|
| 6 | Who | called | yesterday? |
| 7 | What | is happening? | |

GO ONLINE

**3 | Identifying Subjects and Verbs in Questions** What is missing from each question? Look at choices a–e in the box. Write the correct letter above each conversation. Then listen and complete the questions with the words you hear. Correct your labels if necessary.  **14.2 A**

1. ___d___

   A: ___Is_____ Tom in his office?

   B: I think so. He usually comes in at 8:00.

2. ___b___

   A: When is the _____ _new building_ _____ going to open?

   B: In September, I think.

3. ____

   A: Could you _____ the door for me?

   B: Of course. No problem.

4. ____

   A: _____ does the book club meet?

   B: Usually at my house.

5. ____

   A: _____ he wear a uniform every day?

   B: Yeah. He has to.

6. ____

   A: Are _____ expensive?

   B: A little, but I got them on sale.

7. ____

   A: Was _____ a farmer?

   B: Yeah, he was. He grew corn and squash.

a. _wh-_ word
b. subject
c. helping verb
d. _be_ (main verb)
e. main verb (not _be_)

**FYI**

Notice that we often do not answer questions with complete sentences.

A: Where are you going?
**B: To the store.**

A: How's your mom doing?
**B: Pretty well.**

A: Who ate the cake?
**B: Brian.**

squash

8. ____

    A: Who _____ that poem?

    B: I'm not sure. I found it online.

9. ____

    A: _____ is Alan leaving?

    B: He got a new job.

10. ____

    A: What time _____ the show?

    B: 3:00.

11. ____

    A: Who _____ the night class?

    B: Stevenson, I think.

12. ____

    A: Who _____ I talk to?

    B: Why don't you start with the counselor?

**4 | Forming Questions** Look at these statements. Rewrite each statement as a question in the chart below. Change the words *I* and *my* to *you* and *your* where necessary. **14.2 A**

TALKING ABOUT FOOD

### Statements

1. My favorite food is fried chicken.
2. My mother cooks dinner at our house.
3. I ate at a restaurant last night.
4. My friend and I are going shopping tomorrow.
5. My school cafeteria has pretty good food.
6. I'm going out to eat tonight.
7. I like spicy food.
8. My brother is a good cook.
9. I shop at Kelly's Market.
10. I can't eat peanuts.
11. My parents pay for my groceries.
12. My family will eat dinner at 6:00 tonight.

peanuts

### Questions

|  | *Wh*- word | Helping verb or *be* | Subject or *wh*- word as subject | Main verb (not *be*) |  |
|---|---|---|---|---|---|
| 1. | What | is | your favorite food? |  |  |
| 2. |  |  | Who | cooks | dinner at your house? |
| 3. | Where | did | you | eat | last night? |
| 4. |  |  |  |  | shopping tomorrow? |
| 5. |  |  |  |  | good food? |
| 6. |  |  |  |  | out to eat tonight? |
| 7. |  |  |  |  | spicy food? |
| 8. |  |  |  |  | a good cook? |
| 9. |  |  |  | shop? |  |
| 10. |  |  |  |  | peanuts? |
| 11. |  |  |  |  | for your groceries? |
| 12. |  |  |  |  | dinner tonight? |

**Talk about It** Ask and answer the questions with a partner.

*1. A: What's your favorite food?*    *B: My mother's chicken soup.*

**5 | Pronunciation Note: Statements as Questions** Listen to the note. Then do Activity 6.

Sometimes we use a statement with rising intonation as a *yes/no* question. We often do this when we aren't 100% sure that the statement is true. Compare:

**REGULAR STATEMENT**

**1a** My brother's name is Bob.

**STATEMENT AS A QUESTION**

**1b** A: Your brother's name is Bob?
B: That's right.

**ANSWERING STATEMENT-QUESTIONS**

When we use a positive statement to ask a question, we often expect a positive answer.

**2** A: You're from Argentina?
B: **Yes**, I am.

When we use a negative statement to ask a question, we often expect a negative answer.

**3** A: Sal's **not** at home?
B: **Nope.** He'll be home in about an hour.

**6 | Listening for Statements and Questions** Listen to each sentence. Add a question mark (?) or a period (.). `14.2 A`

**AT WORK**

1. You aren't finished yet?
2. Someone called this morning
3. They didn't leave a message
4. The packages are ready to go
5. Mark doesn't work today
6. This call is for you
7. The meeting is at 2:00
8. Kiera didn't call back
9. Break time is over
10. You're leaving early
11. Kim wasn't here yesterday
12. The customers are waiting

**F Y I**

Sometimes we use statements as questions to express surprise or disbelief.

A: He's 70 years old?
B: I know! He looks really young for his age.

Sometimes we use statements as questions to check our understanding of something we heard.

A: Today's Jerome's birthday.
B: Today's Jerome's birthday?

**Talk about It** Look at the sentences above where you added a question mark (?). Ask a partner each of these "statement" questions. Give an "expected" response.

1. A: *You aren't finished yet?*
   B: *No, I'm not.*

Some sentences only have a **subject** and a **verb**. Many sentences have other elements as well.

**STATEMENTS**

Notice: We often use a **prepositional phrase*** or a **time expression** at the end of a sentence.

| | subject | complete verb | prepositional phrase |
|---|---|---|---|
| **1** | This computer | isn't working. | - |
| **2** | My parents | live | in a small town. |

| | subject | complete verb | object (= noun phrase**) | prepositional phrase |
|---|---|---|---|---|
| **3** | His assistant | answered | the phone. | - |
| **4** | Joanne | is taking | her daughter | to work. |

| | subject | linking verb (*be* or other) | adjective phrase | time expression |
|---|---|---|---|---|
| **5** | We | are | excited! | - |
| **6** | The runners | look | really tired. | - |
| **7** | You | seemed | happy | last night. |

| | subject | *be* | |
|---|---|---|---|
| **8** | Mr. Sato | is | a great manager. (noun phrase) |
| **9** | The boxes | were | in the back room. (prepositional phrase) |

*A **prepositional phrase** starts with a preposition (such as *at*, *from*, *in*, *of*, *on*, or *to*) and includes a noun.

**A **noun phrase** includes a noun or a pronoun. For more information, see the Resources, page R-3.

**QUESTIONS**

| | *wh-* word | first helping verb | subject | (other helping verbs +) main verb | object (= noun phrase) | prepositional phrase / time expression |
|---|---|---|---|---|---|---|
| **10** | - | Does | Antonio | work | - | at the mall? |
| **11** | - | Is | the teacher | going to correct | the papers | tonight? |
| **12** | When | did | the class | start? | - | - |

| | | *wh-* word (= subject) | complete verb | object (= noun phrase) | prepositional phrase / time expression |
|---|---|---|---|---|---|
| **13** | - | - | Who | works | - | on Tuesday nights? |
| **14** | - | - | Who | can take | the money | to the bank? |

| | *wh-* word | *be* | subject | |
|---|---|---|---|---|
| **15** | - | Is | Julie | a new student? (noun phrase) |
| **16** | - | Are | you | hungry? (adjective) |
| **17** | - | Was | the new student | in class today? (prepositional phrase) |
| **18** | Where | are | your keys? | - |

**7 | Noticing Statement Patterns** Read these sentences about an artist. Label the <u>underlined</u> words and phrases. Use the labels in the box. `14.3 A`

**ANDY GOLDSWORTHY**

            *S*             *V*   *NP*
1. <u>Andy Goldsworthy</u> <u>is</u> <u>an artist</u>.

2. <u>He</u> <u>grew up</u> <u>in England</u>.

3. <u>He</u> <u>lives</u> <u>in Scotland</u> <u>now</u>.

4. <u>He</u> <u>has</u> <u>four children</u>.

5. <u>Goldsworthy</u> <u>uses</u> <u>natural materials</u> <u>for his art</u>.

6. <u>Most of his artwork</u> <u>is</u> <u>temporary</u>³.

7. <u>He</u> <u>makes</u> <u>sculptures</u>⁴ <u>from snow, leaves, and flowers</u>.

8. <u>The sun, wind, and water</u> <u>erase</u> <u>his work</u>.

9. <u>He</u> <u>has</u> <u>permanent</u>⁵ <u>sculptures</u>, too.

10. <u>His sculptures</u> <u>are</u> <u>at museums around the world</u>.

11. <u>He</u> <u>takes</u> <u>photos</u> <u>of his temporary work</u>.

12. <u>You</u> <u>can see</u> <u>the photos</u> <u>on the Internet</u>.

> *S* = subject
> *V* = verb
> *O* = object
> *A* = adjective
> *NP* = noun phrase after *be*
> *PP* = prepositional phrase
> *T* = time expression

> **F Y I**
> We sometimes use *too* at the end of a sentence to show added information.

temporary artwork by Andy Goldsworthy

permanent sculpture by Andy Goldsworthy

**Write about It** Write five sentences about a famous person or a person you know. Use these sentence patterns.

| | subject | *be* | noun phrase |
|---|---|---|---|
| 1. | *Pele* | *is* | *a famous soccer player.* |

> **F Y I**
> For a list of verbs that are followed by an object, see the Resources, page R-7.
>
> For a list of linking verbs, see the Resources, page R-6.

| | subject | verb | prepositional phrase / time expression |
|---|---|---|---|
| 2. | | | |

| | subject | verb | object | prepositional phrase / time expression |
|---|---|---|---|---|
| 3. | | | | |

³ **temporary:** lasting for a short time
⁴ **sculptures:** works of art often made from stone or wood

⁵ **permanent:** lasting for a long time or forever

|  | subject | linking verb | adjective |
|---|---|---|---|
| 4. | | | |

|  | subject | *be* | prepositional phrase / time expression |
|---|---|---|---|
| 5. | | | |

## 8 | Using Statement Patterns  Complete these statements to make them true for you. Use the sentence elements in parentheses to add information. Then share your sentences with a partner.  `14.3 A`

OPINIONS AND DESIRES

1. Someday I want to live _____ *in Costa Rica* _____.
   (prepositional phrase)
2. I would like to visit _____.
   (object)
3. I would like to see _____ every day.
   (object)
4. The best cities have _____.
   (object)
5. I like to bring _____ _____.
   (object)  (prepositional phrase)
6. I don't _____ _____.
   (main verb)  (prepositional phrase)
7. Fresh vegetables _____ _____.
   (*be*)  (adjective)
8. I shouldn't _____ _____.
   (main verb)  (prepositional phrase)
9. Reporters[6] should _____ _____.
   (main verb)  (object)
10. I will never _____ _____.
    (main verb)  (object)

**Talk about It**  Compare your sentences as a class.

## 9 | Using Question Patterns  Look at this chart. Follow the instructions on page 368 to write eight questions with words and phrases from the chart. Change the form of the main verb where necessary.  `14.3 B`

| Wh- words | Helping verbs or *be* | Subjects | Main verbs | Other sentence parts |
|---|---|---|---|---|
| When | do | you | bring | to school |
| Where | does | your friends | buy | to work |
| What | did | your town | clean | interesting |
| Who | is | your school | come | nice |
| Why | are | who | go | your bills |
| How | was | what | happen | your car |
| | were | | have | your home |
| | can | | make | your lunch |
| | will | | pay | now |
| | | | start | tomorrow |
| | | | work | yesterday |

> **F Y I**
> For an overview of past, present, and future verb forms, see Unit 13, page 334.

---

[6] **reporters:**  people who write for newspapers or speak on the radio or television about things that happened

1.  Write four *yes/no* questions. (You will NOT use words from every column in every question.)

    *Are you coming to school tomorrow?*
    *Did you work yesterday?*

2.  Write four *wh-* questions. Include one question where the *wh-* word is the subject. (You will NOT use words from every column in every question.)

    *When did you buy your car?*
    *Who makes your lunch?*

**Talk about It** Ask and answer your questions with a partner. Write down your partner's answers.

**Write about It** Choose three of your partner's answers and write complete sentences about your partner. Share your sentences with the class.

*Bae works at a Chinese market.*
*She's coming to school tomorrow.*

## 10 | Usage Note: Placement of Adverbs of Frequency   Read the note. Then do Activity 11.

Notice the common location of **adverbs of frequency** in statements and questions.

**STATEMENTS**

| | subject | first helping verb / *be* | adverb of frequency | (other helping verbs +) main verb | rest of the sentence |
|---|---|---|---|---|---|
| 1 | Jill | - | hardly ever | walks | to school. |
| 2 | Brent | can | usually | come | on time. |
| 3 | I | 'm | never | going to fix | this problem. |
| 4 | Those cookies | - | always | smell | delicious. |
| 5 | Alan | is | sometimes | - | late. |
| 6 | My father | wasn't | always | - | an architect. |

| | |
|---|---|
| 7 | **Sometimes** Alan is late. |
| 8 | We take the train **sometimes**. |

◄ We can also use *sometimes* at the beginning or end of a statement.

**QUESTIONS**

| | *wh-* word | first helping verb / *be* | subject | adverb of frequency | (other helping verbs +) main verb | rest of the question |
|---|---|---|---|---|---|---|
| 9 | Where | does | Anna | usually | sit? | |
| 10 | | Are | you | always | going to live | here? |
| 11 | | Were | the meals | usually | - | pretty good? |

| | |
|---|---|
| 12 | Do you come here **often**? |

◄ We often use *often* at the end of a question.

For more information on adverbs of frequency, see Unit 3, page 53.

**11 | Using Adverbs of Frequency** Add the adverb of frequency in parentheses to each sentence. Then check (✓) *Agree* or *Disagree*. 14.3 A

| MODERN TIMES | AGREE | DISAGREE |
|---|---|---|
| 1. In the past, people were <sub>usually</sub> more polite. (usually) | ☐ | ☐ |
| 2. Nowadays, students come late to class. (often) | ☐ | ☐ |
| 3. Technology improves our lives. (always) | ☐ | ☐ |
| 4. Older people don't understand the younger generation[7]. (always) | ☐ | ☐ |
| 5. Popular music is good. (hardly ever) | ☐ | ☐ |
| 6. Video games are bad for children. (usually) | ☐ | ☐ |
| 7. The government can solve people's problems. (never) | ☐ | ☐ |
| 8. Young people have the best ideas. (often) | ☐ | ☐ |
| 9. Technology causes serious problems. (hardly ever) | ☐ | ☐ |
| 10. Children don't respect[8] their parents. (always) | ☐ | ☐ |

*(In sentence 1, "usually" is inserted with a caret between "were" and "more.")*

**Write about It** Rewrite the statements you disagreed with in the survey above. Change the adverb of frequency to write about your opinion. Share your ideas with a partner.

*In the past, people were sometimes more polite.*

**Write about It** Write four questions. Use the patterns below. Then ask and answer your questions with a partner. 14.3 B

| | first helping verb | subject | adverb of frequency | (other helping verbs +) main verb | (rest of the question) |
|---|---|---|---|---|---|
| 1. | | | always | | |

| | first helping verb | subject | (other helping verbs +) main verb | (rest of the question) | adverb of frequency |
|---|---|---|---|---|---|
| 2. | | | | | often? |

| | *wh-* word | first helping verb | subject | adverb of frequency | (other helping verbs +) main verb | (rest of the question) |
|---|---|---|---|---|---|---|
| 3. | | | | usually | | |

| | *be* | subject | adverb of frequency | adjective phrase / prepositional phrase / noun phrase | (rest of the question) |
|---|---|---|---|---|---|
| 4. | | | usually | | |

*1. Does Vicky always eat cereal for breakfast?*
*2. When does your family usually go on vacation?*

---

[7] **generation:** people who were born at around the same time          [8] **respect:** to have a good opinion of someone or something

## A

**SENTENCES WITH ONE CLAUSE**

A simple sentence has one **clause**. A clause includes a subject, a complete verb, and other words.
(Charts 14.1–14.3 are about simple sentences.)

| CLAUSE | | |
|---|---|---|
| subject | complete verb | rest of the clause |
| **1** Some people | are standing | outside the store. |

**SENTENCES WITH TWO CLAUSES**

Many sentences contain more than one clause. We can use the **connecting words *and*, *but*,** and ***so*** to connect two clauses.

| CLAUSE | | | connecting word | CLAUSE | | |
|---|---|---|---|---|---|---|
| subject | complete verb | rest of the clause | | subject | complete verb | rest of the clause |
| **2** Maria | left | at 7:30, | and | she | is going to return | at 4:00. |
| **3** I | love | apples, | but | I | don't like | pears. |
| **4** We | have to work | late tonight, | so | we | can't come | to dinner. |
| **5** Greg | isn't going | on vacation, | so | he | 'll watch | our house. |

Notice: We sometimes use a comma (,) before the connecting word if the sentence is long.

## B

**USING *AND*, *BUT*, AND *SO***

**6** I looked in the closets, **and** Tim searched the living room.

We use ***and*** to add information and to connect related ideas.

**7** It rained yesterday, **but** today it's really sunny.

We use ***but*** to show contrast.

cause — result

**8** We needed more paper, **so** Tim went to the store.

We use ***so*** to introduce a result.

**12 | Identifying Clauses** Underline the clauses in these sentences. Label the subject (*S*) and complete verb (*V*) in each clause. (Some sentences only have one clause.) **14.4 A**

## WORLD LEADERS

**Benito Juarez**

1. Benito Juarez was born very poor, but he became the president of Mexico.
   (S) (V) ... (S) (V)

2. Juarez' parents spoke an Indian language, so he didn't learn Spanish at home.

3. Juarez was a small man (only 4'6″/1.37m tall) with a big heart.

4. He became an important leader, and his birthday is now a national holiday in Mexico.

**Sejong the Great**

5.  Sejong the Great was the king of Korea in the early 1400s.

6.  He was very intelligent and creative, and he helped Korea in many ways.

7.  At that time Koreans used the Chinese writing system, but it didn't work well for the Korean language.

8.  King Sejong wanted a Korean writing system, so he created the Korean alphabet.

Chinese writing system

Korean alphabet

**Mahatma Gandhi**

9.  Mahatma Gandhi helped the poor people of India, and he changed the lives of many people.

10. Gandhi did not believe in violence⁹.

11. His first name was Mohandas, but most people called him Mahatma.

**13 | Using Connecting Words** Complete each conversation with *and*, *but*, or *so*. Then listen and check your answers. `14.4 B`

VACATION QUESTIONS

1.  A: Did you go to Mallorca?
    B: No. We wanted to go there, _____*but*_____ the flight was too expensive.

2.  A: Where did you go?
    B: The tickets to Cancun were pretty cheap, _____ we went there.

3.  A: What did you do in Cancun?
    B: We sat on the beach a lot, _____ one day we went to the pyramids. It was great!

4.  B: How about you? Are you going on vacation soon?
    A: I'd love to take a vacation, _____ I'm really busy at work.

5.  B: Will you have more time this summer?
    A: Yeah. I finish school in June, _____ I might take a vacation then.

6.  B: Where do you want to go?
    A: I want to go to Europe, _____ my husband wants to go to Brazil.

7.  B: Where in Europe do you want to go?
    A: I want to go back to Paris, _____ I'd love to see Switzerland, too.

8.  A: I think you went to Europe a few years ago?
    B: I did! We stayed in Paris for a few days, _____ we didn't go to Switzerland.

pyramid in Cancun

⁹**violence:** behavior that causes physical harm to other people

9. A: How long did you stay in Europe?

   B: We stayed for two weeks, _____ we went to four different countries.

10. A: How was the food?

    B: The food was great, _____ the restaurants were really expensive.

11. A: Was the language a problem?

    B: No. I always try to speak the local[10] language, _____ people are usually friendly to me.

12. B: I went with World Tour Company. You should check their website.

    A: Thanks. I'll look at it, _____ we probably won't take a tour.

**Talk about It** Complete the answers below with your own ideas. Then ask and answer the questions with a partner.

1. A: What did you do last summer?

   B: I _____,

      and I _____.

2. A: What do you want to do next summer?

   B: I want to _____,

      but _____.

3. A: Are you going somewhere next weekend?

   B: I _____,

      so _____.

> **RESEARCH SAYS...**
>
> *And* is the most common connecting word in speaking and writing.
>
> *But* is more common in speaking than in writing.
>
> CORPUS

**14 | Writing with Connecting Words** Choose two phrases from each box. Combine the two ideas with *and*, *but*, or *so* to write sentences about your future plans.  14.4 A–B

**MY FUTURE**

1.
   go to graduate school
   study business
   finish my degree[11]

2.
   get a good job
   work hard
   make a lot of money

3.
   travel around the world
   take a long vacation
   save money

4.
   live in another country
   get a job in Asia
   study Chinese

5.
   get plenty of exercise
   become a professional athlete
   be healthy

6.
   learn to cook
   open a restaurant
   eat delicious food

7.
   improve my computer skills
   design websites
   become a programmer[12]

8.
   become a teacher
   work with small children
   continue my education

9.
   buy a house
   move to a different city
   save money

1. *I'm going to finish my degree, but I'm not going to study business.*
   OR  *I want to go to graduate school, so I'm going to finish my degree.*
   OR  *I don't want to study business, and I'm not going to go to graduate school.*

---

[10] **local:** of the place
[11] **degree:** a certificate from a university, such as a BA (Bachelor of Arts) or MA (Master of Arts)

[12] **programmer:** a person who writes computer programs

**Write about It** Write three more sentences about your future. Use your own ideas.

I'd like to _____, but I don't want to _____.

I want to _____, and I'd like to _____.

I want to _____, so I'm going to _____.

## 14.5 Clauses with *Because*

We can combine two clauses with the connecting word ***because***.

> The clause with ***because*** is called the **reason clause**. It answers the question *why*.

**A**

| MAIN CLAUSE | | | REASON CLAUSE | | | |
|---|---|---|---|---|---|---|
| subject | complete verb | rest of the clause | *because* | subject | complete verb | rest of the clause |
| **1** Tom | moved | to Mexico | **because** | his father | got | a job there. |
| **2** Shaun | didn't get | the job | **because** | he | didn't have | any experience. |
| **3** Kim | is working | extra hours | **because** | she | has to save | money. |

> This clause is called the **main clause**.
> Notice: A main clause can be a complete simple sentence alone.
> ✓ Tom moved to Mexico.  ✓ Shaun didn't get the job.

**WARNING!** In writing, we don't use a reason clause alone. The sentence is not complete.

✗ Because we took the bus.

Notice: In conversation, we often use a reason clause alone when we respond to a question:

A: Why did it take you so long to get here?
B: **Because we took the bus.**

GO ONLINE

## 15 | Noticing Clauses with *Because* Underline the reason clause in each statement. Then check (✓) *Agree* or *Disagree*. 14.5 A

○ ○ ○

# Opinions

|  | AGREE | DISAGREE |
|---|---|---|
| 1. Children misbehave[13] <u>because they're spoiled[14]</u>. | ☐ | ☐ |
| 2. People don't write as well now because they text too often. | ☐ | ☐ |
| 3. Many people are unhealthy because they eat too much sugar. | ☐ | ☐ |

**F Y I**

Sometimes we put the **reason clause** before the **main clause**. When we do this, we add a comma after the reason clause.

**Because people are online too much, they don't get enough exercise.**

---

[13] **misbehave:** to act badly          [14] **spoiled:** A spoiled child gets everything he/she wants

|  | AGREE | DISAGREE |
|---|:---:|:---:|
| 4. Sick people shouldn't go to work because other people will get sick. | ☐ | ☐ |
| 5. Most people don't get enough exercise because they are online too much. | ☐ | ☐ |
| 6. It's OK to take office supplies¹⁵ from work because the company can afford¹⁶ it. | ☐ | ☐ |
| 7. A lot of people get into car accidents because they are on the phone. | ☐ | ☐ |
| 8. Crimes happen because people are naturally violent¹⁷. | ☐ | ☐ |
| 9. Life is better today because we have technology. | ☐ | ☐ |
| 10. Many people are poor because they don't want to work. | ☐ | ☐ |

**Think about It** In the sentences above, label the subject (*S*) and the verb (*V*) in each clause (the main clause and the reason clause).

**Talk about It** Share your answers to the survey as a class.

**16 | Writing Sentences with *Because*** Complete the sentences with *because* and your own ideas. Then share your sentences with a partner. `14.5 A`

EXPLAIN YOURSELF

1. I left the door open ____*because it was hot inside*____.

2. I didn't finish my homework _____
_____.

3. I forgot my lunch _____.

4. I was late _____.

5. I missed the bus _____.

6. I didn't clean the house _____
_____.

7. I didn't come to class _____
_____.

8. I ate too much _____.

9. I didn't call my friend _____
_____.

10. I got sick _____.

11. I'm happy _____.

12. I'm studying English _____
_____.

**Think about It** Label the subject (*S*) and the verb (*V*) in each reason clause you wrote above. Correct your answers if necessary.

**Write about It** Complete these sentences with your own ideas. Complete the main clause and add a reason clause with *because*.

Yesterday I _____.

Tomorrow I _____.

Sometimes I _____.

*Yesterday I called my brother because it was his birthday.*
*Tomorrow I'm going to the mall because I need a new jacket.*
*Sometimes I stay up late because I have to study.*

---

¹⁵ **office supplies:** things you use in an office, such as pens, pencils, paper, etc.

¹⁶ **afford:** to have enough money to buy or do something
¹⁷ **violent:** strong and dangerous; causing physical harm

# 14.6 Past and Present Time Clauses

We can connect a main clause with a **time clause**. The time clause answers the question *when*.
We can begin a time clause with connecting words like ***before***, ***when***, or ***after***.

**A**

**1**  | main clause | time clause |
Maria always eats breakfast | **before** she goes to work.
(1) (2)

(First, she eats breakfast. Second, she goes to work.)

**2**  | main clause | time clause |
Ken checked his email | **when** he got to the office.
(2) (1)

(First, he got to the office. Second, he checked his email.)

**3**  | main clause | time clause |
My roommate usually watches TV | **after** he eats dinner.
(2) (1)

(First, he eats dinner. Second, he watches TV.)

**B**

**TIME CLAUSES WITH THE SIMPLE PRESENT**

We can use time clauses with the simple present to describe general habits and routines.
Notice that we use a **simple present verb** in the main clause and in the time clause.

| main clause | time clause |
| --- | --- |
| **4** I always **do** the dishes | after I **eat** dinner. |
| **5** The teacher usually **closes** the door | when class **begins**. |

**TIME CLAUSES WITH THE SIMPLE PAST**

We can use time clauses with the simple past to describe when two past events happened.
Notice that we use a **simple past verb** in the main clause and in the time clause.

| main clause | time clause |
| --- | --- |
| **6** Sarah **called** me | before she **left**. |
| **7** She **broke** her arm | when she **fell**. |

**WARNING!** In writing, we don't use a time clause by itself. The sentence is not complete.

✗ After you went to bed.

**C**

We often use a time clause after the main clause:

| main clause | time clause |
| --- | --- |
| **8** I met some wonderful people | when I went to Russia. |

We can also use a time clause before the main clause:

| time clause | main clause |
| --- | --- |
| **9** When I went to Russia, | I met some wonderful people. |

Notice: When the time clause is before the main clause, we use a comma (,) to separate the clauses.

**17 | Noticing Time Clauses** Read the information about Marie Curie and Enrico Fermi. Underline the time clause in each sentence. Then number the events in the correct order. `14.6 A`

FAMOUS SCIENTISTS

## Marie Curie

1. Marie Curie began her scientific training in Poland <u>before she moved to Paris in 1891</u>.

    <u> 1 </u> She began her scientific training.

    <u> 2 </u> She moved to Paris.

2. She finished her degrees in physics and chemistry after she moved to Paris.

    ____ She moved to Paris.

    ____ She finished her degrees in physics and chemistry.

3. She and her husband Pierre won a Nobel Prize in physics after they discovered the element radium.

    ____ Marie and Pierre Curie discovered radium.

    ____ Marie and Pierre Curie won a Nobel Prize in physics.

4. She won another Nobel Prize in chemistry after she won the physics prize.

    ____ She won a Nobel Prize in chemistry.

    ____ She won the physics prize.

## Enrico Fermi

5. Enrico Fermi became interested in physics after his brother died.

    ____ He became interested in physics.

    ____ His brother died.

6. Other scientists discovered the parts of the atom[18] before Fermi began his work.

    ____ Scientists discovered the parts of the atom.

    ____ Fermi began his work.

7. He moved to the United States after he won the Nobel Prize for physics in 1938.

    ____ He moved to the United States.

    ____ He won the Nobel Prize.

8. Fermi worked on the atomic bomb[19] after he came to the United States.

    ____ He came to the United States.

    ____ He worked on the atomic bomb.

9. He was very unhappy when he saw the results of the bomb.

    ____ He was unhappy.

    ____ He saw the results of the bomb.

10. He became a professor at the University of Chicago when he finished the atomic bomb project.

    ____ He became a professor at the University of Chicago.

    ____ He finished the atomic bomb project.

Marie Curie

Enrico Fermi

[18] **atom:** one of the very small things that everything is made of

[19] **atomic bomb:** a very powerful thing that explodes and causes a lot of damage. Two atomic bombs exploded in Japan in 1945 (in Hiroshima and Nagasaki).

## 18 | Using Time Clauses
Complete these sentences with the phrases from the box or your own ideas. Underline the time clause in each sentence. Then share your answers with a partner. **14.6 B–C**

**MY DAILY ROUTINES**

1. I usually _____*drink coffee*_____ <u>when I get up in the morning</u>.
2. <u>Before I go to bed</u>, I always _____.
3. <u>When I get home from school</u>, I usually _____.
4. I usually _____ <u>after I eat dinner</u>.
5. <u>When I'm sick</u>, I usually _____.
6. I usually _____ <u>when I have a day off</u>.

**YESTERDAY AND TODAY**

7. <u>When I woke up this morning</u>, I _____*took a shower*_____.
8. I _____ <u>before I came to school today</u>.
9. <u>Yesterday</u> I _____ <u>after I ate lunch</u>.
10. I _____ <u>when I went to bed last night</u>.
11. <u>When I got to school today</u>, I _____.
12. <u>Before I left the house today</u>, I _____.

| |
|---|
| call my parents |
| take a shower |
| eat something |
| exercise |
| go online |
| do my homework |
| watch TV |
| see my friends |
| stay in bed |
| drink a lot of tea |
| go to the park |
| drink coffee |
| text a friend |
| take a nap |
| come to class |
| fall asleep |

**Write about It** Write two present and two past sentences about your partner. Use time clauses.

*Tom brushes his teeth before he goes to bed.*

## 19 | Using Punctuation in Time Clauses
Underline each time clause in the article below. Add a comma (,) where necessary. **14.6 C**

# Negative Feelings

We all have negative feelings sometimes. Maybe you feel anxious[20] <u>before you meet new people</u>. Maybe you feel depressed[21] after you have a bad day. Or maybe you get angry at the customers at work. Here are some ways to deal with common negative emotions[22].

- When you start to feel anxious find a quiet place to sit. Close your eyes and take some deep breaths.
- When someone makes you angry count to 25 before you talk to them.
- After you get home from a hard day at work go outside. Get some exercise or work in the garden.
- Make a list of good things in your life. When you are feeling bad look at the list again.

When you have negative feelings you may not sleep well. Try these tips:
- Before you go to bed listen to calm music or take a warm shower.
- Don't get in bed before you are tired.
- Turn off your computer, phone, and TV 30 minutes before you go to bed.

These tips will help you sleep. When you get enough sleep it's easier to fight negative emotions!

---

[20]**anxious:** worried and afraid
[21]**depressed:** very unhappy

[22]**emotions:** feelings

**Write about It** Add a time clause to make each sentence true for you. Then rewrite the sentences and change the order of the clauses.

1. I get very anxious _____.

2. _____, I feel really good.

3. I was anxious _____.

4. _____, I was very angry.

*I get very anxious when I fly.* → *When I fly, I get very anxious.*

---

**20 | Error Correction** Find and correct the errors. (Some sentences may not have any errors.)

1. He got a promotion[23] because ^*he* worked very hard.

2. I took a shower after I went to bed.

3. He graduated from high school. Before he went to college.

4. After got the good news, she was very happy.

5. Before I made soup, we ate it in the kitchen.

6. I wanted to study English, but this semester I'm taking an English class.

7. I visited my family before I go on vacation.

8. Anton is worried about his grade because the test was very difficult.

9. They went out to dinner. After they went to the movie.

10. I saved money so I wanted to buy a car.

11. When he told us the good news. We were very excited for him.

12. After I take an exercise class, I felt a lot better.

---

## 14.7 Future Time Clauses

We can use connecting words like *when*, *before*, and *after* in **time clauses about the future**. Notice the different verb forms in each clause.

| We use a **future verb form** (*will* or *be going to*) in the **main clause**. | We use a **simple present verb form** in the **time clause**. (Notice: The verb has a future meaning.) |
|---|---|

| | main clause | time clause |
|---|---|---|
| 1 | Bob **will make** dinner | when he **gets** home. |
| 2 | I **am going to talk** to the teacher | before I **register** for the class. |
| 3 | The manager **will lock** the doors | after the last customer **leaves**. |

**A**

The time clause can also come before the main clause:

| | time clause | main clause |
|---|---|---|
| 4 | When I **get** home tonight, | I'm **going to call** my brother. |
| 5 | After Mark **fixes** the car, | he'll **try to sell** it. |
| 6 | Before we **buy** a car, | I'm **going to do** a lot of research. |

simple present form ↑     future form ↑

Remember: When the time clause is before the main clause, we use a comma (,) after the time clause.

**WARNING!** Use a simple present verb form in the time clause. DON'T use a future verb form.

✓ I'll call you when I **get** home.     ✗ I'll call you when I **will get** home.

[23] **promotion:** a more important job

**21 | Noticing Future Time Clauses** Complete these conversations with the verbs you hear. Underline the time clauses. Then read the conversations with a partner. `14.7 A`

MAKING PLANS

1. A: Are you going to make dessert?

    B: No, I _____'ll do_____ that <u>after we</u>

    _____eat_____ dinner.

2. A: When should we buy the flowers?

    B: I _____ them right before

    we _____.

3. A: When do you want to open your presents?

    B: I _____ that when my parents

    _____ home.

4. A: These chairs _____

    wet when it _____.

    B: They're plastic. They'll be fine.

5. A: I _____ you before the movie

    _____.

    B: Thanks.

6. A: Is he coming with us?

    B: No. He _____ after he

    _____ Anna home.

7. A: Do you have any free time this weekend?

    B: I'm not sure. I _____ you after

    I _____ to my boss.

8. A: When you _____ us,

    we _____ camping.

    B: Sounds fun!

9. A: She's not _____ happy

    when she _____ about our plan.

    B: I know.

10. A: What's Miguel going to do?

    B: I don't know. But he _____ to us

    before he _____ a decision.

11. A: I _____ some cash when I

    _____ to the store.

    B: Good idea.

12. A: I _____ you the directions before

    I _____ the office.

    B: OK.

**Think about It** In the sentences above, label the future verb forms *F* and the simple present verb forms *SP*. Are the present verb forms in the time clause or the main clause?

       *F*             *SP*

No, I'll do that after we eat dinner.

**Think about It** Which sentence has the time clause before the main clause?

**22 | Using Future Time Clauses** Circle the correct verb form in each sentence. Then practice the conversations with a partner. `14.7 A`

OFFICE CONVERSATIONS

1. A: Did Tina start the new project?

    B: Not yet. She (starts / (ll start)) that one when she finishes this one.

2. A: We (begin / 'll begin) the meeting after the manager gets here.

    B: When is she coming?

3. A: I (call / 'll call) the customer when I get to the office tomorrow.

    B: OK.

4. A: When the IT person gets back from lunch, I (send / 'll send)

    him up to help you.

    B: Thanks.

5. A: I'll call you back after I (review / 'll review) your problem.

   B: Thanks.

6. A: Do I need to sign this?

   B: Not yet. We'll print a new copy before we (ask / 'll ask) you to sign it.

7. A: So what's next?

   B: We'll test the product before we (show / 'll show) it to customers.

8. A: Is he going to hire someone?

   B: Yes, but he (writes / 'll write) a new job description before he (interviews / 'll interview) anyone.

9. A: I need a new computer.

   B: Don't worry. When the new computers (arrive / 'll arrive), we (set / 'll set) them up right away.

10. A: When the manager (sees / will see) this, she (is / 's going to be) angry.

    B: I know.

11. A: After he (checks / will check) the meeting notes, I (make / 'll make) a copy for everyone.

    B: Thanks.

**Write about It** Complete these sentences with your own ideas. Add a comma (,) where necessary.

1. I'll call you before _____.

2. I'll go shopping after _____.

3. When I get home tomorrow _____.

4. Before I come to the next class _____.

🔊 **23 | Understanding Past, Present, and Future Time Clauses** Listen to each conversation. **Then complete each sentence with information about the conversation. (See Chart 14.6 for help with past and present time clauses.)** `14.7 A`

1. The woman _____*wants*_____ to have children after she _____*gets*_____ married.

2. The man _____ a nap after he _____ home yesterday.

3. The man _____ after Sandra _____ back.

4. The woman _____ to the gym in the morning before she _____ to school.

5. The man _____ to Mexico after he _____ from high school.

6. Martha _____ always happy when her children _____.

7. The man _____ lunch before he _____ to class.

8. The woman _____ her car before she _____ this job.

9. All students _____ the English test before they _____ for classes.

10. Terry _____ after she _____ off work.

11. The woman _____ her mom every night before she _____ to bed.

12. Ken _____ right after she _____.

**Write about It** Complete these statements with a main clause that is true for you. Share your sentences with a partner.

1. When I finish this English class, _____.

2. _____ when I have time.

3. Before I started at this school, _____.

## 14.8 Using Sentence Patterns in Writing

Good writers use a variety of sentence patterns. This makes writing more interesting.

**A**

Alicia Delgado is a nurse at Longwood Hospital in California. She grew up in Oregon, and she graduated from Portland State University in 2007. After she graduated, she moved to Chicago and worked in a medical office. She stayed there for a year and a half. Then she went to nursing school. Alicia moved west in 2012 because she wanted to attend the University of Southern California. Now she is studying and working part-time. She wants to become a nurse educator.

| Simple sentence (one clause) |
|---|
| Sentence with two clauses connected by *and*, *but* or *so* (two main clauses) |
| Sentence with main clause + time clause or reason clause (two clauses) |

**24 | Noticing Sentence Patterns** Read the student's paragraph. Label each sentence. Use a label (*A*, *B*, or *C*) from the box. `14.8 A`

| A Simple sentence (one clause) | B Sentence with two clauses connected by *and*, *but*, or *so* | C Sentence with main clause + reason or time clause |
|---|---|---|

### An Important Person from My Childhood

(1) __A__ My grandmother (Nana) was an important person in my life. (2) ____ She lived with us when I was a child. (3) ____ My parents both worked, so Nana took care of my sister and me. (4) ____ She was very kind to us, but she was also very strict[24]. (5) ____ She wanted us to do well in school because she never had that opportunity[25]. (6) ____ We did our homework every day when we got home.

(7) ____ Nana always looked at each page carefully. (8) ____ The homework had to be complete, and it had to be neat! (9) ____ After we finished our work, Nana always made delicious food.

(10) ____ Nana got sick when I was 11 years old. (11) ____ She couldn't cook for us anymore, but she was always kind and loving. (12) ____ I will always be grateful to her.

**25 | Using Sentence Patterns in Writing** Rewrite this paragraph. Use *when*, *because*, *but*, *after*, *and*, *before*, or *so* to connect some of the sentences. More than one answer may be possible. `14.8 A`

I was 5 years old. We moved to the city. My father wanted to move. There were more opportunities in the city. Life in the city wasn't easy for us. My mother found a job. My parents were able to save some money. They saved money for a few years. They opened a bakery. I helped them in the bakery. I didn't enjoy working there. I worked at the bakery through high school. Then I went to college. I'm living far away now. I can't visit very often. I call every weekend. My parents will retire someday. They will move near me. We'll all be together again.

*When I was 5 years old, we moved to the city. . . .*

**Write about It** Write a short paragraph about your past. Use a variety of sentence patterns.

[24] **strict:** not permitting people to break rules      [25] **opportunity:** a chance to do something

# WRAP-UP

A **GRAMMAR IN READING**  Read the student essay. Underline the complete verb in each clause.

---

Assignment: Describe one of your heroes[26] and explain how the person influenced you.

Some of my heroes <u>are</u> famous people. They <u>are</u> world leaders or great artists or scientists. I<u>'m going to tell</u> you about another kind of hero. My dance teacher, Joy Galen, is not rich or famous, but she is a hero to me.

I started taking dance classes when I was very young. I was shy[27], and I always stood in the back of the class. After I studied dance for several years, I started Joy's class. Joy was not an easy teacher. I had to repeat the same moves again and again. Some steps[28] were easy for other students, but they were difficult for me. I often wanted to quit, but Joy never let me give up[29].

Joy saw the best qualities in every student. When one girl danced in front of the class, the others had to give feedback[30]. Joy was always honest, but she was also kind. We followed her example, and the girls in the class became close friends.

Because we were teenagers, we often had personal problems. Joy always listened to us. After the other teachers went home, Joy usually stayed at the studio with us. We told her all of our problems and she listened patiently.

My experience in Joy's class changed my life. When I started the class, I was very shy. Now I'm not nervous around new people. I feel confident, and I'm also a pretty good dancer!

Joy was a wonderful teacher, but she is also my hero for another reason. She had a full-time job in an office, and she didn't make much money as a dance teacher, but she danced because she loved it. People often say, "Follow your heart," and Joy really did that. I learned that lesson from her.

---

**Think about It**  Answer these questions.

1. What connecting words does the writer use? _____

2. How many time clauses does the writer use? _____

3. How many simple sentences does the writer use? _____

4. How many reason clauses does the writer use? _____

5. There is one sentence with four clauses. What words connect the clauses? _____

B **GRAMMAR IN WRITING**  Write a paragraph about someone you admire[31]. Write 7 or 8 sentences. Answer some of these questions in your paragraph.

- When did you first meet/learn about the person?
- Why do you admire him or her?
- How did the person influence you?

*I admire my friend Martin very much. I met him in high school. He was three years older than me, but he was always very kind to me. He was also an excellent student. After he graduated from high school, Martin went to a university in the United States. He wants to be a doctor. . . .*

---

[26] **hero:** a person who did something brave or good
[27] **shy:** nervous with other people
[28] **steps:** the ways a dancer moves his/her feet

[29] **give up:** to stop trying to do something
[30] **feedback:** information about something you did (if it was good or bad)
[31] **admire:** to think that someone is very good

**SENTENCES WITH ONE CLAUSE**

Every clause must have a **subject** and a **complete verb**. A complete verb includes a **main verb**.
(It may also include one or more helping verbs.)

**SUBJECT + VERB (+ PREPOSITIONAL PHRASE / TIME EXPRESSION)**

| STATEMENT | - | - | Anthony | **works**<br>doesn't **work** | at this restaurant. |
|---|---|---|---|---|---|
| *YES/NO* QUESTION | - | Is | the baby | **sleeping?** | - |
| | - | Did | JoAnn | **help** | with the housework? |
| *WH-* QUESTION | Where | are | the children | going to **go** | tomorrow? |
| | - | - | What | **happened?** | - |

**SUBJECT + VERB + OBJECT (+ PREPOSITIONAL PHRASE / TIME EXPRESSION)**

| STATEMENT | - | - | The students | will **buy**<br>won't **buy** | their books | at Morey's Bookstore. |
|---|---|---|---|---|---|---|
| *YES/NO* QUESTION | - | Are | the students | going to **take** | the test | tomorrow? |
| *WH-* QUESTION | Where | did | Kim | **get** | that computer? | - |
| | - | - | Who | is **taking** | the exam | today? |

**SUBJECT + LINKING VERB + ADJECTIVE PHRASE**

| STATEMENT | - | - | Marcos | **is**<br>isn't | Mexican. |
|---|---|---|---|---|---|
| *YES/NO* QUESTION | - | **Is** | the manager | - | really angry? |
| | - | Doesn't | the soup | **smell** | delicious? |
| *WH-* QUESTION | Why | does | Kathy | **look** | tired? |
| | - | - | Who | **was** | angry? |

**SUBJECT + *BE* + PREPOSITIONAL PHRASE / NOUN PHRASE**

| STATEMENT | - | - | The books | **are**<br>aren't | in the living room. |
|---|---|---|---|---|---|
| | - | - | Sanam | **is**<br>isn't | a student. |
| *YES/NO* QUESTION | - | **Is** | your brother | - | a doctor? |
| *WH-* QUESTION | When | **was** | the teacher | - | in her office? |
| | - | - | Who | will **be** | in class tomorrow? |

**SENTENCES WITH TWO CLAUSES**

| main clause | connecting word | main clause |
|---|---|---|
| He called last night, | **but** | we weren't home. |

| main clause | reason clause / time clause |
|---|---|
| I paid for dinner | **because** he didn't bring any money. |
| The meeting always starts | **before** you get here. |

↑
connecting word

| time clause / reason clause | main clause |
|---|---|
| **After** he finishes the report, | he will share it with everyone. |
| **Because** tomorrow is a holiday, | the school will be closed. |

↑
connecting word

# Resources

## I. Spelling Rules: Possessive Nouns

We sometimes add -**'s** or -**'** after a noun or name to show possession.

| Rules | Examples | |
|---|---|---|
| We add -**'s** after a singular noun and most names. | one student's book | John's book |
| We add -**'** after a name that ends in -**s**. | Bess' family | Chris' book |
| We add -**'s** after an irregular plural noun. | the children's room | the men's group |
| We add -**'** after a plural noun that ends in -**s**. | all of the students' exams | my parents' house |

## II. Common Noncount Nouns

| | | | | | | |
|---|---|---|---|---|---|---|
| advice | coffee* | gasoline (gas) | information | money | rain | traffic |
| air | confidence | glass* | jewelry | music | rice | truth* |
| baggage | electricity | grammar | knowledge | news | safety | water |
| beauty | entertainment | hair* | literature | noise* | salt | weather |
| behavior* | experience* | happiness | luck | organization* | sand | work* |
| blood | flour | health | luggage | oxygen | smoke | |
| bread | fruit* | heat | mathematics | paint* | snow | |
| cash | fun | help | medicine* | pasta | soap | |
| clothing | furniture | homework | milk | peace | sugar | |

*often has a count meaning or a noncount meaning

## III. What Is a Noun Phrase?

A noun phrase can be  (1) a single noun,

(2) a noun + any descriptive words (article, adjective, quantifier, etc.), or

(3) a pronoun.

| (1) NOUN | ARTICLE + NOUN | (2) ARTICLE + ADJECTIVE + NOUN | QUANTIFIER + NOUN | (3) PRONOUN |
|---|---|---|---|---|
| Canada Thomas music money | a friend a school an animal the people | a big city a nice place an unusual person the best food | many friends much work some news no books | I / me you she / her he / him it we / us they / them |

## IV. Common Adjectives

These are the 100 most common adjectives in English in order of frequency.

| | | | | | | |
|---|---|---|---|---|---|---|
| other | little | human | full | current | serious | religious |
| new* | important | local | special | wrong* | ready | cold |
| good* | political | late | easy | private | simple | final |
| high | bad | hard* | clear | past | left | main |
| old* | white* | major | recent | foreign | physical | green |
| great | real | better | certain | fine | general | nice* |
| big* | best | economic | personal | common | environmental | huge |
| American | right* | strong | open | poor | financial | popular |
| small | social | possible | red | natural | blue | traditional |
| large | only | whole* | difficult* | significant | democratic | cultural |
| national | public | free | available | similar | dark | |
| young | sure* | military | likely | hot | various | |
| different* | low | true* | short | dead* | entire | |
| black* | early | federal | single | central | close | |
| long* | able* | international | medical | happy* | legal | |

*common in conversation

## V. Spelling Rules: Doubling the Final Consonant to Form -ing Verbs

The base form of some verbs ends in a **consonant** + **vowel** + **consonant**. For example:

<u>win</u>    for<u>get</u>    pre<u>fer</u>    vi<u>sit</u>

With some (but not all) of these verbs, we double the final consonant and add -ing. For example:

win → wi**nn**ing          forget → forge**tt**ing          prefer → prefe**rr**ing

Follow these rules to decide when to double the final consonant before you add -ing.

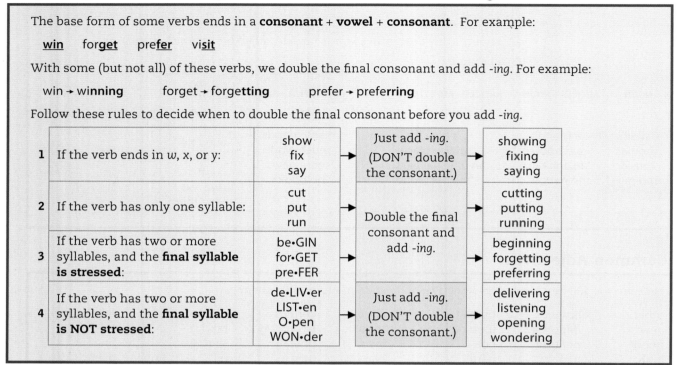

| | | | | |
|---|---|---|---|---|
| **1** | If the verb ends in w, x, or y: | show<br>fix<br>say | → | Just add -ing.<br>(DON'T double<br>the consonant.) | → | showing<br>fixing<br>saying |
| **2** | If the verb has only one syllable: | cut<br>put<br>run | → | Double the final<br>consonant and<br>add -ing. | → | cutting<br>putting<br>running |
| **3** | If the verb has two or more syllables, and the **final syllable is stressed**: | be·GIN<br>for·GET<br>pre·FER | → | | → | beginning<br>forgetting<br>preferring |
| **4** | If the verb has two or more syllables, and the **final syllable is NOT stressed**: | de·LIV·er<br>LIST·en<br>O·pen<br>WON·der | → | Just add -ing.<br>(DON'T double<br>the consonant.) | → | delivering<br>listening<br>opening<br>wondering |

## VI. Spelling Rules: Doubling the Final Consonant to Form -ed Verbs

The base form of some regular verbs ends in a **consonant** + **vowel** + **consonant**. For example:

p<u>lan</u>    d<u>rop</u>    pre<u>fer</u>    deve<u>lop</u>

With some (but not all) of these regular verbs, we double the final consonant and add -ed. For example:

plan → pla**nn**ed          drop → dro**pp**ed          prefer → prefe**rr**ed

Follow these rules to decide when to double the final consonant before you add -ed.

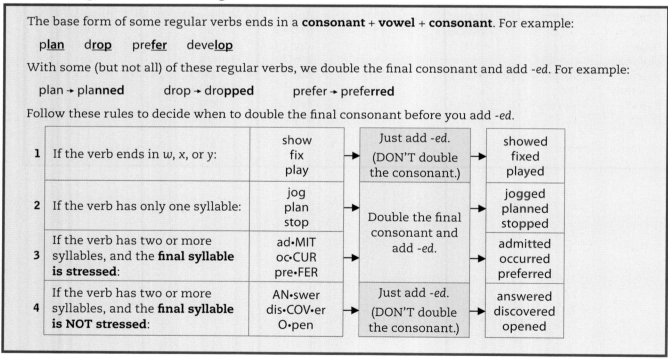

| | | | | |
|---|---|---|---|---|
| **1** | If the verb ends in w, x, or y: | show<br>fix<br>play | → | Just add -ed.<br>(DON'T double<br>the consonant.) | → | showed<br>fixed<br>played |
| **2** | If the verb has only one syllable: | jog<br>plan<br>stop | → | Double the final<br>consonant and<br>add -ed. | → | jogged<br>planned<br>stopped |
| **3** | If the verb has two or more syllables, and the **final syllable is stressed**: | ad·MIT<br>oc·CUR<br>pre·FER | → | | → | admitted<br>occurred<br>preferred |
| **4** | If the verb has two or more syllables, and the **final syllable is NOT stressed**: | AN·swer<br>dis·COV·er<br>O·pen | → | Just add -ed.<br>(DON'T double<br>the consonant.) | → | answered<br>discovered<br>opened |

# VII. Simple Past Form of Irregular Verbs

| BASE FORM | SIMPLE PAST | BASE FORM | SIMPLE PAST | BASE FORM | SIMPLE PAST |
|---|---|---|---|---|---|
| be | was/were | get | got | run | ran |
| become | became | give | gave | say | said |
| begin | began | go | went | see | saw |
| break | broke | grow | grew | sell | sold |
| bring | brought | have | had | send | sent |
| build | built | hear | heard | set | set |
| buy | bought | hide | hid | shake | shook |
| catch | caught | hit | hit | shoot | shot |
| choose | chose | hold | held | shut | shut |
| come | came | hurt | hurt | sing | sang |
| cost | cost | keep | kept | sit | sat |
| cut | cut | know | knew | sleep | slept |
| deal | dealt | lay | laid | speak | spoke |
| do | did | leave | left | spend | spent |
| draw | drew | lend | lent | stand | stood |
| drink | drank | let | let | steal | stole |
| drive | drove | lie | lied | take | took |
| eat | ate | lose | lost | teach | taught |
| fall | fell | make | made | tear | tore |
| feed | fed | mean | meant | tell | told |
| feel | felt | meet | met | think | thought |
| fight | fought | pay | paid | throw | threw |
| find | found | put | put | understand | understood |
| fit | fit | quit | quit | wear | wore |
| fly | flew | read | read* | win | won |
| forget | forgot | ring | rang | write | wrote |
| forgive | forgave | rise | rose | | |

*The past form *read* is pronounced "red."

# VIII. Non-Action Verbs

| | | | | | | |
|---|---|---|---|---|---|---|
| agree | contain | feel | involve | need | remember | understand |
| appear | cost | fit | know | owe | see | want |
| appreciate | dislike | hate | like | own | seem | weigh |
| be | doubt | have | look | possess | smell | wish |
| believe | envy | hear | love | prefer | suppose | |
| belong | equal | imagine | mean | realize | taste | |
| consist of | fear | include | mind | recognize | think | |

Remember:
- A non-action verb describes a state (an unchanging condition).
- Non-action verbs are also called **stative verbs**.
- Some verbs have more than one meaning. They can be a non-action verb in one context and an action verb in another.

## IX. Linking Verbs

**Examples:** *She looks tired. That seems interesting.*

| | | | | | | |
|---|---|---|---|---|---|---|
| appear | become | get* | look | seem | sound | turn* |
| be | feel | grow* | remain | smell | taste | |

*with a meaning of *become*

Remember: A linking verb can be followed by an adjective.

## X. Common Adverbs of Degree

**Examples:** *really big; pretty scary*

| | | | | | | |
|---|---|---|---|---|---|---|
| almost | exactly* | highly | perfectly | real* | so | too* |
| awfully | extremely | kind of* | pretty* | really* | somewhat | totally |
| completely | fairly | more | quite | slightly | terribly | very* |
| definitely | fully | nearly | rather | | | |

*common in conversation

## XI. Common Adjectives + Prepositions

**Examples:** *really afraid of snakes; different from her; good for you*

| ADJECTIVE + *OF* | ADJECTIVE + *FROM* | ADJECTIVE + *ABOUT* | ADJECTIVE + *IN* | ADJECTIVE + *FOR* |
|---|---|---|---|---|
| afraid of | different from | curious about | common in | good for |
| full of | free from | excited about | important in | hard for |
| proud of | safe from | happy about | interested in | important for |
| tired of | tired from | nervous about | involved in | necessary for |
| | | serious about | useful in | ready for |
| | | sorry about | | responsible for |
| | | worried about | | sorry for |
| | | | | useful for |

## XII. Common Multi-Word Verbs

| | | | | | |
|---|---|---|---|---|---|
| believe in | do without | get over | leave out | put away | throw out |
| bring up | dream of | get up | listen to | put on | try on |
| call off | eat out | give away | look after | shut down | turn down |
| call on | feel like | give up | look at | shut off | turn off |
| care about | figure out | grow up | look for | sit down | wait for |
| care for | fill out | hand in | look forward to | slow down | wake up |
| check out | fill up | hand out | look like | take out | worry about |
| check over | find out | help out | look up | talk about | write down |
| come back | finish up | hold off | make up | talk to | write to |
| come over | forget about | keep on | pay for | think about | work out |
| complain about | get along (with) | keep out | pick out | think of | |
| depend on | get off | know about | pick up | think over | |
| do over | get on | lay down | plan on | throw away | |

Remember: Multi-word verbs include *phrasal verbs* and *prepositional verbs*.

# XIII. Common Verbs + Object or No Object

**VERB + OBJECT**

Some verbs need an object to complete their meaning. Verbs that have an object are called *transitive verbs*.

**Examples:**

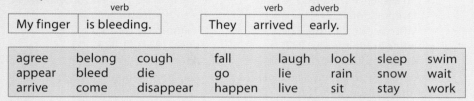

| bring | describe | forgive | love | produce | receive | use |
|-------|----------|---------|------|---------|---------|------|
| buy | discuss | keep | make | provide | send | want |
| carry | enjoy | lend | mean | put | take | wear |
| create | find | like | need | raise | throw | |

**VERB WITH NO OBJECT**

Some verbs are complete without an object. Verbs that do not have an object are called *intransitive verbs*.

**Examples:**

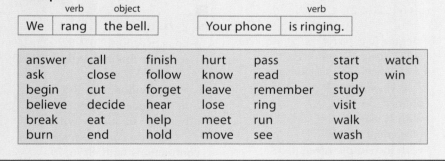

| agree | belong | cough | fall | laugh | look | sleep | swim |
|-------|--------|-------|------|-------|------|-------|------|
| appear | bleed | die | go | lie | rain | snow | wait |
| arrive | come | disappear | happen | live | sit | stay | work |

**VERB + OBJECT OR NO OBJECT**

Many verbs have more than one meaning. With one meaning the verb needs an object. With another meaning the same verb is complete without an object.

**Examples:**

| | verb | object | | | verb | |
|--|------|--------|--|--|------|--|
| We | rang | the bell. | | Your phone | is ringing. | |

| answer | call | finish | hurt | pass | start | watch |
|--------|------|--------|------|------|-------|-------|
| ask | close | follow | know | read | stop | win |
| begin | cut | forget | leave | remember | study | |
| believe | decide | hear | lose | ring | visit | |
| break | eat | help | meet | run | walk | |
| burn | end | hold | move | see | wash | |

# Index

# E

*-ed* form of verbs, 196, 197, 199, R-4. *See also* Simple past

**Enough**
  with adjectives, 226
  with nouns, 255

**-er/more/less** adjectives, 233, 234, 235, 236, 239, 240, 249
  irregular (e.g., *better*), 233
  spelling *-er* adjectives, 234
  with *than*, 236

**-est/most** adjectives, 242, 244, 246, 249
  irregular (e.g., *best*), 242
  prepositional phrases after, 246
  spelling *-est* adjectives, 244

Exclamation mark, use of, 360

# F

Facts, simple present for, 185

**Feel** in simple present and present progressive, 185

Frequency, adverbs of (e.g., *often sometimes, never*), 53, 84

Frequency expressions with simple present, 53, 64, 84, 182

Future forms, 250–277, 334
  *be going to*, 252–261, 334, 357
    with *I think* and *probably*, 258
    negative statements with, 252, 277, 334
    vs. other verb forms, 334, 357
    positive statements with, 252, 277, 334
    vs. present progressive, 266
    pronunciation of (*gonna*), 253
    *there is/there are going to be*, 255
    in time clauses, 378
    *wh-* questions with, 261, 277, 334
    *yes/no* questions and short answers with, 259, 277, 344
  *may* and *might*, 266
  vs. present and past verb forms, 334, 357
  present progressive, 334
    for future plans, 263
    for personal plans, 265
  summary of, 277
  time expressions with, 256, 334, 335
  uses of, 250, 251
  *will*, 269–274, 334, 357
    contractions with (*'ll, won't*), 269
    negative statements with, 269, 277, 334
    vs. other verb forms, 334, 357
    positive statements with, 269, 277, 334

questions with, 274
in time clauses, 378
*wh-* questions with, 274, 277, 334
*yes/no* questions and short answers with, 274, 277, 334

Future time clauses, 378

# G

**Get** in present progressive, 170

**Give** vs. **have** (e.g., *could you give me . . .* ), 298

**Going to**, pronunciation of (*gonna*), 253. See also *Be going to*

# H

Habits, expressing in simple present, 185, 188

**Have/has**, 26–45
  as action verb or non-action verb, 188
  common phrases with, 36
  negative statements with, 31, 45
  positive statements with, 28, 45
  in requests (e.g., *could I have a glass of water?*), 298
  simple present of, 26–45
  summary of, 45
  in talking about food and drink, 29
  uses of, 26–27, 45
  *wh-* questions with, 38, 45
  *yes/no* questions with, 34, 45

**Have to/not have to**, 318–321, 324, 326
  vs. *can* and *should*, 326
  negative statements (*not have to*) with, 318, 322, 324, 326
    vs. *must not*, 324
  positive statements with, 318, 326
  pronunciation of, 319
  questions with, 321

Helping verbs, 360, 365, 383
  defined, 57, 334
  *be*, 166, 252 (See also under *Be*, as helping verb)
    vs. *do*, 96, 213, 182
  *can*, 280
  *could*, 286
  *do* (See also under *Do*, as helping verb and main verb)
    vs. *be*, 96, 182, 213
    *did*, 206
    *didn't*, 204, 206
    *do/does*, 60, 66
    *don't/doesn't*, 57
  *may*, 266
  *might*, 266

*must*, 323
overview of, 334
in sentence patterns, 360, 362, 365, 368, 383
*should*, 311
*will*, 269
*would*, 299

**Here**, 86

**He's** vs. **his**, pronunciation of, 83

**How**, 92, 177, 231
  + adjective (e.g., *how hot is it?*), 231

**How many**, 38, 148, 149, 163

**How much**, 92, 148, 149, 150, 163

**How often**, 66

# I

Imperative sentences, 19, 25, 334, 357
  defined, 19
  subject in, 361

**In**
  adjective + (e.g., *interested in*), 348, R-6
  as preposition of place (e.g., *in Paris*), 86
  in time expressions (e.g., *in July*), 40, 56, 196, 256

Indefinite articles
  defined, 115
  *a/an*, 115, 120, 122, 123, 135 (See also *A/an*)
  *some*, 118, 122, 127, 135
  vs. *the*, 122

**-ing** form of verbs, 166, 168
  as adjectives, 225
  spelling rules for, 168, R-4

**Inside**, 86

Instructions (imperatives), 19, 25

Intonation
  in statements as questions, 364
  in *wh-* questions, 43, 95
  in *yes/no* questions, 38, 43, 61, 91, 95, 364

Intransitive verbs, 343, R-7. *See also under* Verbs, with no object

Introductions (with *this is*), 77

Invitations (*would like* for), 299
  saying yes or no to, 301

Irregular verbs, simple past forms of, 202, R-5

**Is**. See *Be*

**Is there**, 146, 148, 149, 163

**I think/I don't think**
  in statements with *be going to*, 258
  in statements with *should*, 310

**It is** in talking about weather, 91

## V

Verb forms, 334, 357
  future, 250–277, 334. (*See also* Future forms)
    with *be going to*, 252–261, 277, 334, 357
    with present progressive, 263, 265, 334
    with *will*, 269–277, 334, 357
  imperative, 19, 25, 334, 357, 361
  modals, 266, 279–305, 306–331 (*See also* Modals)
  overview of, 334
  present progressive, 164–193, 334, 357 (*See also* Present progressive)
  simple past, 194–219, 334, 357 (*See also* Simple past)
  simple present, 26–45, 46–73, 334, 357 (*See also* Simple present)
    of *be*, 74–101 (See also *Be*)
    of *have*, 26–45 (See also *Have/has*)
  summary of, 357
Verbs, 332–357. *See also* Verb forms
  defined, 15
  action, 15, 185, 188, 193, 336
  *be*, 74–101 (See also *Be*)
  complete, 360, 362
    defined, 360
  -*ed* form of, 196, 197, 199, R-4
  *have*, 26–45 (See also *Have/has*)
  helping, 57, 166, 360, 364
  -*ing* form of, 166, 168, R-4
    as adjective, 225
  intransitive, 343, R-7 (*See also under* Verbs, with no object)
  irregular, 202, R-5
  *let's* +, 19, 25
  linking, 222, 345, R-6 (*See also* Linking verbs)
  main, 334 (*See also* Main verbs)
  multi-word, 351, 353, 354, R-6
  non-action, 15, 185, 188, 193, 336, R-5
  with no object, 343, 344, 346, 357, R-7
  vs. nouns (e.g., *work*), 17
  + object, 340, 346, 357, R-7
    vs. no object, 344, R-7
  in sentence patterns, 365, 383 (*See also* Sentence patterns)
  stative (*See* Non-action verbs)
  transitive, 340, R-7 (*See also under* Verbs, + object)
  types of, 346, 357
  uses of, 332–333
***Very***, 82, 226, 227

## W

***Want***
  + noun phrase (e.g., *do you want a cup of tea?*), 302
  + *to* + verb (e.g., *do you want to go somewhere?*), 302
  vs. *would like*, 302
***Was***, 209–216, 219. *See also under* Simple past
***Was born in***, 209
Weather, use of *it* for, 91, 101
***Well*** as adverb, 281
***Were***, 209, 211, 213, 216, 219, 334
***Were*** vs. ***weren't***, pronunciation of, 211
***When*** in time clauses, 375, 376, 378
***Which***, 233
***Wh-*** questions. *See under* Questions, *wh-*
***Wh-*** words
  contractions with, 178
  *how*, 92, 177
  *how many*, 38, 148, 149, 163
  *how much*, 92, 148, 149, 150, 163
  *how often*, 66
  as subjects, 362
  *what*, 38, 66, 177
    + noun, 38, 45, 66
  *what kind of*, 66
  *what time*, 66, 92
  *when*, 38, 45, 66
  *where*, 66, 92, 177
  *which*, 233
  *who*, 92, 177
  *whose*, 157, 163
  *why*, 177
***Why don't you/we*** for suggestions, 314
***Will***, 269–277, 334, 357. *See also under* Future forms
***Would*** for requests, 295, 305
***Would like***
  for desires (*I'd like*), 299, 305
  vs. *like*, 300
  for offers and invitations (*would you like*), 299, 305
    pronunciation of (*wouldju/wouldja*), 300
  vs. *want*, 302
Writing, sentence patterns in, 381

## Y

***Yes/no*** questions. *See under* Questions, *yes/no*
***You*** as subject in imperatives, 19

# Class Audio Track List

GO ONLINE  For these audio tracks and the audio scripts, go to the Online Practice.

| Unit | Activity | Track File Name |
|------|----------|-----------------|
| Unit 1 | Activity 5, p. 7 | ELM1_U01_Track01_Activity05.mp3 |
| | Activity 13, p. 14 | ELM1_U01_Track02_Activity13.mp3 |
| | Activity 24, p. 21 | ELM1_U01_Track03_Activity24.mp3 |
| Unit 2 | Activity 10, p. 35 | ELM1_U02_Track01_Activity10.mp3 |
| | Activity 12, p. 36 | ELM1_U02_Track02_Activity12.mp3 |
| | Activity 14, p. 37 | ELM1_U02_Track03_Activity14.mp3 |
| | Activity 15, p. 37 | ELM1_U02_Track04_Activity15.mp3 |
| | Activity 16, p. 38 | ELM1_U02_Track05_Activity16.mp3 |
| | Activity 17, p. 38 | ELM1_U02_Track06_Activity17.mp3 |
| | Activity 23, p. 43 | ELM1_U02_Track07_Activity23.mp3 |
| | Activity 24, p. 43 | ELM1_U02_Track08_Activity24.mp3 |
| Unit 3 | Activity 6, p. 51 | ELM1_U03_Track01_Activity06.mp3 |
| | Activity 7, p. 52 | ELM1_U03_Track02_Activity07.mp3 |
| | Activity 8, p. 52 | ELM1_U03_Track03_Activity08.mp3 |
| | Activity 23, p. 63 | ELM1_U03_Track04_Activity23.mp3 |
| Unit 4 | Activity 11, p. 83 | ELM1_U04_Track01_Activity11.mp3 |
| | Activity 12, p. 84 | ELM1_U04_Track02_Activity12.mp3 |
| | Activity 22, p. 93 | ELM1_U04_Track03_Activity22.mp3 |
| | Activity 23, p. 93 | ELM1_U04_Track04_Activity23.mp3 |
| | Activity 28, p. 98 | ELM1_U04_Track05_Activity28.mp3 |
| Unit 5 | Activity 5, p. 107 | ELM1_U05_Track01_Activity05.mp3 |
| | Activity 9, p. 110 | ELM1_U05_Track02_Activity09.mp3 |
| | Activity 10, p. 110 | ELM1_U05_Track03_Activity10.mp3 |
| | Activity 11, p. 111 | ELM1_U05_Track04_Activity11.mp3 |
| | Activity 17, p. 116 | ELM1_U05_Track05_Activity17.mp3 |
| | Activity 27, p. 123 | ELM1_U05_Track06_Activity27.mp3 |
| | Activity 28, p. 124 | ELM1_U05_Track07_Activity28.mp3 |
| | Activity 33, p. 126 | ELM1_U05_Track08_Activity33.mp3 |
| | Activity 39, p. 132 | ELM1_U05_Track09_Activity39.mp3 |
| Unit 6 | Activity 3, p. 141 | ELM1_U06_Track01_Activity03.mp3 |
| | Activity 4, p. 141 | ELM1_U06_Track02_Activity04.mp3 |
| | Activity 5, p. 142 | ELM1_U06_Track03_Activity05.mp3 |
| | Activity 11, p. 147 | ELM1_U06_Track04_Activity11.mp3 |
| | Activity 14, p. 149 | ELM1_U06_Track05_Activity14.mp3 |
| | Activity 15, p. 149 | ELM1_U06_Track06_Activity15.mp3 |
| | Activity 19, p. 154 | ELM1_U06_Track07_Activity19.mp3 |
| | Activity 20, p. 154 | ELM1_U06_Track08_Activity20.mp3 |
| | Activity 21, p. 155 | ELM1_U06_Track09_Activity21.mp3 |
| | Activity 22, p. 156 | ELM1_U06_Track10_Activity22.mp3 |
| | Activity 24, p. 158 | ELM1_U06_Track11_Activity24.mp3 |
| Unit 7 | Activity 9, p. 172 | ELM1_U07_Track01_Activity09.mp3 |
| | Activity 10, p. 173 | ELM1_U07_Track02_Activity10.mp3 |
| | Activity 16, p. 178 | ELM1_U07_Track03_Activity16.mp3 |
| | Activity 17, p. 178 | ELM1_U07_Track04_Activity17.mp3 |
| | Activity 18, p. 179 | ELM1_U07_Track05_Activity18.mp3 |
| | Activity 19, p. 179 | ELM1_U07_Track06_Activity19.mp3 |
| | Activity 23, p. 183 | ELM1_U07_Track07_Activity23.mp3 |
| | Activity 26, p. 186 | ELM1_U07_Track08_Activity26.mp3 |
| | Activity 27, p. 188 | ELM1_U07_Track09_Activity27.mp3 |
| Unit 8 | Activity 5, p. 199 | ELM1_U08_Track01_Activity05.mp3 |
| | Activity 6, p. 200 | ELM1_U08_Track02_Activity06.mp3 |
| | Activity 6, p. 200 | ELM1_U08_Track03_Activity06.mp3 |
| | Activity 7, p. 200 | ELM1_U08_Track04_Activity07.mp3 |
| | Activity 9, p. 202 | ELM1_U08_Track05_Activity09.mp3 |

| Unit | Activity | Track File Name |
|------|----------|-----------------|
| Unit 8 (cont.) | Activity 12, p. 204 | ELM1_U08_Track06_Activity12.mp3 |
| | Activity 15, p. 207 | ELM1_U08_Track07_Activity15.mp3 |
| | Activity 16, p. 208 | ELM1_U08_Track08_Activity16.mp3 |
| | Activity 20, p. 211 | ELM1_U08_Track09_Activity20.mp3 |
| | Activity 21, p. 211 | ELM1_U08_Track10_Activity21.mp3 |
| | Activity 23, p. 214 | ELM1_U08_Track11_Activity23.mp3 |
| | Activity 24, p. 214 | ELM1_U08_Track12_Activity24.mp3 |
| | Activity 26, p. 217 | ELM1_U08_Track13_Activity26.mp3 |
| Unit 9 | Activity 4, p. 225 | ELM1_U09_Track01_Activity04.mp3 |
| | Activity 5, p. 227 | ELM1_U09_Track02_Activity05.mp3 |
| | Activity 7, p. 228 | ELM1_U09_Track03_Activity07.mp3 |
| | Activity 17, p. 239 | ELM1_U09_Track04_Activity17.mp3 |
| Unit 10 | Activity 2, p. 253 | ELM1_U10_Track01_Activity02.mp3 |
| | Activity 3, p. 253 | ELM1_U10_Track02_Activity03.mp3 |
| | Activity 6, p. 255 | ELM1_U10_Track03_Activity06.mp3 |
| | Activity 11, p. 260 | ELM1_U10_Track04_Activity11.mp3 |
| | Activity 13, p. 262 | ELM1_U10_Track05_Activity13.mp3 |
| | Activity 16, p. 265 | ELM1_U10_Track06_Activity16.mp3 |
| | Activity 17, p. 266 | ELM1_U10_Track07_Activity17.mp3 |
| | Activity 21, p. 270 | ELM1_U10_Track08_Activity21.mp3 |
| | Activity 22, p. 271 | ELM1_U10_Track09_Activity22.mp3 |
| | Activity 23, p. 271 | ELM1_U10_Track10_Activity23.mp3 |
| | Activity 25, p. 272 | ELM1_U10_Track11_Activity 25.mp3 |
| Unit 11 | Activity 4, p. 282 | ELM1_U11_Track01_Activity04.mp3 |
| | Activity 5, p. 283 | ELM1_U11_Track02_Activity05.mp3 |
| | Activity 7, p. 284 | ELM1_U11_Track03_Activity07.mp3 |
| | Activity 11, p. 289 | ELM1_U11_Track04_Activity11.mp3 |
| | Activity 18, p. 296 | ELM1_U11_Track05_Activity18.mp3 |
| | Activity 23, p. 300 | ELM1_U11_Track06_Activity23.mp3 |
| | Activity 24, p. 300 | ELM1_U11_Track07_Activity24.mp3 |
| | Activity 25, p. 300 | ELM1_U11_Track08_Activity25.mp3 |
| | Activity 28, p. 302 | ELM1_U11_Track09_Activity28.mp3 |
| | Activity 29, p. 303 | ELM1_U11_Track10_Activity29.mp3 |
| Unit 12 | Activity 1, p. 308 | ELM1_U12_Track01_Activity01.mp3 |
| | Activity 2, p. 308 | ELM1_U12_Track02_Activity02.mp3 |
| | Activity 8, p. 315 | ELM1_U12_Track03_Activity08.mp3 |
| | Activity 10, p. 317 | ELM1_U12_Track04_Activity10.mp3 |
| | Activity 12, p. 319 | ELM1_U12_Track05_Activity12.mp3 |
| | Activity 13, p. 320 | ELM1_U12_Track06_Activity13.mp3 |
| | Activity 14, p. 320 | ELM1_U12_Track07_Activity14.mp3 |
| | Activity 20, p. 326 | ELM1_U12_Track08_Activity20.mp3 |
| Unit 13 | Activity 1, p. 335 | ELM1_U13_Track01_Activity01.mp3 |
| | Activity 4, p. 338 | ELM1_U13_Track02_Activity04.mp3 |
| | Activity 7, p. 340 | ELM1_U13_Track03_Activity07.mp3 |
| | Activity 13, p. 344 | ELM1_U13_Track04_Activity13.mp3 |
| | Activity 18, p. 349 | ELM1_U13_Track05_Activity18.mp3 |
| | Activity 22, p. 352 | ELM1_U13_Track06_Activity22.mp3 |
| | Activity 24, p. 354 | ELM1_U13_Track07_Activity24.mp3 |
| Unit 14 | Activity 3, p. 362 | ELM1_U14_Track01_Activity03.mp3 |
| | Activity 5, p. 364 | ELM1_U14_Track02_Activity05.mp3 |
| | Activity 6, p. 364 | ELM1_U14_Track03_Activity06.mp3 |
| | Activity 13, p. 371 | ELM1_U14_Track04_Activity13.mp3 |
| | Activity 21, p. 379 | ELM1_U14_Track05_Activity21.mp3 |
| | Activity 23, p. 380 | ELM1_U14_Track06_Activity23.mp3 |

OXFORD
UNIVERSITY PRESS

198 Madison Avenue
New York, NY 10016 USA

Great Clarendon Street, Oxford, OX2 6DP, United Kingdom

Oxford University Press is a department of the University of Oxford. It furthers the University's objective of excellence in research, scholarship, and education by publishing worldwide. Oxford is a registered trade mark of Oxford University Press in the UK and in certain other countries.





First published in 2015
2019 2018 2017 2016 2015
10 9 8 7 6 5 4 3 2 1





Director, ELT New York: Laura Pearson
Head of Adult, ELT New York: Stephanie Karras
Publisher: Sharon Sargent
Senior Development Editor: Andrew Gitzy
Senior Development Editor: Rebecca Mostov
Development Editor: Eric Zuarino
Executive Art and Design Manager: Maj-Britt Hagsted
Content Production Manager: Julie Armstrong
Image Manager: Trisha Masterson
Image Editor: Liaht Pashayan
Production Artists: Elissa Santos, Julie Sussman-Perez
Production Coordinator: Brad Tucker

Special thanks to Electra Jablons and Rima Ibrahim for assistance with language data research.

ISBN: 978 0 19 402820 2 Student Book 1 with Online Practice Pack
ISBN: 978 0 19 402839 4 Student Book 1 as pack component
ISBN: 978 0 19 402879 0 Online Practice website

Printed in China

This book is printed on paper from certified and well-managed sources.

ACKNOWLEDGEMENTS

*Illustrations by:* Mark Duffin: 33, 34, 86 (desk), 127, 131, 135. Dermot Flynn: p. 110. John Kaufmann: p. 91. Jerome Mireault: p. 80, 132, 133, 151, 158, 159, 160. Joe Taylor: p. 8, 13, 19, 32, 33, 86, 87, 150, 157, 171, 181, 188, 205, 226, 229, 230, 253, 254, 287, 288, 293, 294, 295, 312, 313, 349, 350. 5W Infographics: p. 20, 21, 30, 35, 41, 82, 91, 128, 129, 138, 139, 144, 149, 169, 196, 201, 233, 239, 242, 256, 258, 266, 287, 314, 323, 324.

*We would also like to thank the following for permission to reproduce the following photographs:* Cover: blinkblink/shutterstock; back cover: lvcandy/Getty Images; global: Rodin Anton/shutterstock; p. 2 Jim Craigmyle/Corbis; p. 3 Robert Deutschman /Getty Images, NicoElNino/shutterstock; p. 4 paulista/shutterstock, Thomas Bethge/shutterstock, OUP/Digital Vision, Mark Hunt/Huntstock/Corbis, michaeljung/shutterstock.com, Nikada/istockphoto, OUP/Image Source, Beau Lark/Corbis, OUP/Corbis, OUP/Thinkstock, GSPhotography/Shutterstock.com; p. 5 EricFerguson/istockphoto, OUP/Okea, Corbis, adventtr/istockphoto, wavebreakmedia/shutterstock, Steve Debenport/Getty Images, OUP/Dennis Kitchen Studio, Inc., Chris Howey/shutterstock, Mrsiraphol/shutterstock, OUP/Mark Mason, mphillips007/istockphoto, Tom Wang/shutterstock; p. 10 Ocean/Corbis, OUP/Asia Images RF, OUP/Beau Lark, OUP/Luminis; p. 12 DJTaylor/shutterstock, CORBIS RM/CUSP/Inmagine, ostill/shutterstock, wavebreakmedia/shutterstock, Radius Images/Alamy; p. 14 Goodluz/shutterstock, Tetra Images/Alamy, Moncherie/Getty Images, Aletia/shutterstock, gchutka/istockphoto, Lithiumphoto/shutterstock; p. 18 OUP/Photodisc; p. 26 guvendemir/istock, Jack Hollingsworth/Getty Images; p. 27 OUP/LePZ, Monkey Business Images/shutterstock, Justin Kase zsixz/Alamy, Brejeq/istockphoto, Joe Gough/shutterstock; p. 28 imagebroker/Alamy; p. 29 Naho Yoshizawa/Aflo/Corbis, Africa Studio/shutterstock, age fotostock/SuperStock, Julia Davila-Lampe/Getty Images, JTB Photo/SuperStock, harikarn/shutterstock; p. 31 cynoclub/shutterstock, Andrew Scherbackov/shutterstock, photobank.ch/shutterstock, karen roach/shutterstock; p. 35 mozcann/istockphoto.com, Ziva_K/istockphoto, vasabii/shutterstock, skodonnell/istockphoto, pockygallery/shutterstock; p. 36 blyjak/istockphoto, Sergii Korolko/shutterstock, OUP/LePZ, haveseen/shutterstock, muharrem öner/istockphoto; p. 39 szefei wong/Alamy; p. 40 Cusp/SuperStock, Henry Westheim Photography/Alamy, Christian Kober/age fotostock; p. 42 r.nagy/shutterstock; p. 46 Johanna Goodyear/shutterstock, Martin Harvey/Getty Images, Craig Dingle/istockphoto, Gleb Tarro/shutterstock, OUP/Corel, OUP/Ingram; p. 47 kickstand/istockphoto, Willie B. Thomas/istockphoto, Stanislaw Pytel/getty Images, OUP/Cultura; p. 48 almgren/shutterstock, Hellen Sergeyeva/shutterstock; p. 49 OUP/Jim Reed, OUP/Digital Vision, OUP/Tom Wang, Minerva Studio/shutterstock; p. 50 Jose Luis Pelaez, Inc./Blend Images/Corbis, OUP/Fuse, bjdlzx/istockphoto, OUP/Digital Vision, Dmitry Kalinovsky/shutterstock, Monkey Business Images/shutterstock; p. 51Minerva Studio/shutterstock, BJI/Blue Jean Images/Getty Images, Alexander Raths/shutterstock, Dave & Les Jacobs/Blend Images/Corbis, Tony Gentile/Reuters/Corbis, Alina Solovyova-Vincent/Getty Images; p. 54 LWA/Getty Images, Radius Images/Alamy; p. 61 shaunl/istockphoto; p. 67 Montreal_Photos/istockphoto; p. 70 OUP/Digital Vision, OUP/Corbis, Konrad Mostert/shutterstock, OUP/Photodisc, Heiko Kiera/shutterstock, skilpad/istockphoto, Matthias Breiter/Minden Pictures/Corbis; p. 71 Ralph Lee Hopkins/National Geographic Society/Corbis; p. 74 arek_malang/shutterstock, Robert Crum/shutterstock, takayuki/shutterstock, ArtisticCaptures/istockphoto; p. 75 Monkey Business Images/shutterstock, Tetra Images/Alamy, Viktor Gladkov/shutterstock, Andrey Arkusha/shutterstock; p. 77 Don Mason/Blend Images/Corbis, Justin Horrocks/Getty Images, Jose Luis Pelaez, Inc./Blend Images/Corbis, Keith Brofsky/Blend Images/Corbis, wavebreakmedia/shutterstock; p. 78 bumihills/shutterstock, OUP/Ocean, Planet Observer/Universal Images Group/Getty Images, Noppasin/shutterstock.com, Blaine Harrington III/Corbis, OUP/Photodisc, Marco Rubino/shutterstock, Celia Mannings/Alamy, Roger De La Harpe; Gallo Images/Corbis, Steven Vidler/Eurasia Press/Corbis; p. 80 Fine Art Photographic Library/SuperStock, Corbis; p. 81 Corbis; p. 83 Yagi Studio/Getty Images, KidStock/Blend Images/Corbis, Hero Images/Corbis, Ocean/Corbis; p. 87 Harvey Silikovitz; p. 88 Rodrigo Reyes MarÃn/AFLO/Nippon News/Corbis; p. 94 OUP/Photodisc; p. 97 Juniors Bildarchiv GmbH/Alamy, blickwinkel/Alamy; p. 102 Olympus/shutterstock, Jinxy Productions/Blend Images/Corbis, Hans-Peter Merten/Robert Harding World Imagery/Corbis, Chad McDermott/shutterstock, Spiderplay/Getty Images, Pichi/shutterstock; p. 103 Klaus Tiedge/Corbis, JDC/LWA/Corbis, Andersen Ross/Blend Images/Corbis, OUP/Mikhail Kokhanchikov, OUP/Andres Rodriguez, OUP/Photodisc, Ensuper/shutterstock, Ed Kashi/VII/Corbis; p. 106 OUP/Mark Mason, OUP/Gareth Boden, Enrique Soriano/Bloomberg/Getty Images; p. 107 lilly3/istockphoto, Jochen Tack/imagebrok/age fotostock; p. 109 Blaine Harrington III/Alamy, Li Muzi/Xinhua Press/Corbis; p. 112 Roobcio/shutterstock, OUP/Photodisc, sandr2002/shutterstock, OZaiachin/shutterstock, Amos Chapple/Getty Images; p. 113 Ted Dayton Photography/Beateworks/Corbis, Hoberman Collection/UIG via Getty Images, Clive Rose/Getty Images; p. 117 Lena Pantiukh/shutterstock; p. 123 Mikulich Alexander Andreevich/shutterstock; p. 124 OUP/Imge Source, djem/shutterstock; p. 136 Jose Luis Pelaez Inc/Blend Image/Blend Images/Corbis, David Wall Photo/Getty Images, Mark Bolton/Getty Images, chsherbakova yuliya/shutterstock; p. 137 JAG IMAGES/age fotostock, Don Mason/Blend Images/Corbis, Turba/Corbis, Erik Mandre/shutterstock, Corepics VOF/shutterstock, Aaron Amat/shutterstock; p. 148 Adam Pass Photography/cultura/Corbis, OUP/Vulkanette; p. 152 OUP/Photodisc; p. 153 Christophe Testi/shutterstock, Vector Market/shutterstock; p. 164 Michael Hall Photography Pty Ltd/Corbis, Stephen Stickler/Getty Images, lithian/shutterstock; p. 165 Sergey Nivens/shutterstock, John Fedele/Getty Images, PhotoTalk/istockphoto, jcarillet/istockphoto; p. 167 michaeljung/shutterstock, urbandevill/istockphoto, Stephen Dalton/Getty Images; p. 172 Brent Winebrenner/Getty Images; p. 185 Reuters/STR New; p. 190 Beau Lark/Corbis, Marcelo Santos/Getty Images, Ariel Skelley/Getty Images, Image Source/Getty Images, Alexander Raths/shutterstock, Moxie Productions/Blend Images/Corbis; p. 191 www.joshneufeld.com. p. 194 P. Coen/Corbis, antos777/shutterstock, Ferenc Szelepcsenyi/shutterstock.com; p. 195 OUP/Photodisc, zhu difeng/shutterstock.com, ImageegamI/istockphoto, Cavan Images/Getty Images; p. 197 cinemafestival/shutterstock.com(2), K2 images/shutterstock.com, DFree/shutterstock.com, Helga Esteb/shutterstock.com, Featureflash/shutterstock.com, LaCameraChiara/shutterstock.com, JStone/shutterstock.com; p. 203 OUP/Dave Crombeen, mbbirdy/istockphoto; p. 204 Ansis Klucis/shutterstock, Myibean/shutterstock, Mike Flippo/shutterstock; p. 211 Underwood & Underwood/Corbis, Oxford Science Archive/Print Collector/Getty Images; p. 212 Erik Isakson/Tetra Images/Corbis; p. 215 Eric Audras/Onoky/Corbis; p. 218 Michael Ochs Archives/Getty Images, Paul Schutzer/Time Life Pictures/Getty Images, Chris Jackson/Getty Images; p. 220 OUP/StockbrokerXtra, SIHASAKPRACHUM/shutterstock, Jean-Paul Ferrero/age fotostock, Tracy Packer Photography/Getty Images; p. 221 John Harper/Corbis, OUP/Songquan Deng, OUP/Corbis/Digital Stock, Whiteway/istockphoto, isoft/istockphoto; p. 222 David Haring/DUPC/Getty Images; p. 223 Mint Images - Frans Lanting/Getty Images, Kazakov Maksim/shutterstock, Christian Musat/shutterstock, Eric Isselee/shutterstock; p. 224 Steve Hickey/Alamy, Sean Nel/shutterstock, LianeM/shutterstock, ollyy/shutterstock; p. 225 OUP/Purestock, Ocean/Corbis, Phase4Studios/shutterstock; p. 230 Foodio/shutterstock; p. 232 OUP/Photodisc; p. 234 OUP/Ingram, Kletr/shutterstock; p. 235 Todor Tsvetkov/istockphoto; p. 240 Jorge Salcedo/shutterstock; p. 241 karamysh/shutterstock, Patrick Poendl/shutterstock.com; p. 243 Tuan Tran/Getty Images; p. 245 TommL/istockphoto, Petar Chernaev/istockphoto; p. 248 Nick Tzolo/Getty Images, Myroslava/shutterstock; p. 250 OUP/LePZ, OUP/Digital Vision, littleny/shutterstock.com, OUP/Blue Jean Images; p. 251 IS_ImageSource/istockphoto, Goodluz/shutterstock, Terrafugia Inc., Universal Images Group Limited/Alamy, Jupiterimages/Getty Images, Pinkcandy/shutterstock; p. 254 Syda Productions/shutterstock, Joshua Dalsimer/Corbis, Tifonimages/shutterstock, James Baigrie/Getty Images, Konstantin Sutyagin/shutterstock, Stokkete/shutterstock, Thomas Kienzle/Getty Images, Corbis; p. 255 Kim Nguyen/shutterstock; p. 262 Flashon Studio/shutterstock; p. 265 Ron Niebrugge/Alamy; p. 268 OUP/HAWKEYE, OJO_Images/istockphoto, Michael Pettigrew/shutterstock, Fotokostic/shutterstock; p. 270 IS_ImageSource/istockphoto; p. 271 Margoe Edwards/shutterstock; p. 276 iconeer/istockphoto; p. 278 Dirk Lindner/Getty Images, Petrified Collection/Getty Images, Tomas Rodriguez/Corbis, incamerastock/Alamy; p. 279 Izabela Habur/Getty Images, Johner Images/Johnér Images/Corbis, mediaphotos/istockphoto, skynesher/istockphoto; p. 280 sampics/Corbis, Christian Hartmann/Reuters/Corbis, Liao Yujie/xh/Xinhua Press/Corbis, Smirnov Vladimir/ITAR-TASS Photo/Corbis, Jewel Samad/AFP/GettyImages, Alex Livesey/Getty Images, Richard Heathcote/Getty Images, PCN/Corbis; p. 284 BlueSkyImage/shutterstock, Marko Tomicic/shutterstock, Art Wolfe/Getty Images, Gillian Holliday/shutterstock, dmvphotos/shutterstock, OUP/Digital Stock, Brian J. Skerry/National Geographic Creative, c-foto/istockphoto, OUP/White, OUP/Amazon-Images, Anton_Ivanov/shutterstock, OUP/Corbis; p. 287 Bloomimage/Corbis, mandygodbehear/istockphoto; p. 291 Josie Elias/Getty Images, Dimitrios Kambouris/Getty Images, Jerry Lodriguss/Science Photo Library; p. 297 Image Source/Getty Images, YinYang/Getty Images, Dmitry Kalinovsky/shutterstock, DAJ/Getty Images; p. 302 Alex Mares-Manton/Getty Images, OJO_Images/istockphoto; p. 304 REUTERS/Danny Moloshok; p. 306 Joshua Blake/Getty Images, Benoit Daoust/shutterstock, Paul Bradbury/Getty Images, Kris Ubach and Quim Roser/cultura/Corbis; p. 307 Topic Photo Agency/Corbis, wavebreakmedia/shutterstock, Bogdan VASILESCU/shutterstock, Fuse/Getty Images; p. 319 Andresr/shutterstock; p. 325 Baloncici/shutterstock, Sonja Pacho/Corbis, pio3/shutterstock, Steve Debenport/istockphoto; p. 326 AP Photo/Paul Sakuma; p. 327 Martina I. Meyer/shutterstock; p. 329 koh sze kiat/shutterstock, Gareth Brown/Corbis; p. 332 Popperfoto/Getty Images, XXLPhoto/shutterstock, olaser/istockphoto, Courtesy Aptera/ZUMA Press/Newscom; p. 333 VOISIN/phanie/Phanie Sarl/Corbis, Justin Horrocks/istockphoto, Subbotina Anna/shutterstock, Jose Azel/Aurora Photos/Corbis, Jess Yu/shutterstock, OJO_Images/istockphoto; p. 336 Bettmann/Corbis; p. 337 Hulton Archive/Getty Images, CB2/ZOB/WENN.com/Newscom; p. 339 Radharc Images/Alamy, muzsy/shutterstock.com; p. 343 wavebreakmedia/shutterstock; p. 345 urii Kachkovskyi/shutterstock; p. 351 INTERFOTO/Alamy, OUP/Photographers Choice, OUP/Art Explosion; p. 356 Gino's Premium Images/Alamy; p. 358 Helen King/Corbis, Photodisc/Getty Images; p. 359 HamsterMan/shutterstock, Grisha Bruev/shutterstock; p. 361 Leonello Calvetti/Stocktrek Images/Corbis, Pablo Corral Vega/Corbis; p. 362 Hurst Photo/shutterstock; p. 363 OUP/Photodisc; p. 366 Jenny Matthews/Alamy, Dennis MacDonald/Alamy; p. 369 Veronica Louro/shutterstock; p. 371 Danilo Ascione/shutterstock; p. 376 Science Source/Science Photo Library, Keystone Pictures USA/Alamy; p. 377 violetblue/shutterstock; p. 379 michaeljung/shutterstock.

# ELEMENTS *of* SUCCESS
## Online Practice

### How to Register for Elements of Success Online Practice

**Follow these steps to register for *Elements of Success Online Practice*:**

1. Go to  www.elementsofsuccessonline.com and click **Register**

2. Read and agree to the terms of use. **I Agree.**

3. Enter the Access Code that came with your Student Book. Your code is written on the inside back cover of your book.

   [ ] [ ] [ ] [ ]    **Enter**

4. Enter your personal information (first and last name, email address, and password).

5. Click the Student Book that you are using for your class.

   > It is very important to select your book.
   > You are using Elements of Success 1.
   > Please click the **RED** Elements of Success 1 cover.

   If you don't know which book to select, **STOP**. Continue when you know your book.

6. Enter your class ID to join your class, and click NEXT. Your class ID is on the line below, or your teacher will give it to you on a different piece of paper.

   _____  **Next**

   You don't need a class ID code. If you do not have a class ID code, click Skip.
   To enter this code later, choose Join a Class from your Home page.

7. Once you're done, click Activities to begin using *Elements of Success Online Practice*.

Next time you want to use *Elements of Success Online Practice*, just go to www.elementsofsuccessonline.com and log in with your email address and password.